Punk Rock and Philosophy

Pop Culture and Philosophy®

General Editor: George A. Reisch

For full details of all Pop Culture and Philosophy® books, and all Open Universe® books, visit www.carusbooks.com

Pop Culture and Philosophy®

Punk Rock and Philosophy

Research and Destroy

Edited by
JOSHUA HETER AND
RICHARD GREENE

OPEN UNIVERSE
Chicago

Volume 7 in the series, Pop Culture and Philosophy®, edited by George A. Reisch

To find out more about Open Universe and Carus Books, visit our website at www.carusbooks.com.

Punk Rock and Philosophy: Research and Destroy

ISBN: 978-1-63770-022-8

This book is also available as an e-book (978-1-63770-023-5).

Library of Congress Control Number: 2021941784

For Wade Fox and Eric Petersen
For Benjamin Crackle

Contents

Thanks

Working on this project has been a pleasure, in no small part because of the many fine folks who have assisted us along the way. In particular, a debt of gratitude is owed to David Ramsay Steele at Carus Books, the contributors to this volume, the School of Humanities at Jefferson College and the Department of Political Science and Philosophy at Weber State University. Finally, we'd like to thank those family members, students, friends, and colleagues with whom we've had fruitful and rewarding conversations on various aspects of all things punk as it relates to philosophical themes.

This Is a Public Service Announcement (with Guitar)

Punk rock was invented on August 16th 1974 when four disaffected young men from Queens, New York, took the stage at the now (in)famous CBGB bar and belted out a new, furious brand of rock'n'roll the world wasn't quite ready for. On that night, the band in question, The Ramones, began a movement of not only music, but of fashion and attitude previously unseen in civilized society. Fast forward a few decades, and what began that fateful summer evening has touched every continent around the globe.

What is perhaps most interesting about this story is that it's all untrue. Or, at the very least, it's oversimplified to the point of absurdity.

As monumental as The Ramones have been to rock'n'roll in general and punk rock in particular, musical genres like punk aren't the type of thing that are brought into existence *ex nihilo*. The seeds that would eventually become punk by way of a *number* of acts in the mid-1970s were being planted almost immediately as rock'n'roll first hit the scene in the early 1950s. Indeed, the origins of punk can be found in the boisterous, rebellious scream of Little Richard, the outlaw persona of Johnny Cash, and the high energy performances of James Brown. Its sound was born from the fuzzy guitar hums of artists like Link Wray, up-tempo surf rock, and the messiness of so-called garage bands. (Ravok and Autumn. "Before 1976 Revisited: How Punk became Punk"). And, it was only after punk was established as its own musical genre that bands like The Stooges, New York Dolls, The Modern Lovers, and The Velvet Underground would receive their due in regard to shaping the burgeoning style.

Just as both the history and development of what would become punk rock are more complex than we might think at first blush, so too are the ideas and themes that embody and epitomize punk. As it turns out, there is a great deal of interesting philosophical content to be found in the lyrics and themes of punk songs and in the attitudes and practices of punk rockers. A host of thought-provoking, challenging questions are raised by only a modest reflection on the movement as a whole. Why do we listen to such dark (punk) songs? What does it mean to be a poseur (and should I care if I am one)? Is anarchy truly defensible as a political ideology, or is it better left merely as something more like an attitude or anthem for punk rock rebelliousness? Can punk be mature, or is it fundamentally tied to youth culture? Does punk rock (successfully) challenge the idea that art is inherently aimed at beauty?

As daunting as answering these questions may be, they are simply the tip of the iceberg. A truly robust accounting of the philosophical issues embedded in and around punk can't be cataloged so easily. That being said, with perhaps the same brash, youthful exuberance that fuels much of punk rock, this book is an attempt to answer some of these questions. Or, at the very least, it's an attempt to sketch out and provide arguments for some of the *possible* answers so that you, dear reader, may answer them for yourself. After all, just *telling you* what the answers are (as if we are some sort of an authority figure) wouldn't be very punk.

I

What Makes It Punk

1
The Essence of Punk

TIMOTHY M. KWIATEK

What holds punk together? I don't just mean how hasn't that scene fallen apart completely (though perhaps you think it has). I mean, what unifies all the things we call 'punk'?

How can things as disparate as a piece of music, an album, a band, a person, an outfit or a zine all share this property? We could start by confining our question to music: what makes The Ramones a band in the same category as Blondie? What makes The Go-Go's fit in the same category as the Bad Brains? When I talk to other punks, these questions are not puzzling. Punks know it when they see it (or hear it). But when other philosophers make the mistake of talking to me about music, I sometimes come up against questions that boil down to this: does punk have an essence? Is there some quality that all and only the things we call 'punk' possess?

Musical Essence

According to one familiar way of thinking, many things have essences. These are qualities that are necessary for that thing being what it is. For example, triangles have three sides. All triangles are like this. To have more or less sides than this is to not be a triangle. So if we're stuck on the question of whether or not something is a triangle, we have a plan for resolving it. Just count the number of sides and then you'll know.

Another example is that bachelors are unmarried men. This is true for all bachelors. Generally speaking, the assumption about things we find out in the world is that they have an essence. And a lot of the time we assume this about categories we create, like 'bachelor'. So what we do to understand these things is try to find out what their essence is. If I offer an analysis of something according to which it has an essence, you are then free to provide me with a counterexample which might disprove my analysis. So if I say the essence of a book is to be written or printed on paper, you can say 'What about audio books or ebooks?' Then, I would have to come up with a better analysis of 'book'.

Music is a tricky case. Music seems more like bachelor than triangle insofar as we create categories for ease of reference. Sometimes those categories are quite precise and it can look as if certain categories of music do have an essence. This is true at the level of types of compositions. Think about a waltz. The rhythm of a waltz is an essential feature. Other things can change, it can be faster or slower, louder or quieter, played by a novice or a professional. But it has to have a certain pattern that your steps can follow to dance the accompanying dance.

Sometimes music distinguished by time period has an essence. Baroque music is from the 1600s. New music made in that style today would be something else. But we can't define punk in either of those ways. Punk songs vary tremendously in rhythms and all other musical patterns. This is especially true earlier on in punk's history. It was wonderfully eclectic. And even if we could agree on when punk started, it's still clearly happening today, so we can't confine it to a time period as we do with something like Baroque music.

In fact, virtually any attempt to find the essence of punk admits of obvious counterexamples. Let's consider a few. Is punk essentially political in its lyrical content? Well, if by that we mean the songs are all about politics, then no. There are paradigmatic examples of punk songs which don't seem to engage with social or political issues. Think of Black Flag's "Six Pack" or The Ramones' "She's the One." Not to mention that there are purely instrumental punk songs. Is punk essentially DIY or underground? Sure, this is true for Crass or whoever your favorite local band is. But The Clash and the Sex Pistols were pretty mainstream. They were on major record labels. It's a stretch to claim they weren't punk bands. Does punk music just come from people who self-identify as punks? That would make this easier. But The Descendants would disagree in the song "I'm Not a Punk" as would Jawbreaker in the song "Boxcar." We all know it can be particularly punk to not try to be punk.

Rebellion

Or maybe these are too easy. Maybe the essence of punk is something more relational between the punk and the wider world. This could be manifested in various ways and no one particular manifestation would be required. Perhaps punk music is about rebellion? This would allow for us to understand our mainstream bands, if they were rebelling against the prevailing sound. At a time of complicated music, The Ramones wrote simple songs. In the face of English propriety, The Sex Pistols wrote improper songs.

But rebellion against what? If punk music is essentially rebellion against prevailing norms, on what scale are we considering? Any action is an action under a description. And virtually any action can be described as rebellion against something else. Conventionally, rebellion seems to be done by a smaller and less powerful contingent against a larger one. But we're all nested within countless such arrangements of power and influence. So The Ramones may have been rebelling by doing their own thing in response to a rock music industry. And The Descendants were rebelling against an increasingly established punk scene that advanced a more homogenized kind of rebellion. So that checks out.

But there seem to be limits to how you can rebel and still be punk. Two words: Green Day. Green Day was associated with the Bay Area's DIY punk scene. Then they signed to a major label and became big rock stars and were ostracized from that scene. You might interpret this act of signing to a major label as just rebellion against the norms of their scene. But at the time, we had a different concept for this. It was called selling out. This concept seems to have been lost to history, which is probably for the best. But logically, we must consider the difference between selling out and rebelling. If the essence of punk is rebellion and selling out is not punk, how do we know which of these is happening? And why was it selling out for Green Day but not for The Descendants?

We might think two different things by rebellion. According to one reading, rebellion is just acting contrary to the values of the people immediately around you. Call this *local rebellion*. A second theory: rebellion is acting contrary to the values of the dominant culture. Call this *global rebellion*. In this sense, Green Day moving to a major label was *local rebellion* but not *global rebellion*. So which one of these might punk be about? If punk is essentially about local rebellion, then signing to a major label was punk. Intuitively, this was not punk. Thus, we might conclude that the only rebellion punk can plausibly be about is *global rebellion*.

But another problem case comes to mind: The Misfits. The Misfits just wrote songs about horror movies. This wasn't any big rebellion against the prevailing culture. It was a reflection of popular culture in the form of horror movies. Yet again, The Misfits are intuitively a punk band. Thus I conclude that neither local nor global rebellion is necessary for something to be punk.

Authenticity

Let's take one more stab at this. Maybe punk isn't about any of those particular things, and it isn't about rebellion as such. Maybe punk is essentially about authenticity. It's about being yourself in the face of a culture that tries to make you something else. That's a certain kind of existentialist ideal. Aging punks like myself love this one because it lets us still say we're punk no matter how we dress, what we listen to, or what we do with our lives now. We should be especially cautious about theories that always say we're doing it right. But we should still consider it.

Of course, authenticity might preclude acting for reasons of rebellion. Because acting in rebellion against the dominant culture, or just against your scene, is ultimately still beholden to that scene. If Y is the opposite of X and my culture all does X, so in response I do Y, my action is still determined by my culture's doing X. I'm not doing what the dominant cultures says—but nor is it obvious that I'm free of its influence, that I'm doing something that comes just from me.

Punk as authenticity has another problem. Sometimes authenticity leads to stuff that seems very not punk. Authentic homophobia, racism, sexism, conformity, fascism and so on seem no less troubling (and no more punk) than their socially enforced counterparts. Also, what if one's authentic self just so happens to perfectly conform to all of the expectations of their community and the broader society? We would then be left saying of such a person is the epitome of punk. This seems like the wrong answer.

Even so, *sometimes* any one or combination of these qualities make for a punk song/band/album. We often say a band or a song is punk because of some particular feature. Examples of these features include, but are not limited to:

- **what the music sounds like (d-beats, breakdowns, speed, and so on . . . .)**

- the skill (or lack thereof) with which it's played
- the identity of those who make the music (punks make punk music)
- the scale on which the music is made (small DIY bands versus big corporate bands)
- the scene from which the music emerges (punk music comes from punk scenes)
- previous bands the artists were in (punk is as punk does)
- the fan base of the artist (punk by association)

• • •

This list could go on and on. None of these are necessary and none of them are sufficient. For any given quality that makes for a punk song, it looks like there's another punk song that's punk in virtue of something different. The more we reflect on it, the more the list tends to grow.

We're a Happy Family

Philosophy can help here. In his *Philosophical Investigations*, Ludwig Wittgenstein considers just this kind of search for essence. But his philosophy can be read as a kind of anti-philosophy (how punk is that?). He claims that a lot of the problems philosophers are preoccupied with come from things like this search for essence. As it happens, not everything has an essence. And that's not a problem. The problem was that we assumed everything does and that if we just looked hard enough, we could find it.

Wittgenstein considers games as an example. Games lack essence. There is no defining attribute shared by all games. Some are played with cards, others with a ball, others still with pieces on a board or controllers on a screen. There is no one feature that unifies all games. He says that things like games lack an essence, but nonetheless have a family resemblance. Just as members of a family don't all exhibit identical features like eye color, hair color or a wide jaw, if we look at enough of them, we can't help but notice that many of them share this feature. And they are all unified by a wide set of such features.

I suggest that the same holds true for punk. Punk just has a contingent family resemblance. Some bands are punk because the people in them are punks. Some are punk because of the scenes they came from or their fan base. Some bands are punk because of their lyrics or the way their music sounds. Just because there isn't one quality that all and only punk things share doesn't mean there's nothing that it is to be punk. The family resemblance of punk is what allows for the timeless activity of playfully arguing over what is or is not punk.

Maybe I think Television was a punk band and you don't, or maybe you think every issue of Cometbus is punk and I think only some of them are. We can talk about these things for hours and in doing so, reveal more of the contours of the concept of punk. We can have these conversations while not really talking past each other when we say "punk." An excess of precision in terms makes for boring conversation anyway. There's nothing interesting to learn about which numbers are odd and which are even. But discussing what is or isn't punk creates an opportunity to explore the fuzzy boundaries of the concept.

Part of what makes these discussions so fun, also part of what makes them so heated, is that we're at once trying to discover something about the world as well as trying to create a world. Punk isn't dead. It isn't over. It's still happening. Even if we sometimes wish it would end so we could finally understand it. The effort to find an essentialist analysis of punk stems from the idea that it's something we've found in the world. In this, as in so many things, we are world projectors who take ourselves to be world detectors. A conclusive decision that punk was essentially political would yield a genre with determined boundaries.

The thing is, we don't just talk about bands, songs, or albums as being punk. We talk about people being punk. We talk about scenes being punk. We talk about punk zines and punk fashion. It's comprehensible to say that someone dresses like a punk but isn't one. We can also say someone is a punk even if they don't obviously look like it. Since punk is historically connected to a kind of music without an essence, the concept is widely applicable outside of music. The lack of essence ripples out into all the other things we talk about as punk or not.

This is where things get wonderfully complicated. There are punks who don't like traditionally punk things. Graffiti near my house says being kind is the most punk thing to do. In my more overtly punk days, we punks were mean and callous people. We prided ourselves on it. Younger punks today seem to be doing quite the opposite. This is punk's family resemblance working just as it should. It's a changing cluster of properties. Since there's no essential feature which makes a type of music punk, punk music cannot be the essential feature that makes a person a punk. When I go to shows, I'm still wearing a tweed sport coat and slacks. I don't think that makes my outfit punk fashion. Nor do I think that not dressing in punk fashion makes me less a punk.

So what does this matter? Maybe philosophical puzzles don't matter; maybe all that matters is punk. And you want an answer about the essence of punk. The answer is there is no essence. There's no piece of information you can gain through study or analysis that will reveal to you the essence of punk because it lacks an essence. I don't care if you were there from the beginning. The concept of punk is more like a game than it is like a triangle. This may seem like a disappointing result, but I assure you it is not. It just means that we aging punks have no special standing to comment on what is or isn't punk. We know what it meant to us. We can talk about that. But that has no bearing on what it is now, what it should be, or what it can be. Punks have always been mutants. Why should we be surprised if they continue to mutate?

This family resemblance understanding of punk does two things for us. First, it gives us a break. We can stop imagining these arguments about what's punk are supposed to produce anything or get us somewhere. Instead, we can finally just enjoy them for what they are. Second, punk's lack of essence serves as an anti-gatekeeping mechanism. With no essence to appeal to, bad-faith actors cannot conclusively interrogate a work, or a person and exclude them from punk. This is not to say that anyone and anything is punk. But it does shift the burden of justification to those who want to exclude other people or music or art from the category of punk, just because it is not identical to punk as they originally came to understand it.

It's harder to get things out from under the umbrella of punk than it is to get things in. This is really quite impressive. Nobody planned it. It just happened this way. Disparate people in disparate lands started making music, scenes grew around that music, groups of friends made music and art together and we ended up with this handy, yet totally underspecified name for it. Punk rockers make punk rock music. But sometimes they don't. Many punks care predominately about baking the perfect vegan brownie, or radical politics, squatting, riding trains, or riding bikes.

We have to learn the difference between playful bantering about what is or isn't punk and genuine gatekeeping. The banter can help us understand ourselves and each other better. Gatekeeping is futile and it betrays a lack of understanding of punk. Anything can and will get in. That's a feature of punk, not a bug. Punk needs no protector, no guardian.

I think we need to walk the middle way between gatekeeping and giving up. One response to this problem of understanding punk is to throw up our arms. Who cares what is or isn't punk? We don't need to give up on something that's clearly been historically important to so many of us. Punk rock changed our lives. It's worth asking what it is that did that. It's just that, in the course of asking, we stop caring about the answer. The value is in the asking.

You might misinterpret what I've said in this chapter to mean that anything is licensed under this understanding of punk. If this is so, don't we just have to allow the worst kinds of people and activity among this community? Of course not! My claim is just that the arguments about what is or isn't punk and the arguments about what should or shouldn't be done in a punk scene cannot be adjudicated with appeal to what punk essentially is.

When I first encountered a punk scene, it was unapologetically homophobic. One of the last shows I saw was a band approvingly singing about trans folks overthrowing society. That's remarkable, and to my mind, a welcome change. What I've said in this chapter is just designed to provide ammunition for those arguing with the old fogies who think they've grasped the essence of punk. They didn't live fast enough to die young.[1]

---

[1] Dedicated to the memory of Jack Terricloth. You convinced me that joy and literacy are punk. You taught me the importance of looking my best at all times. You made me less lonely and you helped me.

2
Why Sting Is More Punk than You

BRIAN HARDING

Punk began with a rejection of canonical rock figures and nostalgic legacy acts from the sixties: "No Elvis, Beatles, or The Rolling Stones," Joe Strummer sang in 1977. Johnny Rotten reminded his audience to "never trust a hippy."

The point of punk rock was to do something *new*, something by and for the kids. Punk represented an alternative to the boring and well-worn paths of Sixties and Seventies rock. Punk meant freedom to experiment musically; the self-conscious amateurism of punk rock radically opened it up to new ideas and techniques.

Punk rock has ossified into precisely what it rebelled against. Rather than celebrate new sounds and new ideas, punk requires the recycling of old ones, and homage paid to titans of the past, often via cover songs. When, in 2011, H_2O told their fans, "Don't forget your roots," they inadvertently demonstrated that punk has become what it rejected. Punk is now a hierarchical system that holds up an older generation of musicians as the standard younger bands offer homage to. While there may be no Elvis, Beatles, or Rolling Stones, punk gives us The Ramones, The Clash, and myriad other "legendary" bands.

Punk has developed its own canonical rock figures and stories of "Lives of the Saints" not only the aforementioned Strummer and Rotten, but also numerous other elder statesmen and legendary bands: Minor Threat, Black Flag, the Exploited, and the list runs on and on. This ossification continues in a more insidious form than merely holding out certain figures as examples: many punk bands could be (uncharitably) described as nothing more than tributes to earlier acts; the clearest example of this is the D-beat scene vis-a-vis Discharge.

This inability to escape Punk's past reaches its nadir in the never-ending stream of documentaries, gallery exhibits, panel discussions (!), and retrospectives on the history of punk. How and why did Punk rock embrace this kind of hidebound traditionalism? Why is it looking in the rear-view mirror?

Sell Outs and Posers

This traditionalism is closely connected to the fear of "selling out" and of being a poser. To see why, we have to look a little more closely at what "selling out" means; after that, we will look at the meaning of a "poser." The two ideas are closely connected. As it happens, there is no general agreement about selling out. I'll begin with three anecdotes, representing three different views.

1. Fat Mike of NOFX maintains that none of the big punk bands from the 1990s (such as Green Day or the Offspring) sold out since they did not change their sound for the sake of popularity.

2. During the punk explosion of the mid 1990s, Tim Yohannon and *Maximum Rock'n'Roll* were quick to label anyone who signed to a major label or sent a video to MTV as sell-outs.

3. Jello Biafra, in *Bedtime for Democracy*'s song "Chickenshit Conformist," complained about punk bands "crossing over" into metal and thereby selling out.

Each anecdotes represents a slightly different conception of selling out. Selling out can either refer 1. to adapting your artistic vision for the sake of commercial success or 2. to betrayal of certain political ideals (DIY ethics and anti-capitalism) that some punks embraced or 3. mixing in non-punk (typically metal or pop) elements into your music.

Jello's criterion is of particular interest insofar as it does not turn on popularity or complicity with big business per se; on this point simply incorporating *verboten* styles of music is enough to sell out. The concern here is violating some unspoken and mysterious essence of punk. The song's earlier complaint about formulaic punk rock or hardcore doesn't entail all or any breaks with the formula. No head-bangers allowed. To be fair to Jello, he later changed his mind and began to appreciate metal bands (Sepultura, Napalm Death), but the lyrics say quite explicitly that "crossover" (mixing punk and metal) is a symptom of "lack of ideas." (Yes, music nerd, I know that Napalm Death and grindcore more generally have a deep-rooted connection to crust and d-beat. That said, by the time of *Utopia Banished* or *Harmony Corruption* Napalm Death had migrated to the metal scene. The common denominator linking grindcore, crust and d-beat, is that it all sucks in the same way).

Notice the confusion that these three concepts engender: you could be a sell-out by one criterion but not by another. Jello's version had it that DRI sold out by adding metal elements on *Crossover*. According to Tim Yo's description, Green Day sold out by signing to a major label, Rancid and the Offspring sold out for sending videos to MTV (even though they stayed with Epitaph). On Fat Mike's account, none of these bands sold out, since they did not change sound for popularity, but Sugar Ray did when the success of "Fly" led them to change their sound. Compare the manic energy of "Mean Machine" with the chill vibes of "Someday." (I love post-Fly Sugar Ray; *14:59* is an underrated and interesting album. I should point out that I have enjoyed the music of *every* band mentioned in this chapter, including Napalm Death.) The point here is not to decide who is right but to point out the disagreement. There is no consensus in the scene as to what counts as selling out. The only agreement is that is bad, uncool, and the worst thing one can do as a punk. Once having sold out, both the band and their fans become *persona non grata* in the scene. Which brings us to posers.

Being a poser, or posing, closely relates to selling out. The poser is, above all else, someone who lacks scene cred. There are, as I see it, two ways of being a poser. First, one could be a poser by having sold out (so, post-*Dookie* Green Day are posers) or by being a fan of a band that sold out (so people that still listened to Green Day after *Dookie* are posers). The second way of being a poser is to have always-already sold out, to have never had scene cred. Corresponding to Fat Mike's version of selling out, you could be a poser because you pretended to be punk to gain popularity (this was the accusation against people like Good Charlotte or The Police). Likewise, according to Crass, The Clash were posers because they did not live up to left-wing political or social ideals. Finally, you could say that bands that incorporate non-punk influences while claiming to play punk are posers. Certain non-punk influences are allowed. Ska and Reggae have been allowed since the 1970s. Since the success of crossover, metal elements are allowable, but not so much before then. However, there are still limits; nothing too pop or popular is allowed. Likewise, nothing 'pretentious' like jazz or classical music is allowed.

So here's the problem: selling out is, as I said above, about the worst thing a punk can do, but it is really hard to avoid, since the scene doesn't agree as to what constitutes selling out. At any moment, the earnest punk rocker does not know if his or her choices will lead to the charge of selling out. This doesn't apply just to musicians and bands: does a punk sell out if work and family obligations mean that you don't "support the scene"? Do you have to live in a squat to be hardcore? Can you be a true punk and listen to Daddy Yankee? And so on. This lack of clarity about what selling out *is,* combined with the opprobrium attached to it, creates uncertainty. The punk has a problem: he or she is *never* certain that they are not a sellout poser. To solve this problem he or she will look to models to imitate. These models will be "successful" punks with tons of scene cred.

In effect, you minimize the risk of selling out by aping the style of a well-known figure or band in the scene. For example: if most people in the scene agree that Fat Mike has not sold out, then I can avoid the charge of selling out by sounding and looking like Fat Mike. If my peers and I agree that Madball are legit, then I can be legit by looking and sounding like Madball. By following these well-worn paths, they immunize themselves against the charge of selling out.

In fact, you can define the different sub-genres within punk solely in terms of which bands they orient themselves with to avoid selling out. The most obvious example is how D-Beat bands imitate Discharge, but you could point to the legion of skate-punk bands that model themselves off the trinity of Bad Religion, Pennywise, and NOFX, or the hardcore bands that look and sound like Agnostic Front or Madball. In short, because the indeterminacy of selling out makes it so hard to navigate a path forward without the risk of selling out, it's safest to look backwards and copy what has come before. The upshot of this is that Punk becomes backwards-looking scene, caught up in imitation of old bands.

Everybody Hates Sting

This brings me to the most controversial bit: Sting. The Police orbited the early punk scene, and played the first punk festival in continental Europe with bands (with loads more scene cred) like The Clash and the Damned. However, they never fully embraced, or were fully embraced by, the London punk scene. They were called posers and sell-outs from the beginning: Sting was too good looking and talented, Andy Summers was too old, and Stewart Copeland's drumming was too complex; in fact, the whole band was too good. Apparently, Sting would watch other bands play and sneer at their lack of chops and sloppy playing. Normally, sneering at people would be precisely what punks in the late 1970s ought to do, but in this case, the sneering was offensive because it indicated a kind of distance from punk ideals.

Precisely this distance allowed them to avoid the trap of punk traditionalism. Sting has continually experimented with different styles of music and musicians (jazz, classical, dancehall, hip-hop) rather than languish in nostalgia and punk conformity. Admittedly, some of his musical experiments fail, but overall, his career has been more true to the anti-nostalgic and non-conformist punk impulse than that of many "real" punks. For fun, you should compare Sting's 2019 collaboration with Congolese-French rapper GIMS, or his 2021 song "Rushing Water" with his early work in The Police, and then compare Bad Religion's most recent album with *How Could Hell Be Any Worse?* Who has followed his artistic vision down whatever road it takes him, and who has been stuck in a musical cul-de-sac?

I mentioned Bad Religion not to criticize them but because of a forgotten album called *Into the Unknown*, which was the follow up to their debut album *How Could Hell Be Any Worse?* It departed from the rules of punk to include more progressive rock elements and a variety of instruments that went beyond the standard guitar-bass-drums-vocals set up of punk rock. Derided as a sell-out by the fans, the band abandoned the vision and returned to good but predictable punk, and they have not varied from that formula since then.

Bad Religion was not the only band which tried to change but were pulled back into punk by charges of selling out. TSOL and Discharge both put out hair metal albums that they do not talk about anymore; they quickly repented of their selling out and recalibrated. When TSOL and Discharge did this in the early 1980s, hair metal was not what we think of it as now. Before being commercialized by Poison and Bon Jovi, early 1980s hair metal had more in common with punk than punk rockers like to think; the common roots in the NY Dolls, Hanoi Rocks, David Bowie and so on made it a cousin to Seventies punk.

AC/DC rocked harder than many bands coming out of CBGB prior to the rise of NYHC ("It's a long way to the top" mixed bagpipes into rock decades before the Dropkick Murphys had the same idea). Guns and Roses' *Appetite for Destruction*, from a certain point of view, is the best-selling punk album of the 1980s. Although they never bought in, and would be sell-outs according to Tim Yo and Jello, I think they pass Fat Mike's test. Other bands, seeing the spite that greets experimentation learn their lesson: stay in your lane. As such, very few bands allow themselves to develop their sound in any meaningful way (AFI is a notable exception). Instead, punk bands and fans, driven by the fear of selling out, circle back to the same styles, scenes and "legendary" bands and, in so doing, stifle the ability of the artist to develop their talents or the fans to develop their interests. In this way, strangely, the most punk thing to do is to cease caring about selling out altogether, and follow your interests without fear or scruple.

In addition to Sting, who I chose to annoy both punks and their indie purist friends, other relevant examples include Steve Aoki, Nick Cave, Chumbawamba, Billy Idol, Moby, Skrillex, even Henry Rollins. Chumbawamba's *English Rebel Songs 1381–1984* is an amazing album, and not at all punk musically, but still, totally punk in spirit.) Nick Cave's last three albums (*Push the Sky Away, Skeleton Key, Ghosteen*) are perhaps his most interesting and engaging work ever in contrast to many punk bands of the same vintage whose best albums are decades behind them. Joe Strummer's work with the Mescaleros is interesting precisely because it did not try to be punk in any meaningful sense. To be sure, The Clash stopped playing punk rock after *Give 'Em Enough Rope. London Calling* is a great album, but it would not be considered a punk album if it were put out by a band without The Clash's pedigree. The same goes for *Sandinista. Combat Rock* is a difficult one: while there are punk elements ("Know your Rights") it's hardly a pure punk album, as "Rock the Casbah" and "Should I Stay or Should I Go" testify, to say nothing of "Ghetto Defendant" and "Straight to Hell." But this is why The Clash is the best of the first-generation punk bands: they had the courage and talent to stop being one.

Turning Pro/It's a Living

Henry Rollins's narrative of life on the road with Black Flag, *Get in the Van*, shows just how much work goes into the life of a punk musician. The working musician works. This is important to keep in mind, and provides an interpretive key to everything said above. An undercurrent to the accusation of selling out is that the sellout does it, in one way or the other, for the money. But what one sees in *Get in the Van* is that even a band as DIY and independent and legit as Black Flag had to work, had to eat, had to earn their daily bread. Which means, in a sense, they played for the money.

To be sure, they didn't play *only* for the money. But, when you quit the proverbial day job at Häagen-Dazs and turn pro, you perforce sell out. Only the amateur can demand absolute purity. This is why although I find Fat Mike's account of selling out the most plausible of the three I discussed, I think it needs an addendum: while changing your sound for the sake of popularity is selling out, it doesn't matter. Scene cred will not pay your rent, and only a lucky few punk celebrities get benefit concerts when they're sick. Mark McGrath from Sugar Ray initially hated "Fly" and nearly quit the band over it: he wanted to stick with Sugar Ray's then current sound, a cross of So-Cal punk and nu-metal. When he saw the success of "Fly," he embraced it and the band leaned into the chill beach vibe of "Fly" on subsequent singles. This was a perfectly reasonable decision, even if it sacrificed whatever scene cred Sugar Ray earned on the 97-Warped Tour. Once you turn pro, it's entirely sensible to want to be a well-paid professional.

What's the alternative? Either the band breaks up or continues in the underground. If it continues, at best it will end up a legacy act playing the old hits at Riot Fest. While I don't blame older bands for doing what they can to earn a living, any pretense that playing the standards at Riot Fest or Punk Rock Bowling isn't as much of a cash grab as any Boomer Rock reunion tour is illusory. In fact—and this is the great paradox of selling out—over time, for some bands, keeping it real becomes more profitable than changing.

This is the lesson Bad Religion learned with *Into the Unknown* and that TSOL and Discharge learned as well. (The dirty secret of keeping it real is that many older punk musicians don't listen to punk anymore and only play it for the money.) The lesson of this paradox is that selling out is unavoidable. The question is, will you lean into it, or stumble into it. If the former, you're at least free to pursue your artistic vision where it takes you; if the latter, you end up trapped by a scene that demands the same thing from you over and over again.

My point is not to criticize any bands or musicians for selling out nor to call out posers. The point is to encourage a *free* relationship with punk rock. Concerns with scene cred stifles this freedom. Punk can be a force for liberation, but it can also become a trap. The desire to be true to the scene, as opposed to selling out, leads to a cul-de-sac of models and sounds.

To escape, you must realize that being called a sellout or a poser doesn't matter: what matters is to follow your path where it takes you, even if it takes you out of punk. The lesson we should learn from punk is to stop caring about being punk. Joe Strummer was right in his declaration of independence: "No Elvis, No Beatles, No Rolling Stones." However, we should add, "No Clash, No Ramones, No Black Flag," "No Agnostic Front, No Bad Religion, No Minor Threat," and so on.

3
Success and Failure of Punk

MICHAEL STOCK

It was so wonderful to have rediscovered at what was already an advanced age the sort of feelings I first had when I heard Little Richard and Elvis Presley as a kid. It was exciting, but there was an element of fear as well—you thought, 'Can this be real?' You went to the gigs and there was a feeling that you were participating in something that had come from another planet, it seemed so remarkable that it was happening at all.

—JOHN PEEL

No Elvis, Beatles or The Rolling Stones in 1977.

—JOE STRUMMER

WE KILLED ELVIS. When these three words appeared on a San Francisco billboard in the fall of 1977, accompanied by an image of a proud, beaming young punk girl in blonde spikes and requisite piercings, they stirred a generational divide—simultaneously, a rallying call for young punks, and virtual blasphemy to their parents. By the time it appeared two years later in the eleventh and final issue of *Search and Destroy*, the all photo-montage issue published by RE/Search Publications in San Francisco in 1979, the proclamation had lost little of its impact, even shrunk as it was to 4 x 6 inches on the page.

By the time I discovered the photograph in the fall of 2006 as I prepared to teach my first class on the History of Punk at the University of California, Irvine, the words still retained their intensity, but the message was no longer the same. While the tone of the photograph and its sentiments were fueled by punk's separation from tradition, and perceived break in the timeline of musical history—the idea that 1976 was Year Zero and nothing before that mattered—the words now provided emblematic evidence not only of the ultimate failure of punk, but of how failure was built into its very origins. For the Punks *did* need Elvis. Very much. Same as they needed Iggy Pop, Lou Reed, David Bowie, and Brian Eno. They needed heroes. They emulated their heroes. What's more . . . they 'covered' their heroes. (Arguably, again following in the footsteps of Elvis and his "Blue Suede Shoes," which was a cover of a song written by Carl Perkins.)

Maybe the original punks of 1976 didn't cover Elvis. (That would have to wait until Dead Kennedys came along in 1980 with "Viva Las Vegas.") But The Sex Pistols did cover Chuck Berry (and, of course, The Stooges). So did Black Flag. The Dickies covered Blue Oyster Cult. Eater covered The Velvet Underground and David Bowie. The Clash covered Sonny Curtis, Junior Murvin, The Maytals, The Melodians, Mikey Dread, and at least a dozen others. The Slits covered Marvin Gaye. Patti Smith covered The Who. Devo covered The Rolling Stones. The Plugz covered Richie Valens. X covered The Doors. The Damned even covered The Beatles, and perhaps more startling, The Ramones covered Jan and Dean, The Trashmen, *and* The Beach Boys.

To me, that was why that photo in *Search and Destroy* summed up the failure of punk so succinctly. The punks failed because they were lying to themselves from the very beginning. Obviously, the point of the billboard in the photo was ironic; its intention was actually to say: "Do we look like we need Elvis? Fuck you." But the fact was: they *did* need Elvis, and all the trappings of rock music and its bloated history of excess. After all, what was punk rock but rock'n'roll turned up loud—on cheap guitars played by a new generation of amateurs? Otherwise, the basic elements were still in place. Still the same perks, the same career goals, the same music industry. Labels, gigs, groupies, drugs. Verse chorus verse, all over again.

Failure *was* fused into the circuit of punk, as crucial to its wiring as to its birth and its death; and in its death, so too in its resurrection; and perhaps in its immortality, its continued insurrection. Punk was both fueled *and* damned by failure all along its trail of lives and deaths, rebirths and reissues, reunions and reiterations. In other words, it was as true to Guy Debord's *Society of the Spectacle* as Malcolm McLaren had proclaimed all along.

Debord may have been first to identify the spectacle and interrogate it (one of the more lasting revolts to surface in Paris in 1967). But it was Malcolm McLaren, The Sex Pistols' manufacturer or Mephistopheles (depending on which version of punk history you're reading), who was responsible for its dissemination on the street level in the UK circa 1976. While Debord warned "The Spectacle is not a collection of images; rather it is a social relationship between people that is mediated by its images" in Thesis 4 of 211 total (*Society of the Spectacle*, p. 12), McLaren plastered his Situationist banners on T-shirts, foisted them on banners behind bands (starting as early as 1974 in New York, when and where he was managing The New York Dolls).

While the Situationists *stated*: 'Boredom is always counter-revolutionary', McLaren *asked*: 'What are the politics of boredom?' While for the Situationists boredom was "pathological," "a fatalism devoid of meaning," and "a modern means of control," for the punks it was "no fun," "no feelings," and "no future." And yes, it was accompanied by a squeal of guitar and clatter of drums such had rarely been heard before. In the end, in many senses, the song remained the same.

So, still true to Debord's treatise, it is this form I return to now: the failure of Punk in these theses:

1. Punk was born from failure—the failure of the hippies to realize the society they envisioned and promised by turning on, tuning in and dropping out. (This, of course, is a society born before spectacle but doesn't the tune already sound familiar?) Hence, the punks' venomous and continually voiced spite in what can be termed the "primary texts" of punk film: *The Blank Generation* (Amos Poe, 1976), *The Punk Rock Movie* (Don Letts, 1978), *Jubilee* (Derek Jarman, 1978), *D.O.A.* (Lech Kowalski, 1980), *The Great Rock'n'Roll Swindle* (Julien Temple, 1980), *Rude Boy* (Jack Hazan, 1980), and *The Decline of Western Civilization* (Penelope Spheeris, 1981). After all, a copper or a politician is true to their natures all along, true to their suits. It was only in the end, in the hippies' failure, that they too put on their suits.

2. In the end, of course, the founding punks of 1976–77 failed, too. As damned as the hippies, as doomed to suits of their own. For skin stretches, nail varnish chips, and adulthood require an altogether different uniform. In fashion, as in culture, the trend is all and the trend is an arc that eventually closes on itself. Or, as primordial punk theorist Dick Hebdige puts it: "Youth cultural styles may begin by issuing symbolic challenges, but they must inevitably end by establishing new sets of conventions."

It wasn't just the style of clothes. It was first and foremost about a simultaneous re-invention and re-negation of rock-

'n'roll. It is this duality John Savage duly summons at the closing of *England's Dreaming*:

> Punk was beaten, but it had also won. If it had been the project of the Sex Pistols to destroy the music industry, then they had failed; but as they gave it new life, they allowed a myriad of new forms to become possible. When Punk entered the music and media industries, its vision of freedom was eventually swamped by New-Right power politics and the accompanying value systems, but its original, gleeful negation remains a beacon. (*England's Dreaming*, p. 541)

3. The originary point of the failure of punk was precisely when it first became spectacle—the first television appearance of The Sex Pistols on *The Bill Grundy Show* on UK television, December 1st 1976. For this was the specific moment when the punk sub-culture came above ground. Once made spectacle for five million people, the threat was dissipated. For it was now no longer all around, amorphous, and endless, in every shadow, pub, spike, and piercing, but easily contained on a thirteen-inch square over TV dinners nationwide.

As Jon Savage points out in *England's Dreaming*: "Most of those involved had always wanted to engage with the mass media, indeed sought self-justification by so doing, and they now had their wish. The movement's growth was accelerated by this free publicity, but it was a Faustian contract" (p. 231). It wasn't just the Pistols who were immortalized that day in fame and in failure. Veteran television promoter Bill Grundy ended his career that day, just as surely as he ensured his primacy in punk history. The Television Personalities were just the first to commemorate his entry into the punk pantheon. "They said he had too much to drink. / They said that he just could not think straight. / He set them up then they knocked him down. / Where's Bill Grundy now?" they sang on their second single in 1978. By 2008, the infamous clip of Grundy attempting to clip the wings of the fledgling Pistols was named the most requested television clip in UK media history—in a poll by the *NME*, no less (*New Musical Express*, July 28th 2008).

4. "The emergence of a spectacular subculture is invariably accompanied by a wave of hysteria in the press. This hysteria is typically ambivalent; it fluctuates between dread and fascination, outrage and amusement." Hebdige tells us this in 1979. But Adorno said it first in 1931—only, he was talking about the New Music of Schoenberg, Shostkovich, et. al.: "The difficulty of understanding the new art has its specific basis in this necessity of consumer consciousness to refer back to an intellectual and social situation in which everything that goes beyond the given realities, every revelation of their contradictions, amounts to a threat" (*Essays on Music*, p. 131). In both cases, the threat is directed at the status quotient consumers precisely because the emergence of these new musicks marks the emergence of a new generation of consumer. This is why, as Hebdige points out, style is both celebrated and reviled. What the punks failed to realize is that the creation of their new music marked just the latest alienation of production from consumption, and eventually the consumer would catch up.

5. Second-generation punk theorist Greil Marcus summarizes Guy Debord just so:

> The spectacle was capital accumulated until it becomes an image. A never-ending accumulation of spectacles—advertisements, entertainments, traffic, skyscrapers, political campaigns, department stores, sports events, newscasts, art tours, foreign wars, space launchings—made a modern world, a world in which all communication flowed in one direction, from the powerful to the powerless. One could not respond, or talk back, or intervene, but one did not want to. In the spectacle, passivity was simultaneously the means and the end of a great hidden project, a project of social control. On the terms of its particular form of hegemony the spectacle naturally produced not actors but spectators: modern men and women, the citizens of the most advanced societies on earth, who were thrilled to watch whatever it was they were given to watch. (*Lipstick Traces*, p. 99)

Of course the punks thrilled. With spit, spikes, swastikas, and sex, their trade and threat, no soundtrack was even necessary. With the neighborhood threat now on national television in both the UK and US, capital quickly accumulated. Johnny Rotten was only the first to name names: "There's unlimited supply / And there is no reason why / I tell you it was all a frame / They only did it 'cos of fame / Who? / EMI." But other pockets were filling fast too: CBS, Virgin, A&M, Warner Brothers, United Artists, Island, Polydor, Mercury and Chrysalis. Even RCA was cashing in on the spectacle of punk, same as it had (and still was cashing in) on pre-punk punk heroes David Bowie, Lou Reed, Iggy Pop, Brian Eno, . . . and Elvis Presley.

6. Consider, too, punk cinema's arc of failure. Most of the first wave of punk movies—*The Punk Rock Movie* (Don Letts,

1978), *The Blank Generation* (Amos Poe, 1976), *D.O.A.* (Lech Kowalski, 1980), and *The Decline of Western Civilization* (Penelope Spheeris, 1981)—was one of documentation, and in their dissemination, spreading the sub-culture. There were no rules. No established standards or reference points. Doing that would have meant recognizing *Don't Look Back* (D.A. Pennebaker, 1967), *Gimme Shelter* (Albert and David Maysles), or, worse yet, *Woodstock* (Michael Wadleigh, 1970), all located deep within the overlapping enemy territories of hippies and history.

The nearest rulebook for punk filmmakers was the recently hand-stapled format of the 'zine, or the DIY. seven-inch single. IF Xerox music really was here to last, as The Desperate Bicycles had promised, then so too were Xerox films: shot, cut, and pasted to life by like-minded amateurs. The mission statement was the same: "the overthrow of the establishment music industry through people seizing the means of production, making their own entertainment, and selling it to other creative and autonomous spirits," as Simon Reynolds would only later describe it (*Rip It Up and Start Again*, pp. 30–31). The technical failings of these films attest to their authenticity. Lack of light, lack of focus, lack of (sync) sound even, all provided markers not only of Being-There but being a Participant; Pioneers creating a new film genre of punk-verité. But the spectacle they projected also quickened punk's absorption into the mainstream. Hence, the second wave of punk cinema marks punk's entry into narrative and, indeed, even genre: the musical, rags to riches (and sometimes back to rags) melodrama, and even comedy—*Rock'n'Roll High School* (Alan Arkush, 1979), *Rude Boy* (Jack Hazan and David Mingay, 1980), *Ladies and Gentlemen the Fabulous Stains* (Lou Adler, 1982), and, of course, *Sid and Nancy* (Alex Cox, 1986). Steeped in tradition and shaped by decades of genre conventions, these were films equally haunted by the spirits of guys and dolls like Busby Berkeley, Fred and Ginger, Rodgers and Hammerstein, Gene Kelly, Judy Garland, Julie Andrews, The Beatles, and of course Elvis.

7. Greil Marcus might argue the point:

> Punk was not a musical genre; it was a moment in time that took shape as a language anticipating its own destruction, and thus sometimes seeking it, seeking the statement of what could be said with neither words nor chords.

But primordial punk historian Jon Savage decries such a statement as the purist's stand on punk, the idealist's. And they're both right. And that's precisely the point. Contradiction is the point. Multivalence is the point. So it's failure that validates punk and authenticates it just as surely as it dooms it.

8. That was the point with the swastika; the multivalence, the contradiction. Because they were everywhere in 1976–77; on T-shirts and armbands and guitar cases and skin. On the one hand, the swastika was two symbolic fingers pointed in the air (in the UK anyway) and directed at mum and at dad and their shared history, having lived through the Second World War. As Siouxsie Sioux later described: "We hated older people—not across the board, but particularly in suburbia—always harping on about Hitler, 'We showed him,' and that smug pride. It was a way of saying, 'Well I think Hitler was very good, actually': a way of watching someone like that go completely red-faced" (*England's Dreaming*, p. 241). The three fingers that remained folded on that hand simultaneously stood for many of the punks' true beliefs in England: 1. it was a country ruled by fascists; 2. it was a country populated by racists; and 3. it was a county poised in the same ramshackle state of unemployment and undirected desperation as the Weimar Germany of the 1930s where and when an Adolf Hitler was welcomed so enthusiastically. (The sort of welcome that both Margaret Thatcher and Ronald Reagan would receive.)

On the other hand entirely (one belonging to Jon Savage): "There was one final point to the swastika that goes to the heart of punk polysemy: the erosion of meaning itself" (p. 242). Not everyone agreed. Not even among punks. As John Lydon was the first to point out, "I thought Siouxsie and Sid were quite foolish . . . Although I know the idea behind it was to debunk all this crap from the past, wipe history clean and have a fresh approach, it doesn't really work that way" (*The Filth and the Fury*). So, long before the end, the punks failed in that, too. Because there is no such thing as wiping history clean, same as there is no wiping meaning from a sign as virulent as the swastika.

9. If only the punks hadn't danced. If only they hadn't failed to break the rockist equation of music = [equals] = dancing. *Because you can't dance to anarchy.* Even if the pogo was a caricature, it was still referential and reactionary, and a "dumbshow of blank robotics" (*The Meaning of Style*, p. 108) was still a show. Pose, pogo or robot were, when set to music, were still an expression of collective activity, participation in the call-and-response machinations of a communal concert experience, a variation on follow the leader no matter the manner of contortion. If punk were truly a Dada-ist movement, perhaps then, there should have been no movement at all.

10.   It was 1976, and Joe Strummer said: "We were strict. We'd look at everything and think: 'Is this retro?' I painted this shirt which said 'Chuck Berry Is Dead.' If it was old, it was out" (*England's Dreaming*, p. 232). But by 1977, The Clash were already on CBS. The Sex Pistols were on Virgin (and had been on EMI, A&M, and Warner Brothers). Buzzcocks were on United Artists, Siouxsie was on Polydor, along with Sham 69, The Ramones were on Warner Brothers, Richard Hell was on Sire, Generation X were on Chrysalis; Blondie, too (although they would go disco soon enough), The Adverts eventually signed to RCA—home of David Bowie, Iggy Pop, Lou Reed, Brian Eno, . . . and Elvis Presley.

Even fledgling Indie labels like Factory Records in Manchester, Zoo Records in Liverpool, and Rough Trade in London, who would debut in the winter of 1977–78, sealed their deals with little more than a handshake; yes, in an effort at being anti-corporate, but at the same time so their bands would be free to sign to a major label. "He no longer denies, / All the failures of the modern man. / No, no, no, he can't pick sides, / Sees the failures of the modern man," Ian Curtis sang on Joy Division's self-released debut DIY single, "An Ideal for Living." released in June of 1978 on seven-inch vinyl in sleeves hand-folded by the band. But by the end of the year they would sign to Factory Records, and in 1986 to Qwest, a subsidiary of Warner Brothers run by Quincy Jones who set up the deal— but only after the label had already released two New Order albums, *Lowlife* and *Brotherhood*.

11.   "I hate hippies," Rotten intoned almost continuously from 1976 to 1979 in patented Cockney snarl. ("Kill all hippies," The Deadbeats sang soon after on Dangerhouse Records, Los Angeles's first DIY punk label, no less, so you knew that they meant it.) But, by 1984, with Rotten now reinvented as Lydon, and front-man of Public Image Limited for nearly half-a-decade, not only were the band in heavy rotation on MTV with their anthem-cum-hit, "Rise," they were all in suits, even as Lydon now spat: "I could be wrong, but I could be right . . ." on endless repeat.

12.   The individual who in the service of the spectacle is placed in stardom's spotlight is in fact the opposite of an individual, and as clearly the enemy of the individual in himself as of the individual in others. In entering the spectacle as a model to be identified with, he renounces all autonomy in order himself to identify with the general laws of obedience to the course of things" (*Society of the Spectacle*, p. 39). Debord told us these things in 1967. But they were as true to punks in 1976 as they are to part-time punks now. Obedience to the course of age. Obedience to the course of culture, be it specious, spectacular, or sub-cultural. Obedience, even, to the rules of the rebel, with cause or without. For who could be more doomed to failure than a rebel *with* a role model?

13. To succeed as a punk is to fail. To fail in punk is to succeed. Welcome to the atrocity exhibition, where all doors open wide onto the circular corridor of history. This is the way, step inside.

14. Sid Vicious was the only real punk who did not fail. And Ian Curtis. They escaped failure for they failed to live. By becoming martyrs, they became pure spectacle. And via their ascension were authenticated. Here *were* the young men— barely men—who swore in life they didn't want to live past the age of twenty-five, and, as it turned out, swore true. And so, in their eternal silence after age twenty-one (Vicious) and twenty-three (Curtis), spake only the truth forevermore. The punks that remain are the true failures. John Lydon who treads his Sex Pistols or Public Image into the rock arena every other year has worn a suit for decades. To reunite, after all, in any costume, is to play to nostalgia.

15. (Which leads us to the alternate title of this chapter: "Society of the Bespectacled: The Dinosaurs that Would Not Die and Other Failures of Punk Rock.")

16. "Something must come after punk, 'cause you can't have permanent revolution." Peter Saville tells us this (Martin Wong interview, pp. 44–45). As graphic designer for Factory Records (arguably, the most important and influential post-punk label of all time), he helped define what would be the new music after punk—a form of music which fused music and art object. But of course, . . . there's no such thing as a new form of music. No such thing as a new Art, even. Theodor Adorno told us this ninety years ago. Expressionism, constructivism, futurism, cubism, atonality, surrealism, are all just catchwords, ultimately as empty and eventually as anachronistic as punk, goth, industrial, darkwave, minimal synth, post-punk, post-rock, grunge, shoegaze, Britpop, Krautrock, and of course rock'n'roll. There has been shock and strangeness with each new term, of course, but only manifested at the time those artistic tendencies were emerging.

Any description is ultimately a catchword, coined by a journalist, whose greatest gift is to name a trend; and by naming it, so dooms it to a specific moment in time. In Adorno's time, the New Music was Schoenberg, Berg, and Krenek. It was atonal and introspective but not emotional. It was, as Adorno described it, music "torn asunder from the immediacy of use." Its crime, so primal, its critics (or, as Adorno refers to them, "The Philistines") pronounced it, *"l'art pour l'art"*: "art for art's sake" and "an isolated aberration—hence correctable by means of a so-called 'recovery'—that is supposed to have something to do with some shortcomings in the psychic makeup of modern artists, who are said to be rootless and alienated from nature." But, as Adorno points out with regards to The New Music, "the roots nowhere reach deeper into the situation than in the case of so-called 'rootlessness'" (*Essays on Music*, p. 128). For Adorno, this was 1931.

By 1977, the separation from the root was all too often an exile voluntarily assumed by most punks. It was a pose informed by the first wave of rock'n'roll in the 1950s. Same chords, same strut, similar sneer. Only this time accessorized with piercings and requisite spikes on a billboard that *should* have read: **ELVIS IS DEAD AND WE *KINGED* HIM.**

4
Punk as Praxis

Nicholas H. Smith

What is Punk? One answer is that it is a genre of popular music, a sub-genre of Rock, pioneered by bands like the Ramones, the Sex Pistols and The Clash in the mid-1970s. At the top of my personal Punk playlist are songs by the Sex Pistols, The Clash, the Stranglers, Buzzcocks, Magazine, the Saints, Stiff Little Fingers, The Ruts, The Fall, Crass, and Dead Kennedys.

Punk, understood this way, is a set of songs, a *playlist*. We can debate which songs exactly should be included on this list—"Anarchy in the UK" definitely, "White Riot" definitely, "Psycho Killer" maybe, and so on—as we can debate which songs best epitomize Punk. However such debates go, the underlying assumption is that Punk is a body of music there to be heard.

A second way of thinking about Punk comes to mind if we ask of Punk songs, What makes them Punk? Punk songs have some distinctive musical features—a quick, simple tempo and basic chord progressions, for instance—but the distinctive sound of a Punk song seems to derive from something else: the *attitude* it expresses. It's not the thrashing of a handful of distorted guitar chords or a pounding bass as such that we intuitively recognize as Punk, but the angst, anger, and rebelliousness expressed in that sound. The distinctive sound of Punk, we could say, is the sound of the Punk attitude. And this attitude gets expressed not just in the songs that make up the Punk playlist, but also in Punk fashion and the lifestyle we associate with Punks.

The playlist view and the attitude view of Punk are both legitimate ways of looking at Punk. But they both miss, or do not properly bring into focus, something which is crucial to the

Punk phenomenon: <u>the fact that Punk involves *action* of sorts.</u>
It's obvious that Punk, like other forms of popular music, only
came into being through various kinds of activity: the formation of bands, the composition of songs, the playing at gigs, the
recording of tracks, the promotion of records and so on. But in
the case of Punk, such activities were carried out in a particular way, and it was by acting in that way that Punks distinguished themselves from others. The particular form of action
in which Punks were engaged and which brings us to the heart
of the Punk phenomenon—so I will argue—is *praxis*.

The Concept of Praxis

Praxis is a Greek word, and it is the sense given to this word
by the ancient philosopher Aristotle (384–322 B.C.), especially
in his *Nicomachean Ethics*, that subsequent use of the term
praxis (in English and other modern languages) invokes.
Aristotle's basic insight was that while human beings, like
other animals, have desires for the goods necessary for life
(food, warmth, and so on), in the human case satisfaction of
such desires is not enough for them to *flourish*. A flourishing
human life, Aristotle thought, also involves engagement in self-
directed activity.

Human activities can be more or less self-directed. Activity
that is exclusively at the command of someone else or in the
service of someone else's needs (such as a slave performs),
barely qualifies as self-directed at all. Activity that makes
something useful in accordance with a design, such as an arti-
san performs, allows more self-directedness, but it is limited by
the demands of the job and the properties of the thing to be
made. Activity that is done neither in the service of a master
nor for the sake of some product, but for its *own* sake, is more
self-directed still. It is activity of this sort, activity that is its
own end ("autotelic" activity), that Aristotle calls *praxis*.

For Aristotle, engagement in *praxis*-like, "autotelic," or fully
self-directed activity makes for human flourishing. But if
praxis is not available to slaves, or artisans, or businessmen
(who act in order to make money), who is able to engage in it?
Only free-persons (non-slaves) not preoccupied with work that
provides them with a living.

For Aristotle, *praxis* was the prerogative of a leisured elite.
But if the members of this elite are to *flourish* through their
praxis, they must act so as to ensure the flourishing of the community of which they are a part. This makes *praxis* an essentially political concept for Aristotle: it is by way of the collective

praxis of a community (Aristotle had in mind the Greek city-state, the *polis*) that the community realizes its common good. While *praxis* wasn't available to everyone, it reached perfection in the self-directing activities of a whole community.

Existentialist Praxis

We owe the modern understanding of *praxis* as much to some highly influential twentieth-century interpreters of Aristotle as to Aristotle's texts themselves. Chief amongst these interpreters was Martin Heidegger (1889–1976). Heidegger's lecture course on Aristotle's *Nicomachean Ethics* at the University of Marburg in 1924 is the stuff of legend: students included Hannah Arendt (1906–1975), Hans-Georg Gadamer (1900–2002), Hans Jonas (1903–1993), and Leo Strauss (1899–1973)—some of the key thinkers of their age—and they were captivated by Heidegger's teaching. Heidegger brought Aristotle's concept of *praxis* to life by reading it *existentially*.

Rather than taking *praxis* to be about human flourishing, Heidegger took it to be essentially about *authentic existence*. *Praxis* was first and foremost a mode of being, Heidegger thought; the mode in which the meaning of Being truly or authentically discloses itself. Being-in-the-mode-of-*praxis* stands in contrast to inauthentic existence, to a mere going along with things, to stale and suffocating convention. As opposed to mere getting by, or just doing what "one" does or saying what "one" says in this or that situation, *praxis* involves a radical questioning of accepted norms, a speaking in one's own voice, and a striking out at something new.

Of Heidegger's students, it was Arendt who would do most to interpret the contemporary world through the lens of the concept of *praxis*. Arendt emphasized the communicative aspect of *praxis* and the self-disclosure that comes from unforced speech. Arendt also stressed the public context of *praxis*-action and the importance of vibrant public spheres for democratic politics. But she lamented the absence of such spheres in contemporary societies, and more generally the dearth of opportunity for *praxis* in modernity. Autotelic activity, action done for its own sake rather than as a means to some external end, is barely possible anymore; such is the modern obsession with strategic thinking, efficiency, productivity, growth and so on. The ideal of the active life, which Aristotle had envisaged as a life of *praxis*, had degenerated in modern times into a mindless frenzy of working and spending, Arendt thought.

Marxist Praxis

While Heidegger and his followers used the idea of praxis to criticize modern society, Marxists wanted to do more than criticize. Marxists such as György Lukács, Antonio Gramsci, Herbert Marcuse, and Jean-Paul Sartre saw *praxis* as the key to *overthrowing* capitalism, not just diagnosing its ills. The transformation of capitalism into communism could not be left to the laws of history playing themselves out, as so-called 'Orthodox' Marxism maintained. Rather, it required self-conscious acts of resistance and self-organization on the part of ordinary working people.

It is primarily in such ground-level acts of opposition and self-organization that *praxis,* and with it the potential for real social change, is to be found. In Western Marxism, the concept of *praxis* becomes intimately bound up not just with political action, as it had been in Aristotle and Arendt, but with revolutionary action.

The Practice of Punk

A concept first introduced in a course of instruction to the political elite of ancient Greece, then adopted by radical philosophers in central Europe between the two world wars, brings us to the heart of Punk.

Negations

Punk involves a "no-saying." It begins with a "no" to how things are currently done, a refusal to carry on as usual.

The no-saying is most literal in the lyrics of some classic Punk songs. "Anarchy in the UK" begins with what many listeners at the time would have found the most shocking negation of all: "I am the *anti*-Christ." Typically, the object of negation is more diffuse, and easier for Catholic kids to sing along to: "*Something* better change," as in the Stranglers' hit. But the targeted negation is more effective, and one of the most persistent targets of Punk negation (at least in its first wave) was the world of *employment.*

In part, this was a matter of calling out the scarcity of decent employment ("No jobs, buddy"), especially for young people, and the drudgery and boredom of the work that was available. But underlying this was a questioning of the *promise* of work and the ideal of a career. The refusal to have your life defined by employment comes across especially powerfully in some of The Clash's early songs ("Career Opportunities" and "Clash City Rockers," for instance).

On the one hand, there is a refusal to fit into established, stultifying occupational roles. On the other, there is a refusal to be given over to the rewards of employment: buying and consuming things. The predominant message of "The Clash" album is: "No to life without *praxis*!"

But the musical communication of this message can *itself* only be a *praxis* if it is not co-opted for external ends, especially commercial ones. Commercialization is fatal to *praxis* and resistance to it in the act of making popular music is one of the most characteristic features of Punk. Punk-rockers are in constant, open battle with the forces that would make money out of them or use them for some other form of gain. Some of the best Punk songs take up this theme: "EMI," "Public Image," and "Garageland," to mention my personal favorites. The "no" to Punk without *praxis* on account of it being co-opted for commercial purposes wasn't just a matter of words. It was backed up by active resistance to the big record companies.

Another way of protecting Punk from commercialization was to refuse to *entertain*. Entertainment is a form of music-making and playing that serves an external purpose (to please people) and in that sense is a form of instrumental action, not autotelic action. The goal of the entertainer is to give pleasure to an audience, typically by engaging their fantasies and distracting them from reality, rather than confronting them with reality. In return for the entertainment provided, the entertainer takes the audience's money. Most Punks, though, did not see themselves as entertainers. They did not refuse payment for their performances (when they were paid for them), but neither the payment nor any pleasure the audience may have enjoyed was the *point* of the performance.

Refusal to go along with the stock-in-trade fantasies of popular music was another mark of Punk *praxis*. The sentimental, cliché-ridden love song (think Donny Osmond or Rod Stewart) was a strict no-no. Some saw the whole love song genre as a fraud and repudiated it completely. In any case, there were more important things than holding hands to worry about—nuclear war, for instance. The arms race looms menacingly in the background—and occasionally the foreground—of Punk, and a "no" to the military-industrial complex was for some (most notably Crass) the first and final responsibility of Punk.

Negation is a vital element of Punk *praxis*. It's a mistake, though, to think of Punk as *just* about negation. Most Punks saw this, but some were fooled into thinking that refusal and destruction are the final ends of Punk action and to be glorified as such. The glamorization of violence that Punk sometimes degenerated into—think, for instance, of Sid Vicious's trick or treat antics in the abject "The Great Rock'n'Roll Swindle," or more generally the on- and off-stage violence at Punk gigs—was an embarrassment to most Punks, and the antithesis of what got them into Punk in the first place.

Affirmations

The appeal of Punk was more due to its affirmative aspect—to what can positively be done through Punk *praxis*—than its sheer negations or refusals. It was the *alternative* it presented to established ways of doing things that attracted people.

The first positive thing about Punk *praxis* is that through it you can say what *you mean,* what comes to *your mind*—as the first line of Buzzcocks' Punk classic "Boredom" goes. You don't just say what "one" says or what "one" means when writing and playing a song. The space Punk provided for speaking in your *own* voice was incredibly liberating for young people at the time. Saying what you mean and speaking your own mind are key features of *praxis* action as distinct from strategic or instrumental action, where speaking is merely a means to some external end, a way of manipulating people to think and act as someone else wants them to.

The Punk song also provides a vehicle for you to say what's *on* your mind. You sing about the things that matter to you, the world as you see it. So, while its important for you to speak in your own voice, you don't just talk about yourself. There are things around you to call out: complacency, decadence, oppression, exploitation, hopelessness, defiance, and so on. But there is also an inner world of feelings to express, and the challenge is to be true to those feelings, to express them authentically. If you do that successfully, the feeling itself can be intensified. Clarity of expression and intensification of feeling are both enhancements of life, and both could be achieved by Punk *praxis*.

In order to speak in your own voice, you first have to find it. But you can only find it by experimenting, and in the course of experimenting, you create your voice, you *self*-create. Experimentation in song-writing and musical form was another important aspect of Punk. Punk *praxis* was fundamentally *creative* action. It's a reflection of this emphasis on creativity that Punk bands were expected to play their own songs; a practice generally carried over into the recordings. In *Punk: Attitude* (the documentary film directed by Don Letts, 2005) Hilly Kristall said he had a policy of only having bands on at CBGB's who played their own music. From recollection, a similar policy held at British Punk venues such as Eric's in Liverpool. There are very few covers on the classic Punk albums, The Clash's cover of Junior Murvin's "Police and Thieves" prominent among them. (Having said that, the song lists for the Sex Pistols' early gigs consisted almost entirely of covers, and this was true for other Punk bands.)

But Punk experimentation was rarely a matter of musical *technique*. You didn't need any particular musical skills or expertise to try it out. You certainly didn't need any qualifications. In principle, anyone could do it.

It wasn't just in song-writing and playing that Punks acted experimentally and creatively. The whole productive process was up for grabs. Don't have a band? Form one. Don't have songs? Write them. Don't have a record label? Set one up. Don't wait for permission to do any of these things; don't wait till you have the qualifications. *Acting* for yourself—self-directed, *praxis* action—was the Punk way.

We shouldn't be misled though into thinking that Punk *praxis* was just about individuals doing their own thing indifferently to each other. The subject (or agent) of Punk *praxis* was an "us" as well as an "I." This is obvious—no individual can play the drums, guitar, and bass at the same time or produce a record all on their own—but it has a significance that is easily overlooked. Punk *praxis* is essentially a form of *social* action: it involves doing something *together* for a shared purpose. In our atomized world, opportunities for social action can be hard to find. Not least amongst the positive effects of Punk was to give people such opportunities.

You could also find community in Punk. There were the squats, of course, but more relevant for *praxis* were the performance and discussion spaces organized around Punk. In the fanzines, the music press, and to a certain extent radio stations, Punk found a vibrant public sphere, a place of passionate discussion and critique. The fanzines would often be sold and read in record shops. Reading the mags and flicking through the records, you got the sense that a higher life and true community were possible. In this respect, a visit to the record shop was like attending a modern art gallery, only less intimidating, less pretentious, more inclusive, and more fun.

Post-Punk *Poiesis*

On 4th June 1976, a gathering took place at the Lesser Free Trade Hall in Manchester, England, that was as consequential for the history of Punk as Heidegger's lectures in Marburg were for the history of the concept of *praxis* half a century earlier. It was the legendary performance by the Sex Pistols to a small audience that included Howard Trafford, Peter McNeish, Peter Hook, Bernard Sumner, and Steven Morrissey. A few weeks later the Sex Pistols did another gig at the same venue to a larger audience that included Tony Wilson, Ian Curtis and Mark E. Smith. (There was no attendance list so we have no proof of who was actually there. I'm relying here on Paul Glynn's account.)

The gigs marked the arrival of the Sex Pistols as a band breaking with the past and opening hitherto unimagined possibilities for popular music-making. These possibilities would be experimented with and developed by the bands those audience members would go on to form: Buzzcocks, Magazine, The Fall, Joy Division, New Order, and the Smiths. The independent record label Tony Wilson would soon set up, Factory, encouraged further experimentation along the lines the Sex Pistols first put on show that night. Increasingly, though, the music produced under the label lost its resemblance to the original Punk sound. That it did so reflects an inherent weakness in Punk *praxis*.

We saw that *praxis* as conceived by Aristotle was distinct from, and in a sense opposed to, activity that involved skill, craft, or technique—what Aristotle called *poiesis*. Punk's refusal of musical virtuosity for its own sake was thus a rejection of a *poiesis* model of music, and this had an empowering effect: punk enabled and encouraged you to say what you meant, to express yourself authentically, and anyone could join in. Punk put *praxis* before *poiesis*. But saying what you mean, and being true to your experience of your inner and outer world, is itself something that can be refined through musical technique. It turns out that you can say more interesting things, and be truer to your experience, if you are more musically equipped. As the first wave of Punks learned this, most left the essentially amateur *praxis* sound of Punk behind to develop the more sophisticated, professional-sounding music of Post-Punk.

This might be one reason why your Post-Punk or "Alternative" playlist is likely to be longer, more diverse, and more interesting to listen to than your Punk list. But as we've seen, there's more to Punk than a playlist.

5
To Resist Despair

BAILIE PETERSON

When someone asks you 'What's punk?' my reply is, 'If you have to ask, you're never going to know'.

—HENRY ROLLINS ("Black Flag," The Rollins Band)

Despite Henry's wry comment, the question remains. What makes something, or someone, punk? Is there an essential nature to punks? Being punk requires striving towards several inter-connected virtues: being authentic to yourself, valuing individual freedom and autonomy, and questioning all forms of authority. While there are other virtues and aesthetic preferences associated with punk, these make up the minimal set of necessary characteristics for punk. These characteristics explain what punk is.

"Punk"?

'Punk rock' is a word used by dilettantes and heartless manipulators.

—IGGY POP, The Stooges

The term 'punk' has created problems from the beginning, as seen in Iggy Pop's 1977 interview with Peter Gzowski on *90 Minutes Live*. At the time, the term was somewhat pejorative or jocular, associated with prison lingo for young male prostitutes and with a more general term for shiftless young ruffians. Before this time, the word appeared as a jibe in Shakespeare's plays and was also used negatively in Victorian times ("From Shakespeare to Rock Music").

By many accounts, "punk" was first connected to the music scene by the creators of *Punk Magazine*, a publication put out beginning in 1976 in New York (*Please Kill Me*). They were looking for a contemptible and silly term that would connect the characteristics they ascribed to themselves and their peers in the scene: "drunk, obnoxious, smart but not pretentious, absurd, funny, ironic," and into "things that appealed to the darker side" (p. 204). Even though early punks tried to reject the term 'punk', it stuck.

Unity Despite Diversity?

Is punk merely a fashion? A musical genre? A countercultural movement? Let's take the community of people who call themselves punk as the starting point and work out what additional ideals and goals are necessary for membership in this group. How do we account for the massive disagreement among punks, both historically and today, while still identifying a cohesive group?

Those less familiar with punk might picture a more or less uniform style and wonder if there is any disagreement or diversity among punks. A google image search for "punk" yields many expected results: mohawks in every color, dog collars, plaid bondage pants, spikes, chains, and vests made up of band patches. But mixed among this trope is a young and shirtless Iggy Pop, long straight hair and heavy eyeliner; The Ramones with their signature T-shirt-and-jeans style, X-Ray Spec's Poly Styrene with full curls tied up in a headband bow, and a recent photo of Debbie Harry of Blondie, who still looks cool and relevant despite the absence of typical punk gear.

Punk music covers very diverse subject matter, as well. There are messages promoting a drug-free life (Minor Threat's "Straight Edge") and those with a less restrictive position (The Ramones "Now I Wanna Sniff Some Glue"). Some songs are intensely political (The Dead Kennedys' "Holiday in Cambodia") while others have a light-hearted (if still critical) feel (like Black Flag's "TV Party"). There are songs criticizing established religion like the Damned's "Anti-Pope," or much of Bad Religion's early catalog, but there are also Christian Punk bands, like MxPx. In addition to the content, the sound of punk varies widely. Some genres, like Surf-punk, are very far stylistically from others, like Hardcore.

While the range of views among punks may create challenges, it may also be worth highlighting that the disagreement present reflects some of punk's best features, including a critical eye towards accepted views. This skepticism naturally leads to a tendency to disagree.

Despite the disagreements among punks, there are also common virtues significant enough to establish a coherent sub-culture. These are themes echoed in punk music, interviews, and personal reflections.

Punk and Authenticity

I've learned that telling the truth is a very good way of life.

—JOHN LYDON, The Sex Pistols; Public Image Limited, *Punk*, Part Four

Authenticity is essential to being punk. It is about being genuine, true to oneself, and honest about what you are doing and why you are doing it. To a large degree, punk requires forging your own path rather than just falling in line with the expectations of peers, family, community, and society. Only you can determine if you are a success or failure, depending on whether your own reflective interests direct your life, according to your own (carefully considered) rules. Henry Rollins provides a basic punk manifesto: "Let's determine our outcome—let's form the future" (*Punk*, Part Four).

In contrast, consider Operation Ivy's "Smiling," in which the song's protagonist criticizes a man for "smiling when his friends are watching," as he throws himself into meaningless sexual exploits, not because this is part of who he really is, but simply as a quest to be accepted by his peers.

Another strong example of this virtue within the punk community is Palmolive of the Slits, one of the legends of early punk. When asked why her band became punk, she said, "we wanted to have the reins of our destiny" (*Punk*, Part Two). As an all-female band at a time when men dominated rock, the Slits broke significant ground. Palmolive's bandmate, Viv Albertine, expresses a similar sentiment in a recent interview: "We weren't going to try and be this constructed ideal of femininity—or masculinity, come to that—that had been put upon us for not just decades but centuries, you know, to be sort of tittering, sort of giggling, smiley, appeasing . . . we absolutely, you know, weren't going to do that" (*Fresh Air* interview). These women created a space to play punk rock at a time when there were no women in rock at all (in fact, Joan Jett found that while the music of her first band, *The Runaways,* may not be considered punk, "the idea of girls playing rock'n'roll was as punk as you get)" (*Punk*, Part Two). What makes these women's actions both authentic and punk is the desire and willingness to forge their paths based on their own values, goals, and sense of self.

Existentialism and Authenticity

Although I've sketched the notion, more work is needed to explain what is meant by 'authenticity'. Consider the definition offered by Somogy Varga and Charles Guignon (2020). They begin by posing a question, "Are one's thoughts, decisions, and actions genuinely expressive of who one is?" They set out a view of authenticity that "describes a person who acts in accordance with desires, motives, ideals or beliefs that are not only hers (as opposed to someone else's), but that also express who she really is." What does it mean to express who you *really* are?

This notion of authenticity is expressed in philosophical writing by Heidegger, Beauvoir, and Sartre. Central to their concept of authenticity is the claim that you're responsible for your actions and for ensuring that your choices and actions reflect who you are. Freedom and autonomy are prerequisites to living authentically. You must first be free to make your own decisions and then free to act on them.

Punk and Freedom

> We're born with a chance
> Rise above! We're gonna rise above!
> I am gonna have my chance.
> Rise above! We're gonna rise above!
>
> —Black Flag, "Rise Above."

Authenticity requires and reflects the metaphysical assumption that humans are free, and free enough to create their selves. If free choices are not possible, then no one can choose to live authentically or even try to do so. Rather than imagining that we're born with a fixed "soul" that dictates our being, Sartre claims that "existence precedes essence." There is no set self beyond the self you create through your free choices and actions. In this Sartrean sense, punks hold individual freedom in high regard. Rejecting the rules and assumptions of parents, teachers, employers, and society is an essential punk virtue.

Punk and Autonomy

As well as metaphysical freedom, there is another prerequisite for authenticity: autonomy, or your capacity for self-governance. While autonomy requires that you guide your life through your own decisions, authenticity goes beyond simply being in control of one's life and further requires that "one's motives and reasons are expressive of who one is" (Varga and Guignon).

Punk authenticity requires understanding that you are responsible for who you are and what you do as an autonomous and free being.

Punk and Questioning Authority

The questioning of authority, pushing back against established structures of authority, of government, of the way it is. Questioning anything and everything to me is punk rock.

—HENRY ROLLINS, "What Is Punk?

The last essential virtue of punk is the push to hold a skeptical eye towards authority. This virtue is also linked to authenticity, which, according to Varga and Guignon, "becomes an implicitly critical concept, often calling into question the reigning social order and public opinion."

Being authentic brings with it a willingness to question authority since it requires you to reflect on the underlying reasons for your decisions and actions, many of which may be due to outside forces, like people, institutions, and social and cultural norms. This entails that your own reasons and expectations are also subject to scrutiny since they can be guided by outside influences that do not reflect your genuine interests.

Even though not all punks are political anarchists (and not all anarchists are punk), they share the virtue of questioning authority. Robert Paul Wolff, for example, claims that mindlessly obeying authority puts a person in a position of servitude and must be rejected (*In Defense of Anarchism*, p. 9). Wolff explains that obeying authority requires acting simply because an act is commanded, which contrasts sharply with our notion of punk authenticity. He argues that authenticity conflicts with autonomy for two main reasons—first, authority requires submission, which rules out self-governance since it requires obedience rather than exercising autonomy, even when doing so conflicts with your use of reason. Second, acting autonomously requires acting from your own reasons in coming to a decision—obeying authority conflicts with this since you are supposed to act in obedience rather than through reason, which strips away your ability to decide for yourself.

While Wolff is making a case for rejecting political authority, in particular, the general move to question sources of authority is a virtue punks must strive towards as a means to live an authentic life.

Crass, a primary example of anarcho-punk, declare, in the final lines of the album *Yes Sir, I Will*: "You must learn to live with your own conscience, your own morality, your own decision, your own self. You alone can do it. There is no authority but yourself."

Authenticity and Authority

You might wonder whether authenticity is a virtue anyone should strive towards, let alone a punk. For example, Varga and Guignon note the objection that authenticity, with its commitment to inwardly focused directives, may be thought to create a sort of narcissistic egoism. If a person only relies on an inward notion of how they ought to be, might they choose to be a self-interested, terrible person?

We might also ask whether shrugging off all sources of authority yields a nihilistic, anything-goes approach, or whether this anti-authority stance supports some sort of mindless rebellion. Punks are often accused of merely seeking shock value. Consider Jayne County's acknowledgment that early punks like her "just wanted to shock people out of their normalcy" (*Punk*, Part Two). It can be tempting to associate this virtue with cheap attention-seeking or with tepid, mass-produced anarchism of the sort that you can buy at Hot Topic. To a large degree, these concerns are raising the same question—do these punk virtues enable one to be a jerk?

However, the virtues in play are not supposed to stand alone, as each criterion makes up only a part of what is essential to punk. The requirements that 1. you attempt to be authentic to yourself while 2. accepting the responsibilities and benefits that stem from your freedom, and also, 3. questioning authority, are inter-related. This set of virtues together suggests a healthy skepticism towards the opinions that you encounter, including your own. Just as you ought to question whether or not the structures of society are justified, you ought to reflect on your choices and values and ask yourself whether you are living authentically.

We can take Jayne's comment in a different light—as a gender-nonconforming punk icon, she was not calling us to mindlessly stand in opposition to everything. Instead, she raised important questions about gender roles and abuse towards queer people, which were not part of the conversation. Far from advocating mindless rebellion, this is a call for necessary change.

Punk also reflects the philosophical virtue of humility. When Operation Ivy declares, "All I know is that I don't know nothing" in the song "Knowledge," this recalls Socrates's famous conclusion that the oracle had named him the wisest man alive because he knew that he knew nothing. We know so little that we cannot act rashly or pretend to have it all figured out. Together, autonomy and freedom yield responsibilities—we're free to make ourselves, but we are also responsible for our choices and the consequences that stem from them. Ultimately, we're accountable for the selves that we create. Taken altogether, the virtues of punk, while they don't rule out the opportunity to be a jerk, at least advocate against selfishness and hubris.

Freedom and Facticity

The role claimed for freedom in this account also draws criticism. You might wonder whether it's a non-starter to create a view dependent upon freedom given how many aspects of our lives are determined. In response, Sartre and Beauvoir argued that we must recognize and respond to our "facticity," or the set of circumstances we are in, beyond our control. Facticity includes things like when and where you are born, the physical body you are born into, the past choices you've made, and even aspects of the human condition like death. We cannot choose to be immortal or born into a wealthy, stable, loving family. We cannot choose our sexual orientation, nor if we live in a time when the world is welcoming or hostile to the various characteristics of our facticity. But given the situation we are thrown into, we are free and responsible for responding to these circumstances from within the range of possible options.

The punk response to facticity explains another common characteristic of the punk ethos—the DIY approach. Consider Alice Bag of the groundbreaking female LA punk band, Bags. "In Los Angeles, almost every band had women in them; Women, people of color, queers—anyone who had been shut out in the past, anybody who felt like "I have to wait until I reach this certain level of proficiency," or "until I see myself reflected." All of a sudden, punk opened the doors, and you were your own role model."

As a punk, you must forge your path, creating opportunities and positive pressure to "rise above." You cannot say, "well, I am not a good enough singer, not attractive enough to be in a band, not wealthy enough to buy a professional bass." Johnny Ramone played a cheap Mosrite guitar (which Lou Reed criticized him for), while The Ramones created a new sound and established themselves as punk rock demigods (*Please Kill Me*, p. 206). Similarly, when Harley Flanagan started playing drums for the Stimulators, he was twelve years old and not tall enough to sit on the stool, resorting to playing drums standing up. As he puts it, "To me punk rock was about being creative with very little, making something out of nothing, not giving a f**** about the rest of the world's standards—just simplicity and freedom" (*Punk*, Part Three).

There are no excuses—punk asks you to do what you freely can, in line with who you are, authentically. You can shrug off as many of the socially imposed shackles as you can—you can decide to go to art school instead of joining the army; you can choose to take a gap year, learn a second language and travel to a new place, or volunteer for Food Not Bombs. You can drop out of high school, run away to an anarchist festival, live under a bridge, and become a philosophy professor later—this was what I freely chose to do, and it was one of the most important decisions of my life. You are the one who decides what a successful life is—you decide what makes your life worthwhile, given your standards.

The opportunity to move beyond circumstances does not deny that many people are dealt a terrible starting hand, nor does it blame those who cannot find success or overcome the impediments in their way. Alice Bag's depiction of her childhood in her memoir, *Violence Girl: East LA Rage to Hollywood Stage, A Chicana Punk Story*, is both devasting and familiar to many other punk bios. In some ways, it's radical for these punks just to attempt to pursue their dreams given their starting points.

Selling Out and the Poseur Problem

Consider the character Stevo from the 1998 movie *SLC, Punk*. He spends much of the film criticizing those who have "sold out" before he decides to follow the very path he had declared anathema.

Can you change your style, go to Harvard, and become a high-profile lawyer, while still being a punk? In my view, you can. This might seem to indicate that this view is too permissive; however, that is not the case. First, I am only considering those who declare themselves punk, so if Stevo doesn't claim to be punk anymore, he isn't. This has the benefit of allowing us to describe non-punks as exemplifying punk's virtues. We can earnestly say that David Hume exemplified many virtues of punk, for example (I think he did), without anachronistically calling him a punk.

Second, my view requires that punks strive to live a life imbued with clear-eyed authenticity. If we meets these goals earnestly, it doesn't matter what they look like, and to suggest otherwise supports a much more shallow view of punk. There is a related concern, the "poseur problem," which bottoms out in a similarly shallow version of punk.

My view implies that genuine punks *strive* to become punks by meeting specific criteria. We could question whether there is something inconsistent, or even pernicious, in insisting that punks must *try* to be punk. In other words, don't we need to rule out inauthentic punks?

While it's aesthetically unappealing to imagine a punk's slow and concerted effort to look disheveled, this stems from a false stereotype of what it is to be punk. Sure, Darby Crash of the Germs puts on a big show that he does not care, refusing to even sing into the microphone during *The Decline of Western Civilization: I*. But this conflicts with the careful efforts he put into songwriting or the countless stories of the concerted efforts of punks to be true to their art. This notion also seems to assume that punks must have some pre-existing ineffable quality of punkness that they are living out, rather than striving towards, which directly conflicts with the view put forth here.

In addition, it seems that this assumption relies on a different concept of authenticity. My notion is an inward, personal quest. In contrast, here, we have a metaphysical notion, capturing the same sense of authenticity we might ascribe when identifying "an authentic Beauguereau painting." I reject this notion because it misses what's actually essential to punk.

My view also entails that there may be mere "fashion punks," since it's feasible that someone could like punk music or adopt punk fashion as a means to conform, as a fashion statement, or even as a way to express that they unquestioningly agree with the status quo. Consider the Halloween that my popular older sister (the Quinn Morgendorffer to my own Daria) borrowed my clothes and dressed as me for Halloween. In doing so, she did not become "punk," and it's a virtue of my view to provide this distinction. Put another way, you can value authenticity without being punk, but you cannot be punk without striving to be authentic.

Capturing Punks

Taken together, the virtues of punk I've supported present a plausible notion while capturing a wide range of punks. Punk urges us to critically examine who we are and who we want to be, make our own path while pausing to subject our choices to scrutiny, and shrug off all that conflicts with the ability to live authentically. This thesis is reflected in the final lines of Operation Ivy's "Sound System": "To resist despair in this world is . . . what it is to be free."

6
When Punks Grow Up

Thomas Meagher

"Punk" is inescapably linked to youth culture. As with the broader cultural framework of rock'n'roll, punk's origins embraced rebellion against older authority figures. Punk, though, goes further, rejecting myriad structures of power.

If rock's framework is rebellion against the teen's exclusion from the privileges of adult life, punk rebels not in order to secure access but to protest adults' status as functionaries of oppressive social relations. Punk manifests an adolescent rage not at its exclusion from adulthood but at the decadence of social structures perpetuated by more powerful older generations. Indeed, punks often define themselves just as strongly in opposition to non-punk peers whose function is to reproduce objectionable modes of power. The punk's ill-will toward "jocks," for instance, is rooted in a conception of the jock as maintaining hierarchical systems of power and privilege passed on by older generations, rather than scorn for athleticism.

The punk, then, emerges as an adolescent who contests the normalcy of established orders through revolt against adults and adolescents alike. So what happens when punks become adults? In the initial punk eruption driven by adolescents and twenty-somethings, an "old punk" was an oxymoron. Old punks would later emerge as those *who had once been young punks*, rather than as elders *becoming* punk.

Punk's association with aggrieved youth presents the aging punk as a cultural contradiction. Subsequent representations of punk, as in movies such as *SLC Punk* (1998), *The Other F Word* (2011), and *Ordinary World* (2016), treat the punk facing adult responsibilities as a paradox. Can we grapple with adult responsibilities while remaining punk? Is punk inescapably juvenile and incompatible with maturity?

47

If maturity is conformity to adult conventions, punk is clearly immature. If familiar admonitions by the powerful to "grow up," "be a man," or "act lady-like" through acceptance of prevailing norms exhaust maturity's meaning, then one who matures ceases to be a punk. However, an alternative conception is possible: the conventional view of maturity might be mistaken and, even, *an immature notion of maturity*. If predecessors insist maturity means conformity, punks may respond by showing they are *wrong* about the meaning of maturity. Hence, the punk may offer an alternative, *punk* conception of maturity.

Punk and Rebellion

The emergence of rock'n'roll in the 1950s was grounded in a spirit of rebellion. Filmic icons of this rebellion are found in *Rebel Without a Cause* (1954) and *The Wild One* (1953). In the latter, Marlon Brando's Johnny Strabler is asked, "Hey Johnny, what are you rebelling against?" His response: "Whadda you got?" Johnny rebels for rebellion's sake. Revolt is thus an end in and of itself, a *telos*. Rock'n'rollers required no cause other than rebellion.

By the 1970s, rock'n'roll had become more hegemonic than resistant. Hippie rockers produced rock with a social aim, but often became so rich or drug-addled in the process that their music served aims alien to the socially-transformative ones they had initially talked about. Progressive rock turned the form into one of ornate "high art." Arena rock maintained a measure of edge and simplicity but for the sake of popular appeal.

Punk rock emerged as a rebellion against these forms, returning to rock'n'roll's stripped-down essentials with a faster pace and radical antipathy to the appearance of professionalism. Yet punk's rebellion transcends musical elements. There are hallmarks of a punk rock *sound*, but punk is not reducible to its sonic dimensions. Punk's sound was a product of a broader ethos of revolt, rather than the other way around. Punk rock as musical form is but one aspect of punk culture, which encompasses elements of dance (moshing), visual art (stenciling, collage), fashion (safety pins, mohawks), nomenclature ("Sid Vicious," "Poly Styrene"), and so on. These various elements unite in subversion of prevailing orders through explicit and aggressive modes of non-conformity and denunciation.

If punk is grounded in rebellion and non-conformity, an internal drama follows. What happens when "punk" becomes a convention? If punk is rebellious, does it mandate conformity to particular modes of rebelling? Does punk sometimes demand rebellion even *against punk*? Is being *against* something so essential that punk can never be *for* anything? Must punk merely rebel against whatever can be rebelled against?

Indeed, the very spirit of rebellion precludes developing a philosophical interpretation of "punk" that would be universally adopted by all punks. Yet all punks face the burden of explaining what punk means *to them*, where any individual's answer is potentially meaningful to others. Though there is no way to define everything punk rebels against, punks nonetheless face the existential question of giving meaning to their rebellions, both individually and collectively, such that what punk rebels against—and what it fights for—are recurring questions.

Seriousness as Immaturity

For Jean-Paul Sartre and Simone de Beauvoir, the characteristic of *freedom* defines human reality. Human existence requires choices. This means we *must* make choices; human reality is "condemned to freedom." Abstractly, freedom sounds appealing. Concretely, though, freedom is often burdensome. When we reflect on freedom as a burden, we realize this condition of *having* to choose invites discomfort, pain, even terror. Such reflection on freedom as burden Sartre terms *anguish*. Because we'd like to evade anguish, we often turn to *bad faith* which for Sartre is consciousness that denies, disavows, or represses awareness of its freedom, hoping to make anguish go away.

A typical form of bad faith is *the spirit of seriousness*. The "serious person" is in bad faith about values. The serious person affirms that their day is full of choices, but each choice is viewed as merely fulfilling an external obligation: "I did it because I had to." The serious person says he simply acts in accordance with what is demanded by God, law, or convention. The serious person acts as if it is always someone or something else determining the values that dictate their choices. The serious person, then, is engaged in self-deception: they could reject these "imposed" values, but they deny their freedom to do so.

Insofar as punk rejects conformism, it can be characterized as a rebellion against the spirit of seriousness. On this interpretation, punk revolts against human tendencies to accept values on the basis of tradition, authority, or presupposition. Ergo, punk can be viewed as embracing freedom to choose your own values, deciding what to live for rather than deferring this decision to those in power.

What, then, is the relationship between the spirit of seriousness and maturity? "Man's unhappiness," de Beauvoir contends, "is due to his having first been a child" (*The Ethics of Ambiguity*, p. 35). The child experiences a world populated by adults whose power seems limitless and benevolence indubitable. The child experiences the freedom of *play* but under the watchful eye of adult guardians. In the sandbox, the child plays and imagines, yet adults dictate where, when, and for how long the sandbox is available. Where the sandbox ends, the child must simply *behave*.

As children grow, they experiment with disobedience, learning the consequences of stepping out of line. Authoritarians seek to make such consequences so extreme that obedience becomes uncontrollable habit. Yet often this gives way to a period of adolescence in which the relation to one's choices becomes complex. The high-school student who must now choose elective classes, for instance, makes choices that at first appear to be about what the student enjoys, or at least tolerates. But then these choices emerge as linked to prospects for college and career. Adolescence offers a preview of adult life: for the adult, choices are laden with *power*, such that choices build the world of actuality and not merely the world imagined in child's play.

This difference between power and play, though, suggests different degrees of anguish. Child's play is low-stakes. Power, though, invites *accountability*. Adult life is saturated with the anguish of standing face-to-face with the burden of choosing what kind of world to produce, not as merely imagined but as actually inhabited by others. Maturity entails dealing with such anguish head on: I am mature when I accept the anguish of adult life and face my responsibility for the world, knowing that even my best effort won't be enough to satisfy every possible mode of accountability. The spirit of seriousness, by contrast, is immature. The serious man evades his anguish by acting as if he still faced the discipline of a disapproving parent: God, convention, Kantian morality, and so forth. For the serious man, while this imagined stern parent who stands in judgment may invite the anxiety of living up to its standards, it ultimately eases the anguish of being held accountable by other actual people; it defuses the anguish of knowing that others are freedom to articulate values of their own and to hold him accountable for failing to live up to them.

The serious person is thus immature because he takes values to be concrete and externally-imposed rather than malleable and constructed; he seeks to evade the anguish and accountability of adult life. If punk is a rebellion against the spirit of seriousness, does it follow, then, that punk is necessarily mature?

Weak Nihilism

What happens when one who has taken seriously these externally-imposed values experiences failure and disappointment? Beauvoir contends that this often prompts rapid descent to *nihilism*. If serious values get you nowhere, you may reject values altogether; everything becomes equally worthless. Straitlaced students who get rejected by their preferred college and jocks who experience career-ending injuries, for instance, sometimes respond by taking solace in punk rebellion. Their initial embrace of punk is driven by the strange *relief* it may offer in suggesting that their old lives didn't matter.

Yet is nihilism only a rejection of values? For Sartre, all valuing is a "nihilation," since to affirm any particular value is to negate competing ones. This suggests that a broader interpretation of "nihilism" would be one in which the agent embraces their freedom to *choose* what to value, as opposed to the spirit of seriousness's insistence that all choices are in service of external values. This is so for the philosopher most often termed nihilist, Friedrich Nietzsche, for whom nihilism's function is to clear away old values *so that new ones can be constructed.*

If nihilism just means rejecting all values, then it's as immature as the spirit of seriousness: both would simply reject the anguished project of choosing values. Hence, to get at our conception of maturity, we may distinguish between *weak nihilism* and *strong nihilism.* Per Devon Johnson, "'weak' nihilism responds to the fall of traditional values by denying the value of human valuing altogether. . . . 'Strong' nihilism . . . not only rejects decadent values, but seeks creation of ways of valuing beyond weak nihilism" (*Black Nihilism*, p. 40). Weak nihilists abandon values, but strong nihilists revolt against decadent values *by creating new ones.* Weak nihilism offers an immature revolt, denying responsibility for producing alternative values.

Johnson argues that weak nihilism came to predominate in Western culture through European colonialism. Christianity could neither offer a coherent rationale for a dehumanizing system of global domination nor could it satisfy the hedonistic impulses of societies enriched by conquest and enslavement. Western Humanism emerged to trample the serious values of Christendom. However, this meant any attempt to impose a humanistic seriousness harbored internal seeds of crisis. These alternative value systems rested on the notion of a "modern" consciousness, "enlightened" and freely choosing its values. Yet attachment to colonialism's spoils rendered Europe incapable of producing a genuine humanism in which *all* human beings freely fashion values. Western Humanism would have to be *externally-imposed* on the globe, which would have to take it seriously at gunpoint rather than contributing equally in constructing its values. Western Humanism's racism meant its philosophical avatars indulged in decadent rationalizations of its compatibility with genocidal empire. Western Humanism thus proved incapable of genuine value-creation: its substitutes for Christian seriousness yielded intellectual veneers for hollow hedonism. Hence, it produced exactly those types of societies against which punk would revolt—societies where human beings have no meaningful power to transform the present and future direct their societies to simply function to reproduce the power of elites by promoting consumerist conformity.

Hence, Johnson surmises, the West's racism and colonialism meant that its toppling of Christian values was weakly nihilistic. It offered no genuine effort to replace decadent values but rather an effort to cloak imperial evils in a "modern" façade. Euromodernity offered the idea of "Man" as global *adult* whose rule would bring the world to maturity. The reality was the reverse: Euromodern "Man" as childish ideologue seeking to impose his will on others through values they'd have to take seriously but he would not. The weak nihilism of Euromodernity immaturely evades the burden of *producing values worth valuing*.

Strong Nihilism

What, then, of those who live under the force of Euromodern domination? Johnson analyzes Black existence in the face of an antiblack racist world order. Many who are dominated take on the values the dominator imposes by force. Others, though, see their suffering as flatly contradicting the premise that fidelity to the dominator's values is redeeming. Hence, many respond with nihilism; antiblack racism, therefore, produces Black nihilism.

Weak Black nihilism, Johnson, notes, attempts to flee anguish. It affirms the pessimism and despair white hegemony inspires. For weak Black nihilism, nothing Black people do matters since they lack the power to build the world; Black values appear as pointless as racist ones. Hence, there is no concern with building the world anew: you simply must wait for it to end.

The alternative is strong Black nihilism. Strong Black nihilism takes seriously that, though the global order seeks to radically undermine Black values and Black power, these nonetheless require cultivation. For Johnson, this is precisely what *maturity* demands: to embrace one's freedom to build the world anew through efforts of value-creation. Strong Black nihilism is thus needed for a mature response to antiblack racism, which demands not the lamentation of an antiblack world but the political project of realizing other possible worlds.

Maturity requires embracing your responsibility for building the world: humanity not merely inhabits a world but *alters* it. Strong nihilism, then, is ultimately necessary for maturity because it is through the creation of values that human existence transforms its world. Punk as strong nihilism cannot simply seek to tear down but must build something: mature punk destroys the values the world has imposed but does so to build values anew.

This should not be interpreted narrowly as merely creating *your own* values. Values are durable products of a human world: a value, having been created, is like toothpaste that can't be put back into the tube. Values are meaningful beyond the moment of their creation. Subsequent generations may embrace or reject them, but their meanings endure even when denounced. To create values is to become responsible for the world those values produce through their reception and negotiation.

Strong nihilism embraces the agent's role as "parent" to values. Parenthood, of course, is an indelible image of maturity. The new parent faces a radical burden not only to care but to *produce a livable world* for the child. This requires working with other adults to produce institutions facilitating health, education, art, and exchange. This calls for politics, which, Hannah Arendt reminds us, in *The Human Condition*, requires many working together to establish shared ends that determine whom we will become, even though this process is necessarily arduous and unpredictable. The familiar divide between those tasked with political agency and those excluded is that between adult and child: children need the safety and comfort of privacy to develop their humanity prior to facing the anguish of an adult responsibility.

This is evident precisely where punks seek to produce punk *scenes* and institutions (record labels, zines, and so forth). These not only produce spaces outside the mainstream for the punks who create them; they function for those who will *become* punks in the future. Punk as weak nihilism aesthetically embraces having a scene, publication, or band for nonconformist self-expression. But punk as strong nihilism goes further toward taking responsibility for the scene such that it is hospitable to subsequent "generations" of punks, who won't simply play in the old punks' sandbox but rather transform it as stewards for future generations.

Maturity and strong nihilism are thus linked in two crucial respects. First, strong nihilism embraces responsibility for the world by producing values for which the strong nihilist must ultimately be held accountable. Second, maturity's demand that one function as *political* agent requires strong nihilism. As Arendt shows, the "politics" of serious men and weak nihilists employ instrumental, means-to-an-end logic, in which governments *rule* to serve fixed values (security, abundance). Such rule merely *imitates* politics. Genuine politics takes seriously that it's an exercise in *freedom* whose purpose is not to serve pre-given ends but to *produce* the values our communities shall serve. Hence, the political demand that adult life presents necessitates that *we* embrace the strong nihilistic function that true politics requires.

Liberation and Mature Punk

The notion of "punk" emerged precisely through projects of value-creation. For punks, sounds, looks, movements, and ideas are valuable *because they are punk*; punks *value* punk. Punk is thus a product of strong nihilism: punk was produced as a set of alternative values in protest against the decadence of serious and weak nihilist values. Does it follow that all punk is a species of strong nihilism and that all punk is mature?

The answer is no. Punk is a broad constellation of value-laden meanings, originating in but irreducible to strong nihilism. Similar to Johnson's conception of Black nihilism, punk is a nihilistic response to the decadence of prevailing values, but whether punk takes the form of producing genuinely alternative modes of valuing depends upon punks.

Weak punk nihilism thus may come in various forms. One emerges where punk becomes a *telos*, an end in and of itself. If *all* that matters is being punk, punk is not in service of anything else. Given that punk is a rebellion against established values, such a logic makes punk a cyclical revolt whose aim is to rebel against every previous articulation of punk. Weakly-nihilistic punks may initially participate in the creation of a punk "scene," but once the scene is created, their function is to decry it as passé, uncool, *unpunk*.

Weak punk nihilism also emerges through punk's commodification. Many who initially embrace punk values achieve commercial success whose pleasures crowd out the commitment to punk. While punks are often too quick to label successful punks sellouts, there are, nonetheless, those who abandon punk principles for wealth; some punk rockers adopt the weak nihilism of market validation. Because they *resent* being labeled sellouts, they often reconfigure the meaning of punk, such that they maintain it's their rebellion against a punk consensus that makes them *more* punk. The followers they attract, in turn, often adopt the same view.

Punk's maturity requires that punk *stand in relation to other values*. If punk is posited as the *only* value, it negates constructive relationships to other values. Since maturity takes responsibility for the world, it must value *others*; this in turn demands valuing the freedom of others *as valuers*. This does not mean I can only be mature where I *accept* another's values. Rather, my freedom demands precisely the pluralistic conduct found in genuine politics where you and I debate each other's values, such that through examining my values and yours we establish *shared* values. In so doing, I value your efforts *to build the world with me.*

Mature punk embraces strong nihilism's call for other values. Chief among these is *liberation*. Weak punk nihilism may rest content with having secured the individual's right to be a source of values or to abandon valuing in favor of the exhilaration of revolt. This reduces the punk to a variation of Beauvoir's figures of the passionate man, who makes himself the only relevant source of values, or the adventurer, who merely seeks to enjoy life's journey without affirming any values.

Strong punk nihilism, by contrast, demands a fight for the value of punk. Punk seeks to seize one's ability to value otherwise and can only do so maturely by recognizing the fight for a *world* of such freedom, rather than simply one's own liberty. Strong punk nihilism demands liberation: the punk produces alternative values toward building a world where others are free to produce values. Given the Euromodern context out of which punk emerges, mature punk thus calls for projects of *decolonization*, through which the world's liberation from Euromodern coloniality is affected.

For weak punk nihilism, punk is *aesthetic*: I am punk because I like it, and since nothing else matters, I might as well do as I like. Existentially mature punk, by contrast, embraces its *political* responsibility to build a world valuing human freedom. This is embedded in the familiar punk slogan, "Do It Yourself." DIY culture rejects the values of the serious while accepting responsibility for building otherwise. If those who dominate and those who accept subordination and conformity can't be trusted to build a better world, one must do it oneself. Crucially, though, the "Y" in DIY need not imply a *singular* "you": punk DIY invokes a decidedly pluralistic "you." The "you" who ought to do it might start with "me," but it's up to me to help make it *us*.

Mature punk thereby faces an inescapable irony. Nietzsche's nihilism called for acknowledging God's death, since we can't appeal to God to tell us what to value (*The Gay Science*, §125). If mature punk requires strong punk nihilism, it must fight for values beyond punk. Where "punk," then, is colonized or becomes decadent, mature punk ironically demands its abandonment.

Hence, Crass asserted as early as 1978 that "Punk is dead." They did so through the existential paradox of a punk band announcing punk's death. We know that decades later, "punk" remains meaningful. The strong nihilism that made it meaningful, though, built a world in which its meaning must continually be contested. To honor that initial upsurge sometimes calls for denouncing punk's subsumption to commodification, as did Crass in pronouncing its death. But to take "punk" as a signifier with many potential meanings is to embrace that punk's death can be followed with its rebirth in many potential forms. Some of these forms are immature and collapse into weak punk nihilisms. Others, though, embrace the link between punk and liberatory projects of value creation.

Mature punk, as a strong nihilism, is thus a rebellion that seizes its freedom to build a world that values human freedom.

II

Punk Values

7

The Paradox of the Poseur

PETER BRIAN BARRY

You're not punk
And I'm telling everyone.
Save your breath
I never was one.

The first lines from "Boxcar," the third track from Jawbreaker's third studio album, *24 Hour Revenge Therapy*, pack a lot into the fourteen words reproduced above. Blake Schwarzenbach, Jawbreaker's lyricist and singer, comes off as a bit of a tattletale here: he's going to tell everybody that someone else is, well, *not* punk.

We learn quickly that Blake's weapons can't be used against him: he's not punk either. But why shouldn't the revelation that he's not punk be just as damning? We're sort of led to the conclusion that while Blake can't be hurt by his admission that he's not punk because he never claimed to be, the song's target has no such protection. They must have represented themselves as punk and now they are about to be exposed as something else, as a *poseur*. (Is it 'poseur' or 'poser'? Why prefer the Frenchified version that I use? I don't know that much matters but traditional dictionaries and the decidedly more democratic *Urban Dictionary* recommend 'poseur' as the preferred spelling. Whatever.)

The word 'poseur' has been a term of abuse for some time. In the ancient Greek comedy, *The Clouds*, Aristophanes dubiously portrays the great philosopher Socrates "in a way calculated to ensure that the impression of a *poseur* is always with us." And while there are other subcultures and sociological groups that use 'poseur' pejoratively, the poseur is an especially familiar figure in punk culture if an unwelcome one. Poseurs are insincere, although their insincerity can be repurposed in ironic ways: Fugazi, the band, is having a bit of fun by adopting a name that implies they are infected by the poseur's insincerity. But no way around it: being called a 'poseur' makes social life hard if it sticks. An alleged poseur's best hope is to deflect the accusation and make the case that the person leveling the charge is themselves a poseur, that they are the ones who are somehow insincere. Things can get pretty comical from the outside if everyone is accusing everyone else of insincerity: bands have broken up over less.

The poseur is a threat to punks in a different, deeper way: reflecting on the poseur and just why the poseur is an offending character reveals a deep tension in the very concept of punk. It at least suggests a real paradox that needs to be resolved. The typical take on what it is to be punk alludes to embracing certain values and aesthetics, but also rejecting conformity and mainstream culture and embracing individuality. This typical take quickly generates the *paradox of the poseur*.

The Paradox Explained

The paradox of the poseur can be motivated by asking some pretty simple questions. If punk is about individual expression and the rejection of conformity, how can the poseur be a fake? Can punks both reject conformity while complaining that poseurs fail to conform? These questions are tricky to answer, and the paradox of the poseur emerges, because two different seemingly plausible assumptions, captured below, are operating in the background. I identify them as *Lemmas* because that's how philosophers talk sometimes:

> LEMMA 1: Punk is about rejecting conformity and embracing individuality.

> LEMMA 2: Not just anyone is punk and saying that you are doesn't make you one.

Both are worth discussing.

Lemma 1 is a *subjectivity criterion* for being punk. It seems to follow from the popular thought, expressed initially by Frank Sinatra and later by Sid Vicious, that a true punk is doing it "my way" partly by rejecting mainstream culture, fashion, music, and much more. I have no metric to measure this, but I've long since lost count of how many times 'punk' and 'individual', or similar words, have been used in the same breath, usually to explain the one in terms of the other. For example, John Lydon, former frontman of the Sex Pistols, is reported to have claimed that "Punk was never about one particular clean-cut imagery . . . it's about many, many individuals coming very loosely together," and Billy Joe Armstrong of Green Day explained that "Punk has always been about doing things your own way" and that "What it represents for me is the ultimate freedom and a sense of individuality." Maybe they aren't your favorite punks, but again, the sentiment that they express—that punk's ideals and ethos are explicated by appeal to individuality—is pretty common and commonly asserted. Individualism and punk seem pretty tightly entwined, a result that speaks in favor of the subjectivity criterion.

That said, Sid Vicious is at least a plausible example of a punk while Frank Sinatra is not, and if that is beyond dispute then we have a reason to think that the *objectivity criterion* expressed by Lemma 2 is also correct. It might seem like it *has* to be true, unless bourgeois suburbanites who shave their head, buy Doc Martens using their trust fund, and tell everyone they've always been punk somehow make the cut.

That we can make sense of the poseur *at all* suggests that Lemma 2 must be true since it's hard to know what it would mean to be a poseur if there were no objective standards for being punk: you can't be fake unless there is standard that distinguishes the real thing from the imposter. It is probably facts about a poseur's genealogy that exposes them: if someone's origin story reveals that they were created and shaped by corporate influences, they're poseurs; if they sold out later in their career, they're poseurs. (Sidenote: there might be some weird metaphysics going on here. Is the idea that facts about a person later affects their status earlier? I remember straight-edge kids with T-shirts bearing slogans like "If you aren't now, you never were" suggesting that someone who previously did everything right—had 'XXX' tattoos, eschewed drugs and alcohol—but years later indulged wasn't ever really straight-edge. That sounds like backwards causation. Or is the idea that even when they seemed to be punk, facts about their future entail that they weren't actually punk? That sounds like denying that there are future contingents. Either way, weird.) But if those facts, independent of anyone's subjective feelings and sentiments, settle whether someone is punk then something like the objectivity criterion must be right.

Philosophers have often been puzzled when offering an objective account of something that cannot account for what appears to be the case from a subjective point of view (Thomas Nagel, "Subjective and Objective"). Can a physical account of the mind account for the qualitative experience of, say, seeing the color red? What to do when the feeling of free will conflicts with scientific explanations of what we do? The conflict between the subjective and objective gets us to the paradox of the poseur too: Lemma 1 suggests that the objectivity criterion expressed by Lemma 2 is false, while Lemma 2 suggests that the subjectivity criterion expressed by Lemma 1 is false. They both seem true, but each implies the other is false. This is the paradox of the poseur.

The Ethics of Authenticity

If the paradox of the poseur is going to be resolved, we have to find a way to dissolve the tension between the objectivity and subjectivity criterion. Thinking a bit about the ethics of authenticity might help.

One of the lower ranked entries for 'poseur' in the *Urban Dictionary* affirms that the poseur is "Somebody acting in a manner inconsistent with their true self," a definition that begs some questions: what *is* a true self? We might be somewhat torn here. The philosopher Charles Taylor offers the oddly mixed suggestion that "Being true to myself means being true to my own originality, and that is something only I can articulate and discover." Talk of originality and the existence of something that only that self can articulate suggests that a true self is the one that springs creative energies. The true self is created, not found. But Taylor's talk of discovering our true self suggests that a true self *is* some extant self, someone who isn't my original product, someone who is found, not created. Can we have it both ways?

The philosopher Kwame Anthony Appiah does better by separating "two rival pictures" of what is involved in shaping one's identity. Apologies for the longish quote but this will help:

> One is a picture that comes from romanticism, the idea of finding one's self—of discovering, by means of reflection or a careful attention to the world, a meaning for one's life that is already there, waiting to be found. This is the vision we can call *authenticity*. It is a matter of being true to who you already really are, or would be if it weren't for distorting influences. . . . the *existentialist* picture, let's call it, is one in which, as the doctrine goes, existence precedes essence: that is, you exist first and then have to decide what to exist *as*, who to be, afterward. (*The Ethics of Identity*, p. 17)

Appiah implicitly suggests what authenticity *isn't*: it isn't just making yourself into any sort of person you want, unencumbered by restriction or obstacle. Only the existentialist conception of identity gets us that sort of radical freedom. But how real is the existentialist conception? How well does it track our actual experience of identifying? None of us create who we are out of thin air: we are born into a certain place and time, with certain familial and social relations, and so forth. We can change over time, abandoning some relations in favor of others and revising previously deeply-held values and concerns, but everyone changes *from someone*. None of us has the freedom to decide who to be prior to first being someone. The existentialist picture is a myth.

That leaves us with the authenticity conception, which isn't the worst thing. The authenticity conception does not rule out changing our identity or revising it significantly, but it does mean that who we are is not entirely up to us. But this tracks with some familiar experiences: many of us talk of finding ourselves or discovering what we really wanted all along. It's not just decidedly non-punk hippie types who engage in self-discovery: many a punk kid would probably admit to learning who they really were only when freed from the trappings of suburban life or capitalist consumer culture. And that's what poseurs lack: authenticity. They're trying to make themselves into a punk, none too successfully, but their attempt at creation just doesn't track their real self, no matter how much they might want it to.

I've suggested that the authenticity conception of shaping one's identity is a better, more accurate conception of what really happens when we sincerely engage in talk of self-creation and such. But the authenticity conception can also help dissolve the paradox of the poseur. It *seems* as though both Lemmas cannot be true, but appearances can be deceiving, kid.

The Paradox Resolved

Remember how the paradox of the poseur is supposed to get started. On the one hand, it seems as if punk is a matter of individuality, a subjective thing. On the other hand, it seems like not just anyone is punk, and saying you are doesn't make you one, an objective matter. And, you might think, if the subjectivity criterion is right, the objectivity criterion is wrong; it goes the other way too, of course. But with the authenticity conception in place, we can dissolve whatever tension might have seemed to be there and the paradox of the poseur along with it.

Start with Lemma 1, the subjectivity criterion. I've denied that any of us has the existentialist freedom to simply create ourselves out of nothing—*ex nihilo*, if you will, which sounds like the name of a metal band—but Appiah's discussion makes it clear just why the authenticity conception demands individuality. According to that conception, authenticity demands being true to whom you already really are, or would be if it weren't for distorting influences constraining you. Your true self might be a mystery given the influence of distorting mainstream influences so if you're going to discover that real self, you, the individual, have to do some work and free yourself from them: think for yourself, punk. Once freed, you can then engage in those acts of creative self-expression and experiment in ways that will help you to find who you really are. Our individuality remains a function of what we're like in conditions in which our real desires and beliefs and values can be reflected upon and put into action, conditions that obtain only when those distorting influences are eliminated or at least mitigated. So, even if we don't literally create ourselves on the authenticity conception, we have work to do and who we, as individuals, are must be separated from those distorting conditions we find ourselves in. So punk really is about individuality after all, albeit *authentic* individuality.

Lemma 2, the objectivity criterion, is even easier to accommodate given the authenticity conception. If your true self isn't punk, then wearing the right clothes, listening to the right music, having the right politics, and so forth are just outward expressions of something else—say, a desire to adopt a particular social identity—but it's just posing and not an expression of who you really are.

But there is something else that is crucial to the authenticity conception that is worth making explicit. Even if we don't have much control over our true self, we can change who we are, at least sometimes; the authenticity conception allows that. Even if we don't have much control, initially, about what our social relations are like, those obviously can and do change. But what is much, much harder to change and beyond us to dictate is how membership in a collective is socially understood: for example, we don't get to stipulate how others interpret membership in a collective, the implications that membership in a collective has for other aspects of our social lives, nor what counts as stereotypical marks of membership. Here too, social facts about group membership can change over time, and marks of group membership can be repurposed or appropriated, but they emphatically do not usually change by individual decision.

What's more, most of us have at least some knowledge of social facts about a collective, even if we're not members of it:

we know something about their values, the stereotypical marks of membership, their relationships with other collectives, and so forth. The idea is simple: it only takes a bit of amateur sociology to learn some social facts about a collective of which you're not a member, facts that are public and observable. Even the bourgeois suburbanite has some knowledge about the culture and sociology of punks, enough that she can probably articulate some tropes and stereotypes.

I bring this up to illustrate another important feature of the poseur's inauthenticity. The poseur too has some knowledge of the social facts about punks, enough that, we suspect, they *know* that they don't make the cut. The poseur surely knows, or is at least worried, that they're a faker: they might bluff and feign bravado, but on some level the poseur knows they aren't punk, having just enough social knowledge about punks to offer up outward expressions that suggest membership in a collective that they don't truly belong to.

This is why poseurs are independently obnoxious: it's not just that they've invaded your precious scene, but that their inauthenticity is inconsistent with a kind of self-knowledge that we tend to think is worth aspiring to. Either the poseur is so cocksure that they count as punk even though they don't know that they are sanctimonious and smug, or they really do know that they are faking it and thus count as insincere and dishonest. The poseur's inauthenticity has moral implications: it suggests that they suffer from character flaws, moral failings suggestive of undesirable vices. Poseurs aren't just annoying; they're *vicious*.

Identities Abound

The paradox of the poseur, like certain other paradoxes, fades away once we've done some good philosophy: punk *is* about individuality since it is facts about individual persons and their social identity that settle such matters, facts that we learn only when distorting influences are controlled for, although those facts which settle the matter are not up to the person who would identify as punk. So, both the subjectivity criterion and the objectivity criterion are true and mutually consistent.

It is worthwhile to consider whether other kinds of identities also allow both subjective and objective criterion. If it's not generally the case that simply saying "I am *Blah*" settles whether a person is a member of the social collective *Blah* then it seems, quite generally, that social identity must be at least partly a function of some objective criterion. But to ignore that person's self-conception entirely might seem cruel or at least neglectful of important information: who is a better source of information about who a person is than *that* person?

Counting both sources of information as relevant, incorporating both subjective and objective criterion, when articulating social identities feels like a happy medium, but it matters for another reason. Some commentators use expressions like "identity politics" in a dismissive manner, but why? Our social identities speak to our deepest sense of who we are and ground many important ethical obligations, and insofar as our social identities have implications for how we live and flourish it's difficult to see why they shouldn't be a subject of political interest.

To allow solitary individuals to determine what social identities are and what they mean is pretty undemocratic, but so is letting unaccountable elites settle these matters. Incorporating both subjective and objective criterion into our understandings of social identities might democratize identity politics in a fortunate way. That would be pretty punk.

8

Straight Edge and How to Live the Good Life

ANN-MARIE TIERNEY

Am I a good person? Could I be better? We've all pondered these questions and the success of the "self-help" and "self-improvement" industry would indicate that not only are humans asking the question, but we're actively seeking answers.

One of the most fundamental questions that humans have been grappling with for centuries is how to optimize ourselves as human beings. This expands to incorporate so many different considerations—can I define myself as a good person or do I have to get endorsement from the community? Should I aim for purity of intention, or can I make a little slip-up now and then and still be okay?

Well, funnily enough, such important questions have not just been mulled over by the philosophy crowd, but punks have done their fair share of soul-searching and navel-gazing as well. From the Lyceum in Ancient Greece to Club Minimal in 1980s Sacramento, ideas have been shared by civilized debate in the former and by screaming into a microphone in the latter. Did either group actually get anywhere with this question or are we all still none the wiser?

Go Hardcore or Go Home

Punk means a lot of things to a lot of people, but one aspect that is often either dismissed or ignored is the desire to create a better life—for yourself, your community and perhaps the world. In the original 1970s cohort of punk bands, there were certainly political ideas thrown around but not a huge amount on morality and ethics. But the American hardcore scene that sprang up in the 1980s, advocated a stronger, more overt fusion of punk and politics, underpinned by the belief that the individuals in the community, and their actions, could be galvanized for the greater good.

And the point of philosophy, surely, is to make sense of the world? Not just to understand it, but perhaps be able to influence it starting from within. Punk and philosophy are not so different—both can be deep, radical, and thought provoking—and the likes of Ian Mackaye, Henry Rollins, and Jello Biafra are the Platos and Aristotles of the Hermosa Beach and Washington DC areas. The hardcore punk movement of America was, in many ways perhaps the punkest punk there has been, built upon a catalogue of philosophical, literary, and ideological positions that were at times complementary and at other times jarring.

It wasn't just the music that was not for the faint-hearted—everything about hardcore punk required either a lifestyle commitment or a demonstrative disregard for bourgeois concepts and norms. It examined the individual and how they lived their life and whether it was good or bad. American hardcore demanded something of its listeners and being excessive and like rock stars of old was not it. Getting drunk, taking drugs, being promiscuous, were suddenly *persona non grata*—this era of punk had a grave sense of responsibility.

Perhaps punk is an unlikely place to find guidance on being the best version of you that you can be. As you listen to Henry Rollins, Keith Morris, or D. Boon shouting about Reagan, nuclear war, and nervous breakdowns, maybe it doesn't occur to the uninitiated that these figures are just as concerned with the complexities of the human character as the traditional chin-scratchers of the past. But that would be to misunderstand the underpinning ethics that have always been present in punk and all its subsequent waves, to varying extents.

When we get to the hardcore acts of 1980s America, the political becomes the personal and the ideological and the existential combine. It was a combination of the primal and intellectual. There was plenty of government bashing and political commentary as well as satire (particularly aimed at then-president Reagan), but it wasn't enough to just sing along to the likes of Reagan Youth or Dead Kennedys.

For people like Ian Mackaye from Minor Threat or Ray Cappo from Youth of Today, your behavior has to reflect the ethics you espouse. It's a sure-fire way of both weeding out hypocrites and the weak-willed, whilst also legitimizing punk as a meaningful way of life and not just loud music. This very much fits in with the preoccupation in this period to try and define punk, not just by what it is but by what it isn't. A frequently fraught debate was hashed out in the pages of zines such as

Maximum Rock'n'Roll and *Profane Existence*, where writers and editors went back and forth with fans and musicians about where to set the parameters for the genre and who could or couldn't use the label. It even came to fisticuffs in some instances: Jello Biafra was beaten up when attending punk mecca, The Gilman Street Project to cries of "sell out"—an event Biafra laid responsibility for at the feet of *Maximum Rock'n'Roll* founder Tim Yohannen. This was serious stuff.

Life on the Straight Edge

Straight Edge (sXe) as a subculture of hardcore punk, sprang out of the west coast of America during the first wave of American hardcore. The term was taken from the name of a song by Minor Threat with lyrics that had an anti-drugs message and featured the line "I've got straight edge." What started out as a gesture to enable underage gig-goers to get access to punk shows, grew into a bona fide ideology that influenced adherents' political beliefs; relationships; lifestyles, and ultimately the punk scene as a whole.

Minor Threat and Fugazi vocalist Ian MacKaye is widely credited with beginning the sXe movement—much to his chagrin. Like many punks before him, he looked around and saw the shallow decadence demonstrated by his (largely male) peers and felt that punk should strive to do better. And by better he meant avoiding falling into the same traps as the rest of mainstream society—self-destruction, self-absorption, getting drunk, taking drugs, getting laid, and acting like jerks at gigs.

To ensure that punk was accessible to those too young to drink, bands agreed to play at venues where alcohol would not be served at all or where underage gig-goers would be required to have a big black 'X' on their hand, guaranteeing they would not be served the bad stuff. This was soon adopted by people like Mackaye who wanted to refrain from drinking by choice. The movement started by advocating abstention from drug use or alcohol consumption, but also stretched to an embargo on smoking, causal sex, and in some cases, meat.

The abstinence had a few functions, one of which being to deliver a blow to the mass commercial companies who push their alcohol, tobacco, and processed foods to the masses, furthering their profits whilst eroding our bodies and the environment. It provided a safe space at punk gigs—no drunken brawling in the pit; no concert unfit for minors; women not being picked up like chattel for conquests at the end of the night. But even more fundamental than this was an exercise in self-control, and by extension, self-improvement. And if everyone is walking around as the best version of themselves—lean, clean, and morally engaged—imagine how great our communities would be!

The idea that our communal contribution is an important part of our individual morality is a view that has been shared by many philosophers including David Hume, Adam Smith, and Arthur Schopenhauer. For them, altruism is a natural state for us to be in. And whilst Straight Edge talks about the individual benefits gained from adhering to the lifestyle, there are wider benefits—making a safe and inclusive environment for all, undermining damaging capitalist entities, and providing positive role models. The benefits were both internal and external. So, if all the philosophers walked into a seven-seconds gig and heard all that sXe talk, how many of them would agree that the sXe-ers are on the right track to optimum human-ness?

One dude who would definitely be able to share an orange juice with the likes of Henry Rollins, would be Aristotle.

For Aristotle, we are bodies in a world and that world is observable. Our lives matter in the present and therefore our actions matter. Aristotle was trying to identify the ingredients for happiness and meaning or, to us his word, *eudaimonia*. (This Greek word has been variously translated as 'happiness', 'living well', or 'flourishing'.) For Aristotle, that meant community and being around other people. In order to live well amongst people (not to hurt them or piss them off) people need to acquire virtues—good habits that promote stable, productive behavior and inspire co-operation. He believed you could acquire these habits by practicing conscious thoughts and decisions about what to do and how to do it that would soon become second nature. He said: "We are what we repeatedly do. Excellence, then, is not an act but a habit." This is exactly what Straight Edge preached—by improving yourself, you elevate the community around you and collectively you make a better world. Simples!

Keep Stoic and Carry On . . .

Another ancient Greek thinker who would have enjoyed having a chat with someone like Mackaye is Epicurus. He saw philosophy as a route to happiness—find the answers to help build a better life—one of happiness (*eudaimonic*) with freedom from worry (*ataraxia*) and freedom from pain (*aponia*). For him, part of how you get to this state (which sounds nice) is by living a virtuous and ethical life, surrounded by friends and community.

That way, you don't have to worry about vexation and guilt, caused by doing the wrong thing. Epicurus acknowledged fondness for pleasure as natural and he has gained a reputation for being in favor of pursuing these pleasures. After all, then you're living a life free from pain. But Epicurus was actually in favor of a simpler life and opposed overindulgence.

For Epicurus and mates, you want to have a peaceful life. But does a life free from fear or pain—a pretty pleasurable and peaceful one—necessarily deliver anything beyond an immediate sense of happiness? If the punks are saying you need to contribute to the overall happiness and safety of the community, then surely an Epicurean approach won't cut it. Maybe take a leaf out of the Buddha's book and accept that a certain level of pain, suffering and discomfort is an essential part of your development as a person. One of the key beliefs of Buddhism is that your mind precedes all mental states. Therefore, ridding yourself of impure motives is essential. Take the first three of the noble truths:

1. **DUKKHA—life is unsatisfactory and full of suffering (ain't that the truth?). While desires might be temporarily fulfilled, physical, emotional, or mental suffering cannot be avoided. So, you can get drunk and do drugs but you're not going to outrun your suffering.**

2. **SAMUDAYA—suffering is caused by desire or craving. So that need to get pissed at a punk show is actually causing you suffering.**

3. **NIRODHA—an end to craving is an end to suffering. So, get off the booze and the drugs; you'll stop craving them because you'll realize how much sharper and more focused and alert you are, and your suffering will end.**

If that's not a basis for Straight Edge then I don't know what is: life is difficult. Alcohol, drugs, and sex might help in the short term, but will not lead to any long-term good. Once you conquer your cravings, you have control over yourself and therefore your life. I mean, it fits like a glove.

Consider the three poisons which (according to Buddhism) form the basis of human suffering—greed, ignorance, and hatred. If you expand the Straight Edge experience and look at the accompanying anti-fascism, progressive politics, community co-operation ideals, then the sXe also agree that those three attributes are a real drag and should not be indulged.

The Stoics were all over this too. Epictetus left us the longest surviving treatises on Stoicism, a doctrine that offered a comprehensive theory of existence which at its heart, gives us the basis for a good life. For Stoics like Epictetus, we should only concern ourselves with what is *eph'hēmin* (within our power), and not sweat the other stuff. Pursue meaningful things that add to the collective happiness and not all the shallow stuff like wealth and esteem. And whatever you do, make your decisions rationally and maintain control over yourself. Overindulging is a quick ticket to Sadville and rather, you should just act justly and pursue strong relationships. Living in a self-sufficient way with your friends around you will lead you to *ataraxia*—peace and freedom from fear.

That was exactly what Ian Mackaye was trying to cultivate by shunning major label funding and starting his own label Dischord Records that could nurture and promote the bands in the hardcore movement. Mackaye was quoted as saying "I'm not a religious person, and I'm not too interested in being a part of a religion, but I do like having some sort of communal gathering and having some sense of peoples."

Trouble in Paradise

But what if you disagree on what makes a better world? If Aristotle and Rollins sat down to hash it out, what if they don't agree? And there were plenty of punks in the hardcore scene who did not agree with the sober crowd and who felt the sXe-ers should tone it down a bit. SXe-ers were often considered rather zealous in their attitudes towards sobriety with many members of the early punk scene in the US claiming that they were ostracized heavily (and some say violently) with guilt and shame if they did not adhere to the "code." Henry Rollins would reputedly read a list of names of people who had died from drug use to the crowd at the beginning of Black Flag gigs to demonstrate the real consequences of the "getting high" lifestyle. Bit of a drag

Someone who would probably also find the Buddha, and the whole hardcore punk crowd a right bore is John Stuart Mill. He reckoned that pleasure is one of the main contributing factors to our wellbeing and conversely, pain makes us worse off. For Mill, a life is going well if it is a happy life and generally speaking, that means a life filled with lots of lovely pleasure and freedom from pain. And this should all be self-evident because people seek out pleasure and why would they do that if it didn't have some inherent value? Take that, Buddha!

To be fair, although Mill is considered to be advocating some sort of hedonism, he did clarify that there are distinct types of pleasures and some are 'higher' than others, with pleasures of intellect and moral sentiments being better in the long run that just feelings or sensations.

In his *Utilitarianism* Mill describes the best life as "an existence exempt as far as possible from pain, and as rich as possible in enjoyments." Enjoyments? Not particularly punk. Not amongst the likes of Gorilla Biscuits and DYS anyway. How can pursuing pleasure make for a better world? How can a load of hedonists and self-indulgent creeps actually find time or motivation to work for their community? Imagine life where we all do our own thing seeking only the pleasurable . . . it probably wouldn't lead to very cohesive society, motivated by bringing about the common good. For that, sometimes you gotta do the hard thing, take the hard path. As Rollins says: *"Pain is not my enemy. It is my call to greatness."*

Rollins can be accused of glorifying pain and struggle somewhat but there is a seriousness behind the idea that we don't want to get too caught up in pursuing the shallow. For Dutch philosopher Benedict de Spinoza, the reason we should try and avoid riches, glory and fleeting pleasures is because other than satisfying individual vanity, there isn't really much point to them. They are finite things and when they go, all that pleasure does too. Anyone who has nursed a monster hangover and cursed the day you ever let a by-product of the fermentation process cross your lips would probably relate. But we choose these things anyway because we are ruled by our emotions. And these emotional decisions are likely to be substandard and lead to a substandard life—not what punk wants for you! In 1980s America, punks were demonized by the press, by conservative politicians, by religious leaders. Footage of violent melees at punk shows were broadcast via the local news into TV sets all over the nation. Punks were dragged onto talk shows like *The Phil Donahue Show* and paraded in front of good, god-fearing people who were horrified at this new youth cult that would tear apart the delicate fabric of America. No morals, no God, no respect for authority—bad. With those dominant messages, it was an act of defiance in itself to take a higher path and not conform to the caricature that society had drawn of punks. That is another rebellious angle to sXe—in a hostile system (which most punks believe is the case), and a world that doesn't care about you, to take care of yourself, expand your mind and live up to your potential is an act of rebellion. Black Flag put it succinctly in their song "Rise Above":

We are born with a chance
And I'm gonna have my chance.

Masters of Destiny

In the spirit of Do-It-Yourself, you can take control of your life.
That's another thing Spinoza would have approved of—self-love
(not that sort of self-love you filthy beasts). This is a virtue. And
not only is that great for us, but once we have this virtue, we can
then want it for other people. And the more people obtain this
virtue, the more harmonious our world becomes. For those zealous sXe-ers, this is why it needs a community response. If we let
some people get drunk, drugged up and display obnoxious
behaviors to others at shows and other punk gatherings, it taints
their experience as well. Like or not, it is for the greater good—
so for god's sake, PUT DOWN THAT BEER.

It's certainly true that Straight Edge was considered a
choice rooted in ethics—ethical consumerism, ethical relations
with others, and ethical responsibility. Ethics established by
the community—guidelines and codes that were, at least in
principle, endorsed. But was it also a matter of morals? Is it
the same thing?

If our moral codes are more subjective and based on our own
individual sense of right and wrong, was it moral to be Straight
Edge and therefore by extension, those who weren't doing it
were *immoral* individuals? Should it in fact be left to the individual to make up their own mind whether they felt it morally
necessary to observe SxE? Judging by the reputation sXe had
for being in-your-face and all judge-y, it would seem some people took the moral absolute position that some things are right,
some things are wrong, and sXe is the former. Our own sense
of morality rarely just guides us and our own behavior, we usually apply it to other people—if I shouldn't be doing something,
then neither should you or anyone else.

A moral relativist would take a slightly more chilled view.
For a relativist, it's not that there is no right or wrong, it's more
that we're all going to have different ideas on what right or
wrong is and slight variations can co-exist. Philosophers such
as David Wong suggest a sort of pluralistic relativism: depending on different social contexts, different rules would be acceptable. Have minimum standards but allow a certain amount of
reasonable deviation.

Making space for dissent, for opposing views and for "slip
ups" has been echoed by philosopher Cheshire Calhoun who
has written on the subject of integrity as a social virtue. In

Calhoun's view, there is a difference between maintaining integrity and becoming a fanatical zealot. Some, like Hugh Breakey, argue that integrity is a potentially dangerous trait in that possession of it can lead strong-minded people to act without proper regard for the needs and perspectives of others.

In the punk world, we can look at the ideological conflicts in the American hardcore scene to see where a steadfast passion for a certain set of values can lead to intolerance of those who may not share the same feeling. Publications like *Maximum Rock'n'Roll* stoked a lot of debate since its beginnings in 1982 by gatekeeping the concept of punk—some labels boycotted advertising in the zine due to it being perceived as unnecessarily elitist and confrontational. The unapologetic founder of *Maximum Rock'n'Roll*—Tim Yohannan—and many of its readers would argue that they were upholding the integrity of the punk scene and calling out slipping standards and striving for authenticity to protect the scene. For others, they had strayed into fanaticism—appointing themselves the arbiters and setting impossible or insignificant standards.

Mackaye did grow to lament what sXe became in terms of becoming so reactionary and exclusionary:

> I think that the idea of straight edge, the song that I wrote, and the way people have related it, there's some people who have abused it, they've allowed their fundamentalism to interfere with the real message, which in my mind, was that people should be allowed to live their lives the way they want to.

To Beer or not to Beer?

With no consensus on how to achieve that elusive happy and productive life, we're left with the same questions the Stoics mulled over thousands of years ago: how can I judge I've lived a good life? For Straight Edgers there were clear choices to make that remove you from things that could lead to a *bad* life. The reality of substance misuse amongst their community prompted them to take a stand. For others, it doesn't just have to come down to tough lifestyle choices and making extreme gestures. Instead, your heart and intent—if pure— will eventually lead to good in the world. Even if we don't have answers, just asking the questions demonstrates that the will is there. And where's there's a will . . . there just might be a way. And there's a lot of hope to be found in that fact alone.

I'll end with a quote from Tony Nineteen of the Dils, a California punk band who split in 1980, just as hardcore was taking off. "Punk has to move from a stance of mindless, stupid outrage to a threat . . . It's not good if it doesn't challenge anything and change anything."

I'll drink to that.

9

The Seven P's of Real Punk

JESSE PRINZ

"I am a poseur and I don't care / I like to make people stare." These words, belted out by the X-Ray Spex's frontwoman, Poly Styrene, ooze with irony. Punks do care about posers. They care a lot.

Punk subculture has a notorious habit of weaponizing the p-word to decide who is in and who is out. Authenticity is a cardinal virtue in punk, and there are many gatekeepers eager to keep fakers out. Yet there is something paradoxical lurking in this attitude—one might even say hypocritical. Poly Styrene helped to invent British punk—she was a true original. But the rest of us arrived on our respective scenes when many aspects of the subculture were already well-formed: the music, the fashion, the attitude. For those who adopt a prefab identity, can there be any such thing as authenticity? Aren't we all posers? Should we care?

Here I'm going to try to wriggle out of the paradox, or perhaps to embrace it. The poser paradox can teach us much about punk, and there are more general lessons for the philosophy of personal identity as well.

Punk's Poser Policing

We've all met them, those assholes who spend energy thinking about who is punk enough (or cool enough, or gay enough, or trans enough, or Black enough, or Jewish enough, or feminist enough, or progressive enough, or conservative enough—you can fill in whatever term you like). We've all probably also contributed to the exercise. Each of us has multiple "social identities." These are ties to social groups that help us define who we take ourselves to be. Social identities have boundaries, but they tend to be pretty blurry, all of us often spend time thinking about the membership criteria. We worry about infiltration, dilution, and contamination. There are at least two good reasons for this First, when others co-opt aspects of our subculture, it is a kind of identity theft, and that threatens our capacity to defend ourselves—this, I believe, is the cardinal sin of cultural appropriation. Second, our safe spaces can be undermined by interlopers. For example, with the rise of hardcore, American punk clubs became increasingly violent, making dance floors treacherous for many, and that was perceived by some as a kind of invasion. The desire for purity is not just snobbery, it can feel like a matter of survival. Still, the urge to decide who qualifies as a real punk can, at times, look a bit absurd. Here I want to survey some of the charges levied against people in doubt. There are many ways to out a poser.

No Newbies

I used to quip that the "poser" could be defined as someone who got into punk a day later than you. There was often suspicion about newcomers, and much bragging about having been on the scene for ages. Those who just got into punk were on probation—at least for a few months, and then they could start harassing neophytes themselves.

Scene Unseen

For some, punk standing depends on presence in the punk community. Punk scenes are usually centered around music venues, but also include social networks, with likeminded people socializing together, and supporting each other in various ways. It's not uncommon these days to get a crowdfunding request for a punk in need. For those of us who like keeping to ourselves, there can be credible costs. True punks, some think, support local scenes.

Prêt-à-Porter Punk

Punk has been commodified from the earliest days. The Sex Pistols hung out in two King's road fashion boutiques: SEX, which was run by Vivianne Westwood and Malcolm McLaren, and Acme Attractions, managed by Don Letts. Acolytes could go to these places and purchase a punk wardrobe right off the rack. In New York, we have Trash and Vaudeville, D.C. had Commander Salamander, and American shopping malls have

Hot Topic. Kids who found their threads in these emporia might lose points if they didn't also do any thrifting, or DIY demolitions jobs on stuff bought off the shelves.

Taste Tests

Oh, the hours we spent signaling coolness! To gain respect in the punk world, you had to love the right bands and hate the right bands, and you also had to have the right preferences for clothes, toys, books, television, and other products of pop culture. If you weren't into serial killers and Herschell Gordon Lewis splatter films, you might raise a few eyebrows among punk peers.

Spineless Sellouts

Punk fans judge bands even harsher than they judge each other. The cardinal sin is selling out. We old punks shuddered when The Clash became popular and had a video ("Rock the Kasbah") on MTV. As early as 1978, Crass released a song called "Punk Is Dead," which whined: "CBS promote The Clash / But it ain't for revolution, it's just for cash." In contrast, the Sex Pistols gained points for getting kicked off two labels.

Puerile Politics

Some punks are very particular about their politics. When Crass complained about The Clash, they saw success as compromising political integrity. In the US, straightedge punks were similarly doctrinaire. These anarcho-punks tended to take themselves very seriously, and those who fell short in their fervency were sometimes written off.

Pop Punk

We did talk about pop punk back in the day, but it was not a pejorative. Examples included the Dead Boys who had an old-school rock'n'roll sensibility, or Buzzcocks, who were incredibly catchy. A little later, we got Social Distortion, with their energizing power chords, and Bad Religion, with their harmonies. I don't recall anyone being ostracized for liking these bands. Then Green Day happened. And the Offspring. And Blink-182. And Avril Lavigne, oh my. Many old-timers refuse to recognize this as punk. Regardless of the music, performers are discredited for playing to fans who did not identify as punk rockers. Equally, fans who admit affection for popular bands risk being dismissed as inauthentic. Punk's status as an underground counterculture is threatened when outsiders have heard of your favorite bands.

Punky Pop

Even more sinister, from the perspective of the poser police, are pop bands that capitalize on a punk image while playing music that lacks trademark features of the genre. P!nk comes to mind here. When I first saw the dyed hair and the fauxhawk, I was pretty confused. These days people who have adopted aspects of punk style without the full package (music, politics, and taste, for example) are commonplace. Think of Kim and Kourtney Kardashian. Post-modern sociologists, like Andy Bennett, say we've entered a post-subculture era, in which people can pick and choose from a smorgasbord of styles without any expectations of consistency (*Subcultures or Neo-Tribes?*). For punk diehards that amounts to false advertising.

We-Is-Me Identity

Having looked at the policing of posers, we can step back and ask about what is being policed. What is it to be a punk? I have talked about policing as gatekeeping, as if punk were a club. But this metaphor has limitations. Punk is not a place; punk is an identity. Poser-police are always trying to decide not just where you belong but who you really are.

When philosophers discuss identity they usually ask what makes someone count as the same person over time. The most popular answers to this question make no reference to social groups. We are said to be linked to our past through autobiographical memories. Marya Schechtman, for example, argues (p. 207) that personal identity is formed through the narratives we tell about our lives. Such proposals implicitly treat personal identity as fundamentally different from social identity. My memories are distinctive to me, whereas group memberships are something I share with others. For many philosophers, who you are has little to do with your social affiliations. I think we should resist this division between the personal and the social. If you want to tell someone who you are, you don't tell stories from your childhood; you say something about the things you're about and the things that play a role in guiding your life. That can include your political outlook, your dietary habits, your occupation, and your favorite pastimes. It can also include the social groups you belong to, such as your religion and, yes, the subcultures you belong to. Being a punk rocker can help define who you are. Personal identity encompasses social identity.

Some philosophers might resist this idea. Punk may seem too superficial. It is, for many, an aesthetic category: a genre of music, a style of dress. Isn't it a stretch to suppose that aesthetic preferences are part of personal identity? I don't think so. I conducted a survey with my collaborators in which we asked participants to imagine individuals whose taste in art or music changed dramatically. Would someone be the same person, we asked, after that transformation? Most answered no; a change in taste was perceived as a change in identity (Fingerhut et al., "The Aesthetic Self"). People evidently presume that, if I stop liking punk, I will have become a different person.

This is striking for two reasons. First, we tend to think of aesthetic preferences as incidental facts about people, but they may be integral to identity. Second, my aesthetic preferences are not unique to me. Being into punk is something I share with countless others. Being a punk rocker is a matter of adopting tastes that others had cultivated before I ever took any interest. If so, what makes me me, has a lot to do with who I call 'we'. For those of us who identify as punk, that means we define who we are, in part, by the group with which affiliate.

All this may sound perfectly plausible, but it creates a puzzle when juxtaposed to our earlier observation about policing posers. When punk rockers decree who counts as an authentic member of the group, they seem to presuppose that one can be authentically punk. But, aside from the originators, punk is a borrowed identity: we pick from others. Once we grant that personal identity is social, it's hard to make much sense of authenticity. When I insist this identity is really me, while granting that I got it from others, I seem to be contradicting myself. This leads to a paradox:

> *The Poser Paradox*: Posers are people who simply act as if they were punk by iimitating genuine punks. But everyone who claims to be punk is playing a social role created by others. Therefore, everyone who claims to be punk is a poser. It follows from this that there are no genuine punks. And if there are no genuine punks to copy, there can't be any posers.

Genuine Fakery

To squirm out of this embarrassing paradox, we need an account of authenticity that allows for a distinction between genuine punks and phonies. Here we may get a hint from Poly Styrene. Poly could get away with calling herself a "poseur." She was as authentic as they came: a member of punk's first generation in the UK, and one of the scene's true originals. Poly designed her own clothes, masterminded the punk critique of consumerism, and produced what is arguably the greatest punk LP of all time (*Germfree Adolescents*). Poly was born to a Scottish-Irish single mum and a Somali-born dad, and she suffered from bipolar disorder, giving her claim to a marginalized status on several dimensions. As a teen runaway and squatter, she also had plenty of street cred. Poly was the epitome of punk.

What about the rest of us? Well, those who came around after punk's inception can hardly compete with a legend like Poly Styrene, but there may still be ways to earn accreditation as *bone fide* punks. Sociologists claim that there are ways to earn "subcultural capital"—insider knowledge and other traits that establish identity is the eyes of one's peers (1995). Building on this idea, I want to suggest "Seven P's" of punk authenticity. There are things that confer subcultural capital; the more you have, the more likely you are to be granted punk status member of the group:

> *Priority.* Exhibiting tendencies towards punk traits (such as an irreverent attitude of disregard for mainstream fashion norms) before joining the subculture. Poly Styrene's street cred would also belong here.

> *Pansophy.* This refers to knowledge across a range of dimensions: knowing about punk bands, venues, styles, people, and history.

> *Preferences.* Liking punk music and other aspects of punk culture.

> *Performance.* Acting in accordance with punk preferences: listening to punk regularly, going to shows, dressing in ways that signal punk identity.

> *Proficiency.* Punk performance should be effortless, or second nature. Never try too hard

> *Peril.* Willingness to take risks or incur costs. For example, violating a school dress code or playing music too loud.

> *Persistence.* Demonstrating long-term allegiance to punk.

Two of these P's are epistemic: Panosophy encompasses knowledge of punk and Proficiency is a kind of know-how. Two are measures of sincerity: Preferences constitute a real taste for punk and Priority indicates that you're drawn to punk honestly. The remaining three reflect commitment: Performance, Persistence, and Peril each indicate investment in punk lifeways.

Punks need not exhibit all seven P's. Some may dress down, for example, because they resent the way punk styles have been co-opted by big capital. Indeed, dressing punk can be a red flag in the eyes of poser police, since it can indicate that someone is adoping punk style as a fashion statement rather than a deeper commitment (Andes 2002, p. 218).

I am not sure that any P is necessary. It may not even be necessary to have punk taste (Preferences). Britney Spears's spontaneous decision to shave her head can be regarded as a punk gesture. Headshaving enacts a punk aesthetic (Performance) and doing so at the height of pop success appeared reckless to many (Peril). It may have come from a lot of pain, but that's what made it so empowering: Britney's fuck-all-y'all attitude toward mistreatment indicated a disposition toward shocking acts of defiance (Priority). In that moment, Britney earned honorary punk status. To make this case—or contest it—you can tabulate a person's P score.

Put simply, having a good number of these P's is a sure way to confirm that your punk pretentions are legit. Sometimes a single gesture can indicate several of these at once. In 1982, my older brother—a veteran of the New York scene—gave himself a sloppy, stick-and-poke tattoo that said "T.P.L.F." meaning true punks last forever. The tattoo signaled Persistence, Peril, Performance, and a Preference for punk aesthetics. At the time tattoos were neither trendy nor legal in New York. He since covered it up with something even more punk: a cluster of cockroaches.

You might want to add or subtract from this list. I intentionally left out any strong connection to a scene or a community, which I mentioned in the discussion of punk policing. As a socially anxious introvert, I always resented the expectation that punks be active in a scene, but others might give that more weight. Scene participation can also be gendered; Angela McRobbie (1991) argues variety of pressures make it easier for some young women to participate in subcultures from home. I also left off a purity condition. We used to scoff at punks who liked disco, for example, but history has shown that crosspollination is a source of punk innovation: The Stooges draw on jazz, The Slits incorporate dub, ESG exhibits funk influences, The Contortions bring in dance music, Le Tigre goes electro, Go!Go!7188 builds in surf, pop, and Japanese enka, and artists like JPEGMAFIA bring a punk sensibility to hip-hop. There is ska punk, gypsy punk, Latin punk, and cowpunk, to name a few more. These days, the Internet is fostering unprecedented eclecticism (Adegoke, 2021), so we can expect to see even more intersectional punk identities. Those who are mixing up new punk cocktails can retain a genuine predilection the punk spirit that gives these concoctions their kick.

Punk police can be understood as looking for signs of authenticity. Some of their demands might be rejected (must punks like splatter films?), but others seem perfectly defensible (a punk wardrobe may make you punky but not punk). Oftentimes punk police may miss the mark. If you compare the Seven P's to that earlier list, you will see that punk police focus on things that are not, by my lights, crucial for authenticity. Some of the poser tests make contact with the Seven P's.

Can a newbie qualify as punk? Well sure, but the court will be out, at that stage, about Persistence. Other poser tests seem too demanding: a suburban kid who buys punk clothes at the mall may fail the prêt-à-porter test, but in her world, there may still be some risk in choosing that wardrobe, and there may be much sincerity in her preferences. What about Spineless Sell-outs? I'm going to risk heresy and say that authenticity is not undermined by profit. Selling out risks inauthenticity: the corporate machine might start dictating your taste, and you might start displaying your punk attitude for a lucrative photo-shoot rather than as an expression of sincerely felt attitudes (violating Preferences and Proficiency). But there is nothing wrong with getting well compensated for your passions and hard work. Put differently, there's a difference between cashing in and selling out. Likewise, when we older punks scoff at those who cut their teeth on Blink-182, we should remember that commercial bands may open up a new world and refuge to those who feel disenchanted with mainstream culture. Pop punk is a gateway drug, and those who with whom it resonates may be on a path to self-discovery and self-construction that deserves recognition and respect. Punk police can be judgmental and elitist. We might do well to focus more on the Seven P's.

The Seven P's can also help with the Poser Paradox. They provide an account of authenticity that allows for social influence. A genuine punk is not someone who magically acquires punk taste *ex nihilo*. Some precursors to punk were remarkably original: outlandish nonconformists from the past, like Alfred Jarry or the Baroness Elsa von Freytag-Loringhoven, are visionaries who embodied a punk ethos before there were any clear models to emulate. Pioneers of the modern punk movement, like Poly Styrene, were spectacularly innovative as well. But even these individuals were bouncing off all that came before. The rest of us are less creative; we are copycats. But a genuine punk need not originate anything. They need only exhibit the preponderance of Ps. Anyone with a high P score demonstrates knowledge, sincerity, and commitment. That is enough to qualify as punk.

Does this solve the paradox? Yes and no. One the one hand, the Seven P's provide a measure of authenticity. They allow us to distinguish genuine punks from appropriators and wanna-bes. On the other hand, they concede that punk is a social role we learn from others. Punk is something we copy and act out, even if we add a personal touch. Indeed, we would cease being punk if we didn't like what prior punks had created. In a discussion of Black identity, Paul Taylor (2016, p. 151) argues that questions of authenticity are inherently social; communities must deliberate together about what counts. He concludes, "authenticity talk seems most useful not as a resource for distinguishing the really real from the faked, the mistaken, or the confused. It can be a way to take inventory on our own commitments" (p. 153). If we define a poser as someone who fails the Seven P test, not all punks are posers. But a poser might also be defined as someone who plays a role scripted by others. By that definition, all punks are posers. On that reading the paradox is not so much escaped as embraced. All punks can sing along with Poly Styrene: "I am a poseur, and I don't care." We are genuine fakes.

10

The Post-Punk Struggle for Authenticity

Markus Kohl

In the sub-cultural context of late 1970s/early1980s post-punk, the ideal of an authentic lifestyle is shaped by three interrelated concerns.

First, there is the wish to live in a manner true to your *individuality*, your personal feelings and characteristics, even (indeed, especially) if these are not encouraged by society at large.

Second, the pursuit of authenticity involves the ambition to develop unique, *original* modes of artistic self-expression which give voice to your distinctive personality, which defy common tastes and established modes of (pseudo-)artistic production.

Third, authenticity in this context is tightly connected to purity and personal *integrity*. This involves living and creating without caving in to diluted mainstream tastes, without insincerely playing some public role for the sake of money and fame. As Jennifer Bickerdike stresses, "the 'inauthentic'" here becomes synonymous with "the fake, the insincere, that which is only for show, for fattening the coffers, extolling for a quick PR hit" (*Fandom*, p. 11).

Fear of Corruption

The modern quest for authentic lifestyles and artforms is infected with a simultaneous fear of being corrupted by the inauthentic. As Somogy Varga observes, "the fear that the 'authentic' might turn out to be a 'fake' . . . has followed the ideal of authenticity as its shadow" (*Authenticity*, p. 4).

The worry here does not pertain to any deliberate decision to fake some role in order to gain more money or fame. Rather, the modern fear of the inauthentic rests on a deep-seated suspicion that you are duped or *deceive yourself* into believing that you think, act, and create authentically. This suspicion derives from a growing awareness of the pervasive influence the culture industry exerts upon all of us, thereby turning *everyone* into a willing or unwilling participant in mainstream practices, modes of feeling, and behavior—even if the participants fail to recognize this and continue to flatter themselves with a self-image of swimming against the mainstream, duly and sincerely performing the rituals and gestures of non-conformism.

The problem is that those very rituals and gestures are themselves liable to be infiltrated by the culture industry, which surreptitiously exploits our longing for sincerity and uniqueness by feeding us fake simulacra of authenticity: through materialistic education, work models (consider, for instance, how corporate culture has utilized the language of self-realization and empowerment) and above all (increasingly, *social*) media exposure. If you value living authentically and are also aware of these insidious co-option mechanisms, you should worry that your struggle for authenticity is already infected by inauthentic desires, values, and categories. You might then also feel, as Richard Rorty puts it, the "horror of finding" yourself "to be only a copy or a replica" (*Contingency, Irony, and Solidarity*, p. 24) of a mere authenticity-template that has been carefully designed by the strategists of mainstream production.

This dialectic has a particular bite in regard to the subcultures invested in musical genres like post-punk. Dan Jacobson and Ian Jeffrey diagnose that "Among fans of underground music, there tends to be an insistence on artists that are characterized as raw or deskilled, signifying a contrarian individuality and an 'authentically' real, countercultural experience. This is positioned in opposition to a mainstream culture seen as contrived and artificial . . ."

As various cultural theorists have stressed, this stance of countercultural aesthetic creativity and experience is threatened by "how alert the dominant" mainstream "culture . . . is to anything that can be seen as emergent" (*Marxism and Literature*, p. 122), as something ripe to be exploited for the purposes of the culture industry. A particularly insidious and effective strategy here is to remove the sting from sub-cultural challenges to the reigning socio-cultural order by transforming "doubts about authority into questions of self-image. Once dissent becomes a question of image, it can be magically resolved by purchasing commodities, by getting into style" (*The Contest of Meaning*, pp. 261–283). Once the dissenting rebels have been swayed (via clever methods of marketing and advertising) to trade in their original concerns about neo-liberal culture for a pre-occupation with *signaling and performing* such concerns to an audience of fellow party attendees and Instagram followers, they no longer pose a recalcitrant threat to mainstream culture. Instead, they contribute to that culture by spending their money on expensive limited editions, T-shirts, and Doc Martens. The real struggle for authenticity becomes a mere show parade whose participants flaunt tangible markers of "authenticity" that can impress others in a game of one-upmanship played according to the rulebook of capitalist logic.

From Punk to Post-Punk

The growing awareness of the mainstream assimilation techniques contributes to the—gradual, non-linear—transition from punk to post-punk, and to a corresponding shift from an *outward* to an *inward* model of authenticity.

The outward model is closely linked with the beginnings of punk music in the 1970s. Here the ideal of sincerely expressing your inner feelings in an original, upright fashion incorporates the goal to connect in meaningful ways with your society and to contribute towards progressive sociopolitical changes. This outward model can take several forms. One prominent form is participation in activist political movements. For instance, the Leeds-based, Marx- and Brecht-inspired Gang of Four participated in the 1979 Rock Against Racism's "Militant Entertainment" tour which was directed against the National Front and the impending Conservative turn under Thatcher (*Rip It Up and Start Again*, p. 123). Likewise, Bristol's The Pop Group performed in an anti-nuclear rally in Trafalgar Square in 1980 (p. 89).

Another incarnation of the outward model is "shock effect" tactics where musicians externalize their inner feelings through actions that drastically break with ordinary conventions in order to alienate, incense, or provoke audiences or even the larger public. A famous example of an early punk attempt to enact authentic counter-culture via shock effects is the Sex Pistols with their, as Joy Division/New Order bassist Peter Hook enthusiastically recalls, "aura of violence," their "reputation for fighting at every gig" (*Unknown Pleasures*, p. 26), or—according to the equally lyrical reminiscences of Alan Vega (founding member of the New York-based band Suicide, and a former member of a militant socialist group that barricaded the Museum of Modern Art)—Iggy Pop's "flying into the audience . . . cutting himself up with drumsticks, bleeding"

(Reynolds, p. 54). This category also includes the public display of *verbotene* political symbols, as when the Sex Pistols' Sid Vicious appeared in a swastika T-shirt, or when The Fall's Mark E. Smith and Siouxsie and the Banshees's frontwoman (and avid Sex Pistols fan) Siouxsie Sioux sported swastika armbands. She conceived this "as an anti-mums-and-dads-things . . . a way of watching" older folks with their "smug pride" about defeating Hitler "go completely red-faced . . . a way of getting back at the older generation that we hated" (*England's Dreaming*, p. 340).

Co-optation

But the outward model of authenticity is especially liable to co-option by the mainstream. This is particularly clear in regard to the shock-effect model whose linchpin is crass, extreme, or aggressively provocative behavior. However disturbing this may seem to sedate elderly generations, it has a widespread mainstream appeal simply because human nature is inherently volatile, ripe with aggressive instincts which are particularly pronounced in younger folks that typically (nowadays) have money to spend. Moreover, the shrill, flamboyant aspects of the shock-effect model, its focus on immediately tangible effects that incite strong emotions and its corresponding lack of subtlety or ambiguity, provide a golden key for clever marketing strategists.

Any mode of behavior that seeks to evoke specific feelings in audiences and whose *modus operandi* is the theatrical display of those feelings via easily identifiable gestures, symbols and sounds can be effectively designed and then *performed* according to the design plan: in which case it is no longer a spontaneous, sincere expression of truly felt and owned personal characteristics but, rather, a calculated attempt to impress targeted audiences, to get them hooked on a product that competes with other products for their attention and spending habits. The Sex Pistols are a case in point here. Hook felt that "what made them special, without a shadow of a doubt, was Johnny Rotten," for "who was going to close their eyes when he . . . was standing there? Sneering and snarling at you, looking at you like he hated you, hated being there, hated everyone. What he embodied was the *attitude* of the Pistols, the attitude of punk . . . complete nihilism" (p. 38).

Likewise, Hook was hooked on punk when he first set eyes on Sex Pistols manager Malcolm McLaren, "dressed head to toe in black leather—leather jacket, leather trousers and leather boots—with a shock of bright-orange hair, a manic grin and the air of a circus ringmaster . . . We were like, *Wow*" (p. 36). Actually, however, Rottens's aka John Lydon's, real persona was that of a pensive, sensitive individual who shared his vulnerability and feelings of humiliation after being demonized by the tabloids and attacked by Conservative street thugs. He also revealed (during a 1977 radio show) that his musical taste is much more wide-ranging (encompassing Lou Reed, John Cale, Tim Buckley, and Can, among others) than punk dogmatism allowed. This led McLaren to accuse Rotten of undermining "the band's threat," revealing himself as "a constructive sissy rather than a destructive lunatic." As Simon Reynolds observes, Lydon earned McLaren's rage for breaking "with his . . . McLaren-scripted role as a cultural terrorist by effectively outing himself as an aesthete" (p. 4). This exemplifies the dubious character of the shock-effect model as a self-proclaimed exhibition of authenticity, its inherent liability to be instrumentalized as part of marketing ploys which are designed to dupe and draw money from gullible, naive (angry, vulgar) audiences.

Unshockable

A further problem here is that shock tactics quickly lose their efficacy. Nowadays, the standard methods of provoking or antagonizing the mainstream have been overdone and no longer strike people as startling or shocking. Moreover, due to a massive over-exposure to crass, violent behavior in the media, the larger public has become jaded and indifferent to things that might have raised eyebrows (and more) thirty years ago. (Perhaps, though, a new golden age of different shock tactics is looming due to the new hyper-sensibility of millennial/Gen-Z folks.)

The political activist model of outward authenticity also faces salient threats of co-option by the mainstream culture industry. This is partly because the professed values of political agendas are typically condensed to buzzwords—such as "social equality," "racial justice," or "fight oppression"—gestures and symbols that have a widespread appeal and that can easily be incorporated into the commercial strategies of established brands.

The performative display of the relevant values—such as wearing a "Black Lives Matter" T-shirt—evokes discernible positive reactions from like mind-people, which is a well-established mechanism for building up a positive self-image (if you feel that people feel good about you, you feel good about yourself); thus the external markers (T-shirts, pins, bandanas) for signaling one's virtue to others can be sold at great profit. Moreover, capitalist brands can increase their customer base by joining in the virtue-signaling game and feigning their solidarity with the underprivileged (as when Amazon Prime Video introduces a "Hispanic and Latino Voices" series). The fact that a supposedly authentic counter-culture that focuses on rebellious sociopolitical agendas invites mainstream infiltration was not lost on the pioneers of post-punk music who felt disillusioned by the punk movement. For instance, Mark Mothersbaugh from the Akron-based New Wave band Devo recalls that he and his bandmates in the mid to late 1970s "thought the punks never learned from the hippies. Rebellion always gets co-opted into another marketing device" (*Rip It Up and Start Again*, p. 41).

Foundational post-punk figures had further grounds for dissatisfaction with the notion that authenticity should manifest itself as political activism. Their main intellectual influences included Ballard, Burroughs, Beckett, Camus, Dostoevsky, Huysmans, Schopenhauer, and Nietzsche rather than Marx or Lukacs. These sources are apt to undermine confidence in progressive leftist agendas, partly because they suggest a principled pessimism about human nature. They convey the point that a tendency towards (self-)destructiveness, aggression and hostility is an inherent and insuperable aspect of humanity.

Hollow Ideals

This point impugns socialist calls for progressive activism in pursuit of an allegedly "more equal" and peaceful society, because it implies that the ideals of solidarity and community which inspire the socialist birdcall are hollow. We find an expression of this fatalistic-pessimistic sentiment in Ian Curtis's lyrics for the song "Heart and Soul" from Joy Division's 1980 album *Closer*: "An abyss that laughs at creation, a circus complete with all fools, foundations that lasted the ages, then ripped apart at their roots. Beyond all this good is the terror, the grip of a mercenary hand, when savagery turns all good reason, there's no turning back, no last stand" (*Touching from a Distance*, p. 179).

If you have such an image of humanity, it makes sense to hold onto a political system that secures some degree of order, stability and protection against the savagery of uninhibited human destructiveness, rather than placing vain hope in some allegedly better social world that requires a revolution of the reigning status quo. Accordingly, Curtis always voted

Conservative, that is: *pro-Thatcher*, against "progressive" ideas (p. 35). Likewise, we can suspect an influence of Camus's existentialist-pessimist masterpiece novel *The Stranger* on the Manchester band The Fall, which used to play "numerous Rock Against Racism benefits but, like many post-punk groups . . . became disenchanted with RAR's treatment of music as a mere vehicle for politicking youth. Soon, they distanced themselves from anything remotely resembling agit-prop or right-on trendy leftyism" (*Rip It Up*, pp. 178–79.

Beyond their pessimistic implications, these intellectual sources sap the appeal of progressive political activism as a model of living authentically in further ways. They inspire strong skepticism about whether the moral values (such as equality, solidarity or beneficence) that animate activist projects have any legitimate foundation in the modern world. Such skepticism can encourage a mindset that avoids commitments to definitive ethical goals or socio-political causes and instead embraces a detached stance of experimental individualism. Such a mindset is expressed in Richard Kirk's (Cabaret Voltaire) confession that he never took his dad's staunch commitment to the Young Communist League seriously, that he was instead (as Reynolds comments) "drawn to Dada's unconstructive revolt and intoxicating irrationalism" (p. 151).

We can witness a related attitude in initial Buzzcocks and later Magazine frontman Howard Devoto, who reports frustrating his socialist girlfriend by "playing my devil's advocate role, saying, 'Yes, but . . .'", and who commended "the true enlightenment" as involving "somehow making the paradoxical and contradictory the focal point of your life, just holding on to them and making them dance" (p. 21). This calls to mind Nietzsche's *Zarathustra's* admonition, "I say unto you: one must still have chaos in oneself to be able to give birth to a dancing star."

In the same paragraph, Nietzsche's prophet expresses his horror towards "the last man" who has realized the socialist-Christian dream of perfect equality and universal neighborly love, of a social order where everybody "loves one's neighbor and rubs against him, for one needs warmth." For Nietzsche, this is not a hopeful vision but the horrid nightmare of a world where insipid mediocrity has become the normal standard, of a "herd" where "Everybody wants the same, everybody is the same: whoever feels different goes voluntarily into a madhouse" (*Also Sprach Zarathustra*, Prologue, §5). In Magazine's debut single "Shot by Both Sides," Devoto proclaims his disgust with the herd and his return to defiant individualism when he sings, "I wormed my way into the heart of crowd, I was shocked by what was allowed, I didn't lose myself in the crowd" (*Rip It Up*, p. 21)

A stark rejection of herds or crowds is a key aspect not only in Nietzsche but also of Kierkegaard, for whom "the crowd . . . is the untruth" (Kaufman, *Existentialism*, p. 95). Identifying yourself as part of human communities amounts to becoming "a copy, a number, a mass man . . . instead of a self . . . just one more repetition of this everlasting *Einerlei*" (Marino, *Basic Writings*, pp. 62–63). Accordingly, Kierkegaard rejects the idea that living authentically is a matter of producing tangible outward effects. Instead, he argues that "subjectivity, inwardness, is the truth," and "one becomes mature only through" a particularly "intense" "inwardness in existing" (*Existentialism*, pp 117–19). Such dissatisfaction with the outward model propelled founding post-punk figures towards something like the Kierkegaardian idea that living and creating authentically is primarily a matter of turning inwardly, directing one's attention away from the chattering of the crowd and towards one's own subjectivity, struggling with—but also drawing creative energy from—one's inner chaos and contradictions, and doing so with uncompromising focus and intensity.

The movement from outward to inward models of authenticity is mirrored by post-punk's shift in musical style: away from the crude, stifling three-chord guitar rock-punk ethos towards more experimental forms of musical self-expression. Devoto's stance of "recoiling from the rabble-rousing vulgarity that typified most punk gigs by the middle of 1977" (*Rip It Up*, p. 21). leads to his pronouncement, when recruiting bandmates for Magazine, that "Punk mentality is not essential" (p. 19). Similarly, the transgression from Warsaw's (the predecessor of Joy Division) rather simplistic punk-aggression towards the more complex, darker sound of Joy Division (carefully enriched with experimental techniques by producer Martin Hannett) is accompanied by a turn in Ian Curtis's lyrics which become increasingly personal and cryptic. As the (then) pioneering underground music journal *Zillo* puts it in a 1990 retrospective analysis, the directive was "no longer 'Get pissed, destroy' but 'This is the way, step inside'"—the latter being the key line in Joy Division's "Atrocity Exhibition," the first track on *Closer* (April 1990). Tony Wilson (founder of the iconic independent label *Factory Records*) expressed the spirit of this transition as follows: "Punk enabled you to say 'Fuck you,' but somehow it couldn't go any further . . . sooner or later someone was going to want to say . . . 'I'm fucked,' and it was Joy Division who were the first band to do that . . . to express more complex emotions" (*This Searing Light*, p. 191).

Two Challenges for the Inward Model

These problems for outward models of authenticity seem more pertinent than ever nowadays, due to the rise of the mass and social media (which provide ever more effective mechanisms for influencing external practices and communities in ways that are congenial to the reigning capitalist paradigms), recent socio-political developments (such as ever-increasing polarization), and the total collapse of olden metaphysical (for instance, theocentric) ideas that once supported beliefs in universally binding moral values. This explains the lasting, increasing appeal of inward models.

Inward models are not immune to challenges either. First, you might object that the very idea of a *truly* inward form of authentic lifestyle is incoherent, since we always strive to make the outer world conform to our inner conception of how the world ought to be by seeking to realize our inner passions through external achievements. This worry seems especially salient in regard to authentic forms of sub- or counter-cultural aesthetics, since (you might argue) artistic inwardness is always inherently directed towards outward, performative expression (in gigs or record productions). But in response, we might question whether it is indeed essential to all human agency that it must seek fulfilment in the outer world. The inward model is animated precisely by the sense that this is a futile project: authentic self-fulfillment cannot be fully realized outwardly because corrupt social practices, pseudo-communities and mediocre crowds have a leveling effect on the individual, reducing its strongest passions and talents to the lowly common mass denominator.

In regard to *artistic* inwardness, it may perhaps be true that internal creative efforts are inherently geared towards external expressions and towards (actual or imaginary-idealized) audiences. But at least in the case of foundational post-punk figures, acts of external authentic self-expression do not involve the ambition to change or influence others in any specific way. This is the crucial difference between such figures and those who seek to provoke specific reactions in others via shock effect tactics, or those who aim to facilitate "progressive" socio-political changes via their political activism. Insofar as the inward model relinquishes such aspirations, it also releases the pressure on artists to conform to external conventions in ways that undermine their personal integrity and sap their unique passions and talents. Notably, once creative energies and efforts are stripped of specific outward intentions, the externally accessible creative output becomes increasingly *ambiguous*.

Such ambiguity, the refusal to commit to a clear "message" or to preach determinate values, is a key marker for a lot of late 1970s/early 1980s post-punk aesthetics. We can witness it, for instance, in Ian Curtis's points that "I wouldn't like to sort of make a statement on sort of a vast . . . subject" (Radio Blackburn Interview). or that "we haven't got any message really; the lyrics are open to interpretation. They're multi-dimensional. You can read into them whatever you like" (*Touching from a Distance*, p. 75).

Another common worry about the inward approach is that it compromises the appeal of authenticity as an *ethical-political* ideal: stripped of the ambition to make positive moral contributions or to responsibly engage with one's socio-political community, the inward struggle for authenticity acquires an individualistic character where the emphasis is chiefly on self-exploration and self-realization, ethically uncommitted experimentation, and creativity for its own sake. This worry may, again, seem especially relevant in sub-cultural contexts where the turn towards inward authenticity often goes along with an aestheticist, quietist orientation that involves a stance of ethical-political ambiguity or indifference.

In response to this worry, defenders of inwardly oriented authenticity can vigorously turn the tables on the objector: after all, the inward model is typically motivated in the first place (in part) by doubts about whether appeals to universalist ethical values or solidaric human communities have any legitimate basis. The burden of proof is on those who complain about the ethically-politically uncommitted connotations of the inward model: they must show that the moral values and anti-individualistic prescriptions which they seek to impose on defiant or indifferent individuals can retain their normative purchase in the fragmented, disenchanted modern world.

Aestheticists can defend their uncommitted stance via the Nietzschean insight that the religious or secular preachers' values manifest no more than petty human needs, are borne out of resentment, fear and weakness. They can also invoke the soberly realistic-pessimistic recognition that the invocation of solidaric communities is a mere sham, since human beings are inherently aggressive, competitive, combative, (self-)destructive creatures who only ever preach rather than practice true solidarity.

III

Punk and the Corpse of Philosophy

11

A Punk by Any Other Name Would Smell as Rotten

GWENDA-LIN GREWAL

Punk is a comedy of opposition to what authorities take in earnest. Punks are forward-thinking pessimists, at once on the fringe and the cutting edge, their tough appearances more often than not clashing with their unwillingness to make good on their apparent anarchism. No matter the reigning dictum, punk will denounce it as fake: governments, corporations, manners—Bad Religion, Dead Kennedys, The Clash—rage against any and all machines.

At the same time, the punk manifesto is set to self-destruct the moment it catches on. As a counter-culture, punk must negate even its own claims to legitimacy. Once it begins to invoke a group ethos, it can no longer be pulling itself up by the bootstraps and striking out on its own. Punk's marginal stance is thus at odds with its call to arms. Any complacency or agreement must be contested, including punks who become too punk. For a comparative punk is no punk at all. Punks don't carry identification. They don't have parents.

They don't need chapters in books to tell them who they are either. They set their own standards and cannot be typed. Yet if Punk's MO is to always shirk patterns and rules, how can you ever call punk "punk" without subjecting it to the sickening embrace of a term? Punks are usually deemed "punks" by other people. The word materializes *ex nihilo* like a spitball. It aims close-range to gutturally malign its target as worthless: "stupid punk." But once spat on, punks become notorious spitters—salivating at no one in particular, but rather, for the sake of self-affirming ejaculation.

Etymologically, "punk" may come from "spunk," the bastard child of "spark" and "funk." "Funk," in turn, comes from the Latin word *fumus* ("smoke"), which is related to the Greek word *thumos*. *Thumos* means something like "spirit," "anger," or perhaps, "the will to live." The will to live is the kind of thing you need in order to be willing to die. Soldiers, therefore, need *thumos*, as do ideologues or anyone who believes in anything, including sentences.

In Plato's *Republic*, Socrates tells a story about Leontius "going up" from the Piraeus. On his way, Leontius sees some corpses lying outside of the public execution house. He wants to look, but is also repulsed by his own desire. Finally overpowered, Leontius's *thumos* rises to his defense. It divides him against his own eyes: "Look you miserable wretches (*kakodaimones*)," Leontius cries, "have your fill of the beautiful sight!" (439e–440a). Leontius's eyes, the miserable little punks, charge forward into the doom of necrophilia—doing exactly what they were told not to. But as the eyes engage in the punky act of looking, the corpses take on their own punk appearance. The dead seem to have set their sights on Leontius before he sees them. Punk is the site of a conflict between subject and object. The goal is to not submit. But punks assert their agency only in a refusal to allow any claims to agency. Punks are the living dead, and *kakodaimôn* (an untranslatable word that combines "bad" with "surprise") a sort of ancient spitball.

"Punk" once meant "prostitute," and that may be helpful here—in the words of William Burroughs, "I always thought a punk was someone who takes it up the ass" (quoted in *Please Kill Me*, p. 357). A prostitute is a punk in the sense of dwelling on the outskirts of society: a sign of social distortion, unassimilated and undermining the ordinary sensibilities of passers-by. Yet it is only because society has noticed what is not-to-be noticed that it can give the prostitute a title. Society's own absurdity thus lies in those it ostracizes. Calling outsiders names gives civility significance. Without the exile of the wilderness, the "Suburban Home" ceases to look so safe (The Descendents, 1982). The punk, then, is the loner that the herd's aggregation attentively maligns and begrudgingly covets. As the punk aggravates the aggregate, he/she/it also signifies individual worth. Punks are the antisocial antiheros we all want to be. They don't need help, unlike all the other sorry lemmings suckled by association.

Even to speak of a movement called "punk," is to badmouth it—to suggest it has certain "class" (ugh) characteristics. If there are characteristics, there is a way to fit or not fit the punk mold. But punks are misfits. How can one punk, then, fit in more than another? Shouldn't the fake punk—the "punk" in scare quotes—always be the true punk? Surely any loser who thinks they are *truly* punk is fodder for the tongue-in-cheek revelation that they are not? In any case, real punks have to be somehow more truly false than falsely true. Punk is non sequitur.

It can't be solely a social, political, and aesthetic movement beginning in the 1970s either. This helps to put a name to a face, but musical references won't any more supply the innards to punk's periphery than a list of hard drugs. Punks are crooked but also straight edge: they are an inside on the outside: an interior outer limit. Their metaphysical attitude by its own lights resists being pigeonholed, and punk itself is perpetually alienated from particular places and times. It is homeless, rootless, ungirded from the grand maw of convention.

Poor old punk, thou prun'st a rotten tree. Punk can hardly be a modern phenomenon. In Lux Interior sporting a top hat and tails you can see the roughed-up specter of Beau Brummell. The nineteenth-century dandies, too, once had a fancy for torn clothes, since they were already primping to attack those aristocratic phantoms we now call "suits." Maybe the punk of now is the prude of yesterday? Maybe after the stale antiquarians were ousted by the penchants of slang, the new punk can only be the rogue who would dare to speak properly?

Diogenes the Punk

There was anarchy in Thebes when the Maenads lost their minds to Dionysus. The Bacchae were perhaps an early example of an anti-establishment "group"—again, whatever "group" means in punk's case. "Punk community" is an oxymoron too. Where everyone is gathering together around some icon, fracturing their individuality in the face of the ghost of unity, you need a punk to crash the party. You need a punk to tell you: "You're praying to an ass" and "It's all a lie." Thus spoke Zarathustra, another punk of old.

As to the greatest of all lies—life—it's here that punk strikes the high note of Greek tragedy: "I was saying let me out of here before I was even born," sings Richard Hell in the song, "Blank Generation," channeling the chorus of *Oedipus at Colonus* (Richard Hell and the Voidoids, 1977). But tragic characters don't usually know that they are rebelling. Life may be the charged pursuit of nothing, but you need a punk like Antigone or Socrates to announce it.

Socrates roamed around barefoot (mostly), unmoored from conventional trappings, and only professing to know his own ignorance. He was also quite ugly, though it's hard to know whether this image came from his appearance or from his manner. His execution, both his own and that of others, seems to have followed from his apparent public demonstrations. It's said that he trolled the marketplace critiquing the knowledge of artisans, politicians, and poets, and leaving them in *aporia*: without resource, impoverished, safety-pinning their principles back together. But Socrates criticized his fellow lowlifes, too. Upon seeing Antisthenes reveal a hole in his cloak, Socrates remarked, "I see your love of reputation in the tear in your cloak" (*Lives*, 6.8). The tear ventures to say I am miserable—but so are you.

More dramatically, there was Antisthenes's student, Diogenes of Sinope. He was so-called because of his birthplace, but renamed "Diogenes the Dog" on account of his attitude. When someone inquired, "What sort do you think Diogenes is?" he replied, "Socrates gone mad" (6.54). In Plato's *Sophist*, Socrates himself remarks that philosophers sometimes give the impression of being complete madmen (216d).

Diogenes learned how to live from a mouse—sleeping in Zeus's portico on his folded cloak, wandering around with his middle finger out, giving himself hand jobs in public "continuously" (*suneches*), urinating on crowds, and defacing statues. You can imagine him temple hopping with a switchblade. At Delphi, he scratched into a newly-sculpted mold of golden Aphrodite, "from the unrestraint of the Greeks" (6.60). He was once beaten up for having a mohawk (in Greek, the word is *hêmi-xurêtos*, "half-shaved"). In retaliation he wrote the names of the bullies on a sign that he wore around his neck until they were ridiculed and blamed by everyone (6.33).

Apparently, it was Plato who deemed Diogenes a "dog" (*cyôn*), to which Diogenes replied, "Sure, because I come back again and again to the ones who've sold me" (640). "I Wanna Be Your Dog," sing The Stooges (1969). Socrates used to swear with the words, "by the dog," invoking an Egyptian god with a dog head, Anubis. Doggy Diogenes, it's true, was up for sale, and Menippus's lost *Sale of Diogenes* told of his capture and auction. On the slave market, he professed to a single talent—"ruling over men" (6.29). Diogenes's master baiting knew no end.

His first name should not be neglected either. "Diogenes," means "God-born," or, more figuratively, "divine." When Alexander introduced himself as "Alexander the great king," Diogenes replied, "And I'm God-born dog," or, taking liberties, "a divine son-of-a-bitch." When further asked what he'd done to be called "dog," he said, "Wagging my tail at those who give me things, barking at those who don't, and biting the wicked" (6.60). Diogenes is the sly dog who'll dog you. From his dogeared persona emerged the more tasteful moniker, "cynic" (*cynikos*), or "doglike."

So, before Sid Vicious and Siouxsie Sioux, before The Cramps and Minor Threat, there was Diogenes the Punk, barking at the moon since the late Eighties, that is, the late 380s, B.C. At any rate, Plato was making a joke. It was originally Antisthenes who was called "Dog," and he got the name from the gymnasium he used to haunt—Cynosarges, meaning, "shining dog." The Cynosarges was *just outside* the Athenian walls. Diogenes trotted out after Antisthenes like a puppy.

But when he arrived in Athens, Diogenes was already an exile. In one story, he had been forced to leave his native Sinope because of counterfeiting (either his father's or his own). In another, "exile" was the answer the Delphic oracle gave when Diogenes asked how to gain the greatest reputation. Either way, Diogenes seems to have identified expatriation with philosophy. In response to someone reproaching him for his exile, he quipped: "But, you miserable punk (*kakodaimôn*), because of this, I philosophized" (6.49).

Is philosophy slinking around on the outskirts of town, masturbating in public, and pissing on (and off) unsuspecting revelers? Jerking off might be another name for a kind of thinking concerned solely with its own activity. Thinking touches itself as if it were another, but in the act of getting itself off, it turns itself on. So, Diogenes is said to masturbate *suneches*, "continuously" or "without end" (6.69). He is in constant conjugal cogitation, eternal spring, endlessly erecting the philosophical question. "Would that one could stop hunger by rubbing the belly!" he remarked. Hunger, in contrast to sexual urges, is not so easily quelled by turning inward. While sophists hawk their loogies to the starving masses, philosophers eat themselves. The sophist is a gigolo; the philosopher a wanker.

But Antisthenes is said to be responsible for "leading" Diogenes into "apathy." The phrasing is strange. How is it possible to rope someone into indifference? Apathy (*a-pathia*) seems to involve the opposite of "being led." Rather, it resists as much as possible undergoing any *pathos*. The apathetic must be *de facto* disinterested in extravagant claims and ways of life. They must live like mice and vagabonds. Yet in such apathy the skeptical spirit of contrarianism rears its comic head: "Should I Stay or Should I Go?" (The Clash, 1982). Coming out of the public baths, Diogenes told one man that the bath was crowded, another that it was not.

Punks beware: where shabby attitudes turn swanky, twee is but a heartbeat away. Diogenes himself was bested in his simple drinking cup when he saw a child drinking out of his hands. The lower you go, the better you do? Is the underdog the top dog? Whatever the wholesome cloth, punk can cynically shred it. But in its exposure of the shreds, it seems impossible to refrain from asserting that the rips are more genuine than the garment. The distinction of chaff over wheat lurks in another motto: *the meek shall inherit the Earth.*

Punk thus threatens to turn itself into the iconic anti-icon of the very icons it mocks, smashes, or ignores. In its quest to uphold meaninglessness, a cry of existential horror rings out. Punk suddenly finds itself waving the flag of non-being with a flair of troublingly familiar school spirit, just before it limps off into the shadows of its opposite, lest it suffer that cruel fate of becoming mainstream.

Exile and Adultery

The connection between punk and exile seems especially critical. And it is here that we might pell-mell discover punk's philosophical moment.

In Simone de Beauvoir's account of the trap of domestic life, a woman experiences freedom from her house by becoming an adulteress. She goes punk, striking out on her own and turning away from her vanilla life as if it were newly meaningless. Forget the manicure of marriage:

> Her husband's too mundane gaze no longer nurtures her image; she needs eyes still full of mystery to discover her as mystery; she needs a sovereign consciousness before her to receive her confidences, to revive the faded photographs, to bring to life that dimple in the corner of her mouth, the fluttering eyelashes that are hers alone; she is only desirable, lovable, if she is desired, loved. (*The Second Sex*, p. 592)

A tryst dissolves patterned behavior. It imitates serendipity by negating everyday existence and revamping the agency lost in the objectification of commitment. Cheating opens secret chambers in a hackneyed house.

Indeed, an exile from any loyalty or allegiance—parents, friends, cities, spouses, lovers, words—might birth a joyous fount of self-immolation in the form of caprice, decay, and bad brains. What once was a mummified image of who-you-are and what-you-believe reveals itself to keep mutable walls. It therefore becomes important that you don't replicate a new attachment within the experience of contingency: the brains must remain bad; the decay must not turn into a beautified flaw.

Such is the manner of a digression on an argument, too: where implications begin to force necessary conclusions, an adulterous detour recalibrates the author's will. Beauvoir's style is interesting in this regard. She describes the female plight with a boldly luxurious affair of words. Today's academics would never dare it. They are too prudish. They long for the marriage of prose to truth, avoiding at all costs the masturbatory insult. Meanwhile, poets continue to engage in perfidious diction, bringing back the ripples that scholarship so scrupulously tries to iron out (lest an author seduce the reader beside the point). In this punk divergence, in the digression outside the walls, the possibility of philosophy flickers.

Philosophy Gone Punk

So punk, as if to begin in wonder, regularly adulterates what is with what's not. The negation, though serial, must remain noncommittal, if it is not to accidentally renew its vows to the very being it was and is inclined to question. Punk, then, seems to be an action that reveals action to be inaction upon reflection. Or is it that inaction is action upon reflection? Reflection is action too: a flash in the pan, gone before it can begin to argue its case. To see it spark is to foresee its imminent extinction; yet when it flies under the radar, it is not exactly going punk. Maybe you don't know what's punk till it's gone. Maybe masturbation loses its fun, when it begins to be more "rom" than "com" ("Longview," Green Day, 1992).

Still, in its affinity for shocking statements, punk seems more like a Diogenes than a Socrates. Ozzy Osbourne bit the head off a bat and drank his own urine; Ozzy was not quite a punk (maybe he was more so in the Black Sabbath days), but then there was Iggy Pop puking on his audience. More disturbing is the early punk usage of the Nazi swastika. The Nazis themselves had already misappropriated the swastika, which was originally an ancient symbol meaning "good fortune." The punks then mis-mis-appropriated it, and they did so (for the most part) not intending to become Nazis but rather to identify themselves with a group with whom it would seem shocking to identify. Punk did not lack a counter-counter-shock either: "Nazi Punks Fuck Off," sing the Dead Kennedys (1983).

The longing for disapproval is as old as the longing for approval. But to stun is not the end game. The goal is to overhaul the power of approbation entire. Here, Rousseau emerges as a prime punk. He became more liberated to the degree that he was cast out by society. But it wasn't about being hated so much as it was about being ignored. The more he was ignored, the more nonexistent he felt. And as he channeled the negation of his own being, he began to feel godlike: "and here I am, tranquil at the bottom of the abyss, a poor unfortunate mortal, but unperturbed, like God himself" (*Reveries of a Solitary Walker*, p. 5). Cut yourself off from human judgment; release yourself from mortal anxiety.

And yet—and yet—the holier-than-thou is the flip side of thou as nothing. Christian Punk occupies its own genre. Some argue that it is disqualified from being punk because of its allegiance to a higher authority. Others say it is novel in its attempt to be punk while not being punk. Punks can only scream to an empty room. They must reject the concept of followers. They must remain hardly a they, for punk runs on the heels of the winged subject, always in adultery and never wedded to a band. Punk is the ruthless pursuit of the rootless: the thrill of being in a continual flirtation with denial.

In this, punks seem to mock any ascent from the cave. "Holi-days in the Sun" are, after all, miserable and cheap (Sex Pistols, 1977). And pure sunlight is so blinding it replicates total darkness: "To be enlightened is to be brainwashed" (*Socrates' Second Sailing*, p. 179). When Socrates was trying to save the young Cleinias from being hazed by two unrelenting sophists, Euthydemus and Dionysodorus, he asked Dionysodorus in a whisper, "When will this end?" To which Dionysodorus replied, "All the things we ask, Socrates, are the sort with no escape" (*Euthydemus*, 276e). Is there no escape from the cynical skepticism about all things? No escape from the *kakodaimôn* attitude? If everything can be negated, "I Wanna Be Sedated" (The Ramones, 1978).

Perhaps the true punk is time itself—time which cheats on our certainty about nearly everything, but especially our own existence. Meanwhile, the human punk throws off the chains of objectification as a means to take back agency, only to "Search and Destroy" it all over again in the face of their own detestable triumph (The Stooges, 1973).

To say 'No' and 'Don't bother' is to deny the future from progressing. To do this repeatedly is to try to forge the escape of no escape: a vicarious freedom from time's wedlock in the incessant exile of every new belief. God is dead; God Save the Queen. Loyalty and doubt meet again. But in the bug of indecision, in the getaway of the "Young, Loud, and Snotty" (Dead Boys, 1977), the engine of complaint buzzes, the denial of what is as what was finds that its own is must be was anew—a "Personality Crisis" or the inverted desire for "Complete Control"? (The New York Dolls, 1973; The Clash, 1977). What good is knowledge these days anyway? Oh bollocks, never mind.

12
Early Punk and the Dionysian Lion-Child

Casey Rentmeester

A crystallizing contrast of punk and professionalism can be found in the 1977 interview of punk rock star Iggy Pop by the Canadian Broadcasting Corporation host Peter Gzowski, colloquially called "Mr. Canada" and generally embodying the reserved nature and politeness of that amicable ethos, on the late-night show *90 Minutes Live*.

Although Pop was scheduled to play a concert on the show that night, arrangements between the Canadian Broadcasting Corporation and the American Federation of Musicians disallowed it, so they interviewed him instead and asked him about punk rock. Pop's response to the question as to the nature of punk rock is legendary: "Punk rock is a word used by dilettantes and heartless manipulators about music that takes up the energies, the bodies, the hearts, the souls, the time, and the minds of young men who give everything they have to it" (*90 Minutes Live*, March 11th 1977).

The interview features Gzowski donning a buttoned-up suit, thick glasses, neatly styled hair and a professional demeanor (that, admittedly, gets tested by Pop's shenanigans) while Pop is baring his chest centered with a crucifix emblem, sporting his distinctive mullet and looking around for a lighter for his cigarette. Pop's countercultural, anti-establishment mentality is apparent, as is his frustration with corporate arrangements dictating whether or not he can play music. Equally apparent is his commitment to authenticity, honesty, and the dedication to his craft that he explicitly compares to the work of Sigmund Freud.

If there's one figure in the history of philosophy who embodied the punk mentality of Iggy Pop it is Friedrich Nietzsche, who, as it happens, had a strong influence on Freud. Born into a deeply religious family (his father and grandfather were both pastors) in the small village of Röcken, Germany, Nietzsche was a child prodigy who became the youngest person ever to hold the Chair of Classical Philology at the University of Basel at the ripe age of twenty-four.

Disillusioned by the formalities and pompous nature of academia and partially due to health reasons, he left roughly ten years later to live by himself in the Swiss Alps, going on to write some of the most provocative and scathingly critical philosophy the world has ever seen in books that hardly anyone ever read in his lifetime, prompting him at one point to say that some are born posthumously, an acknowledgement that few people alive during his time could understand him (Friedrich Nietzsche, *The Antichrist*, p. 1). A similar narrative can be found in Pop's commentary during the Gzowski interview: "What sounds to you like a big load of trashy old noise is in fact the brilliant music of a genius—myself."

Famously proclaiming that God is dead and dedicating much of his later thoughts to questioning not just Christianity—he called himself "the Antichrist" long before the famous lyric from the Sex Pistols' "Anarchy in the UK," "I am an antichrist"—but also morality, justice and *truth itself*, Nietzsche described himself not as a man but as dynamite and only trusted those who had the courage to write with blood (*Ecce Homo*, p. 326; *Thus Spake Zarathustra*, p. 65). Nietzsche made no distinction between his life and his craft, a similarity that can be found not only in Iggy Pop's commentary but generally in punk rock culture.

Any examination of early punk rock from the perspective of Nietzsche's philosophy should begin with *Thus Spake Zarathustra*, which Nietzsche considered to be his masterpiece; in fact, summoning hyperbole befitting to the punk scene, he called it "the greatest present that has ever been made to mankind so far" (*Ecce Homo*, p. 219).

In *Zarathustra* he speaks of three metamorphoses of the spirit: the camel, who bears the burden of traditional values not posited by oneself; the lion, who destroys worn-out, life-denying values; and the child, who creatively posits new values with a "sacred Yes" sort of attitude towards life. At first glance, the countercultural, anti-establishment mentality of punk rock most obviously signifies the lion, as seen clearly in songs like "God Save the Queen," the song that inspired the subtitle of this volume, or the aforementioned "Anarchy in the UK" by the Sex Pistols. At the same time, though, the coveted ideals of authenticity and freedom in punk rock seen, for instance, in early classics like The Stooges' "I Wanna Be Your Dog" or their

1973 album *Raw Power* evoke the ideal of Nietzsche's child in that they are beautiful in their pure simplicity.

While punk rock sometimes teeters on the edge of nihilism, it really is a movement embracing what Nietzsche in *The Birth of Tragedy from the Spirit of Music* calls "the Dionysian," which venerates the raw, instinctual, and libidinous aspects of life. As an instantiation of a Nietzschean hybrid, a destructive creator, a "lion-child," punk rock simultaneously unmasks and destroys the privileged and pompous aspects of life through irreverent figures like Johnny Rotten and Sid Vicious while celebrating the brash and the crass elements, that is, the raw components of what Nietzsche referred to as "the will to power," through Iggy Pop and The Stooges and other bands who expel "raw power."

In the end, punk is an attitude, a mentality, and a way of life that embraces the instinctual and raw aspects of life that Nietzsche called the Dionysian over what he referred to as the Apollonian—the drive for ordered, reasoned, calm and mea- sured restraint. In this way, punk highlights aspects of human nature that are primal, real, and animalistic, though all-too- often covered over when we frame ourselves as the *rational* animal, a famous definition of the human being dating all the way back to Aristotle.

From Camel to Lion-Child

The camel, for Nietzsche, is the person who doesn't question anything but simply obeys, blindly taking up the gestures and values to sustain the status quo. Think, for instance, of a per- son who was born and raised in a certain religious tradition and never questioned any of the doctrines of that faith. Nietzsche calls such persons members of "the herd" in that they are only capable of following but are incapable of engaging in any sort of critical thought on their own, noting that such persons are common since "it is more comfortable to obey than to examine" (*The Will to Power*, p. 248).

These sorts of people prefer a world in which "everybody's doing just what they're told," to quote a famous line from The Clash's iconic song, "White Riot." The camel simply perpetuates what has already been without questioning it. As a pianist, improviser, and composer in his own right, Nietzsche had a lot to say about music and claimed famously that "without music, life would be an error" (*Twilight of the Idols*, p. 10).

If we are to apply the label of the camel to genres of music, we can say that the mindless, easily replaceable, and shallow nature of pop music exemplifies aspects of the camel in that, in the words of Nietzsche, the music "serves only as a diversion or as a kind of vain ostentation." (quoted in Young, *Friedrich Nietzsche*, p. 37). Perhaps the most fitting critique of "camelistic" music in the realm of philosophy comes from Max Horkheimer and Theodor Adorno's critique of the culture industry in which they criticize pop songs following short and catchy interval sequences with "ready-made clichés to be slotted in anywhere" (*Dialectic of Enlightenment*, p. 125). Soft rock music—a patently oxymoronic genre—that arose in the 1970s just before the punk rock revolution of the mid-1970s is also a clear candidate for being a musical instantiation of the camel, which might be why, for instance, Pop (in the movie *Gimme Danger*) calls the Crosby, Stills, and Nash song "Marrakesh Express," a soft rock staple, "the worst song ever written."

Whereas the camel obeys blindly, the fundamental feature of the lion, the second metamorphosis of the Nietzschean spirit, is destruction. The lion destroys traditional values found so clearly in the phrase "Thou shalt," to put it in Biblical terms, or "Obey," if you prefer a secular context. Those who have the courage to challenge the status quo exemplify features of the lion. In the realm of punk rock, the Sex Pistols' 1977 single "God Save the Queen" is a perfect embodiment of the lion. Explicitly titled to mock the British National Anthem of the same name and released during Queen Elizabeth II's "Silver Jubilee" to celebrate twenty-five years of her rule, the song exemplifies a full-on resentment of the monarchy, including references to the queen's regime as fascist and to her not being a human being but rather simply a figurehead.

The mantra during the song's closing refrain—"No future"—has rightly become the motto of the punk rock movement in that it captures the rebellious and nihilistic elements so crucial to its ethos. Moreover, you could argue that the band's attempt to perform the song from a boat named *Queen Elizabeth* on the River Thames during the actual celebration that ended in multiple arrests is one of the more iconic moments in punk rock history. Nietzsche's lion, to be sure, was alive and well on that occasion. Instantiations of the lion can be found in genres beyond punk rock as well, as in, for instance, in some versions of hip hop, particularly in the group N.W.A., and certain metal and hard rock groups, especially Rage Against the Machine.

However, if all there is to punk rock is rebellion and disobedience, the movement would be sheerly nihilistic rather than providing an ethos of its own. Nietzsche referred to the negative version of nihilism as "the radical repudiation of value, meaning, and desirability" so well encompassed in the phrase "everything lacks meaning," a viewpoint he considered to be merely "a *transitional stage*" to a higher point of view. The higher, *more enlightened* perspective is found symbolically in the child who, rather than going along with the crowd as the camel or merely criticizing the values of others as the lion, asserts their *own* values in a creative and authentic manner. The child takes on a "sacred Yes" mentality by living in accordance with their own values, thereby achieving true freedom.

As Nietzsche puts it, "for the game of creating . . . there is needed a sacred Yes to life: *its own* will, wills now the spirit; *his own* world wins the world's outcast" (*Zarathustra*, p. 53). The Stooges' "I Wanna Be Your Dog" is a nice embodiment of such creativity in that its iconic riff is composed of only three cords accompanied by a continuously repeated piano note by John Cale, the co-founding member of the Velvet Underground who produced the track. This simplicity, combined with the distortion-heavy guitar play in the beginning complemented by the sleigh bells that are played throughout, and the sexual nature of the lyrical content that somehow is fittingly paired with aspects of self-loathing and disillusionment, make for a highly unique style that has rightly inspired many punk musicians ever since.

As Brett Callwood notes, "The Stooges . . . influenced hundreds if not thousands of bands that followed in their wake . . . with a completely unconventional approach to rock music. They tore up the rulebook and created something completely fresh" (*The Stooges*, p. xv). Iggy Pop is thus rightly regarded as the "Godfather of Punk" in that in embodying the Nietzschean child he breathed life into an entirely new approach to music that we now call "punk," and, in doing so, won the world's outcast, to paraphrase Nietzsche. Paul Trynka's book does a nice job of chronicling how Pop's provocations led audiences to revile him in the beginning. We don't, however, necessarily have to be an outcast to embody the Nietzschean child: anyone willing to throw out the rulebook, capable "of being able *to go it alone*, of being able *to be different*" (*Will to Power*, p. 196), traits seen in various artists from Beethoven to the Beatles, demonstrate elements of Nietzsche's child.

Punk Rock's Dionysian Nature

While the Stooges certainly embodied the attitude of punk even as early as "I Wanna Be Your Dog," the unique sound of punk really didn't come forth until their third album, *Raw*

Power. Bill Janovitz credits the first song of the album—
"Search and Destroy"—for laying down an archetype for punk
rock and heavily influencing subsequent punk heavy hitters
like the Sex Pistols and The Ramones. During this era, Pop's
stage presence and outrageous antics reached legendary status: the audience didn't know whether they would witness
(merely) lewd and obscene behavior (Pop often pulled out his
penis on stage) or straight-up self-mutilation (on one occasion
he carved an "X" in blood on his chest with a broken drum stick
and on another he writhed around in broken shards of glass
mid-show only to continue performing, ending the night by
being driven to the emergency room by Alice Cooper). What *is*
clear is that Iggy and the Stooges had a raw, primal, energetic,
intoxicating presence and a fast-paced and hard-edged sound
to match it, both key ingredients for the punk rock revolution
of the mid-1970s that was stoked and highlighted so well by
the Sex Pistols during the Silver Jubilee.

The primal, creative-yet-destructive force that has become
synonymous with punk rock can be understood from the perspective of Nietzsche's metamorphoses of the spirit as a lion-
child hybrid of sorts in that it embraces an anti-establishment
mentality and a passionate dedication to creativity all at the
same time. From a broader perspective, Nietzsche explained
the simultaneity of destruction-and-creation through what he
referred to as "Dionysian wisdom," which destroys the past and
affirms the future all at once in a way that more perfectly
affirms "the principle of life," that is, *instinct*, since "one acts
perfectly only when one acts instinctively" (*Will to Power*, pp.
224, 243). His most famous phrase for this instinctual drive is
"the will to power." In order to explain the instinctual, primal,
raw, and visceral aspects of life as opposed to the rational, measured, and calculated ones, Nietzsche utilizes a dichotomous
metaphor related to the Greek god Dionysius—the god of wine,
fertility, festivity, ecstasy, and intoxication—and his counterpart Apollo—the god of truth, knowledge, order, and harmony.

The most robust commentary on the difference between the
Dionysian and the Apollonian as applied to music is found in
Nietzsche's first work, *The Birth of Tragedy from the Spirit of
Music*, where he juxtaposes the calm and measured restraint of
Apollonian music with the primitive, libidinous, and joyous
nature of Dionysian music, which, as he puts it, allows us to
experience "primordial joy even in pain" (*Birth of Tragedy*, p.
141), as it is an expulsion of raw energy or, to put it in punk
rock terms, *raw power*. Punk rock is certainly Dionysian,
rather than Apollonian, in nature since it values power over

musical perfection and authenticity and freedom over sticking to the rules, which Pop explicitly points out in an interview featured toward the end of the 2016 documentary *Gimme Danger* in referring to his music as "Dionysian art." We're reminded again of the commentary from that notorious interview between Pop and Gzowski when Pop states "that music is so powerful that it's quite beyond my control. And when I'm in the grips of it, I don't feel pleasure and I don't feel pain, either physically or emotionally." Rather than a conscious reflection on emotions or one's physical state, raw power entails a primal expulsion of instincts, which might explain Pop's ability to go on performing even after engaging in self-mutilating acts.

Whereas Apollonian music follows the rules pertaining to rhythm, dynamics, melody, harmony, tone, texture, and form, Dionysian music throws all of that out the window and is more geared toward expelling emotions authentically, that is, in their rawest form, through the means of music, even if—or rather, *especially if*—it flies in the face of convention or the status quo, as the politically incorrect or the positively indecent is more likely to be more honest than the pompous, which can easily bleed into the pretentious (in the literal sense of that word).

The politically-charged nature of many of the classics in early punk rock history showcase this well: above and beyond "Anarchy in the UK," which provides a scathing critique of the British government from the perspective of disenfranchised youth, it's notable that The Ramones' "Blitzkrieg Bop" utilizes a reference to Nazi war tactics in World War II to give voice to youth disillusionment with the state of the world and that The Clash's "London Calling" is rife with critical commentary on the political state of England at the time.

From a Nietzschean perspective, these commentaries are best interpreted not as merely critical and thus nihilistic in nature: rather, they should be understood as honest emotional expulsions in the form of music. Nietzsche argued that modern society has led humans to be too civilized, which for him meant too out of touch with their primal instincts and wilder emotions to the point where we repress them, to use a term made famous by Freud. Dionysian music, though, allows for "all the rigid, hostile barriers that necessity, caprice, or 'impudent convention' have fixed between man and man to be broken" to such an extent that "the barbarian in each of us is affirmed; also the wild beast," thereby allowing us to enter a more natural, primal state (*Birth of Tragedy*, p. 37; *Will to Power*, p. 78). This primal state explicitly goes against the privileged and pompous aspects of normal, "civilized" life and instead opens us up to more brash and crass behaviors as can be seen, for instance, not only in the lyrics of many early punk rock classics or in Iggy Pop's famous on-stage antics, but also in the Sex Pistols' frontman Johnny Rotten's rage-infused rebellious attitude that has become a voice of the subculture or the even-more-outlandish behaviors of his bandmate, Sid Vicious, which included drug-addled violence towards himself and others—instantiations of Freud's death drive par excellence, which is Freud's name for the instinctual drive toward death and destruction (*Beyond the Pleasure Principle*). Joe Strummer of The Clash may have put it best in stating that "punk rock is an attitude, and the essence of that attitude is 'give us some truth'" (Quoted in D'Ambrosio, *Let Fury Have the Hour*, p. 233). While the truth is uncomfortable and downright ugly at times (Think of Iggy Pop's penchant for vomiting on stage or the violent riots common at punk rock concerts throughout the mid-1970s), it is true nonetheless.

Awakening the Dionysian Lion-Child

Early punk rock can be understood as a Dionysian lion-child from the lens of Nietzsche's philosophy. Since the first wave of punk rock in the mid-1970s—"early punk rock"—there have been several instantiations of punk and legitimate debate as to whether some punk bands are truly punk or merely shams or sellouts, a crucial question given punk's commitment to authenticity and truth.

Rather than engage in that debate, I want to end with a statement Pop gave at The Stooges' induction into the Rock'n' Roll Hall of Fame: "Music is life, and life is not a business" (*Gimme Danger*).

Those who "never mind the bollocks," to reference one of the greatest albums in punk rock history and the only album by the Sex Pistols, and stay true to the inner essence of punk—the dedication to the truth, even when it hurts, and the courageous commitment to authenticity, even when it risks making you a social pariah—are truly punk. May those contemporary artists who carry the punk rock torch into the new generation heed this message and awaken their own version of the Dionysian lion-child.[1]

---

[1] I thank Josh Heter, Richard Greene, and Mary Roffers for comments on earlier versions of this chapter.

13
Punk's Not Dead

RANDALL E. AUXIER

I walked past this message every day in the fall of 2021, painted on the side of a dormitory at the University of Warsaw in Poland. You can't help noticing the anarchy symbol of course, but the very presence of the epigraph suggests that maybe there is a problem. If no one was saying 'Punk is dead' there would be little reason to contradict that little assertion.

Origins, or, If that Ain't Punk . . .

I take the position supported by the artist here, but we have to think about what punk *is* before we can judge its health, or lack thereof. A cultural movement doesn't get a name until it has been around for a while, maybe a long while. Punk didn't start when people started *calling* it that. Everyone probably wants to identify "punk" with the break out of The Sex Pistols, which came to the consciousness of American teenagers in about 1976. That was certainly when the name became household, but the music, by which I mean the sounds we associate with the bands of the punk era, is a good bit older. So is the attitude. It's a little like Justice Powell's account of obscenity: we know it when we see it, or, in this case, hear it.

To take a couple of classic examples, listen to "She Said Yeah" by The Rolling Stones, released in July of 1965 in the UK, and it was cut number one on *December's Children (and Everyone Elses's)*, December 1965 in the US. If that isn't punk music, nothing is. About the same time The Who were experimenting with auto-destruction as a stage gimmick. Earlier that year Suzie Quatro and her sister released "What a Way to Die," which really has to be classified as punk—"I may not live past twenty-one, but ooooh what a way to die." The Troggs certainly had a punk moment right at the same time. The Ramones and The Buzzcocks both cited them as influences. Definitely by 1968 *punk exists*, since MC5 exists, and, to repeat, if that isn't punk, nothing is.

It begins to seem we ought to date the movement to 1965 or so, but this isn't a quest for the origin of punk. My point is that it was coming well before it arrived, even if we didn't quite see it coming. This kind of discussion can go on forever. I don't have forever. I'm reminded of Johnny Rotten's remark to the journalist who suggested the Sex Pistols could use some more rehearsal: "We don't want to spend ten years learning a million chords, we want to play *now!*"

Essences, or . . . Nothing Is

I'm after the *essence* of punk, not in a definition, but in the sort of description where a lot of people would say 'Yeah, that's pretty much it'. You'll say that by the end of this chapter. Betcha five bucks. It needs to be functional, so no matter where you go you can point and say 'Now *that's* fucking punk." *Elements* of punk pre-date punk, even if it's MC5. Kids have always been able to piss off their parents with the sort of music they favor, which is why Plato banned all the rockers and the bluesmen from his Republic. He let in hymn writers, and John Philip Sousa, and Mozart. No Leadbelly, no Zeppelin, and certainly no Sex Pistols. You would think that with The Ramones' fondness for major chords, maybe they'd at least get an audition. I feel confident Plato would give them a laurel and send them to another town, say, Thebes. (And if you don't get this pointy-headed, elitist, bullshit-filled inside joke, forget it. It's not important.)

Yeah, punk's a lot more than just pissing off your parents, but *that* has to be there. If your parents like it, it ain't punk. Or, screw what they like or don't. One or the other. What else? Loud. Yes, it has to be loud. Not just loud, painful, and bullocks to your eardrums, and do you think you want to listen to *this* fucked up world when you're old? Okay then. Rebellious? Yes, that too. But so far, and I'm not kidding, we could still include early Frank Sinatra as punk. All this stuff is so common it makes me want to vomit, on your vacant face, frankly. Okay, not really. Just your shoes.

I think we have to allow that punk must be a kind of *rock* music. We can add that it is, most of the time, guitar-driven, and kind of hard to imagine it coming from a piano, but then there is Jerry Lee Lewis, proving that it can be done. He is still telling the world where to stick it as of this writing. The man is a punk. And by the way, don't marry him. It isn't good for your health. Still, a small number of songs that are clearly punk are not guitar-driven, like "Rock the Casbah," and "Lost in the Supermarket" by The Clash.

And then there's the whole ugly issue of whether Talking Heads (and a bunch of other edgy New Wave bands like Devo) are punk. And what about Bowie? Lou Reed? What will we say with our lists of 'necessary conditions' for 'x to be punk'. We have parent-pissing-off, loud, rebellious, guitar-driven, which is not a bad start. But my dad, at ninety, might like "Rock the Casbah," because of the cool bass-piano trade-off. Jesus that's cool. But no. Just no. Nothing my father could possibly like is punk, right?

So the list of necessary conditions could continue. And it would be bullshit. Philosophers like lists of necessary conditions. It makes them feel important. You pile up necessary conditions until you arrive at something they pronounce 'sufficiency', and then you try to see if you can subtract anything on the list and still *have* sufficiency. It's simpler than Super Mario Brothers without even the barrels. It is, quite possibly, the most useless game ever invented, but we would now need a list of *what* is necessary to call something useless, wouldn't we? Fuck that. I am going at this another way. (Impatience is very punk.)

Gabba Gabba Hey!

So, pissing people off is a big part of punk. If you're not pissing *anyone* off you're definitely not punk. Taking shots at your own audience is included—Johnny Rotten saying, "I'm not here for your amusement, you're here for mine." In an interview, Steve Jones said "we're not into music, we're into chaos." But I, your loyal narrator, *played* in some of those punk bands –even as a drummer in one (in my opinion, it's the most demanding role in this kind of music), and I can tell you from experience, it's not easy to sound that *kind* of bad. You have to be good at being bad. It takes at least some talent and practice to be bad in just the best way.

I don't think that there's a magic bullet that strikes your brain and make you able to be punk. It is something performative, not intellectual. You may know when you're doing it, and you may not. But you don't know why or how, and if you do, or think you do, you're wrong, you're off. What is this music that so completely rejects reflective self-awareness and all of its associated bullshit? In a way it's like being 'cool', with the paradox that if you *try*, you'll fail. If you don't try, you might fail too, but you're sure to miss if you don't take the step at all.

A Line in the Sand

So, putting yourself out there to *see* whether others *see you* as punk is about the best you can do. From experience: During a shining few months of 1983, I was playing in three bands at once. The punk scene had developed by then, had become somewhat refined (if that's possible) and genre-fied. The initial confusion had passed and it had become clear that Tom Petty and Cheap Trick were not punk, not even New Wave. The New Wave had defined itself along lines of Blondie, The Cars, Talking Heads, The Police, and their ilk. Very pop. The opposite of Iggy Pop. One of my bands was like that. There was a second division of punk that we called Hard Core. This was Sex Pistols-inspired: Black Flag, Dead Kennedys, and included (at this moment) the surf punk crowd (like Circle Jerks). One of my bands was like this. Then there was Art Punk, very New York City, admirers of Lou Reed, even Bowie and the Stones, but anti-glam, a forerunner of Grunge, but likely to dig through older music and play it with a punk twist. One of my bands was like this.

The Ramones were New Wave but without the pop leaning. The Clash was Art Rock but more London than New York. The Sex Pistols were Hard Core, but strangely tuneful and accessible, and the lyrics were comprehensible, which later went away. So none of my exemplars fell exactly into these categories. They were all good musicians, exception of Sid Vicious, who might have been a passable drummer, but bass player he was not. Icon? He *was* that. But here is an interesting test, from before we needed to say 'Punk's not dead'. (It's hard not to notice that the graffiti artist apparently cared about the apostrophe. Not very punk?)

My New Wave band played Clash and Ramones, but no Sex Pistols. They chose the most popular tunes—"Should I Stay or Should I Go," and "Train in Vain," and "'Rock-'n-'Roll High School," and "Do You Wanna Dance." I dare say we tended to take the edge *off* of those songs. There was plenty of Blondie and Cars and what not, as well as Cheap Trick and Tom Petty—it was the South, and ordinary hard rock wasn't dead, nor was Southern Rock (although it was dying, even if Tom Petty wasn't).

My Hard Core band would never have played Clash, but they might have put a nasty edge on a Ramones song—I never suggested it, but I could have. Sex Pistols was the center of that show. It was important for the music to be angry, which Clash and Ramones sometimes were, but not in the right way, somehow. Those other bands were plenty self-destructive, as people, but their music really wasn't. It needed to be self-destructive—you know, "Don't know what I want but I know how to get it, I wanna destroy punk supply," *that* sort of self-destructive. Pretty vacant.

My Art Rock band wouldn't have played any Sex Pistols, but the other two exemplars wouldn't have been automatically off the table. But here is what they would have said about all of the exemplars: "Everybody else is doing that." And *that* is condemnation from an Art Punk perspective. So as a matter of fact, we didn't play any of the three, but we did do Joy Division and Flippers, some of which might have appealed to the Hard Core band. On the other hand, the Art Rock band was willing to take Neil Young in his rocker mode and play that, which would have been out of the question for the other two.

This makes my three exemplars "boundary cases," with the Sex Pistols being the boundary the other two genres *would not cross*, and the other two boundary-crossers being not quite radical enough to be cool for the Hard Core purist. That was the punk 'line in the sand'.

Birds of a Feather

This threefold form of genre dissociation came with three (almost) completely different audiences, three completely different sets of stage costumes, and almost no overlap of musical communities. My New Wave band hated that I even associated with the Hard Core crowd, and they thought the Art Punk band was a joke ("the same bad joke for four hours," our guitar player said). The Hardcore band had a grudging respect for the Art Punk band, but didn't want to hang out. Since I played drums in the Art Punk band and bass in the Hardcore band, they (strangely) did not see it as a conflict of interest. The Hard Core band thought the New Wave band was a bunch of pussies and didn't understand how I could play that shit. The Art Punk band didn't give a shit what the other bands were like and didn't judge anybody's musical tastes.

And the crowds followed these norms. Hardcore crowds were pissed off working class kids who wanted to let off steam. It was male-dominated, misogynist, violent, and self-destructive. The lead singer for the Hard Core band had a gorgeous girlfriend, who was a nurse but liked to go slumming with the bad boys. When the guitar player remarked on her looks during rehearsal once, the singer said "Yeah, I fucked her in the ass first, just so she'd know how it's gonna be." I thought to myself, "she needs a different boyfriend," but I surely didn't say it.

It was all part of coming to understand I really didn't belong, as they eventually figured out. I could play the music (on bass it isn't very demanding, as Sid Vicious sort of proved), but I was a middle-class kid who just happened to live in a black neighborhood and had gone to a rough school (so I had some weird creds from that). And I was non-violent (a follower of MLK, then and now), and unlikely to fuck anybody in the ass, since it really hadn't occurred to me before that moment that it was possible. (Long before the Internet, you young guys. Believe it. *Playboy* didn't depict anal sex, or any other kind, and I wasn't reading the articles, so I don't know if that act was discussed. Even *Hustler* didn't depict penetration back then. If there was something "harder," I didn't know about it—illegal in the South.) Oh, and I didn't drink or smoke pot (at that time).

There. We have some on-the-ground history from what might be called the late phase of early punk. There were oh so many mutations and mutants after that. It kept morphing and never dying—surf punk, thrash, speed metal, death metal, grunge, whatever the hell Flaming Lips is (Art Punk?), and after that I lose track. I do know that certain characters kept re-appearing, Frank Zappa, Lou Reed, Violent Femmes, the changeling Bowie, but The Ramones all died and The Clash got old (and then died), and The Sex Pistols have become something akin to a novelty, like Andy Kaufman.

A Punk

Now, there was a punk, back in the day, who also keeps popping up. His name was Arthur Schopenhauer (1788–1860). He really hated almost everyone, and almost everyone returned the favor, except his dog. We don't really know how the dog felt about him, but Schopenhauer treated that poodle better than any human being, so we assume. Except that we should not. I wouldn't have wanted to be his dog, except that all of us were his dogs, here for his amusement, so to speak. His mother said: "You are unbearable and burdensome, and very hard to live with; all your good qualities are overshadowed by your conceit, and made useless to the world simply because you cannot restrain your propensity to pick holes in other people."

When that's your own mother's opinion, what must others think? And how does such an asshole become so very famous? (I know you've at least *heard* of him, which is better brand recognition than most philosophers manage.) As he said to his mother, people will still be reading his books when they have forgotten hers. Which is true. How can revenge on your mother be sweet? Best served cold I guess.

Well, this punk got a bunch of stuff just plain *right* that others had missed. Simple things, really. So simple that everyone overlooked them. I won't bore you with details, but I dare you to start reading his essays and say he doesn't have a lot of shit right. He was also a really good writer (rare for philosophers), so people increasingly liked to read his essays and books. He lived to enjoy his own fame, except that he didn't enjoy anything very much.

The boy inherited sufficient wealth to live a gentleman's life, and to pay his prostitutes, so he didn't give a shit whether people liked him or his ideas. He never married, never had legitimate children (two bastards, both died in infancy), and never held a regular job if he could help it. He had respect for his father, but more for his memory than his time on Earth. After his father offed himself, young Arthur took his part of the inheritance and did what he bloody well pleased. He didn't feel any obligation to take care of his own mother and sister when they were later ruined in a bank crash. He warned them about how they handled money, so fuck 'em.

This bunch had been in the city of Danzig (now Gdansk) and then Hamburg, which, while nice enough, were far removed from the beating heart of German civilization. They were pretty rough and tumble port cities and Schopenhauer lived not far from the docks and shipyards. Very drab and windy stuff. So his social butterfly of a mother removed *to* that beating heart, which was Weimar, post-haste. There she befriended Goethe, and then proceeded to embarrass the young man in Goethe's presence.

That's probably when he became a true punk. He hated everyone. He hated women, although he didn't mind fucking the working-class wenches who passed his way. He probably knew things I did not by the age of twenty-three (his correspondence with a French friend makes it pretty clear that he did). He detested other philosophers, with a particular place in Hell reserved for Hegel. He hated God, especially the Anglican God for some strange reason, whom he finally relegated to non-existence. He despised the stupidity of ordinary people, and that was pretty much everyone, including you, no matter how smart you think you are.

Asshole Geniuses

On occasion Arthur the Asshole allowed that another man was a genius, such as Kant or Goethe, the latter even becoming his mentor. But then Schopenhauer began correcting Goethe's "errors" condescendingly, so that didn't last. He later grudgingly admitted that Goethe's work was a passable introduction to his own theories. His faith in his own special genius was boundless. Arthur allowed that the Buddha might be an equal, but too weak. On the other hand, it's pretty hard to deny Schopenhauer was *almost* as smart as he believed he was, which chaps my ass, frankly. He will always have followers and many admirers.

The Savage Breast

Why am I telling you this? There is a reason. In all this hatred, there was one exception: Schopenhauer loved music, played flute himself. He refined his taste and in time came to see music as something ultimate, really the only thing that redeemed our miserable lives and brought us into the immediate presence of Being. (Not that Being is very nice to us, but at least it isn't a bullshit lie, like everything else.) He elevated music to a place in the order of the cosmos above anyone before him, except possibly Pythagoras. But Schopenhauer *hated* noise. He wrote an essay condemning noise as the murderer of thought. In that essay he singled out the cracking of whips as the worst noise in the world.

I had never thought of it, really, as being so bad. Granting, I never lived in a city where people were cracking whips in the street below my house all day and most of the night. But I actually find that sound rather pleasant, and it isn't unlike the sound of milled ash hitting cowhide and cork, which is the best sound I have ever heard. (Baseball fans will all agree.) I think we could assume that Schopenhauer would have hated Devo's big hit, and the theme from *Rawhide*, but let's adjust the story a little bit. He said stupid people don't mind noise, so maybe I'm just stupid. But he said he hated loud, sudden noises that interrupted his thinking, and gave the cracking of whips as the prime example. We rarely hear a whip anymore. But loud motorcycles? Okay, Schop Dog would have hated Harleys. I love motorcycles, but I like the quiet ones, I must admit, so maybe I'm not an idiot.

That led me to wonder: would Schopenhauer, who believes that music is the ultimate experience, have regarded punk rock as part of *that*, or as noise? I am sure the Schopenhauer who actually lived would have hated it, but not so fast, hombre. When Schopenhauer was growing up, there was a musician and composer who broke every rule, whose music they called "noise," and who fomented actual fighting among the crowds of music-lovers. His name was Beethoven, and he was a punk. And Schopenhauer couldn't get enough of it. He certainly didn't think "Ludwig Van" (as Alex the punk calls him in *A Clockwork Orange*) was noise.

So it isn't obvious to me that if Schopenhauer had grown up when I did, he might still have had similar ideas, but his taste in music might be more like mine. There is a way to test this however. The man said that the problem with noise is that it crowds out the kind of concentration that a genuinely intelligent person can manage, and ordinary people can't. Their brains are full of noise anyway, so they don't mind it when there is more. But people who can really bring the whole of the mind to bear on a single thought? They hate noise. But do genuinely smart people today like punk rock or think it sucks, just noise?

I hang around universities where the people thought to be the smartest hang out. I'll confess I haven't met anyone I thought was in Schopenhauer's league, unless it's me, and his work is an adequate introduction to mine, but my mother gets upset when I talk that way, says my conceit is overshadowing all my good qualities. So no, we aren't talking geniuses here at the university, but sure Schopenhauer would allow that some of them are not stupid. And among my acquaintances across many disciplines, I find many people around my age who like punk quite well. I find younger colleagues who genuinely like hip-hop. It isn't to my taste, but David Foster Wallace was my age and liked it. I think Schopenhauer might have been impressed with *him*.

My Body, My Music

Anyway, I think the test is not whether we like one kind of music or another, but whether we can *concentrate* when it is playing. I know many smart people who do their best work listening to music. Obviously classical music is popular among my older colleagues, and some younger ones, but I can't work with that stuff on. My attention is drawn to the music because it is not noise, it is interesting. I don't see how people can put it in the background and concentrate. The same is true for any kind of music we choose to aid concentration. That stuff will never be noise. Schopenhauer didn't really have this option because recorded music didn't exist. But some people do demand complete silence for concentration, and that is what Schopy-Doo liked. I can work in silence easily. But it isn't necessary. The question is whether you can concentrate when music comes to the body uninvited.

Music is a fair example or "order" itself, of how measure and proportion find a home in our pre-cognitive experiential processes. These processes yield, upon reflection, all sorts of dynamic formalizations that serve as genuine reasons why some vibratings of the world-process *do* settle within our bodies while others do not. There is such a thing, in actuality, as "aesthetic value," and it can be formalized in many ways without destroying the experience itself, or its value to us.

By "settling within the body," I mean the dynamic joining of one "history," one "physical route" (my body *is* a history, after all) with another route (the physicality of the music), in a sufficiently intense way as to contribute to the "life" of the dominant route (my body). Schopenhauer was all about "life"—he studied medicine and credited it with grounding his philosophy. Such "settling" is always an accretion of value, and an intensification, *but it is not always invited*. These are not always "elective affinities," to use Goethe's phrase. And musical *experience* is often nonesuch.

Music is sometimes an invader, but sometimes it is more like an annoying street evangelist with a religious tract, or a vacuum cleaner salesman at the front door, or even a lost traveler asking directions. Music is often a ringing at the ears, the side doors of the body, but it is sometimes a rumbling beneath one's seat, a tormenter in the elevator. But *as* such a visitor, it enters not as a primitive or meaningless noise. It's already a fully formed *symbol* by the time it knocks. Otherwise it is not music. This is as true of punk as it is of Beethoven. That second physical route, the music, that settles and joins itself to our physical history has *its own order*. It is a symbol of something the world accommodates as possible and as actual.

At the physical level, sound waves are heavy (relative to other waves), and thus difficult to propagate. Their form of organization has a high entropy, so they dissipate quickly. But encoded as information, with a lower entropy, whether organically, mechanically, or digitally, they can be revived, almost resurrected, and re-released with much of their form intact. As symbolic forms of existing, they have almost no entropy and can be carried in a human body with very little drag on the system, and then re-projected on command or entirely spontaneously, as when a melody simply "comes to mind."

Uninvited Guests

Together, these three overlapping modes of organization (physical sound, encoding, and pure symbol) make up the "music" as a positive actuality that subsists in the present, waiting to be activated. How many songs do you know well enough to just put them out there right now? A bunch I'll wager. An organism is no longer required for the subsistence of the potential music, as it was in Schopenhauer's day; it is encoded mechanically or digitally, but as far as we know, the organic encoding is how nature conserves music when unassisted by technology. For most of the time humans have existed, the mechanical and digital types of organization were merely possible and had not been brought to actuality. We also must admit that the actuality of mechanical and digital music need never have been organized in the fashion we have achieved in the past 150 years (250 if one includes the music box, which did exist in Schopenhauer's time). They might have remained forever implicit in the flux.

When the routes cross, and we did not choose it, we have an uninvited guest. Is that guest an interruption? I think people will differ here. I write most of my work in a noisy bar, with music playing. The bartender chooses the Spotify list. I know when I walk in what will be playing because I know all the bartenders. I also sometimes play at this bar with various bands. It's a good one. The bartender who plays Eighties music messes with my concentration, because I know all the words and want to sing along. But the bartender who likes death metal? I get some of my best work done when he's working. Hip hop is somewhere in between. I can work through and over the noisiest bar crowd. I don't exactly shut it out. Rather, and here is the answer you have been waiting for, all that noise is energy and I absorb it into my body and re-direct it onto the page.

Work

And that, me Droogies, is the key to it all. Music is energy, and energy, as physics defines it, is the capacity for work. I think that the question of noise is whether you can *use* the energy or not. I see the crowd in the mosh pit using the energy. I see the convicts on the chain gang using the energy. I see the secretary with her Miranda Lambert list using the energy. And I use the energy, and it can bloody well be The Sex Pistols or The Clash or The Ramones. It depends on what I'm doing. Apparently death metal is good for writing energy, but for cooking energy, well, I don't know what I want but I know how to get it. I cannot use the energy from a loud Harley. That is noise, interruption. But punk? It is physical and musical order, and it purveys and delivers energy we can use. So no, it doesn't suck, and here is a video you should watch:

<https://www.youtube.com/watch?v=0GKiMvnpqW4>

14
Revolting Punks

CHRISTOPHER M. INNES

The manager of the Sex Pistols was asked during a 1976 interview for a BBC local news show in the Midlands of England, "How do you react to the reputation that your group is the most revolting in the country?" Malcolm McLaren's reply was that a younger generation is not happy with the state of the country and that "every kid has enjoyment in being known as revolting."

Punk rock has a way of being revolting with its onslaught of insults, obscenities, taunts, and general questioning of the rotten state of society. This was done with shared music on seven-inch vinyl singles, with expressing defiance in basic fashion, with its own artistic view, and with a moral attack that shocked the establishment.

The Sex Pistols' "Anarchy in the UK" incited youth to be disruptive and not to conform to the values of society. Later there was "God Save the Queen" which placed the monarchy next to fascism in a way that not only insulted the establishment, but provoked people to question established moral values. Drenched in the memory of defeating European tyranny and safeguarding freedom in the UK, questions were asked whether such virtuous values could be found in practice. The Angelic Upstarts, in "Police Oppression," say "walking down the street" is a crime, suggesting there is something to revolt against. There was a milieu that led to deep social, political, and moral dissatisfaction, as they later sang in "Teenage Warning" where there's frustration and no one's listening.

What was this milieu? Pure, unadulterated cynicism about the moral, social, and political situation in the late 1970s. This is not to be confused with skepticism, which is only a sense of doubt about the state of things. To be cynical is to believe that the government, parents, schoolteachers, and everyone connected to the established order are motivated to keep things as they stand, and that this established order shouldn't be kept as it is. In other words, you don't trust them! This gives rise to revolt. And here lies the double meaning. The establishment sees punks as revolting, a pejorative; McLaren uses the word in its original meaning: rebellion against an established order. It's as Poly Styrene sang in her band, X-ray Spex, "Oh Bondage Up Yours," that women are not free and are held in bondage by the established order. Such bondage applies to us all. Any suggestion of reform by the establishment was not seen as genuine. The order is seen as a moral code that cynically-minded punks rejected for its inability to promote needed social change.

Diogenes, the First Punk

Punks get their inspiration from a tradition of revolt. Back in Greek times, there was a philosopher called Diogenes who came from Sinope. He was not like most philosophers such as Plato and Aristotle whose political, social, and moral thought is abstract, with little application to the world and real life. In fact, Diogenes revolted against abstraction because it had little to do with people and everyday ways of living.

Athens had a code of virtue that dictated its manners and conduct. The majority of Athenians thought this the only moral way to act. Diogenes instead thought Athenian virtue was too abstract, too self-righteous, and led to people being subservient to those values and to those in power. For Diogenes it was a sucker's game. He had little praise for wider society's unthinking fools. It's rather like The Ruts in "Babylon's Burning" saying that people are full of "anxiety," uneasy about the established way of doing things. The implication is to revolt and make the establishment pay for wrongdoing.

This revolt rejects abstract virtue and argues that virtue in agreement with nature be put in its place. There are demands for creating a way of living that is natural to the person. With this comes a rejection of the values of wealth and possessions, fame, reputation, and being emotionally dependent on your family. Humans have complicated the simplest of things. Plato and Aristotle have created social, political, and moral reasoning that have made simple aspects of life far too complex. In fact, Plato rightly described Diogenes as "Socrates gone mad." Diogenes helped create cynical thinking by taking strands of Socrates's more vigorous notions of virtue and rejecting his more conformist notions, thus turning virtue into an authentic and enlightened expression of human conduct. This view of virtue allows people to be who they are and not feel forced into following an abstract code of conduct unnatural to human behavior. This is where people are aware of their community and willfully create a true sense of happiness.

Diogenes was well known for not only voicing discontent with the customs, mannerisms, and ideals of Athens. He would literally trample on them. He was well known for living in a giant ceramic wine barrel, keeping dogs as friends, and walking around the marketplace with a lit lantern in midday searching for an honest man. Most of all Diogenes would interrupt Plato's lectures. He would bring food to share with others and question what Plato argued.

One of Plato's best-known dialogues found in his major work called *the Republic* is between Socrates and Glaucon. This dialogue can be used to illustrate the source of Diogenes's revulsion. Justice is seen by Socrates as almost obvious and something that is done for its own sake. Glaucon disagrees and says it is a code of conduct set up to protect the interests of those with political and social power and to create a moral climate that suits *their* interests.

Glaucon argues that morality is a social contract where people are equal and agree to act in a certain way, and that they agree to not burden each other. People shouldn't agree with Plato's notion of justice and instead see it as a burden, and a burden they will gladly rid themselves. Glaucon supports this with the famous story of "the ring of Gyges." This ring makes the person wearing it invisible, and though they behave justly when visible, they will act in an unjust way when invisible. Virtue for Plato is abstract and has little to do with the community. Diogenes sees it as a fiction that has no role to play in actual social and political circumstances.

This is morality according to Diogenes, who rejected the idealized pretenses of the establishment and went his own way. He was virtuous, but in a genuine way, viewing people in their community and in the time they are living. Diogenes didn't reject virtue. He did reject the abstract type of virtue that got in the way of genuine human behavior where people get to know each other as people, have a say in government, and generally accept others as who they are.

Hippy Values Were Never Going to Work

It's a well-known irony in punk culture that the hippies took on the mantle of Diogenes only to very quickly 'sell out'. To sell out is to give up on your values for personal gain. It can result in becoming part of the group you claimed to not trust. Progressive rock groups like Pink Floyd come to mind. Johnny Rotten, of the Sex Pistols, was notorious for wearing a Pink Floyd T-shirt with "I HATE" penned in above the name Pink Floyd. This is an example of a jaded rock group that is spewing out conceptual music that has little to do with what is happening in the world. Much like the other horrific dinosaur bands, their views on freedom and love relationships were out of touch. Much like Plato and Aristotle, their idealism meant little to the actual world.

Pink Floyd's "Another Brick in the Wall" stirred up feelings about education, but to what purpose? The notion of "thought control" was well received by Floyd fans but called for no actual revolt. "I Hate School" by the punk band Suburban Studs revolted against education and screamed out for freedom after pointing out actual faults such as having to stand in lines and wear uniforms. They sang about freedom to learn on one's own terms, which is more progressive than any prog-rock band could ever hope to express. Here we got a picture of what was happening and what should be done about the poor state of education.

No better example of sarcastic mocking of the hippies' "selling out" is the Dead Kennedys' seven-inch single "California Über Alles," which questions the new hippy establishment. This is about Jerry Brown who once carried the hippy mantle challenging the ideals of the establishment only to happily join them when becoming the California Governor. He becomes tyrannical and the specter of him employing "suede denim secret police" to arrest those who are not hip to his notion of virtue when he becomes President becomes all too clear. There is an air of scorn as lead singer Jello Biafra mocks the Californian elitist who, when in the White House, will introduce mandatory meditation in all state schools.

Punks and Their Seven-inch Singles

The seven-inch punk single was a vital part of the punk arsenal. It would often be a quick track that would last no longer than three minutes. The Clash's "White Riot" lasted for one minute and fifty-eight seconds. For punk, music is to be quick and frantic, unlike the prog-rock track that often could not fit on a single because of its exhausting length. It was a return to good old fashion rock'n'roll, rejecting prog-rock's self-indulgent music.

Steve Jones of the Sex Pistols talked about music losing its way. He saw his band's music as a return to the rock'n'roll of the 1950s. Numbers like "No Fun" were good examples of rock'n'roll with its A-Side "Pretty Vacant" being a punk anthem as part of the revolt, saying that this generation was tuned-out of what society had to offer. Sid Vicious, later, ever revolting, showed-off his singing skills with his brilliant performances of Eddy Cochran's "Something Else" and "C'mon Everybody." These were good rock'n'roll songs played in punk style that captured the spirit of revolt.

Young punk fans were part of the revolt. They could afford to buy seven-inch singles from independent record shops with their pocket money. Buying a seven-inch single was part of a tactile and almost visceral experience. It was not simply getting an idea of the music; you were getting an experience. You were not giving up by owning objects, which Diogenes said are unnecessary luxuries, but you were part of the rejection of extravagant concept albums made by the dinosaur prog-rock bands and major record companies.

This is basic music with the record often in colored vinyl instead of the normal black. You would take the record from an often bright picture sleeve. The artwork, in many cases alternative art, often depicted the song's message. The Sex Pistols' "Holiday in the Sun" had the lyrics on the sleeve accompanying a mock holiday brochure. On the other hand, the Undertones' "Teenage Kicks" sleeve is a simple piece of folded white paper with bold black print that opens up showing a picture of the band standing in a brick alleyway in Belfast. Rumor has it that the group folded the sleeves themselves, meaning that you had in your hands a record once held and processed by the group. This is the story of how many of the groups released their records with the independent labels.

The seven-inch records, often made by independent record companies such as Rough Trade, New Hormones, Pogo, Rigid Digits, and Good Vibrations were also part of the revolt. They released punk that the main companies refused to touch. You were buying material objects and still being part of the revolt.

Punks' music was typically produced by those who did not have access to approved cultural expression or social contacts in the music industry. Punk does not require long hours of training or a wide breadth of knowledge acquired through an expensive music education. This made playing punk accessible to most. All you needed was a cheap set of drums, a singer, and a bass and treble guitar.

Punks are the Anabaptists of rock, rejecting the idea that only those anointed by the music industry can play rock music. This is not just a revolt against hippy and established values, but also against rock itself "selling out" and becoming part of the establishment. What was accepted as music was decided by the establishment. You, as a punk, participated in the revolt against this notion.

Gigs with No Cig' Lighters

Punk gigs were part of the revolt. You could get into the gig for a nominal price, usually in the back room of a pub or in a larger venue such as an old ball room or assembly room. You were now with the band and participating in a revolt against the large "festival" cattle shed venues. For the punk, being up close to the band was not enough. Like Diogenes, who carried out acts in public that the wider Athenian society considered offensive, to show you liked the band you would spit at them. Hurling verbal abuse was not uncommon and was considered a sign of appreciation. The greatest compliment was a good stage invasion. This rejection of the old custom of leaving the band alone as a passive crowd was a sign that the group was doing well, and though punks would clap hands in appreciation, shouting at the band was a good sign all was well.

This is not the way we remember the prog-rock or the hippy bands. There was the specter of slow and tedious songs accompanied by the crowd swaying side to side holding lit cigarette lighters up high. This might be a civil and virtuous way to end a gig, but it was a sign of an unbearably boring set of songs.

The Sex Pistols' gig at Randy's Rodeo, a Country and Western night club in San Antonio, on January 8th 1978 was one with a fully-involved audience. By all accounts, Malcolm McLaren booked the Sex Pistols as an ironic and antagonizing act of defiance, revolting against custom and tradition. Aristotelian pretenses and ideals about correct conduct were set aside. Beer cans and discarded fast food were hurled at the band. Steve Jones whimsically dodged beer cans while Johnny Rotten antagonized the Texas cowboy crowd and got a discarded burrito in the face. His characteristic accentuation of the second syllable of vacant in "Pretty Vacant" might have upset the small-town sensitivities. Sid Vicious certainly upset one audience member as he smashed his Fender Precision Bass over his head. This is what a good punk concert looks like. Diogenes would have cheered the genuine human behavior, unfettered by establishment "norms," where there was no chance of someone holding up a cigarette lighter.

A Cynic in Cheap Clothing

The gig was a great place to wear offensive clothes to express dissatisfaction. The punk look can be a bit obscene. Remember that obscenity is a legitimate tool in the cynic's toolbox of questions and devices used to revolt against the trumped-up virtue of mainstream society. It was cynics like Diogenes who considered being offensive as a way to defy Athenian virtue for its pretenses, hypocrisy and sanctimonious claim to being a universal truth. It's part of the revolt. Offensive clothes are a way to be truly revolting and show parents and government that general established unquestioned values are just as oppressive as what they claim to be arguing against. Rumor has it that Diogenes often wore very little clothing, which may have revolted Athenians!

Vivian Westward is an anti-fashion designer who took bedroom bondage wear and turned it into high street punk wear. The straps, zips, and bum-flaps gave the appearance of obscenity. Siouxsie Sioux of Siouxsie and the Banshees wore bondage wear showing her breasts with the accompanying swastika on her left arm. Poly Styrene of the X-Ray Spex, on a few occasions, dressed in an outfit that resembled Benito Mussolini. John Lydon, a.k.a. Johnny Rotten, likens clothing to architecture. His clothes have become more expensive over the years but are at times revolting; like other punks they aim to offend.

Sid Vicious was the one well known for wearing a swastika T-shirt. We might think that he was being offensive for the sake of it being offensive, but Viv Albertine of the Slits says otherwise. She said, "Sid was clever and understood concepts." This fashion concept was the wearing of a leather jacket, jeans, black buckle boots, a padlock and chain necklace, and the swastika T-shirt with the red background. Sid would walk in public areas and gather looks of disgust from passersby. His usual turned up lip and frown caused even more offense. This image is on the front of his single "Something Else," and sums up the revolt.

Satire at Its Best

The rejection of established ideals, the condemning of the hippy music selling out, buying 7-inch vinyl singles, going to uproarious gigs, and being offensive and outrageous in appearance and language to promote a cause is a serious part of music history. We might ask whether the punk scene should take itself too seriously. John Lydon, a.k.a. Johnny Rotten, commented on the punk scene and being part of it as a really good laugh. Making "God Save the Queen" was a serious comment, but a satirical one as well. Invective and stirring up the complacent hippies was a joy. Criticizing the monarchy as outmoded was fun. And the songs were hilarious. He is much like the cynics who used satire and sarcasm as a way to revolt against the virtue of others. Like Diogenes, Lydon said that there are few if any honest people and with his lit lamp he is looking for an honest person.

Diogenes rejected the pretenses of Plato, Aristotle, and to an extent Socrates, but was at the same time virtuous. To be virtuous is to be happy in your life, a life that is genuine and based on natural values. Many a punk got married and raised their children to be happy and contented. Lydon and his wife Nora adopted the three children of Nora's sister, Arianna, a.k.a. Ari Up, the lead singer of the Slits. The children were out of control, almost feral in nature, until Uncle John and Auntie Nora stepped in and gave structure. Both believed that children need a father and mother. This might sound traditional, but it's a chosen virtue and not one forced. This is part of the cynic's outlook. Virtue exists where there are values, with such values being down to Earth and part of the community.

The cynics thought life was not to be taken too seriously and that satire is a good way to point out that real life can never aspire to be the virtuous place the likes of Plato and Aristotle thought that it might. We take a look at Jello Biafra's "California Über Allas" that presented a menacing specter reminiscent of George Orwell's *Nineteen Eighty-Four*. Satirizing Jerry Brown and his threat of "organic poison gas" was a funny and effective way to revolt. On the other hand, Jake Burns was dead serious and just as effective in Stiff Little Fingers' "Alternative Ulster" when he tells youth to "get up and grab" freedom from the grip of British and paramilitary control.

For much of punk the purpose of the revolt was merely to let those in charge know they were wrong and things needed to change. Nonetheless, it was a revolt, and like all revolts, it was short lived, and, in this case, well appreciated.

IV

Punk Politics

15
Punk Political Philosophy

Marty Sulek

Punk Rock is not susceptible to precise definition. It's like the problem of defining pornography: I can't say precisely what it is, but I know it when I see it.

Several criteria are usually employed to identify Punk, usually relating to musical style and fashion sense, but these things have radically changed over time. One of the more enduring features of Punk, though, is its contempt for authority and challenging of established norms and power structures. Rebellion is its most immutable feature. The consistency of its political philosophy ends there, though.

Punks have variously identified with virtually every point on the political spectrum. Joe Strummer of The Clash, and Paul Weller of the Jam strongly identified with and supported socialist and communist ideologies and causes. We can see this in Strummer's discussion with Ray Gange in *Rude Boy* (1980) and in the Jam's "Eton Rifles," inspired by clashes between demonstrators on a Right to Work March, a campaign initiated by the left-wing Socialist Workers' Party, and pupils from Eton College, an elite English boys' school.

Clark Martell of Skrewdriver identified with Neo-Nazis, while The Dead Kennedys condemned them in their 1981 single, "Nazi Punks Fuck Off!" In Johnny Ramone's acceptance speech at the induction of The Ramones into the Rock'n'Roll Hall of Fame in 2002, he intoned "God bless President Bush." In *I Was a Teenage Sex Pistol*, Glen Matlock considers the Sex Pistols to be essentially apolitical, whereas Johnny Rotten (born John Joseph Lydon) praises President Trump in his latest book. Definitions of what constitutes Punk political philosophy are thus inherently perspective-laden.

Anarchy and Civil Society

Punk political philosophy is somewhat of a contradiction in terms. Its most familiar political symbol is the anarchy logo. The Sex Pistols' "Anarchy in the UK" serves as something of a Punk anthem in this regard. But as a political philosophy, anarchy is full of contradictions. It derives from the ancient Greek term ἀναρχία, variously understood as 'lawless', 'without a ruler', or 'ungoverned'. In modern parlance anarchy is defined as: "a state of disorder due to absence or non-recognition of authority or other controlling system"; and as a political ideal, the "absence of government and absolute freedom of the individual" (*Oxford English Dictionary*). Given these definitions, a political philosophy of anarchy is something of an oxymoron; for how can there be an apolitical political philosophy?

How can there be a political society without rules, rulers, or those ruled over? Furthermore, if Punk's defining political stance is defiance of authority, what happens when that becomes the established norm?

According to Adam Seligman, The first modern political theorists to seriously examine the idea of self-organizing and self-regulating political entities, with no central command structure, were the Scottish Enlightenment thinkers. Adam Smith found that people pursuing their own self-interest in the marketplace unintentionally served the public good so well, it was as if they were directed by an "invisible hand." Adam Ferguson developed similar insights into the self-regulating behavior of civil society, understood as free and responsible citizens regulating their personal and economic affairs independent of government, and as mediated by various forms of voluntary association, such as family, friends, church, and various other community organizations.

While economics became an established academic discipline in the nineteenth century, the idea of civil society came to be discredited by prominent political theorists. Hegel and Marx contemptuously refer to *"bürgerliche Gesellschaft"* [civil society] as merely a transitory phase of social organization situated between family and state, whose purposes and functions were destined to be eventually superseded by the advent of the modern nation-state. Political philosophy's contemplation of civil society was thus eclipsed by political science's empirical study of government and the state.

Civil Society theory remained a dormant concept in political studies until the late twentieth century, when it was resurrected and adopted by several prominent east European dissidents, most notably Václav Havel, to describe their vision of a just society beyond the strictures of communist ideology and the totalitarian state. Since then, the concept of civil society has been considered by a number of prominent political theorists, including Michael Walzer, Robert Putnam, and Ernest Gellner. Within this rubric, it becomes possible to conceive of the anarchic political philosophy of Punk, as an apolitical politics without rulers or ruled, the order of which spontaneously arises from out of the aggregate desires and aspirations of its individual members.

Bob Geldof and Band Aid

In analyzing Punk political philosophy, it helps to look to deeds rather than words. Punk bands have a fairly extensive history of supporting various political and charitable causes. The Clash, the Buzzcocks, Elvis Costello, and Stiff Little Fingers, for instance, performed at music concerts organized in 1978 by the political and cultural movement Rock Against Racism.

Sting of the Police, and Bob Geldof of the Boomtown Rats performed in 1981 at The Secret Policeman's Other Ball, a benefit concert in support of Amnesty International. Paul Weller, formerly of the Jam, worked with his new band, The Style Council, in 1984 to release a charity single, Soul Deep, the proceeds from which went to support families of striking coal miners. By far the most significant example of Punk political philosophy translated into political action, though, was Bob Geldof's organization of Band Aid and Live Aid, in support of famine relief in Ethiopia.

In late 1984, Geldof was desperately working to get the Rats' sixth album, *In The Long Grass*, released. he went home that day "in a state of blank resignation and switched on the television." The images that greeted him there placed his "worries in a ghastly new perspective" (*Is That It?*, p. 215). What he saw was the results of the famine in Ethiopia, the worst to hit the country in a century, in which 1.2 million people would eventually die. He was so struck by what he saw that he resolved to do something about it.

Using his contacts in the music industry, Geldof organized Band Aid, a collective of the top British pop music stars, which released a charity single, *Do They Know It's Christmas?* It became the fastest and biggest selling single of all time in the UK, and raised more than $24 million for famine relief. It also spawned many imitators around the world, the biggest of which was USA for Africa, an *ad hoc* supergroup that recorded a charity single, *We Are the World*, that raised $10.8 million for famine relief. These efforts culminated in Live Aid, a benefit concert held on July 13, 1985, which raised approximately 150 million for famine relief.

Geldof's efforts did not end with staging Band Aid and Live Aid. He began a round of TV, radio, and newspaper interviews to spur greater efforts for famine relief. As he observes, "The mouth that had got me into trouble so often now talked about the simple idea of personal responsibility" (p. 233). He also assumed responsibility for disbursing the funds in Ethiopia and East Africa. In the process, he came to more fully realize his own political philosophy.

In Ethiopia, Geldof was toured around Addis Ababa by Berhane Deressa, then deputy commissioner of the Ethiopian government's Relief and Rehabilitation Commission. Upon entering the city, they drove under a massive concrete arch replete with gaudy trappings and a sign that read "Long Live Proletarian Internationalism," above which was a hammer and sickle.

> What the fuck is that? Geldof asked.
>
> It's the arch of the revolution.
>
> Christ, no wonder there's a famine here if you insist on putting up crap like that. In any case, it's palpably not true. If there really was any proletarian internationalism you wouldn't have millions dying here. (*Is That It?*, p. 239)

Geldof was no political neophyte. After *The Fine Art of Surfacing* was released in 1980, he travelled extensively through the Soviet Union, Mongolia, and China. He was thus acutely aware of the inherent drawbacks of Communism and forced collectivism to human health and well-being.

Geldof also quickly became aware of the potential political power Band Aid wielded, particularly over recalcitrant government officials overly sensitive to criticism who could thwart his efforts. This power primarily stemmed from the financial backing Band Aid enjoyed, but also resided in Geldof's ability and willingness to speak uncomfortable truths. He writes of when this thought first occurred to him:

> It was with the Minister for the Interior, Berhane Biyug, that I first realized what enormous potential there was for me in particular and Band Aid in general for saying the unsayable and confronting those in power with problems which aid workers and even diplomats dared not raise for fear of jeopardizing long-term relationships. (p. 249)

He goes on to write:

Suddenly I saw the purpose of Band Aid. They had to listen because I had not only the money but the constituency of support which that money represented. And it was a populist, non-governmental constituency. I represented nobody but myself and the millions who wanted to help. A constituency of compassion. (p. 250)

He then got into a heated debate with the Minister, a committed Soviet Marxist. Accountable to no-one but himself and his supporters, Geldof bluntly and forcefully spoke his mind in critiquing the famine relief efforts of government officials. This approach later came to be termed "Punk diplomacy," which may be roughly defined as frankly confronting those in power with uncomfortable truths by saying the unsayable, and engaging in honest and open ended debate unrestrained by diplomatic niceties.

Another remarkable aspect of Band Aid / Live Aid was how Geldof wound down its operations once its objectives had been achieved. The refusal to make an institution out of it was integral to Geldof's philosophy. As he writes:

Band Aid must never become what I have always most detested—an institution. Its purpose, were it to continue, would get lost in the mine of professionalism and bureaucracy designed to nurture it, but only serving to obscure it. Band Aid would be more powerful in memory, where it will live as something that was wholly good and incorruptible and that worked. (p. 351)

In Geldof's work with Band Aid, Live Aid, and Ethiopian famine relief, then, we may discern some hallmarks of Punk political philosophy: a deep skepticism toward all established authority, stemming from a recognition of the inherently corrupting influence of power, ideology, and vested interests. But it also has some more positive aspects. A libertarianism, for in-stance, that values the freedom and autonomy of the individual as an independent moral agent. A populism that taps into a broad base of popular support. A discontent with mere protest, and instead engaging the powers-that-be to advance policies that better serve the public good.

From the Velvet Underground to the Velvet Revolution

Lou Reed and his band, the Velvet Underground ("VU"), are widely acknowledged as the most influential forerunners of Punk. The VU was a leading element of New York's *avant-garde* scene in the late Sixties and early Seventies. As such, not many of its songs are identifiably Punk. *White Light/White Heat*, released in 1968, probably comes the closest in terms of sound. What most strongly distinguishes the VU's Punk sensibilities, though, is the gritty realism of their song lyrics, many of which deal with the darker side of life, including: drug abuse, addiction, overdose, sadomasochism, promiscuity, homosexuality, transvestitism, poverty, prostitution, violence, depression, dysfunctional relationships, domestic abuse, child abuse and neglect, paranoia, suicide, disease, death, loss, electro-shock therapy, and of course a deep-seated suspicion of vested authority.

The VU's revolutionary approach confronted its listener with ugly truths ofttimes wrapped in dissonant music. The VU were not an emphatically "political" band. Reed himself was an intensely private person, but supported political causes that defended and advanced the cause of freedom (John Nicols, "Lou Reed's Politics"). However, his unflinching portrayals of the seedier aspects of life in New York shone a light on the darker side of society that often acted as a spur to wider political discussion. What is truly remarkable about the VU, though, is how, by almost pure serendipity, its music fomented revolution in eastern Europe.

In the spring of 1968, a young and upcoming Czech playwright named Václav Havel spent six weeks in New York for the English language premiere of his play, *The Memorandum*, an absurdist comedy that lampooned ideology and authority, and won a prestigious Obie prize. While in New York, Havel deeply imbibed its underground music scene, and brought back several records to Prague. Among these was the recently re-leased VU album, *White Light/White Heat*, which he circulated among his friends.

A couple of months after Havel's return, on the night of August 20–21, the military forces of the Warsaw Pact invaded Czechoslovakia, and installed a new hardline regime under Gustáv Husák. The liberalizing reforms of the "Prague Spring" introduced by the previous Communist leader, Alexander Dubček, were quickly rolled back under the banner of "normalization," and a regime of repression and censorship was reinstated.

Less than a month after the invasion, bassist Milan Hlavsa formed a band called the Plastic People of the Universe ("the Plastics"), largely inspired by the VU. The following year he was joined by Ivan Jirous, who became the band's artistic director. As the process of normalization progressed under the hardline Husák regime, many bands changed their look and sound to survive the transition. Most quickly adapted the "aesthetics of banality" that sought not to provoke or disturb, but only to reiterate conventional ideas in soothing tones. The Plastics refused to change, leading the government to ban their performances.

In response to the government's repression, Jirous organized the first Music Festival of the Second Culture in 1974.
His idea was to establish a separate and vibrant culture
entirely independent of the banal and totalitarian First
Culture supported by authorities. Havel credits this concept of
a "second culture" with playing a critical role in the formulation of opposition to the Communist regime:

> Although at first Jirous was thinking chiefly of nonconformist rock
> music and only certain literary, artistic or performance events close to
> the sensibilities of those nonconformist rock musical groups, the term
> "second culture" very rapidly came to be used for the whole area of
> independent and repressed culture, that is, not only for art and its var-
> ious currents but also for the humanities, the social sciences and
> philosophical thought. (Havel, "The Power of the Powerless," p. 101)

The second Second Culture festival was held on February 21st
1976. Soon after, on March 17th, the Secret Police arrested
twenty-seven musicians and their friends who had attended
the festival, including the Plastics.

Six months later, on September 21st 1976, four of the musicians arrested were put on trial, including two of the Plastics,
Ivan Jirous and Vratislav Brabenec. They were charged under
article 202, paragraph 2, of the Czechoslovak criminal code for
"disturbing the peace," a catch-all law commonly invoked by
Communist authorities to suppress public demonstrations
directed against the government. This charge stemmed from
"obscene lyrics" in some of the songs they performed. In reality,
though, the group's only crime, if it could be labeled as such,
was "the adoption of "their own stance toward life," which in its
very independence constituted a challenge to the Communist
party" (Skilling, *Charter 77*, p. 7).

Havel, whom Jirous had met earlier that year, recognized
the threat the Plastics' trial posed to freedom of thought and
expression. He therefore enlisted a prominent group of artists
and intellectuals to help defend the musicians. As a result of
these efforts, many of those arrested were released, and only
four went to trial. They were, of course, found guilty, but their
sentences were relatively light, with most given time served in
custody. The exception was Jirous, who was sentenced to eigh-
teen months in prison.

The following month, Havel composed a famous essay on
the trial condemning the government's attempt to forcibly cen-
sor freedom of expression. It was first published in a book, *The
Merry Ghetto*, that was included in the Plastics' first record

album, *Egon Bondy's Happy Hearts Club Banned*. On January 1st 1977, the individuals who aided in their defense formed a human rights organization called Charter 77 to combat political persecution on an ongoing basis. With Havel as its acknowledged leader, it quickly became the premier dissident organization in Czechoslovakia, and the *de facto* political opposition to the Communist regime.

On November 17th 1989, police brutally suppressed student demonstrators in Prague. In response, an *ad hoc* organization was created, called Civic Forum, to give voice to public opposition to the government. Given Charter 77's long experience in challenging the government, its leading members naturally played a pivotal role in the formation and direction of Civic Forum. On Friday, November 24th 1989, Havel gave a speech to a cheering crowd of 500,000 people in Wenceslas Square where he outlined Civic Forum's plan for the transition from Communism to democracy:

> Civic Forum wants to be a bridge between totalitarianism and a real, pluralistic democracy, which will subsequently be legitimized by a free election. We further want truth, humanity, freedom. Henceforth we are all directing this country of ours and therefore all bear responsibility for its fate. (Bradley, *Czechoslovakia's Velvet Revolution*, p. 102)

The legitimacy and power of the Communist regime crumbled so quickly there wasn't even time to arrange for democratic elections to choose a new government. Civic Forum formed an interim government largely based upon the legitimacy Havel had acquired through his dissident activity with Charter 77. On December 29th 1989, he was appointed interim President of Czechoslovakia by a unanimous vote of the Federal Assembly. An election was quickly slated for the following June to choose a new Assembly and President.

In recognition of the peaceful and bloodless nature of the transfer of power—and with the Velvet Underground likely providing no small inspiration—this event was dubbed the Velvet Revolution by Havel's translator and spokesperson, Rita Klímová (Victor Sebetsyen, *Revolution 1989*, p. 367).

Punk Political Philosophy—Doing the Right Thing

Havel's discussions of the nature of totalitarianism in his political writings has considerable bearing on Punk political philosophy. Regarding totalitarian ideology, he notes that:

> As the interpretation of reality by the power structure, ideology is always subordinated to the interests of the structure. Therefore it has a natural tendency to disengage itself from reality, to create a world of appearances, to become ritual. ("The Power of the Powerless," pp. 46–47)

An existing power structure relies on ideology to both interpret the world and legitimize the ways in which it exercises its power. In the process of serving the interests of the power structure, ideology gradually degenerates into mere ritual, a language of appearances primarily employed to disguise and or obscure the real motives underlying its use. It becomes a "formalized language deprived of semantic contact with reality." As a result, this rigid ideology inexorably alienates the regime from the lived reality of the people it rules; to such a degree, in fact, that truthful depictions of that reality pose an ever-greater threat to it.

The pre-political existence of people's lived reality, as authentically expressed in the arts and culture, invariably reveals the regime's ideology, its world view and source of legitimacy, to be a lie. The instinct of the regime is thus to suppress all such expressions of truth as subversive and dangerous. Ideology attempts to shape reality, rather than reality shaping ideology. Life is not so easily controlled, though. For while an entropic regime is highly dependent on the lived reality of people, they are in no way dependent on the decaying regime.

> Just as the constant increase of entropy is the basic law of the universe, so it is the basic law of life to be ever more highly structured and to struggle against entropy. (Havel, "Letter to Dr. Gustáv Husák")

People "living in truth" will therefore invariably seek to create an alternative, a 'second culture,' an underground movement, a parallel *polis*, that both turns its back on the mainstream culture controlled by the regime, and serves as its most trenchant critic.

This is the essence of Punk political philosophy: the realization that every regime, every ideology, every power structure is entropic by nature, and eventually becomes antithetical to life. This includes authorities, ideologies, and fashions within the sphere of culture, which provides the essential pre-political grounding for political life. When culture becomes stagnant and mechanical, simply repeating a complacent *status quo*, Punk's role is to act as a counterculture; to offer a critique of the dominant culture, even to destroy its institutions and ideologies, in

the faith that newer and more vital things will grow from authentic expressions of life's truths.

But Punk's role does not end there. Having destroyed an
existing paradigm, there is a corresponding responsibility,
somewhat counter to Punk's alleged nihilism, to build something back in its place. This dynamic can be seen in the music
industry, which seeks to control musical culture to serve its
financial interests by merely repeating successful past formu-
las. In the process, though, music becomes banal and stagnant,
thereby pushing the alternative culture to formulate a
response. This resulted in first-wave Punk's challenge to the
pop music of the 1970s, whether mindless Disco, overwrought
Prog Rock, or vacant Top-40.

Whenever popular musical forms become repetitive, stale,
and unlistenable, the alternative culture—whether Rock,
avant-guard, Punk, New Wave, or Grunge—overthrows them
in a revolution of musical tastes and replaces them with a new,
more authentic sound. Punk is not distillable to a formula.
Rather, it's the manifestation of an eros that drives this eternal
process of destruction and re-creation that is life itself.

Punk critiques of and alternatives to existing regimes also
often extend well beyond musical fashion. The Clash and the
Jam critiqued capitalism and consumerist society, and staged
benefit concerts in support of anti-racism and striking workers.
Geldof organized Band Aid and Live Aid to raise money for
famine relief, and critiqued deficiencies in the world's food system. These exemplars of the Punk spirit not only criticized
existing power structures, but sought to create concrete alternatives besides.

Ironically, thought, the most powerful ramifications of Punk
political philosophy were exercised by those musicians most
aloof from politics *per se*. The VU and Lou Reed generally eschewed public expression of their political views, preferring
instead to honestly depict life as they experienced it, however
disturbing it often appeared to others. That was their philanthropy. In so doing, they found particularly receptive audiences
and imitators among dissident artists in the totalitarian societies of Communist eastern Europe.

The Plastics emulated this Punk aesthetic to create a "second culture" that allowed dissenters to "live in truth" within an
oppressive political regime that had become dependent on a
turgid totalitarian ideology and its lie of providing people a better life and future. Ultimately, truth prevailed.

16
Punk Politics

JESSE PRINZ

The Paradoxical Politics of Punk

Punk is often regarded as political. Unlike mods, goths, head-bangers, or ravers, punk rockers are known for their antago-nistic stance toward the prevailing social and political order. Punk lyrics are often politically inflected, and punk styles initially appeared as an assault on the political status quo.

Punk rock is not the only musical genre to foreground pol-itics—folk, Afrobeat, and underground hip hop are other examples—but few genres have been so overtly political. It would seem silly to inquire into the politics of synth pop, shoegaze, or math rock, even if certain tracks or artists have taken a political stance. Exploring the politics of punk, in con-trast, seems inevitable for any serious examination of the movement. But that line of inquiry immediately slams into a hard brick wall.

On the one hand, punk is associated with anarchism. The most famous punk song of all time is the Sex Pistols' "Anarchy in the UK," and thousands of punk rockers have scrawled anar-chy signs on their clothing, skin, or city streets. On the other hand, the most notorious subculture associated with punk is the Nazi skinheads, and the pervasive use of swastikas in punk visual culture suggests a longstanding courtship with fascism, which is the opposite of anarchy.

So which is it? Are punk rockers anarchists or fascists? Is political ideology integral to punk or just an incoherent façade? I think there is some terra firma below this boggy muck. Beneath countless contradictions and endless adolescent pos-turing, there is a politics of punk.

Anarchy Burger

"Anarchy in the UK" was the first single released by the Sex Pistols. It made the British charts when it was released in 1976, but was quickly withdrawn by the record label, EMI, after Pistols guitarist Steve Jones called the daytime television celebrity, Bill Grundy, a "fuckin' rotter" during a live broadcast. Grundy had evidently been hitting on the nineteen-year-old Siouxsie Sioux, who had come along for the recording. The song, penned by front man John Lydon (a.k.a. Johnny Rotten), threatens that anarchy is coming to the UK. Lydon was not espousing any specific political philosophy. People in his orbit, especially the artist Jamie Reid, who designed the iconic image for the Pistols' subsequent "God Save the Queen" single, were familiar with anarchist thought, and might have exerted an influence (*England's Dreaming*, p. 204). But the song itself makes no references to Kropotkin, Goldman, or Durruti. Rather it alludes to political dissolution and oppression (such as the conflict in Northern Ireland). Other themes include housing projects ("council tenancies"), consumerism ("shopping scheme"), and menial labor ("dogsbody"). There's an allusion to the leftist liberation of Angola ("the MPLA"), but no call for an organized revolution. Rather the song expresses a desire to "be" anarchy, and a call for destruction. The song defines anarchy as an assault on authority and prevailing social structures.

Since the release of that single, punk has been strongly associated with anarchy, and the encircled A has become emblematic of the movement. Some have followed the Sex Pistols in their amorphous formulation of this political ethos. For them, anarchy means chaos. In practice, anarchy means violating social norms through self-expression. Punk fashion includes ripped clothing, threatening spikes, violation of gender norms, BDSM accouterments, and provocative iconography; punk music is aggressive, confrontational, anti-romantic, irrelevant, and amateurish; punk dance, is jerky, graceless, and sometimes violent; punk artwork gravitates toward shock value and wears do-it-yourself imperfection as a badge of honor.' Such practices are meant to offend polite society, and destabilize prevailing norms, and to divest from corporate interests. Of course, those aspirations failed almost immediately as punk was appropriated by mainstream culture, but the underlying ideology remained.

So-described, punk anarchism is more of a fashion statement than a political movement. It is a cultural intervention, not an effort to change how societies are governed. When a socialist wrote an open letter to the Sex Pistols, asking them to join forces, the call went unanswered (*No Future*, p. 40). But there have also been individuals within punk who are political in a more conventional sense. Consider the example of The Clash. The band sang about the oppression of the working class ("Career Opportunities" and "Clampdown"), the Spanish Civil War ("Spanish Bombs"), and imperialism ("Washington Bullets"). They also joined the socialist Anti-Nazi League and an organization called Rock Against Racism, which emerged in response to some allegedly racist remarks by Eric Clapton, David Bowie, and others in the white music world.

Other punk performers joined Rock Against Racism, including Angelic Upstarts, Au Pairs, the Beat, Buzzcocks, Delta 5, the Fall, Patrik Fitzgerald, Gang of Four, the Mekons, the Members, Jimmy Pursey, Tom Robinson, the Ruts, and X-Ray Spex. These concerts also featured reggae bands such as Aswad, Misty in Roots, and Steel Pulse. Many British punk bands were heavily influenced by reggae (for example Generation X, Vivien Goldman, the Ruts, and the Slits), and The Clash recorded reggae covers ("Police and Thieves"). These artistic trends had political import: punks were inspired by the activist ethos of England's Afro-Caribbean community (*Culture Clash*, p. 87). Two Clash members, Paul Simonon and Joe Strummer, had been present at a riot in Noting Hill, which was fuelled, in part, by racist policing. When The Clash wrote "White Riot," they were hoping to inspire their largely white audience to follow the activism they witnessed and admired among English people of color. Likewise, in "(White Man) In Hammersmith Palais" they accuse other punk bands of clamoring for the spotlight rather than fighting fascism.

We wouldn't want to canonize The Clash too quickly, of course. They've been accused of mere posturing, of naivety, or appropriating Black music, and of selling out. Still, they represent a left-leaning political consciousness that was emerging in British punk. The epitome of this trend can be found in the music collective, Crass, that formed in 1977, along with affiliated artists such as Honey Bane, Flux of Pink Indians, The Mob, Omega Tribe, Poison Girls, and Zounds. These performers fostered the development of on overt subculture that became known as anarcho-punk. They performed songs about war, capitalism, feminism, environmentalism, and other leftwing causes (though they eschew the labels "left" and "right"). They also wrote songs criticizing what they regarded as empty acts of protests by other punk acts, include Rock Against Racism ("White Punks on Hope"). Anarcho-punks engaged in activism in various ways: creating a communal living space, political vandalism, and benefit concerts for an anarchist community center, disarmament, animal rights, striking minors. They were largely pacifist but advocated acts of destructive disobedience (for examples, listen to the Zounds song "Subvert"). They also avoided corporate record companies, and made sure their albums and concerts were affordable, or even free. Anarcho-punk evolved into an enduring global movement, with like-minded bands and fans in Argentina, China, Mexico, Indonesia, South Africa, and throughout Europe. One of Björk's early bands, Kukl, released two records on Crass's label.

What about the United States? In some ways, the whole anar-cho-punk movement harks back to the MC5 from Detroit, an American proto-punk band; they lived communally, joined the White Panther Party in the late 1960s—a counterpart to the Black Panthers—and wrote songs denouncing the government ("American Ruse"). But, in early American punk, the MC5 were more the exception than the rule. Proto-punk legends, the Velvet Underground, came out of Andy Warhol's art scene; Iggy Pop and the Stooges mostly wrote sexually themed songs; Patti Smith and Richard Hell (Neon Boys, Television, the Heartbreakers, and the Voidoids) came to punk through poetry; and The Ramones were comprised of two left-leaning Democrats and two rightwing Republicans. Their hit song, Blitzkrieg Bop, captures this ambi-guity; though devised by Tommy Ramone, a Hungarian Jew whose parents survived the Holocaust, the title turns a bit of Nazi terminology into an upbeat injunction to dance.

The Ramones album, *Rocket to Russia*, depicts a pinhead riding a nuclear warhead on the back cover, but the tracks are largely apolitical. Malcolm McLaren tried to inject more poli-tics into the New York scene when he managed the New York Dolls; he dressed them in red outfits to represent Maoism, but it didn't go over well. Gail Higgins, who lived with singer Johnny Thunders at the time, recounts: "We HATED Malcolm. He was putting the Dolls in those red commie-inspired suits and doing the whole political thing, and the Dolls had nothing to do with politics. None of them knew anything about politics. We just thought it was ridiculous" (*Please Kill Me*, p. 191). Likewise, Walter Lure, guitarist for the Heartbreakers, said, "We concentrated on being no more than we were—a great rock'n' roll band—and left the politics to everybody else" (*To Hell and Back*, p. 141).

From Lure's perspective, politics was more of a British thing, but this impression wasn't entirely accurate. Anarchist themes were already prevalent in the San Francisco punk scene of the late 1970s with bands such as the Avengers, the Dead

Kennedys, the Dils, the Nuns, and U.X.A. The Bay Area fanzine, *Search and Destroy* published left-themed articles on the politics of punk by editor Nico Ordway, as well as a history of anarchism (Issue 4, 1977). (Ordway wrote the leftist Dils' song "Class War", then converted to Sufi Islam and became a neoconservative; later she came out as a trans woman.) Los Angeles, which became the epicenter of hardcore in the late Seventies, was less political, but pioneers Black Flag named their band after the anarchist banner, and had their albums illustrated by the progressive artist, Raymond Pettibon, brother of the band's main songwriter, Greg Ginn. Another Southern California band, the Vandals, embodied a playful attitude toward punk politics. With a logo that looks like an inverted anarchy sign and a penchant for kitschy Americana, they amused fans with the track, "Anarchy Burger (Hold the Government)."

In 1980, Reagan's presidential ascent further deepened the anarchist spirit American Punk, injecting a sense of urgency that rivaled British scenes. Examples include New York's Reagan Youth and D.C.'s Minor Threat. Minor Threat front man, Ian MacKaye, coined the term "straight edge," which was used to advocate for a lifestyle free from alcohol, recreational drugs, smoking, and casual sex. In some punk scenes they develop a reputation for bullying, but were mostly benign, and MacKaye shared Crass's commitment to making music that was both political and affordable.

Though hardly cohesive or doctrinaire, these examples forged an enduring image of punk as an anarchist movement. Many bands and fans identified themselves with left-wing causes and openly embraced anarchy, either as a political philosophy or as a creative expression of contempt for societal rules. Interest ranged from silly and sophomoric to self-righteously serious, and everywhere on this spectrum, endorsement of anarchy seemed emblematic of the subculture. But things were more complicated. While some punks became infatuated with anarchy, others were flirting with fascism.

White Noise

Well before the first British punk bands emerged, white working-class youth were embracing skinhead identities. Skinheads have Jamaican roots. There was an influx of West Indian immigrants to UK that began in 1948 and continued into the 1960s. Jamaican youth cultures were imported during this time. These included the rude boys or rudies, who presage many aspects of punk. Here is a description from Obika Gray:

The rude boys flouted conventional norms and turned social etiquette on its head. Likewise, the content of popular songs, the costumes of the rebellious young and the inclination to heroic criminality became means of acquiring reputation and social honor . . . raw aggression became vehicles for the assertion of popular alienation. (p. 216)

Whites who lived in council housing alongside Afro-Caribbean neighbors were exposed to the rude boys' ethos, along with their musical taste—ska, rocksteady, and, later, reggae. In the 1970s, this cultural mix would lead to racially integrated hybrids, such as "two-tone" ska. The skinhead subculture emerged even earlier, in the 1960s, and was also a hybrid. Skinheads listened to Jamaican music and wore short-cropped hair, flannel shirts, Doctor Martens (a uniform of the white working class). But this period of subcultural integration would not last. As Britain slipped into economic decline, an ultra-rightwing political party, the National Front, swept in, espousing anti-immigrant politics and authoritarian nationalism. Their politics resonated with white working-class men who felt entitled to the jobs that were diminishing. Racism, anti-Semitism, nationalism, imperialism, and fascism looked like remedies for white working-class woes, and some white skinheads forgot their Jamaican roots. As punk gained popularity in the UK, it was co-opted as a musical outlet for these attitudes.

There was a deep divide between the Nazi skinhead movement and other punks. While many punks were working class, others were art school students, and they dressed flamboyantly and cultivated interests in fashion, visual art, poetry and other trappings of highbrow culture. The working-class punks, too, were divided. Working-class bands such as Sham 69 were vocally anti-racist, as were some early proponents of a skinhead-dominated subgenre called Oi!, such as the Angelic Upstarts. But Nazi skinheads formed bands of their own, such as No Remorse, Skullhead, and Skrewdriver. Skrewdriver began as a conventional punk band, but changed appearance and musical themes with their 1983 "White Power" single, released on White Noise records. Subsequent album releases included *Hail the New Dawn*, *Blood and Honor*, and *White Rider*, with a Klansman on the cover. The movement also brought more violence into the punk scene, with confrontations between factions at clubs, and confrontations between skinheads and Britain's marginalized communities on the streets.

The news media presented skinheads as universally committed to Nazi ideology, and this impacted the mainstream understanding of punk politics. It must be said that punk had already done much to raise eyebrows before the schism with skins. Sid Vicious donned a swastika T-shirt and wrote a song about Bergen-Belsen. Vivienne Westwood sold swastika-emblazed tops in her punk boutique. Siouxsie Sioux wore a Nazi armband, and wrote anti-Semitic lyrics ("Love in a Void"). Joy Division named their band after a forced prostitution program in concentration camps.

Nazi themes were commonplace on both sides of the Atlantic. Ron Ashton, guitarist for the Stooges, collected Nazi regalia. The Viletones, from Toronto, had a singer named Nazi Dog and a song called "Swastika Girl." The Ramones sing, "I'm a Nazi baby" in a song written by Dee Dee, a right-winger raised in Germany ("Today Your Love, Tomorrow the World"). Darby Crash, from the Germs, was a self-described fascist, who admired Hitler: "I can respect Hitler for being a genius in doing what he did, but not for killing off innocent people . . . The only [form of government] that will work is a complete fascism" (*Lexicon Devil*, p. 128).

By the late Seventies Nazi symbols were ubiquitous in punk culture, even among those who claimed to be anarchists. The explanation is nicely expressed in a 1979 song by a Belgian band called the Kids: "I love the way they dressed, they seemed so decadent / I love to wear their medals, they make some people mad at me." But the song continues: "Do you love the Nazis? And do you like the Gestapo? And do you like the fascists? Oh no, oh no, oh no." Of course, this attitude was not without critics. Lucy Toothpaste, who created the first feminist punk fanzine, complained that "it's stupid for punks to wear swastikas . . . it's just supposed to shock our parents . . . but . . . deep down most of our parents are fascists." Still, for kids trying to provoke strong reactions, the swastika was a seductive symbol. And, for kids too naive to understand history, it was easy to blur the line between ironic reclamation and tacit endorsement. Against this background, an association between punk and fascism was easy to form.

The association was so strong, in fact, that by the late 1970s many punks felt a need to strongly signal a commitment to progressive causes. Rock Against Racism can be understood in this light, and many punks joined the Anti-Nazi League. In the 1980s a group called S.H.A.R.P., Skinheads Against Racial Prejudice, was formed and the Dead Kennedys released a single called "Nazi Punks Fuck Off."

Clearly, leftwing politics was not inherent to punk, and some left-leaning punks may have accentuated their political orientation to overcome the public perception that the movement had fascist and racist tendencies. It's not surprising, then, that these ostentatious gestures on the left were sometimes viewed with cynicism and suspicion. Speaking of The Clash, John Lydon said, "those boys took the wimpy route out with their Marxist nonsense. They had a university kind of rocky attitude: what were they challenging? Really when it boils down to it, it was meaningless and nice." Lydon would later express his support for Donald Trump.

So we're left with a conundrum. While it's easy to find punks espousing anarchist ideology (or some watered-down version thereof), it is also easy to find punks endorsing fascism, either as a provocation or with earnest zeal. It's also easy to find punks who claim to be apolitical. We're left with an incoherent mess.

The Politics of Disaffection

At this point we might be inclined to throw in the towel. Maybe there's no politics of punk, perhaps it's just a grab bag of diverging and conflicting views. Perhaps most punk is apolitical or at least not serious enough to warrant the label 'political'. I am sympathetic to these expressions of futility. Why expect a global movement, spanning decades, to have any ideological uniformity? Why think a movement that is most fundamentally a matter of style (music, fashion, art, dance) would come prepackaged with any political commitments? At the outset, we should expect and accept a high degree of pluralism. No account that insists on a single politics of punk could ever be credible. At the same time, the division that I've been examining here—the division between anarchism and fascism—raises the question: why did two opposing views find expression in punk? Is there something both extremes recognized? Is there a common denominator? If so, can that common denominator be expressed in political terms?

First, we might propose that punk politics is fundamentally anti-authoritarian. This has a ring of truth, but it's really a non-starter when it comes to Nazi punks. The whole problematic here is, can we find a political umbrella that covers both leftwing and rightwing punk? Those on the right actively argued for authoritarian government. Granted, they sometimes express frustration with the current government, but they were happy to back the National Front, and expressed few qualms about Reagan and Thatcher.

Second, we might equate the overarching politics of punk with nihilism. Describing the New York scene, Mary Harron, who wrote for *Punk* magazine, puts it this way: "It took a long time to realize that this attitude was called nihilism . . . People needed to say something that negative, there was something liberating about that negativity . . . this was a search-and-destroy aesthetic" (*The England's Dreaming Tapes*, p. 137).

This characterization resonates with the Sex Pistols' penchant for chaos and menacing incantation of the word "destroy." But it cannot be the whole story. Describing the Ulster scene, Guy Trelford exclaims:

> Nihilistic? Negative? No siree! Ulster punk was creative, positive. Kids were creating their own bands, venues, magazines. They were experimenting with fashion, making records, and kicking down the barriers . . . Other kids were out throwing petrol bombs, joining the youth wings of paramilitary organizations, burning cars and getting sucked into the whole sectarian merry-go-round. Not the punks. (*Punk Rock: An Oral History*, p. 305).

As compared to other politicized youth movements, says Trelford, punk was about creation, not destruction.

Third, we might surmise that punk is politically unified by a commitment to individualism, or non-conformity. The flipside of the "Anarchy in the UK" single is a great track called "I Wanna Be Me." That theme can be found throughout punk. The Avengers have a song called "I Believe in Me," and, when the X-Ray Spex complain about consumerism (as in the song "Art-I-Ficial"), they seem to be worrying about a process of homogenization. As *Punk* magazine's Leggs McNeil sees it:

> Punk . . . wasn't political. I mean, maybe that is political. I mean the great thing about punk was that it had no political agenda. It was about real freedom, personal freedom. (*Please Kill Me*, p. 299)

This, however, is one sided. For many, punk was about collectivist political causes, not about individual freedom. As for non-conformity, punk often became a template that set rigid constraints on taste in fashion and music. Punk was commodified, packaged, and sold in shopping malls. Less cynically, joining a punk scene was, for many, all about community—finding like-minded peers, not crafting yourself into isolating uniqueness.

A fourth suggestion is that punk expressed the politics of boredom. This phrase was promoted by Malcolm McLaren when he was managing the New York Dolls (*No Future*, p. iv and Chapter 4). Boredom is a (boringly!) constant theme in punk music. Examples include the Stooges song "1969" ("Another year with nothin' to do"), the Nixe's "Boring City," Honey Bane's "Boring Conversations," The Clash's "I'm So Bored with the U.S.A.," the Adverts' "Bored Teenages," Androids of Mu's "Bored Housewives," Snatch's "When I'm Bored," Magazine's "Boredom," and Peter and the Test Tube Babies' "U Bore Me," among many others.

There were also punk movements emerging in suburbia that can be understood as a reaction to the uniformity and monotony of suburban life. Examples include the UK's Bromley contingent—a group of punk scenesters that included Siouxsie Sioux—and the hardcore bands from Orange County. The Members, from a London suburb called Camberley, re-leased a song called "The Sound of the Suburbs," which opens: "Same old boring Sunday morning, old men out washing their cars / Mum's in the kitchen cooking Sunday dinner, Herbert's still moaning for food /And Johnny's upstairs in his bedroom sitting in the dark / Annoying the neighbors with his punk rock electric guitar / This is the sound, This is the sound of the suburbs."

Such examples make it clear that boredom is a trope in punk music, and perceived impetus, and a battle cry. Complaints of boredom can be wielding an indictment of a society that offer soulless drudgery in work and family life. At the same time, it would be reductive to equate punk with the politics of boredom. If you consider some of the politically focused punk subcultures, the complaints often concern societal ills that have little to do with boredom. For example, when straightedge punks complain about alcohol, they often have domestic violence in mind. Or consider the Riot Grrrl movement that emerged in Washington State in the early 1990s: members of that movement were feminists complaining about patriarchy and homophobia. Bigotry and abuse are commonplace but hardly boring.

A theory I find more compelling than any of these is that punk rock characteristically embodies a politics of disaffection. Disaffection is a state of being alienated and harboring negative attitudes, especially towards prevailing norms, expectations, or power structures. Etymologically, it refers to having emotions ("affects") directed away from something. It originally referred to disloyalty, but now refers to something more like dislocation or estrangement. The negative emotions include both a feeling of disconnection from others and resentment towards those individuals, institutions, or structures that you regard as impacting your life in some undesirable way. Punk disaffection has no fixed target. It can be directed towards government (as in the case of anarchists), religion (as in the Germ's song "No God"), family (as in the Descendents' "Parents"), or mainstream norms. Sometimes, it's directed in many directions at once, as when the Avengers sing, "We are not Jesus Christ / We are not fascist pigs / We are not capitalist industrialists / We are not communists / We are the one."

Disaffection applies both to punks on the left, who resent the government, and punks on the right, who resent immigrants and multiculturalism. (It may also have resonance in these polarized times, when we see people on the right and left aligned in their exasperation with the status quo.) Disaffection even applies to self-described apolitical punks, since they feel equaly alienated from prevailing norms.. The Ramones, for example, identified with the sideshow performers in Todd Browning's movie, *Freaks*, and punk has always been a bastion for those who don't fit in.

Disaffection can even capture the kernel of truth in the other proposals I surveyed. Nihilist punks may want to destroy because they see the world as hideous or a mess; anti-authoritarianism reflects distrust for the prevailing social or political order; individualism expresses contempt for normative standards of style and identity; the politics of boredom stems from a perception that contemporary life is suffocating. In each case there is a sense of disdain for the *status quo*. The world expects life to look a certain way, and many people all around robotically conform to those expectations. For those who feel disconnected from the scripts they are handed, there is a feeling of alienation. That alienation need not lead you to radical individualism; you might align yourself with others who are disaffected. It need not lead to anarchism; you can protest by becoming a hooligan, a drop out, a drug user, a prankster, a slacker, or in any number of other ways. Each of punk's many manifestations can be read as a rejection of some kind, as a resounding 'No'.

Disaffection helps the aesthetics of punk. Outlandish appearance and abrasive music serve to challenge polite society. They make those who already feel alienated even more so, but in a way that takes ownership of that feeling and finds pride in it. The preference for do-it-yourself aesthetics and amateurism serve to reject norms of acceptability and merit. They convey a refusal to embrace the standards of a society that you don't relate to. They relocate creative energies in the ground floor, refusing dictates from on high. There are, of course, many gatekeepers within punk communities dictating what counts as punk style. Even so, punk aesthetics emphasizes things that each of us can do without special training or resources: anyone can start a band, anyone can customize their wardrobe and color their hair, anyone can create a photomontage.

Aren't all youth groups disaffected? Some are, but others are not. Preppies are not disaffected, for example. In her analysis of club cultures, Sarah Thornton argues that ravers are not disaffected either; they do not define themselves as breaking away from the mainstream. Sociologists reserve the term counterculture for subcultures that have an us-versus-them mentality. Punk is a counterculture. Countercultures tend to be disaffected.

Still, I wouldn't say that all countercultures embrace a politics of disaffection. Consider goths. They tend to be apolitical. They separate themselves from the mainstream with their tastes, interests, and worldview, but they are not at war with society. Punk is confrontational. It's in-your-face. It has a volatile, jeering stance. Goth songs talk about death and horror; they do not assail against prevailing institutions. By comparison to Goths, even so-called apolitical punks are political. The Punk tend to be irreverent and antagonistic, even if playfully so. Goths and punks overlap, so this is not a sharp divide, but the punkness of goth appears at just those moments when goths raise their upper lip or extend their middle finger.

Its sometimes objected that all the swagger of punk is mere style: it doesn't effect meaningful social change. There may be exceptions to this, but it's noteworthy that punks, unlike hippies, never helped end a war or usher in a social revolution. Punk helped to make gender-nonconformity fashionable, and it created an outlet for kids who feel alienated from their peers, but also has a history of being racially homogenous, at times homophobic, and hostile to women.

Punk cannot be credited with significant societal change. This is due in part to the divided agenda of punk, but perhaps also to the politics of disaffection. Some hippies may have felt disaffected, but their politics had more specific contours: pacifism and sexual liberation. I don't mean to suggest that they were especially decisive in these efforts, but the agenda was narrowly focused and it had specific, constructive goals. The politics of disaffection is more about saying 'No' than building alternatives. It's more cynical that utopian.

That doesn't mean that punk is mere posturing—mere style. Those who embraced punk early on faced considerable harassment and violence. Those who embrace it today are often people who feel vulnerable elsewhere and find a safe haven in punk. Punk scenes have championed weirdos everywhere. They have given voice to the disenfranchised. They have supported squatters' rights for homeless kids. Punk has encouraged a skeptical attitude toward the mainstream, and cultivated gestures of defiance. All this is impactful, at least at a local level. These are all aspects of the politics of disaffection.

Punk breaks away from prevailing conventions, but it doesn't isolate itself; it takes aim, it fires. Those bullets may do little to change the world, but, for those firing the gun, they can be empowering.

The politics of punk says 'Fuck you', but with a self-satisfied sneer. Surely there is some good in that.

17
Nazi Punks Fuck Off!

Ryan Falcioni

Defining what counts as punk (and more significantly what does not count) is a favorite pastime of many punks. Documentaries, memoirs, and retrospectives on punk are often packed with aging punks telling their tales of the glory days of their punk youth. And no story about the golden age of punk is complete without uttering some disparaging remarks about the tragic downfall of punk music and culture.

Such accounts generally succeed in answering questions about punk's origins (whether UK or American), its fundamental substance (music, subculture, aesthetic, or ethos), and when it ended. If these stories have a lowest common denominator, it is that punk was once great and then x came along and changed/ruined things.

For many 1970s punks, hardcore came along, bringing its aggression and jockishness with it. The early punk that was the voice of the outcasts, misfits, androgyny, and women, was usurped by this faster, whiter, and more aggressive hardcore bully. Another way this story is told involves the evolution (or devolution) of early punk into its lighter, friendly, poppier iteration, New Wave. Not all bemoan this development, but many are clear to distance punk (and by extension, themselves) from these new musical and cultural forces. It may have punk lineage, but it is decidedly not punk!

Now for hardcore punks, the emergent grunge and pop punk (and their alternative and emo cousins) are often viewed as watered down, derivative, or just plain different. (The debate over the role of grunge in punk and post-punk history is a particularly intriguing phenomenon.) If you care to witness the intensity of such gatekeeping, casually mention to a group of hardcore punks that Blink-182 is your favorite punk band . . . and then hunker down for the inevitably ensuing verbal (and potentially physical) beatdown.

There are innumerable ways that such stories about the punk history and identity are told. The point here is not to provide a full taxonomy or ethnography of these punk recollections and histories. Rather, it is merely to point out that such stories are told, generally with great conviction and then palpable condescension. Not sure that this is as ubiquitous as described? Just ask the most grizzled, aging punk at your next punk show: how did punk get started? Or better yet: what happened to the original or real punk? If you don't get some version of the narratives provided above, I will provide a full refund of this book!

(Thanks for following up on this generous offer. Unfortunately, I cannot actually authorize such a refund. I just wanted to show commitment to these claims. But, if you are ever in Southern California and want to talk about any of this stuff, just shoot me an email and I would love to meet up at a punk-friendly bar or coffee shop!)

Many punks also have strong opinions about various sub-genre distinctions and classifications of both musical and cultural aspects of punk. Such efforts at boundary drawing and gatekeeping are central to many movements, but appear to reach a certain zenith in punk circles. These gatekeeping battles over the essence of punk rock are as contentious as they are ubiquitous. But, no battle has greater significance and engenders greater vitriol, than that over the role of neo-Nazi, white nationalist, and generally racist, punk. Often termed "hatecore," this form of punk has been a central part of many nationalist and racist movements across the globe. (The term 'hatecore' is sometimes used as a general umbrella term, to include racist hardcore punk as well as racist metal and other racist musical styles.) Hate group researcher, Devin Burghart, claims, "This music became not only the No. 1 recruiting tool, but also the biggest revenue source for the movement" (Devin Burghart, quoted in Dao and Kovalski).

But beyond the varying accounts given by punks and punk fans of all stripes and ages, there are serious historical, cultural, methodological, and philosophical obstacles to defining punk identity and establishing the essence of punk. Such difficulties are partially revealed by the stories told about punk. Punk involves various historical origin stories. In some iterations it is strongly characterized by its social and ideological components. In others, the focus seems to be on a punk aesthetic or style. And at the bottom of most versions is, of course, the music. But, should we even be concerned with such historical approaches in trying to really capture the essence of punk? And if so, which/whose history is primary? If we pick one, let's say the history of British punk in the 1970s that many claim was the brainchild of Malcolm McLaren (and to some degree, Vivienne Westwood) as a response to their disdain for hippie culture and a disillusionment with economic and class issues in the UK . . . how do we narrow down the central features and figures? To McClaren and friends, it may be more of a cultural protest, focusing on music and fashion as new vehicles of expression (see *England's Dreaming*). For his musical progeny, the Sex Pistols and their soon ascendant fan base, it might be more about the music itself and pissing off those in power. Or, should we excavate deeper into the musical and ideological origins of proto-punk and earlier punk music in America? Or ahead to what punk was becoming? Furthermore, which features of any of these accounts of punk are the most "essential"? Wherever there are two punks, there are three opinions.

You Can't Put Punk in a Box

There is also something seemingly anti-punk about even attempting to define "punk." To many, if there is a common thread in the various movements calling themselves punk, it is something involving non-conformity and pushing back against accepted norms and traditions. Trying to put something in a box that often prides itself on breaking boxes and defying labels goes against the punk ethos. Yet, if we are to have any meaningful discussion of punk, we must be referring to something.

We have gotten this far in this chapter and have made many assumptions about punk history, music, and culture. Referring to a punk ethos involving personal expression, non-conformity, anti-authoritarianism, and so forth, is engaging in an act of defining. This is an unavoidable feature of the nature of language. By mentioning these features and some of the histories and stories above, I am hoping to orient the reader to the concepts of punk as they function in our collective experience and memory.

I am not making any normative claims about what punk is or must be. In light of the work of Wittgenstein, and echoing the claims of William James, it is important to do justice to the varieties of punk experience! While punks are entitled to make judgments from within their world of punk about what is good punk, what punk values are or should be, and who counts and who doesn't, scholars should not be in the business of making such claims. We have a duty to do justice to the various phenomena that are connected with punk. We need to resist the temptation to say more than we know . . . or we need to do as Wittgenstein admonished and recognize that "What's ragged should be left ragged" (*Culture and Value*, paragraph 45e).

The Case of Neo-Nazi Punks

Many punks and punk scholars seem to treat the hatecore phenomenon of neo-Nazi, racist skinhead, and generally racist punk as an unfortunate aberration in the history of an otherwise progressive subculture. The Dead Kennedys' song title (for which this chapter is named) represents a common attitude toward both neo-Nazis and any attempts they might make to appropriate punk for their purposes.

Indeed, for over forty years, many punks have specifically targeted neo-Nazis, nationalists, and racists with special ire in their songs and writings. There are many reasons for such a dismissive stance. In most of its earliest forms, punk was indeed very progressive on issues of race, class, and gender. As many see this history, punk culture just was a coming together of the most marginalized groups in society to create and project their collective voice. Thus, in describing the early punk scene (and other such movements) in England, punk journalist John Savage states:

> England is a highly static society, with a strongly defined ruling class and a narrow definition of the acceptable. If you fall outside it for any reason, you're marginal. As with any cluster of minorities, if you put them together, you make a majority: pop—a marginal industry in itself—is a place where many of them meet, as dreamers and misfits from all classes, to transform, if not *the* world, then their world. (*England's Dreaming*, p. 12)

So for many, the idea of a racist or fascist punk is something of an oxymoron. Punk "is" the voice of the voiceless in opposition to the ruling class and institutional authority. However, neo-Nazi punks did emerge alongside (and often within) these otherwise marginalized punk subcultures. They may be usurpers of a certain sort, borrowing the music, fashion, and momentum of the early punk movements. But this history is a bit more entangled than many progressives might want it to be. Neo-Nazi punk stands in a family resemblance relationship with many forms of punk. It shares many of the musical forms, aesthetics, and even an interwoven history, with the much more common punk rock that is generally at the other end of most political and ideological spectra.

Returning for a second to the Dead Kennedys' anti-Nazi anthem, there is an uncomfortable truth that emerges, embedded in the very fact that such songs exists: *Punk culture has a Nazi problem.* It has this problem in a way that is relatively unique to punk. Humor me for a minute here. Try to imagine a similar industry of anti-Nazi or anti-fascist anthems emerging out of the music and culture of country, blue grass, or even just traditional rock'n'roll. Now, I am sure that such songs exist in one form or another in these other musical cultures. But, this need to consistently preach against racism, fascism, and neo-Nazi ideals in efforts of rooting out that element from your ranks is nearly exclusive to punk. And lest you think that this issue is merely a case of petty infighting between subcultures and subgenres of punk, it is important that we take a look at the broader significance of hatecore.

The Curious Case of Neo-Nazi Skinhead Christian Picciolini

White power musician and former neo-Nazi skinhead Christian Picciolini has discussed the pivotal role that hatecore music played in his own neo-Nazi punk rock education and subsequent efforts to recruit and brainwash others (Picciolini, *White American Youth*). Punk was the vehicle for indoctrination. It was also the tool for recruitment. This is what hooked Picciolini and also became one of his main tools to recruit others in his role as one of the leaders of the Hammer Skin Nation, one of the most violent neo-Nazi hate groups in America, and as the leader of a couple of racist punk bands (Final Solution and White American Youth).

It was one of his racist anthems that was found to be influential in radicalizing neo-Nazi terrorist Dylann Roof (Lipman, "Christian Picciolini"). Roof killed nine African-American parishioners at Emanuel AME Church in Charleston, South Carolina in 2015. So, the stakes couldn't be higher when discussing the historical and current effectiveness of neo-Nazi hatecore in recruiting, indoctrinating, and mobilizing some of the most violent acts of neo-Nazi, racist, and ethnonationalist groups and individuals. Picciolini is now a former neo-Nazi skinhead and is an Emmy award winning activist against hate and the racist skinhead music and culture that often undergirds it.

Picciolini's own conversion (and his eventual deconversion) story is a testament to the power and embeddedness of hatecore music in neo-Nazi recruitment and violence. And, it is a further testament to the power of punk music and style as vehicles for creating culture, educating or indoctrinating its members, and motivating people to act. This realization is often a tough pill to swallow as it, in one sense validates, the power and profundity of punk music and culture. It shows how significant a tool punk can be. This flip side can be very dark. When cultivated by hands that mean the world ill, its power becomes a detriment to humanity and a formidable foe for those who fight for justice and equality.

Ludwig Wittgenstein: Punk Philosopher

So where do we go from here? How should we define punk and how might this be connected to (and instructive for) the broader project of getting Nazi punks to fuck off? Enter the philosopher Ludwig Wittgenstein (1889–1951)! (For a brief but insightful overview of the life and works of Wittgenstein, please see the "Ludwig Wittgenstein" entry in *The Stanford Encyclopedia of Philosophy*.

There are at least two major ways in which Wittgenstein is significant for punk. First, his life and work embody the spirit of punk rock. Second, his particular contributions to philosophy are extremely illuminating and clarifying on this issue of defining punk, and help point to a path forward in dealing with the scourge of neo-Nazi punk.

Wittgenstein was placed near Karl Marx, but still short of Diogenes, on a chart titled, "Philosophers Ranked by Their Punk Credentials" in a recent post on Reddit. Ludwig Wittgenstein was born into one of the wealthiest families in Europe. His father was a steel magnate and his family was deeply imbedded in Viennese high society. Johannes Brahms was a regular guest in the Wittgenstein home, and Gustav Klimt painted Wittgenstein's sister's wedding portrait (McGuinness, *Wittgenstein: A Life*). Although he no doubt benefitted from such a privileged upbringing, he was never truly comfortable with the trappings of wealth and rebelled against them . . . ultimately giving away his entire inheritance. He studied aeronautics and engineering at university, but his obsession with theoretical matters in mathematics led him to philosophy. He studied under Bertrand Russell at Cambridge, making a huge impression on Russell and his colleagues and students there. He made such an impact on Russell (who was arguably the most prominent philosopher in the world at the time) that it made Russell doubt his own abilities. In a letter from 1916, Russell stated:

I wrote a lot of stuff about Theory of Knowledge, which Wittgenstein criticised with the greatest severity. His criticism, tho' I don't think I realised it at the time, was an event of first-rate importance in my life, and affected everything I have done since. I saw he was right, and I saw that I could not hope ever again to do fundamental work in philosophy. My impulse was shattered, like a wave dashed to pieces against a breakwater. (*The Autobiography of Bertrand Russell*, p. 282)

The particular ways in which this engineering student could bring a Cambridge don to his knees embodies the heart of punk. Wittgenstein did this through flouting convention, tradition, and academic norms. He simply read the work of the world's most prominent philosopher and promptly told him that it was rubbish! He spoke truth to power. Furthermore, he did not appear to have significant interest in (or respect for) much of the history of philosophy. He seemed to have a disdain for the traditional canon of historical philosophers and philosophies.

Other than Kierkegaard, Augustine and the Russian novelists, Tolstoy and Dostoevsky, Wittgenstein did not seem to engage much with the history of philosophy. He charted his own course. He was more interested in solving philosophical problems and believed that much of the history of philosophy was mired in conceptual confusions. He believed that it was his task to get rid of many of the pseudo problems that philosophy had created. In his words, he was trying to "show the fly the way out of the fly-bottle" (*Philosophical Investigations*, paragraph 309).

For Wittgenstein, most philosophers were not helping to see the world more clearly, but were actively muddying the waters with senseless theories and metaphysical systems. Philosopher Alain Badiou described this spirit of Wittgenstein's (as well as Nietzsche's for that matter) philosophy well as "a certain form of philosophical contempt for philosophy" (*Wittgenstein's Antiphilosophy*, p. 74). It was his duty to dismantle these institutional obstacles to understanding the world around us. This no fucks given approach made Wittgenstein many enemies but also many lifelong devotees. He pursued both ethical convictions and philosophical truth with reckless abandon.

And just in case you think that Wittgenstein's rebellious streak might be creditable to his youth or was otherwise anomalous, consider the events of one fateful night in October of 1946. At a meeting of the Moral Sciences Club at Cambridge University, he (allegedly) threatened the famed philosopher Karl Popper with a fireplace poker when he couldn't get Popper to admit that philosophy's problems were generally mired in confusions about language and were lacking in substance. For a book-length discussion of this event, see Edmonds and Eldinow, *Wittgenstein's Poker*.

Wittgenstein's experiences as a gay Jew in Austria during the Nazis' ascent to power make him a particularly salient voice in any conversation involving the call for Nazi punks to fuck off! (see the article by Michael Peters). An even more curious historical point is that Wittgenstein and Hitler were born just a few days apart and were schoolmates in Linz during the first decade of the 1900s (see Monk's biography of Wittgenstein).

Wittgenstein to the Rescue?

One of Wittgenstein's most significant insights is that language is not fixed. Many earlier (and current) philosophical views about the relationship between language and the world holds that words describe objects and states of affairs in the world. On such views of language, words like punk should correspond to some reality in the world. This relatively narrow view of language seems to be embedded in many of the efforts to define and gatekeep punk. For, if punk refers to some fixed object or phenomenon, then we can exclude all other people, movements, or ideas that are not picked out by these words. Wittgenstein's later work cautions us against taking such a narrow approach. This language-world relationship is much more diverse and flexible. The same words can be used in many different ways. A common Wittgensteinian mantra is that the meaning of a word is to be found in its use. We can see what words mean by how they are used in the communities which use them.

So for Wittgenstein, it would be a fool's errand for philosophers to attempt to define punk (or anything else) in an absolute way. For Wittgenstein, meaning lies in the use of language and the use of language occurs in a given historical, cultural, and linguistic context. If we apply these insights to this intra-punk debate about who or what is really punk, or what the essence of punk is or must be, we can see that philosophy is ill equipped to settle the matter. And more importantly, that this matter could not ever be really settled with regard to any type of philosophical investigation. There are answers to be found, of course, about what or what does not count as punk. But these answers are just as regional as the varieties of punk music and culture.

It is in this way then that there is or can be a profound meaning to a group of hardcore punks saying that pop punk,

New Wave, neo-Nazi punk, or post-punk is not really punk. For to them, it's simply does not embody the core meaning of punk that their experience and context bears out. However, these other punk genres and subcultures also make judgments and draw boundaries around what they consider to be punk. And as frustrating as this may be, there is no absolute or universal concept of punk that can be appealed to, to arbitrate these intra-punk disputes. Each group simply cultivates its own meaning for both what counts as punk and what decidedly does not count as punk through their experiences and connections with these related ideas. These different worlds of experiences and connections provide the context and embed the meaning of the different ways that language is used.

To some readers I'm sure this all starts to sound a bit circular: Punk is what various "punks" do or say. How does this help us understand punk or help us combat neo-Nazi punk? This is where an additional feature of Wittgenstein's philosophy seems instructive. We've looked at various definitions and accounts of 'punk'. Many of them stand in opposition to each other on various matters of music taste, aesthetics, and ethos. However, the very fact that all of us can see these connections and recognize the various ways in which all of these accounts are involved with something called 'punk' reveals an additional feature of language.

To be understood across a variety of uses, words often stand in family resemblance relationships to each other. The ways that these uses are connected reveal many shared features. Think of these shared features portrayed as a large Venn diagram, with various degrees of overlapping. Not all words or concepts that are used in different ways will share all of these features in common. But, the degree to which they share these common features reveals their interconnectedness. It is this family resemblance feature of language that might be useful in finding a way forward in this discussion about the meaning of punk and the particular and peculiar role that movements like neo-Nazi punks play in this history.

Now we could take these insights from Wittgenstein and use them to draw even sharper boundaries between the various modes and forms of punk. It seems to justify a certain type of gatekeeping because after all, our meanings are different than their meanings. But I hope that we would not take this path. Rather, we can see this as an opportunity to build bridges. If we recognize that all of these forms of punk share so many elements of musical and cultural history, there are many inroads to make for dialogue, intervention, and inclusion. Furthermore, we can recognize that one of the common family resemblance components of punk is giving voice to those who feel marginalized, cultivating identity, and empowering individuals and groups to change the world around them. This gives us a profound occasion for connection. Getting Nazi punks to fuck off might still be occasionally necessary at punk shows or in defense of others in the short run. But, appealing to the shared traditions of punk might be part of the process for reforming lives.

So How Do We Get Nazi Punks to Finally Fuck Off?

Hopefully the discussion in this chapter has given us a few relevant insights towards accomplishing this goal. Seeing the various ways in which neo-Nazi punks are connected with the history, music, and ethos of other punks is a necessary first step for any constructive path ahead. Christian Picciolini often speaks of the identity, community, and purpose that racist punk provided him. These also seem to be components of the family resemblance that racist punk shares with punk more broadly. Taking the time to really grapple with how profound these elements are reveals what is so appealing about neo-Nazi punk.

So rather than digging in one's heels in an effort to distance your self, your music, and your slice of punk culture from neo-Nazi punks, you can come to see the parts of yourself reflected in them. In looking at potential paths forward, it only seems appropriate to return back to the stories of the glory days told by the aging grizzled punk in the corner. There are profound lessons to be learned through his or her waxing nostalgic about the golden age of punk. It seems particularly poetic for the path forward to be rooted in punk's past.

Getting Nazi punks to fuck off will not happen through physical violence (as appealing and reasonable as that may sound in the era of the 'punch a Nazi' meme). As we have seen, this is the currency of many neo-Nazi groups. In addition to the punk ethos, they have added the tools of violence and the compelling narrative of grievance. To many disaffected youths, it is this totalizing ideology with its Manichean story of white versus black, good versus evil, that is so appealing. These movements don't just give you a voice, they give you an identity, and a mission. But again, neo-Nazi punk culture has been effective precisely because it has been able to utilize the tools of punk that were already present in the good ol' days. Through re-engaging with punk's ability to create a voice and to cultivate identities and even missions for disaffected youth and others in need, the lure of neo-Nazism can be diminished. Punk can and should be utilized to educate, and help provide meaning and purpose towards noble ends. Punk has always had this power. And there are groups of punks who have maintained this part of the movement since its inception. Growing these movements and starting new ones is a key to combatting the appeal of neo-Nazi punk.

At the risk of sounding like the aging grizzled punk myself, punk is at its best when it is experienced in communities and unites us around shared values and shared goals. It's my hope that new and even more profound forms of punk continue to emerge and that they find ways of understanding and including those who might be drawn into neo-Nazi iterations. New punks can draw on the deep wellspring of a shared history of music, culture, and values to build bridges to those on the margins.

There is no panacea here. But, any constructive path forward must both understand neo-Nazi punk and also engage with its prospective (and possibly active) members in ways that provide real opportunities for identity, community, and purpose. So, for all of those interested in creating a more just and equitable world, let's focus our efforts on building bridges more than gatekeeping. Because although necessary at times, I would rather live in a world where I seldom had to believe (and utter) the phrase: Nazi punks fuck off!

18

Wartime Propaganda as Punk Critique

KAREN FOURNIER

Early punk is known for its visual art, which constructed mashups of images borrowed liberally from existing sources. In Britain, these sources often included tokens of the ruling class (the Monarch, her Royal Stewart tartan) and of national patriotism (the Union Jack), many of which were defaced by punk artists not only as a show of punk's contempt for authority, but also to signify the precariousness of the British Empire: in the hands of one of punk's pre-eminent artists, Jamie Reid, the Union Jack was famously torn and pinned together in a blatant representation of an empire that was both literally and figur- atively "coming apart at the seams."

Punk's visual art has been the subject of much scholarship by art historians and punk scholars who have focused their attention on the assemblages that have populated punk fanzines, promotional material, album covers, visual art, and other forms of still imagery. By contrast, the moving image in punk has been comparatively undertheorized.

Julien Temple's 1979 film short, *Punk Can Take It*, provides an illustration of "mashup" in film that borrows from, and modifies, an existing mainstream source: in this case, a wartime propaganda movie created twenty-nine years earlier entitled *London Can Take It!* This nine-minute wartime propaganda movie is replete with patriotic imagery. With particular scorn directed towards the central message of wartime sacrifice that marks its source film, *Punk Can Take It* creates a counternarrative about classism, exclusion, and the emptiness of modern consumerism.

Using "warfare" as its central premise, Temple's movie locates its enemy in an invisible corporate culture, which takes

the place of the faceless German night-time bombers who ter-
rorized London in the original movie. In Temple's film, the corporate enemy, threatened by the individualism that punk
promotes, seeks to annex the subculture, and to drain it of its
power to challenge the cultural (and financial) hegemony of
mainstream society. But as we see at the end of the movie,
punk can take it.

London Can Take It!

London Can Take It!, which can be seen at

<www.youtube.com/watch?v=yoS-CQKvAZA>,

was directed by Humphrey Jennings and Harry Watt and was
designed to combat American anti-interventionism in the war
by demonstrating that Britain was not a lost cause. It became
popular in the United States, where it was widely distributed
through Warner Brothers to twelve thousand movie theaters
and watched by over sixty million viewers.

After seeing the film, the New York Times film critic Bosley
Crowther shared his impression that "there is no one in the
world today—not even the Nazi leaders—who can doubt for
one moment the magnificent courage and determination of the
Londoners as their homes come crashing down around them
and they carry on with confidence" ("The War on the Screen").
The film was nominated for an Academy Award in 1941 in the
category of Best Live Action Short. For British viewers, *London
Can Take It!* served as an important piece of domestic propaganda whose patriotic themes and "stiff upper lip" messaging
helped to bolster sagging wartime morale and to remind its
viewers of the importance of their sacrifices as Britain moved
towards an assumed victory.

The movie stressed that the British wartime effort was a
collective one that mobilized participants across the social
spectrum. King George VI and his wife, Queen Elizabeth, make
an appearance in the film to survey the damage to their own
home and to show that, despite their social status, they were
not immune to the German attacks on London.

Using the technique of mass-observation which had been pioneered by Jennings in 1937 to document the "realities" of everyday life in Britain, *London Can Take It!* offers an eye-witness
account of a single day in the city in September 1940, at the
beginning of the Blitz. The story begins in the evening, as
Londoners head home from work to prepare either to fight the
impending German air-raid on the city as members of a "people's

army" or to seek refuge in the safety of the London Underground. Footage of the night-time bombings is violent and heartbreaking but, as day breaks and the Luftwaffe retreats, Londoners emerge onto the streets to resume their everyday routines: they make their way to jobs, do their shopping, gather on street corners to gossip with friends, and sweep away debris from damaged homes and businesses. A voiceover helps to locate the events as the day unfolds by referencing time with lines like "it is late afternoon," "now it's eight o'clock," "it's just 6 A.M.," and "London looks upwards towards the dawn." The city emerges battered from the overnight attacks, but landmarks like St. Paul's Cathedral, Nelson's Column, and Westminster appear structurally intact in the film as if to signify British resilience. In its closing minutes, the movie repeats its central message, that the seemingly endless German raids are no match for "the unconquerable spirit and courage of the people of London. London can take it!"

The Bricolage Concept

So how does Temple suggest that we resist the absorption of punk into mainstream culture? One answer is to hijack tokens of mainstream culture *first* and subject them to "bricolage," so that these could be turned back against the predatory culture to expose its empty consumerism. In his surrealist manifesto *The Crisis of the Object*, André Breton defines the bricolage concept as

> a total revolution of the object: acting to divert the object from its ends by coupling it to a new name and signing it . . . objects thus reassembled have in common the fact that they derive from and yet succeed in differing from the objects which surround us, by simple *change of role*.

Bricolage invites an artist to create an image from a collage of unrelated "found" objects which are dislocated from their source and whose meanings become infused by their proximity to other objects with which they co-exist in an artwork. This is a common device in punk's still imagery, but bricolage can also inform moving imagery. On the surface of a punk movie, visual artifacts can enter into a dynamic relationship with other borrowed or newly created artifacts that move in and out of its orbit and contribute dynamically to the creation of new meanings.

Like the safety-pin on the Union Jack, the appearance of war-vintage steel helmets, uniforms, and or rifles in a staged punk vignette signifies a specific time and place (wartime

Britain), but the interaction of these artifacts with signifiers of punk (like bondage trousers or safety pins) invites the viewer to map the concept of "wartime" onto punk's performance of "socio-economic class" and to interpret the movie as a depiction of class warfare in which working-class punks resist the incorporation of their subculture into mainstream consumer culture. Bricolage can also inform the structure of a film, where entire scenes borrowed from a source film are inserted into a new film or, more specific to Temple's film, where segments of narrated text are cut out of a source film and rearticulated or rearranged to create a new text that tells a "wartime" story from a different perspective.

Punk Can Take It

Given its assumption, in 1940, that Britain's wartime sacrifices would be rewarded with a better future, *London Can Take It!* seems like an obvious choice for critique by those who found themselves alienated and disillusioned in 1970s Britain. The British youth who coalesced into the punk scene in 1977 represented a generation for whom the postwar promise of a better future rang particularly hollow.

Their experiences were shaped by a decade that had been marked by staggering unemployment and few job prospects, stagflation, nationwide strikes, and an ongoing energy crisis triggered by the 1973 OPEC oil embargo. The working-class, with which many punk artists identified, was affected disproportionately by a decade of hapless political maneuvers like the Three-Day Week and statutory wage and price limits. Designed to curb the economic volatility of the time, these measures managed, instead, to overburden those Britons who were already financially insecure. By the end of 1978, the misery of Britain's mounting and multiplying domestic crises was compounded by a record-breaking cold snap, prompting some to describe the period as Britain's "winter of discontent."

London Can Take It! touted the contributions of a "people's army" of British citizens whose sacrifices would be rewarded equally after victory had been secured, but this had been exposed as a lie by the 1970s. Temple's response to the reality of the social and economic crises that surrounded him and other punks in 1979 was to intercut restaged references to Jennings's movie with modern enactments of punk disaffection. Described by one critic as "a glorious picture of England in a punk rock 'identity crisis'," *Punk Can Take It*, asks us to reconsider our preconceived notions about victor and vanquished in a post-war society that appeared to offer no future to its working-class.

The movie frames this "identity crisis" as a class struggle and asks the viewer to question where the threat to British society in the 1970s actually lies: in the punk scene or in the halls of power. While the question might seem rhetorical today, it was *punk* that was seen by many at the time to pose a very real threat to British values. Consider, for example, the sentiment expressed by Bernard Brook-Partridge that "the whole world would be vastly improved by punk's total and utter nonexistence." Sentiments like these would often place punks in danger of physical violence, either from members of the public or from members of other subcultures. But punks faced a more insidious, existential issue that is explored in Temple's film: the "identity crisis" examined in the film is threat of punk's absorption into mainstream consumer culture, where it would be reduced to a set of empty signifiers and transformed into mass-produced "punk" products.

Punk Can Take It, which can be seen at

<www.youtube.com/watch?v=JDuAtJhqo2k>,

is built around documentary footage of six songs performed in live concert by the UK Subs, interrupted by short fictional scenes that depict various attacks on the integrity of punk. In the first scene, punks seek refuge from an impending attack in the London Underground (as Londoners did in Jennings' wartime film). Above ground, a lone punk is attacked by a trio of journalists disguised as vampires who attempt to suck the essence of punk out of him as he sleeps in a car (signifying the dangers of being overground during wartime). The film cuts to a television craft-show that shows children how they might modify their school uniforms to fit the punk aesthetic (hinting at the infantile co-option of punk by non-punks). This is followed by a scene in which store mannequins, clothed in the latest punk styles, attack a window dresser for her complicity in the commodification of punk. In another part of town, a media executive makes a vain attempt to sign a punk artist to mainstream label while dining at a restaurant. The penultimate scene features an angry punk mob that emerges from the darkness to gather on the bank of the Thames, where they appear in daylight for the first time. They destroy a statue of Johnny Rotten in a move to resist any artist perceived to sell out to the music industry. The movie ends with a darkened funeral scene in which the claim that punk is dead is met with a resurrection and gunfire. The film's vignettes provide localized examples of the bricolage concept, while the film is also stitched together with a narration that illustrates how bricolage can also inform the structure of a punk film.

Localized Bricolage Examples

The bricolage concept is used in individual scenes in different ways, though space permits only a couple of examples. In the opening sequence of the movie, the searchlights that scanned the sky for German aircraft in Jennings's film are transported into Temple's film (at 1:13), where they scan across an aggressive punk audience to reveal the anger felt by the descendents of a "people's army" that was duped by the ruling class.

This new army comprises those who have reaped no benefits from the wartime sacrifices made by their parents and grandparents. A punk "people's army" prepares for war in the ensuing scene (at 2:05), as three working-class punks prepare for battle beneath their own variant of the "steel helmet" (the hoods of three hairdryers). This opening sequence shows the bricolage concept at work in various visual cues drawn from the source film: searchlights that once scanned the sky for the invisible German enemy are now pointed downwards at an audience, to expose punk anger in the darkness of the concert venue, while helmets that once protected soldiers on the streets of Blitz-era London now contribute to the hairstyles that mark punk's difference from the invaders from mainstream culture.

Tokens of wartime are appropriated by Temple to expose the contradictions of post-war Britain, where the descents of those who sacrificed during the war are now vilified as social outcasts in 1970s Britain. In the hands of punks, the searchlight, the gasmask, and the steel helmet point both to the "people's army" who would have used these items in the war and to the post-war generation that continued to fight for promises of equality to be fulfilled.

Concert space in the movie is metonymic with punk space as a place where punks can engage safely in behaviors that would have called for their "total and utter nonexistence" by the enemies who reside beyond the walls of the subculture. Punk space is breached in the film during one of concert scenes (at 10:00), when outsiders in fancy dress suddenly appear in the audience. They pogo in their tuxedos, chest-bump with punks, engage in fights, and gesticulate rudely to the camera in an incongruous performance of punk behaviors. Tokens of "high culture," like the tuxedo, are unmoored in this scene from the semiotic environment that sustains them in the preceding scene, where men and women in fancy dress stroll the shores of the Thames in the afternoon sun and punt along the river. The obvious references to Oxford and Cambridge via the punt makes the appearance of the tuxedo in punk's darkened concert space starker. In the concert scene, "high-culture" appears to wage a war for hegemony with a subculture that it seeks contain, but members of dominant class quickly learn that cooption is the quickest route to punk's commodification. Within a few minutes, the invaders abandon their tuxedos for punk outfits and disappear into the crowd. The film cuts to the next vignette (at 12:31) as the narration, borrowed from two wartime propaganda phrases, warns that "careless talk costs lives" and "the enemy is always listening." The scene relies on a bricolage of class markers to make the film's central point: that punk authenticity needs protection against appropriation by those on the outside who would seek to commodify punk.

Structural Bricolage

Where the use of bricolage in individual scenes in *Punk Can Take It* draws the film into dialogue with its source about the nature of warfare and resistance through shared visual artifacts, *Punk Can Take It* also cues its wartime source in the movie's voiceover monologue, whose script draws from a variety of sources that are fused together through bricolage.

Temple enlisted the help of the BBC wartime announcer, John Snagge, to provide a voice-over to connect the film's disjointed scenes. During the war, Snagge was known to BBC listeners as the journalist who announced the start of the D-Day invasion June 6th 1944. Like any other token of wartime Britain, Snagge's voice signifies the war era and is hijacked from its original newsreel source and inserted into the sonic environment of the punk film, where it contributes to the film's narrative of class warfare. This represents another example of bricolage.

Snagge's script puts also the bricolage concept to work as a text stitched together from direct quotations from the *London Can Take It!*, other phrases of wartime propaganda, and newly-composed text. *Punk Can Take It* draws its first and final lines from the earlier film, for example, and frames its story of class warfare with text originally written to describe *actual* warfare. Snagge sets the scene for the punk's resistance to its incorporation into mainstream culture with the following phrase (at 1:16), lifted almost verbatim from the earlier film:

> The searchlights poke long, white, inquisitive fingers into the blackness of the night. . . . These are not Hollywood sound effects. This is the music they play every night, the symphony of war.

In *London Can Take It!*, the musical metaphor downplays the fear that would have been experienced by the people's army on the ground and assures the viewer that the sounds of war, while real, have simply become part of the aural landscape of wartime London. In Temple's script, by contrast, the word "symphony" has deeper resonances of class and infers the weaponization of punk music against those who would view it as affront to their musical tastes. As Snagge narrates these borrowed lines, the searchlight described earlier pans across punk's "people's army." Three punks are isolated for particular attention as the camera cuts away to a hairdressing salon and are characterized as "hairdressers, bank clerks, and street urchins by day" who prepare to be punk "heroes by night." This phrase is also borrowed from the source film, which describes a "people's army" comprised of "brokers, clerks, peddlers, and merchants by day" who similarly become "heroes by night." In combination with punk imagery, this part of the bricolaged text draws a stark distinction between the wartime and punk armies, the latter of which is comprised largely of unemployed youth who embody the hopeless of their generation.

At the end of the film, the narration hijacks further segments of the source script. In the original film, the viewer is assured that

a bomb has its limitations. It can only destroy buildings and kill people. It cannot kill the unconquerable spirit and courage of the people of London. London can take it!

In the context of punk, Snagge similarly asserts (at 17:40) that

The enemy will continue to devise its vile and treacherous stratagems, but it cannot kill the unconquerable will of Britain's punks. Punk can take it!

These framing quotations establish the basic idea of both films: that punk will be victorious in its fight against the invisible enemy of post-war consumer culture just as Londoners will be victorious in their fight against the German invaders. Despite its spoof of the earlier film, *Punk Can Take It* concludes with the similar utopian sentiment that "right will prevail."

Within the movie itself, the nature of the attack against punk and its alleged perpetrators from the dominant culture is brought into focus in a script that appropriates references to the British wartime Nazi sympathizer Lord Haw-Haw (at 9:19), who was enlisted by the Germans to broadcast propaganda in

English into British homes on the medium-wave *Reichssender Hamburg* radio station, and to the famous British propaganda phrases "Careless talk costs lives, the enemy is always listening" (at 12:31) recreate wartime paranoia about the double agent. In the case of punk, the spy is one who is enlisted by the dominant culture to masquerade as a punk to reproduce elements of the subculture for *their* enjoyment and profit. The film ends in a display of gunfire and resurrection as if to signal punk's ultimate resistance to commodification and to the dominant consumer class.

A Powerful Social Critique

As a multidimensional art form that unfolds in time, punk cinema can mobilize bricolage in ways that still imagery cannot: as Temple's film demonstrates, collaged elements can appear and disappear as individual scenes unfold and can also inform dialogue and narration. In the case of *Punk Can Take It*, references to an earlier wartime short and their combination with punk imagery help to critique post-war British society, where the promises of equal benefit afforded to those who made wartime sacrifices had yet to be realized in some sectors of British society. This movie uses tokens of warfare both to expose that lie and to critique a post-war consumer culture that increasingly excluded working-class Britons.

As an example of social critique in film, *Punk Can Take It!* stands alongside Temple's better-known 1980 punk mockumentary, *The Great Rock and Roll Swindle* and Derek Jarman's 1978 cult classic, *Jubilee*. In all three cases, tokens of the dominant culture are appropriated and turned against that culture: in the case of Temple's 1980 film, the familiar detective genre is adapted to a story that seeks to solve the "mystery" of the demise of the Sex Pistols and the infiltration of mainstream culture into punk, while Jarman's film lampoons the monarchy through its appropriations of markers of the British ruling class. This trio of films illustrates how bricolage was not simply a tool for punk's visual artists but was also a powerful form of critique in punk films of the period.

19

Punk Consciousness and Class Consciousness

TIFFANY MONTOYA

Punk rock started as a musical subculture for and by young, disaffected, working-class youth, and it provided them a space to turn their grievances into music and feel less alone. It was a home for the outcasts, the "losers," and the downtrodden of society. (This can be true while simultaneously acknowledging that it has also been predominantly White and male.)

Consider the band names: the Subhumans, the Unseen, the Exploited, Lower Class Brats, the Misfits, Cockney Rejects . . . the list is long). But the music itself—both in content and form—was a clear expression or artistic representation of an emerging *class consciousness*; and the culture, or the "scene" was a learning site for this growing consciousness and an example of a *proletarian culture*.

It wasn't just that the lyrics shouted anti-establishment or anti-capitalist messages, or that the music style energized a revolutionary fervor, but the scene itself attempted to create alternative realities through a DIY culture, egalitarianism, and mutual aid. Yet the revolutionary potential of punk as a subculture remains up for question and hinges on its ability to hold steadfast to its original values.

What Is Class Consciousness?

We're the first ones to starve, we're the first ones to die
The first ones in line for that pie-in-the-sky
And we're always the last when the cream is shared out
For the worker is working when the fat cat's about.

— "Workers' Song" by Ed Pickford, covered by Dropkick Murphys

183

Class consciousness is a process of gradual awareness of the mechanisms of a class-based society and your role within it. The philosopher Karl Marx spends his whole career studying and writing about the mechanisms of capitalism and the antagonism between two classes within it: the proletariat and the bourgeoisie, or the working class and the capitalist class.

Marx and his collaborator Frederick Engels define the proletariat as a class of laborers, who *must* work as a means of survival, but can only work if their labor produces profit for the owner. They consider this *exploitative* because the relationship is not only forced through circumstance but also because the capitalist extracts a profit out of the wealth that the *worker* produces. Marx goes on to explain how this process creates further residual effects such as alienation from your work and from other humans, it commodifies everything, and compels conformity to a single culture and ideology. Punk songs illustrate these phenomena well.

Alienation is the feeling that the work you do is meaningless and bears no relation to your *true self* (your "species-essence" for Marx). The song "Work" by Screeching Weasel describes this mundanity. Alienation also arises because wage laborers are a *commodity* for capitalists. As the Briggs illustrate, "A pound of flesh, bought and sold / it grows back, it's only bone . . . trade his collar for your dime . . ." ("Common and Unknown"). Or as Propaghandi said, "They own us, they produce us, they consume us" (". . .And We Thought that Nation-States Were a Bad Idea").

As we ourselves are commodified, we begin to view others as mere objects like ourselves. In this way we become alienated from our peers and view them as competition. Although the Hudson Falcons saw through this capitalist ruse: ". . . all they do is pit us against our neighbors / They say, 'shut up, or we'll give them your job' . . . but United we stand divided we fall / Injustice to one, hurts us all" ("Working Class War"). This process of alienating humans or objectifying subjects as passive, expendable, and determined, is what the philosopher Georg Lukács calls *reification*. In other words, we become cogs in a machine.

All of this is perpetuated by maintaining a status quo ideology. "Superstructure" is a term that the philosopher Antonio Gramsci used to describe the institutions and structures of society that *create* ideology and culture such as art, music, the media, or even school curriculum or religion (see "Your Emotions" or "Trust Your Mechanic" by the Dead Kennedys).

"Hegemony" as Gramsci describes it, is the culture which holds overarching power and domination. So, "hegemonic superstructure" would be the Marxist equivalent of "mainstream" culture, which ideologically undergirds capitalism. But the proletariat have the potential to dismantle this hegemonic superstructure by unifying and collectively fighting for their own class interests if and when they *become aware* or *conscious* of the "relations of production," that is, the relationship between who controls wealth and who does the work to produce it. Lukács theorizes about this process of becoming aware, this *class consciousness*, by asking the question: how could the proletariat break free from the ruling ideology if the ruling ideology dominates everything? Or, to put it another way, how did punk arise out of a sea of mainstream culture? Where do radical ideas come from if the mainstream is, well . . . mainstream? (*History and Class Consciousness*, pp. 46–82).

The answer that Lukács comes to is perspective and community. He thought that the advantage that the proletariat has over the bourgeoisie is their "ability to see society from the center, as a coherent whole" (p. 69). But this perspective that "everything sucks" is not enough to bring about punk rebellion. This would simply be misanthropic individualism (a symptom of reification). Rather, the irony of rebellion is that it is only successful through community. Punk culture doesn't exist without the people who make it up; likewise, the proletariat cannot emancipate itself without uniting.

There is a common misconception that punk is about *individuals* who don't need anybody—oneself against the world. But it is strategically impossible to escape the "hegemonic superstructure" on one's own. So, punk rebellion arose through the *unity* of likeminded, people coming together to combat the status quo. Just as the proletariat, working side by side in a factory, can begin to see and then share their grievances with one another, so too did punks recognize and share their societal grievances among their peers in the scene. ("Just take a look around you, what do you see? / Kids with feelings like you and me / Understand him and he'll understand you / For you are him and he is you . . . If we stand together it will just be the start," Sham 69, "If the Kids Are United").

This collective socioeconomic vantage point and its general cultural attitude has developed into the only music genre that has so thoroughly wrestled with peeling itself away from the mainstream/hegemonic culture. Through this process, punk, as a general culture and artform, has developed an unmistakable *class consciousness*.

From 'No Future for You' to 'No War but the Class War'

We can see three main stages of awareness *en route* to class consciousness within the lyrics. They range from 1. a general discontent with your lot in life, to 2. an awareness that your misfortunes have systemic causes, to 3. full class consciousness as the realization of the social relations of production in tandem with empowerment of the proletariat. Your sense of agency also evolves through these stages. The first stage is devoid of class consciousness but expresses a general nihilistic discontent which is nevertheless effective in creating a sense of not being alone in one's struggles. The second stage is a chrysalis where one not only sees that their struggles are not unique, but also the veils of reification begin to fall, gradually revealing the inner mechanisms of capitalism. In the final stage, class consciousness allows you to see yourself as a catalyst of history thus turning, what Lukács calls a mere "psychological state of consciousness" into strategy and praxis.

Songs of nihilism and alienation are plentiful in punk. They portray degradation ("Kids of the Black Hole," the Adolescents; "Gimmie Heroin," Morning Glory; "Dumpster to the Grave," Star Fucking Hipsters; "Easy Way Out," The Adicts), despondent individualism ("Misanthropic Drunken Loner," Days N Daze), or boredom ("Nowhere to Go", the Varukers; or "Living Dead," A Global Threat). Many songs in this first stage of consciousness are about the particular class of people that Marx calls, the "lumpenproletariat," the lowest rung of the proletariat, the unemployed, the vagabonds, criminals, the 'junkies', or 'squatters'. These people are necessary for capitalism because they serve as a "reserve army of labor" (a surplus population of unemployed people) to keep labor costs low. But while their financial and existential precarity is the result of the forces and relations of capitalist production, the degree of social awareness portrayed in these songs stops at individual experience. This stage of consciousness also applies to the songs depicting the comfortable middle-class who have the 'privilege' of experiencing boredom and consumerist alienation ("TV Party," Black Flag or "Lost in the Supermarket," the Clash).

The songs that lie in the second stage of consciousness evolve from solipsistic nihilism to a systemic awareness of its causes. The lyrics don't point to any solution, there's not yet a development of proletarian agency. But there is more recognition of general systemic exploitation, with the complexity of their analysis lying on a spectrum ("Provide To Be Exploited," Discharger;

"Outrage," the Interrupters; "Fascist," the Minutemen; "Those Anarcho Punks Are Mysterious . . .," Against Me!).

"Franco Un-American" by NOFX is a good illustration of a budding political consciousness. Many of the songs in this second stage are critical of power and authority generally and this topic of anti-authoritarianism and anti-establishment may actually make up the largest number of punk songs. But within this stage, there are also many songs that extend beyond a "fuck the system" mentality to a more specific *class* antagonism, meaning they recognize that the interests of "the bosses," "the businessmen," or "the elites" don't align with the interests of the workers or the common people ("Essential," Branded Identity; . . . "And the world files for Chapter 11," The Flatliners). Take these lyrics for example: "The businessman whose master plan controls the world each day / Is blind to indications of his species' slow decay . . . The masses of humanity have always had to suffer" (Bad Religion, "Suffer"); or "Working forty hours for a corporate fuck / a pinhead with power, make your life suck / No Chance for a raise, and no more dough / Say you're a punk, and go too slow" (River City Rebels, "Here or to Go").

However, even the songs that express a more explicit understanding of class relations, would not yet be considered *full* class consciousness or "revolutionary consciousness" because, as Lukács and Gramsci would add, they have yet to describe the moral or historical role of the subject/worker.

The final stage, when we can say that punk is an expression of full class consciousness, arises in the instances where the lyrics express not only an understanding of the *source* of alienation and exploitation but also return agency back to the proletariat. The song "Class War" (originally by The Dils in 1977, then covered by D.O.A. in 1982, and again recently by the Adolescents) states its goals clearly: "I want a war, between the rich and the poor," and confidently, "I wanna fight and know what I'm fighting for." You would discover a very long list if you searched for all the punk songs with "class war" somewhere in the title, lyrics, or theme ("Class War 2000," Good Riddance; "Glass War," NOFX; "Class War," The Baboon Show).

The subject in these songs is no longer pushed around by the whims of capitalist society but is empowered through identification with their class. For example, in the song "Strike" by The Suicide Machines, there is not only an explanation for social ills ("The division of society into two separate classes / there are those of us who work and we make up the masses / slaving for the corporations ranking in the profit . . .") but rather than a nihilistic reprise, there is a call to action: "Unite and you will find that strength is truly found in numbers / and you possess the power to destroy those that you work under / their machine won't operate unless is has an operator . . ." You can also see examples of this third class consciousness stage in the instances when bands, such as the Dropkick Murphys ("Which Side Are You On"), Street Dogs ("There Is Power in a Union"), Anti-Flag ("1915"), Rancid ("Union Blood" and "Harry Bridges"), among others, cover or make reference to the pro-labor folk songs (or movements) of the American progressive and depression era. The lyrics of these songs have straightforward, usually pro-union, messages of mobilizing the proletariat.

Noise for the Masses

Finally, the elements of the music itself (the tempo, dynamics, and structure) when combined with the lyrics, create an affect that induces comradery and the semblance of class agitation. *Affect* is a concept referring to an externally induced shift in our experiential state or an "intensity" that induces, or *moves,* us to act. This concept of 'affect' was developed by various philosophers like Baruch Spinoza (1677), Henri Bergson (1896), Gilles Deleuze and Felix Guattari (1980), and more recently by Brian Massumi and Eve Sedgwick in "affect theory." According to Deleuze, artists create affects, which gives them a powerful potential for inducing social change.

A faster than average tempo and *forte/fortissimo* dynamics is frequently a defining feature of punk which creates a sense of youthful enthusiasm, as well as urgency, agitation, and restlessness—a good jolt, perhaps, to wake from the "dogmatic slumber" of suburban complacency and working-class woes. The affective states generated by these songs, whether they be a fast and loud cacophony or a driving anthem, energize the crowd into a paradoxically unified undulation of chaos.

However, there is an interesting structural and rhythmic commonality among the punk songs that are *explicitly* class conscious (those that fall into subgenres sometimes called "street punk" or "Oi!"). These songs embrace a simpler and melodic style, often with sing-along choruses. Similar to old pro-labor folk songs, the simplicity of the form allows it to be remembered and repeated. This subgenre of punk often contains "gang vocals," a portion of the song that is yelled/sung by a crowd (The Briggs, P.O. Box, Bombshell Rocks). All of this together, the simplicity of form and easy-to-remember lyrics with gang vocals is emulating the style of military cadence and traditional work songs—songs sung/chanted while marching or working. The call-and-response that one often hears shouted at protests is also derived from military cadence.

The purpose of military cadence and work songs is to create and maintain unity among the ranks of soldiers or workers (or protestors) *through* its simplicity of form and rhythm. Many Celtic punk bands use the style of a sea shanty, which is a specific type of work song whose cadence accompanied the rhythmic cadence of laborers on a ship ("The Galley Slave," Flatfoot 56). Their purpose was to synchronize group effort (the same purpose as land-based work songs). Rudimental snare drumming originated in martial music to boost soldiers' morale and arouse enthusiasm (or demoralize the enemy); this is also incorporated into many punk songs (usually in the introduction, bridge, or breakdown) with a similar intended effect on the psyche of the crowd. As working-class punk songs adopt these elements, they create the same effect of engendering a sense of unity and camaraderie among the crowd, as well as invoking a sense of group empowerment as your voice becomes incorporated into a single powerful call.

There are hundreds of songs that contain these elements and fit into the various stages of class consciousness. But we can use "The Power's Out," by Flogging Molly, to illustrate the creative use of musical elements in combination with lyrics that narrate a transformation of class consciousness. First, the drumbeat of the song maintains a simplistic rhythm, reminiscent of work songs and even chain gang songs. Moreover, the drum is made to sound mechanical or hammer-like since the reverb in which it is recorded is distant and open creating an ambience like that of a large industrial warehouse. The guitar is also overdriven, invoking a similar industrial tone, add to that the actual machine sounds in the first couple of choruses, and you have a perfect setting for the content of the song. The lyrics in the beginning of the song use a first-person singular point of view and describe a Detroit worker who's lost his job and is scraping to get by with a "pending foreclosure and mountains of debt." This is the first stage of consciousness, where the subject only sees his powerlessness at the mercy of the "natural" laws of capitalism.

By the end of the second verse, he recognizes that these "natural" laws *do* seem to benefit some people: "Yeah the power's out / Guess it's par for the course / Unless you're a blood sucking leech CEO..." At this point we've reached the second stage of consciousness—a recognition of class antagonisms, and a critique of the very functioning of the political economy (the line, "it's the trickle effect" is taking a jab at trickle-down economic theory). By now, the drumming style has evolved from maintaining a simple half-note beat on the 2 and 4, to the rudimentary style of military drumming. Now we are creating an effect of arousing class agitation or rallying the workers. In these middle verses, the subject is now becoming aware of the *value* he creates as a worker ("I could build him a cross with one hand behind back").

In the final section, after a bridge and stripped-down breakdown, the instrumentation returns with a bang—a sudden increase in dynamics and the introduction of gang vocals. The lyrics also suddenly change into first-person *plural*, from an "I" to "we" and depict a collective, fully conscious, unified front ("From the town of Detroit where we fight till we drop . . . / We don't want your pity we just want a job . . . / There's no shame in us asking with some self-respect / But don't leave it much longer; we're human at best"). This last part of the song, with the combination of class-conscious lyrics, with musical elements such as gang vocals, rudimentary drumming, and the simple work-song tempo and form, create an affect-inducing artistic representation of the final stage of class consciousness.

However, Lukács and Gramsci add one more qualification. It's not enough that we become *aware* of class conflict; thereafter, there must be unified collective action, theory must turn to praxis, agitation must turn to mobilization. Because it's only when we understand the historical role and moral responsibility of our class that we can be said to be fully conscious. Punk is not only a music form, but also a community that attempts to sustain itself outside of and in opposition to mainstream culture. But this is oftentimes an uphill battle.

Gramsci and Lukács rejected the "determinist interpretation" of Marx—the belief in the historical inevitability of capitalism's demise due to economic forces and the material conditions of the proletariat being so dire as to invoke revolution. Rather, class consciousness is only a possibility; overcoming reification is a never-ending laborious process that requires discipline from all workers as *active* subjects. So, the question is, will punk be able to maintain its revolutionary potential?

Rock for Sustainable Capitalism

They're gonna destroy what we worked so hard to create
A subculture of consciousness against a bourgeois society state.

—Against All Authority, "Corporate Takeover"

Punk exemplifies a general culture of egalitarianism where hierarchical lines of division can be blurred. The musicians are not meant to be celebritized and seen as more important than the audience. The crowd could jump on stage and the band could jump into the crowd. Mosh pits are a site of unified aggression, but if someone falls, they are immediately helped back up. People in the scene establish practices of mutual aid, such as allowing traveling bands to sleep in their homes or using the money earned from a show to contribute to a local cause. The idea of mutual aid was developed by the anarchist philosopher Peter Kropotkin who claimed that evolutionarily, "sociability is the greatest advantage in the struggle for life" (*Mutual Aid*, 1902). These punks intuitively know that the only way to survive is together.

As a vanguard of *full* class consciousness, the scene takes the "means of production" into their own hands (owning their own work materials and the resulting profits of their labor through communal organization and decision making). So, rather than relying on a record company or studio, a band will record their own music and distribute it in makeshift cardboard cases or digital links. Rather than conforming to the influence of consumer culture, people will use thrift stores or customize their own clothes. Rather than relying on promoters, bands will organize their own shows in dingy local dive bars, abandoned oil-stained warehouses, a local skatepark, or the basement of their friend's friend. Rather than relying on mainstream sources of media, people will create handmade zines; patches and buttons are DIY publicity; and bands get free advertising spots by pasting their band stickers on the crumbling, graffiti and piss-stained walls of punk venue bathrooms. Although much of this is done out of economic necessity, it is still true that necessity is the mother of invention. Besides, the modest destitution of it all is embraced as quintessentially "punk."

This cultural resistance to bourgeois ideology is what Antonio Gramsci calls a "proletarian culture." But this is not always easy to maintain. It's difficult to escape the material confines of capitalism, and "selling out" begins to gain more appeal. Lukács warns that class consciousness will lose its revolutionary potential when the unified community of the proletariat begins to disintegrate and loses its self-awareness and self-efficacy as the historically revolutionary class that it is. This problem, Lukács says, can be avoided with a political party; but punks can keep *their* "party" going through continual community building and a clear and consistent message.

A more insidious threat is pointed out by Gramsci who warns that the capitalist state appropriates subversive culture. He says that the capitalist state will try to maintain legitimacy by allowing dissonant voices to express themselves, ultimately turning them into, what author Ben Davis calls, "meaningless symbolic theater" (*9.5 Theses*, p. 68).

We can see this capitalist appropriation occurring when bands (even those with subversive messages) get signed on major record labels, when big multi-staged festivals like Warped Tour or Riot Fest are manacled to a slew of corporate sponsors, when new radio-friendly bands emerge and imitate the sound/style but not the message ("Just can't stop it, got it at Hot Topic / No need to read the lyric sheet / It's the same old song, the same old harmony . . . Get all my ideas from MTV . . . Prepackaged punk conformity." Pop Punk Band, *Avoid One Thing*). This is a continual internal conflict within punk: bands try their best to distance themselves from this process of self-commodification, or "selling-out," while also attempting to survive / 'make a living' in the industry.

The roads to revolution are long and hard, and each one of them is necessary though not sufficient. One of those necessary roads is the battle for ideology. The original punk ideology was birthed through the recognition of common working-class struggles and all its symptoms (alienation, reification, precarious living and employment, addiction, consumerism, and its resulting debt).

Punk grew into the global anathema of mainstream culture and music *because* of its existence within, and vantage point from a disenfranchised class. It has played a significant role in disrupting the corporate music industry—a hegemonic disseminator of bourgeois ideology. Punk is now at a formidable crossroads. Will it maintain its vanguard, or will it simply become "rock for sustainable capitalism"?

V

---

*Punk and the
Wider Culture*

20
Punks Pissing People Off

JUNEKO J. ROBINSON, A.K.A. GITTE SYNDROME

Punk rock: a style of rock'n'roll characterized by lyrics dealing with anarchy, violence, sex, drugs, and other subculture themes and by performers, dressed outlandishly, who engage in odd or disgusting behavior.

—1979 *Hammond Almanac*

Persecution is a recurring theme in punk. "Up Against the Wall Punk Rockers" by author, January 1981, featuring lyrics from the Circle Jerks' "Back Against the Wall."

Being stared at is a problem for punks. But not in the way you would think. After coaxing my mom to buy me my first punk rock album—the Sex Pistols' *Never Mind the Bollocks* on January 21st 1978 (yes, I dated my albums)—I finally pulled the trigger in 1980: I bought a thrift-store men's trench coat, blazer, and dress shirt (which I covered with graffiti), bleached half of my hair yellow, and fully adopted the punk aesthetic.

I wasn't surprised that my new friends and I were stared at. Coming home from fashion school, my older sister's chic appearance garnered stares in our small suburban town. What did surprise me, however, was the level of hostility and harassment that we encountered.

Those who weren't punk in the suburbs, small towns, and rural parts of America circa 1980 cannot fathom the level of hostility and violence that we routinely experienced. Although individual experiences varied, something we all shared to some degree was continual discrimination, harassment, threats, and, at times, physical violence at the hands of non-punks. We weren't alone. Attacks on punks by the rightwing National Front were a staple of 1970s London. Decades later, moral panics about "crusty" punks, sometimes-homeless itinerant punks, encouraged public harassment and police brutality from Montreal to New Orleans (*Pretty in Punk*, p. 63). The 1997 murder of Brian Deneke exemplified how looking punk could be fatal (Alioto 2012). But, apart from Lauraine Leblanc's *Pretty in Punk,* these experiences have rarely been shared with outsiders. The common wisdom was that we "got shit," "because you look like you're ready for a fight," according to a former teacher, "because you dress provocatively" or were "trying to get a reaction." Some punks have said as much. Yet none of these answers explain the constant policing of our appearance or the criminal behavior we experienced. Just what was it that pissed so many people off about punk?

Getting Shit

San Francisco Bay Area's "punk problem," circa 1980, was a group of youngsters who 1. organized around a new form of music; 2. dressed unconventionally; 3. purportedly engaged in deviant behavior; and 4. expressed controversial sentiments. The local news coverage of the Sex Pistols' 1978 North American tour entailed constant updates on the band's visa status with footage of them traversing airports surrounded by reporters. Beneath all the news anchor prattle, there was a barely-concealed panic reminiscent of *The Invasion of the Body*

Snatchers ("They're Coming! They're Coming! They're Here!").
As an eleven-year-old, I thought it was bizarre.

For a time after Sid Vicious's death, there was a dearth of
local media interest until the early 1980s when media discovered the "new" music scene, which actually started back in
1976. Despite this, our presence on the streets was routinely
met with hostility, threats, and violence. A survey of friends
revealed what I already knew: we were routinely spit on and
had food and garbage thrown at us. Bottles and other objects
were hurled from passing cars. Young men bared their posteri-
ors or urinated out of car windows at us. Groups of "rednecks,"
dressed in cowboy gear, or "jocks" (athletes, especially football
players) would drive from surrounding exurbs into San
Francisco searching for victims to attack for fun. If they
couldn't find gay men, they would look for punks to beat up. (I
know this because that's what many of these lunkheads would
disclose to us when they were threatening us.) Our unisex
appearance routinely elicited being called "punk-rock-faggots"
and "punk-rock-dyke-whores."

Guys I knew were repeatedly threatened with guns or
beaten up. One was seriously injured when struck by a beer
bottle thrown from a passing car. As he lost consciousness and
two female friends tried to staunch the bleeding, passersby,
including an elderly woman, jeered at them. As teenaged girls,
we were sexually harassed and threatened with violence,
including rape. Being female didn't protect us: Leblanc wrote
about a sanitation worker attempting to kick her in the head
while riding by on the back of his garbage truck and other
unprovoked attacks by men and boys (p. 166). A fifteen-year-old
friend had her face cut with a scalpel in an unprovoked attack.
The EMTs laughed as they loaded her into the ambulance.
Most harassers were men who felt it was their privilege to
police our appearance. They'd demand to know why we "fucked
up" our appearance to make ourselves unattractive to them,
though that didn't stop them from coming onto me when I was
fourteen. What was it that pissed people off about our appearance? Even our detractors couldn't articulate it.

Cease to Exist

As a philosophy of human existence, existentialism's kinship
with punk might not be apparent, but for some, like Stuart
Hanscomb, it's obvious (Hanscomb, p. 4). My dissertation advi-
sor once remarked that she found something rather "adolescent" about existentialism due to its unrelenting scrutiny of

Punks protest alleged police harassment in September at the Delmonte Deli, 339 Eddy St.
They claim police use curfew and noise laws on their music, and claim police ordered
"punks" to leave the Deli at around 3:00 a.m. and arrested them for curfew violations. They
maintain that they had parents' permission to be there that late.   Photo by Bob Dey

"Why is punk rock against the law?" Punks protest police harassment and
the closure of their clubs. I refused to pose for the camera. S.F. Progress,
October 12th 1980.

every minute action and its high level of responsibility, which
both Jean-Paul Sartre and Simone de Beauvoir saw as the fundamental burden of humans. She wasn't far off. In existentialism, thinking is action. Humans create values by acting in the
world therefore we are fully responsible for them even when
there are unintended consequences. For existentialists, freedom is our unlimited ability to think. It is *ontological* freedom,
meaning that it's an integral feature of our being. That doesn't
mean that there aren't consequences for this freedom.
Existentialists understood the difficulties of living with other
free people. However, although we all face obstacles, how we
respond to them is not causally determined. We can laugh, cry,
conform, rebel, adapt, despair, sublimate, revolutionize or rede-
fine the same situation. If every human action creates (or
affirms) value and we are responsible for the results of those
values, which in turn spur other activities that create value,
there's no escaping, which is why philosophically existentialism is seen as so unrelenting and existentialists see our freedom as burdensome. Punk is too. While most focus on punk's

purported rejection of many mainstream values, equally important is our unrelenting judgment of ourselves, both as a collec-
tivity and as individuals.

Both punk and existentialism recognize certain features of
the human condition, locate individual struggle within it, and
share certain attitudes and responses to it (p. 4). Hanscomb
also sees a shared emphasis on freedom (conceptualized as
the rejection of many mainstream values and a creative do-it-
yourself or "DIY" ethic), anti-complacency, and authenticity. For
existentialists, freedom is the defining characteristic of human
existence. It is for punks too. Hanscomb emphasizes punk's
desire for alternative ways of life, extending it beyond mere
social freedoms to a "desire to be, or feel, a certain way" (p. 11).
For me, punk's exaltation of freedom stems from a desire to be
unshackled by authority, tradition, dogma, popularity, and
"common sense." Thus, punk freedom is a skepticism about
what existentialists term "facticity," those pre-existing facts
about the world, which are beyond individual control.

We might be unable to control everything in the world, but
we can choose what attitude to adopt towards it. Regarding
complacency, existentialists and punks believe in the critical
examination of everything, especially that which most avoid
questioning out of habit, laziness, deference to authority or
peer pressure. The point isn't criticism or rebellion for their
own sakes, but to live according to (hard)core values that allow
for individuality and, maybe, a better world. Questioning leads
to another key value: authenticity. For existentialists, authenticity means taking responsibility for your freedom by recognizing that, while nothing objectively guarantees the validity
of your choices, you must still choose which values to live by
and follow through. It also means embracing ambiguity by recognizing that we are both factitious (consisting of things we
cannot change) and transcendent (consisting of how we choose
to react to our facticity). Authenticity is also key in punk:
People should live according to their most deeply held values
and assume (transcendence) the consequences regardless of
difficulty or social disapproval (facticity).

Although Sartre and Beauvoir were activists, existentialism doesn't require any particular political stance. Authenticity applies to individuals not groups, which are inherently
unreliable. Similarly, punk was too individualistic to ever
become a unified political movement. Punks don't agree on
everything, though values like freedom and a DIY ethic, are
shared by most. But although Hanscomb doesn't articulate
what that punk desire is, beyond a DIY ethic, I think it's

about deliberately assuming a sometimes-difficult way of life. Punks admire toughness, courage, resolve. For many, it was all about the struggle: what Sartre and Beauvoir called "existential responsibility." Given these similarities, existentialism is a perfect tool for examining punk.

I Am a Cliché

To existentialists, warring is constant between our conception of ourselves and that of others. In *Being and Nothingness*, Sartre describes being caught peeping through a keyhole out of "jealousy, curiosity, or vice" (p. 347). Upon discovery, the "peeper" suddenly realizes that *he* is the object of the other person's gaze. Although this may be his only transgression, he becomes, in the eyes of the witness, a deviant whose actions permanently stain his identity and social standing.

Punk has also largely been seen as deviant. Public opinion built on existing tropes about youth in general, since even "good" teenagers were a suspect class requiring constant monitoring. Movies such as *Rebel Without a Cause* (1955) and *The Wild Ones* (1953), created an iconography of delinquency, and TV depictions of punk on *CPO Sharkey* (1978), *CHiPs* (1982), and *Quincy ME* (1982), reinforced them. If hippies raised concerns, the Manson Family whose most notorious members were from white, middle-class, church-going families, sounded an alarm. Popular magazines in the 1970s lamented the epidemic of delinquency, drugs, dropping out, running away, and pregnancy amongst white middle-class youth while movies such as *Last Summer* (1969), *Go Ask Alice* (1973), *Outrage!* (1973), *Born Innocent* (1974), *Sara T.: Portrait of a Teenage Alcoholic* (1975), *The Death of Ritchie* (1977), and *Over the Edge* (1979) reflected widespread fears about incorrigible, amoral middle-class white suburban kids. Although some early programs portrayed punk as a cultural or artistic phenomenon, it was still interpreted within the context of an already-existing unease with youth in general.

The lack of scholarly research to counter media sensationalism added to punk's dangerous image. Those behind the mid-Eighties moral panic were what Howard S. Becker referred to as self-appointed moral entrepreneurs: rule enforcers largely from law enforcement and education who equated punk with delinquency. One 1988 report alleged that, far beyond white supremacist gangs, "the most troublesome and numerous of the white gangs are youths involved in punk rock" (National School Safety Center, p. 18). The lack of evidence establishing a causal connection between punk and delinquency was irrelevant (Rosenbaum and Prinsky 1991). Parents were urged to enroll in "de-punking" programs like Back in Control for training in authoritarian parenting and martial arts (Kobayashi, p. 4). Predictably, one study found that ten out of twelve hospitals recommended *psychiatric commitment* for a teenager described over the phone by a fictitious father as getting good grades, not abusing drugs or alcohol, and neither suicidal, violent, nor depressed but dressing "weird" and listening to "horrible" music. To a hammer, everything looks like a nail. According to Becker, prior to 1963, deviance research was primarily concerned with why people do it (*Outsiders*, p. 39). The assumption was that there was "something about the wrongdoers that led people . . . to violate otherwise widely accepted norms" (p. 210). Although deviance studies moved on, "get-tough" policies against what was predominately a music subculture continued to be touted by moral entrepreneurs interested in maximizing their power (p. 143) and legitimizing their specious interpretations of punk as if it was 1962.

Unlike criminal subcultures, however, punk is a consciously reflective subculture: its purpose is to illuminate features of the dominant culture while providing succor, common knowledge, shared values, and a codified system of symbolism to its adherents not widely-shared by outsiders (Levine and Stumpf 1983). Some studies note that "many of the values of deviant groups reiterate in a distorted or heightened form the concerns of outside adults (Hebdige, p. 76). Others hold that a subculture's function is to express and attempt to resolve the hidden or unresolved contradictions in the dominant culture (p. 77). Thus, societies get the deviance they deserve (Schur 1980). Punk's relationship to society is complex, dynamic, symbiotic, and dialectical with both incorporating, influencing, accommodating, rejecting, and reflecting one another. Its criticism of the dominant culture and use of certain visual tropes were aestheticized into forms of visual and auditory resistance.

The London punk scene emerged during a "strange apocalyptic summer" of unprecedented heatwaves, drought, economic turmoil, racial conflict, labor unrest, rightwing extremism, IRA bombings, and a general feeling of doom (Hebdige, pp. 23–25). "Apo-calypse was in the air" in many other far-flung locales. Golnar Nikpour sees punk's simultaneous emergence in 1970s Istanbul, São Paulo, Tokyo, Mexico City, Stockholm, and Warsaw as a reaction to twentieth-century globalization (Nikpour 2012). Water-gate, skyrocketing crime, stagflation, urban decay, gas shortages, the Vietnam War, the Three Mile Island nuclear accident, and public anger at corporate shenanigans such as the exploding Ford Pinto, poisonous products, and cancer caused by the environmental contamination of places like Love Canal, ravaged American optimism and idealism. Beset by drought and floods, California's retreat from Sixties idealism was especially acute with the rise of the "yuppies" (young, upwardly mobile urbanites), increasing conservativism, growing homelessness, the assassination of the first openly gay politician Harvey Milk, the Jonestown massacre, and an ageing rock music industry that became more concerned with exclusivity, money, escapism, and treating fans like cattle in huge concert arenas, than with providing creative responses to social turmoil.

Even though most of the rule-breaking on public display was foul language, dressing funny, and slam dancing, punk was singled out as "nihilistic" which, for those who equated the breaking of rules with their absence, meant that punks "didn't believe in anything." This was false. Punks embraced the gap between idealism and reality, which John Marmysz calls "nihilistic incongruity," by self-legislating our own virtue ethics. Seventies society may have been alienated from ideals such as Truth, Goodness, and Justice but we gleaned something worthwhile out of it all.

American Waste

Marmysz sees nihilism as part of the human experience rather than a few angry punks. But nihilism needn't imply despair as Parents of Punkers feared: it can also serve "as a spur to liveliness, activity, and the celebration of life" (p. 5). Punks witnessed society's hypocrisies and failings, which paid lip service to ideals while simultaneously undermining them. As a bi-racial-working-class-female-teenager, I felt I was exposing the hypocrisy of a community that prided itself in its "liberalism" but whose children called me the n-word. When I testified at the trial of the woman who slashed my friend with a scalpel, the prosecuting attorney asked me about our look. Knowing what was on the line, I said:

> It would be considered a rebellious movement. It is anti-racism, anti-colonialism, anti-Naziism. There are no leaders . . . It's totally an individual movement . . . It resembles . . . the hippie movement. Only we are just going about it a different way. They believe in love and peace . . . But that is not what we see when we look at society. We look like we are violent, the way we dress, the leather and chains and whatever. That is simply what we see in society. So, we are kind of reflecting that by the way that we look.

Q: When you say "rebellious" do you mean physically rebellious or do you mean politically rebellious?

A: Politically rebellious. (*People of the State of California v. Lee*, December 13th 1982, pp. 297–98)

Punk's aggressive "witnessing" was creatively incorporated into music, art, and was literally writ large upon our bodies. But we didn't do it *just* to piss people off. We did it for ourselves: as a show of unity, an expression of a shared worldview, and because we loved the aesthetic, which was powerful, artistic, and beautiful. We fused virtually every post-war subculture, every polarizing symbol—from the crucifix to the swastika— and signifier of race, class, and gender, with a good dose of humor and satire, into a complex, highly-localized aesthetic. The reactions of outsiders, while necessary for the spectacle, were tertiary.

The author in 1981. The antithesis of *America's Next Top Model*.

This aesthetic, while initially not overtly labeled as "delinquent" (Dick Hebdige reports, p. 93, that, in England, as soon as the media discovered punk, they invented punk deviance) and "political" only in some vague, contradictory manner, was viscerally provocative because of the inherent power struggle between the seer and the seen. Ideally, human interaction involves mutual respect for one another's autonomy. But, instead of taking existential responsibility for their values, people in bad faith are overly dependent on how others see them. By trying to control how another person sees them, they deny the other's freedom. They also deny their own by regarding themselves as objects just as the keyhole peeper sees himself through the eyes of the witness who objectifies him as a deviant. In contrast, punk revealed the contingency and arbitrariness of peoples' knee-jerk attitudes, but the recipients of our gaze didn't appreciate being exposed for whatever hypocrisy, shallowness, or ignorance we thought they had. With so much at stake, during turbulent times, *this* more than anything, is what enraged people about us.

In Sartre's *No Exit*, three characters find themselves locked in a room together, which they soon realize is Hell. Estelle frantically searches for a mirror to reflect how she sees herself: a seductress whose worth depends upon being desired by men. Executed for desertion, Joseph needs to believe that he is not cowardly. Only Inèz takes responsibility for the cruelty and manipulativeness that led to her murder. Attempting to flee, Joseph can't bear to leave, preferring to eternally try to convince the others to see him as he needs to be seen. This is why, toward the end of the play, Joseph says that Hell is other people.

The anger we provoked was not, to paraphrase Sartre, an idea: it was a passion (*Anti-Semite and Jew*, p. 17). The Seventies were a destabilizing time and our appearance reflected that. If punks didn't exist, someone else would have emerged to provide a scapegoat for peoples' angst. Although the reasons for punks' appropriation of the swastika were complex, controversial within the scene, and differed according to person and place, at the time, many of us felt it represented what was rotten about America: a society steeped in rhetoric about freedom and individuality, but which was deeply conformist, racist, classist, and sexist. Once we saw this, though burdensome, we couldn't un-see it. To paraphrse Black Flag, freedom "holds a double-edge" for punks. As their songwriter Chuck Dukowski wrote:

I don't wanna think
I'm stuck here and I know it
I don't wanna see
Make me close my eyes
I wanna live
I wish I was dead· ("What I See")

By reflecting the wrongfulness of our society, we represented all its artificiality and its arbitrariness. Far from being the peepers, we were the witnesses who exposed and objectified our harassers as they attempted to do to us. Sometimes they called us "unnatural." Because they saw their beliefs and values as 'natural', we were often called 'unnatural'. And, because 'natural' ways of living absolved them from having to assume the "agonizing and infinite" responsibility for their own destiny, they rejected 'aquired opinions' (*Anti-Semite and Jew*, pp. 40 and 19). Someone once told me that punks should be taken to an island and shot. For such people, "There was no question of building a new society . . . only of purifying" the one that already existed (p. 93) because, in the words of Flipper, "Those too afraid to live, demand a sacrifice."

> Can you hear the war cry?
> It's time to enlist.
> The People think as one. The cattle. The crowd.
> Those who are afraid to live demand a sacrifice. They demand a sacrifice. ("Sacrifice")

Some say that we "brought it upon" ourselves. This is partly correct. Those of us who considered ourselves "hardcore" never wavered in the face of public opposition. "Radically transforming your appearance can be an exercise of personal power in a life that feels out of control" (Chapkis, p. 83) so, as young people, we did what we could and accepted the consequences. Eventually, as we aged, many of us moderated our appearances, not because we surrendered, but because we knew who we were and what we believed in, regardless of appearance.

As Sartre said, "I could feel irritability or anger . . . as before a bad portrait of myself, but I could not be touched to the quick" (*Being and Nothingness*, p. 302) because we never accepted society's view of us. As angry youth, we were self-propelled, sometimes unsuccessfully, towards an imperfect ideal, but most of us turned out just fine. The difference now is that people think we've "outgrown" punk. They don't even realize that we're still watching, still reflecting, and still choosing freedom over conformity.

21
Jesus the Punk Rocker

JOSH CANGELOSI

Some punks purport to be "Christian," but does this even make sense? Christian punk may strike many people, especially Christians and punks, as an oxymoron. Indeed, if Christians and punks agree about anything, it's probably that Christianity and punk don't mix.

Christians may consider it offensive to compare what they regard as Jesus "Son of God" to punk "sons of Satan" (the proud title of many punk songs), the sign of the cross to the Number of the Beast (666, also decorating many punk albums), or the virgin birth to sex, drugs, and rock'n'roll. Many Christian pastors vehemently decry punk rock and related musical genres in such terms (Loudwire 2020). In the words of one televangelist, ". . . real rock music is nothing more than Satanic cyanide. Get it out of your house. Throw it out and burn it. It has no place in the house of the righteous" (Hagee 2013).

Punks, often even fiercer critics of Christianity, may consider it a joke to compare their rebellion against religion to the religion against which they rebel. In the words of Leftöver Crack, "if you wanna join us: dial six—six—six / spit on the holy bible and the crucifix" ("The Good, the Bad, and the Leftöver Crack"). Or, as the Dead Kennedys declare, "All religions make me wanna throw up / All religions make me sick / . . . All religions suck" ("Religious Vomit").

Punks' tendency to reject religion should come as no surprise. Religion preaches obedience to God's authority, while punks scream, "Fuck authority" (Pennywise, "Fuck Authority"). Religion enjoys social hegemony, while punks enjoy being social misfits. Religion enjoys the moral majority, which the Dead Kennedys address by saying, "God must be dead if you're alive" ("Moral Majority")—urging listeners to "take your social regulations . . . [and] shove 'em up your ass" ("Halloween"). As critics of society and its religious influence, punks scorn as wrong what the majority preaches as right, when punks regard those norms as oppressive or unjust. In that case, punks profane the sacrosanct and curse those who curse them—as when NOFX, the self-proclaimed "reverend of irreverence" shouts, "Blasphemy / Blasphe-you / . . . I'm gonna projectile puke off a pew / . . . I'm gonna turn your other cheek for you / . . . My intelligence has been insulted / So my tongue lashes out in defense / Anything that is your holy or sacred / I'm gonna desecrate and use in jest" ("Blasphemy"). At first glance, it appears that religion rejects punk, and punk rejects religion.

Upon deeper investigation, however, Christianity and punk are more compatible than many Christians and punks realize. In fact, Christians must become blasphemous punks if they hope to live up to their name, "followers of Christ." After all, just as some Christians reject punk as Satanic, some religious leaders of Jesus's day reportedly denounced him as in league with "the prince of demons" (Matthew 12:24). According to the gospels, they continually labeled Jesus a "blasphemer" and "sinner" for associating with social outcasts (such as prostitutes, foreigners, and others considered "unclean" or "inferior"), for feasting and drinking, and for flouting sacrosanct social/religious norms (such as those mandating ritualistic washing or prohibiting public association with women or Samaritans). When they shamed Jesus, he shamed them right back, often in quite in-your-face fashion: "Woe to you, teachers of the law and Pharisees, you hypocrites! . . . You snakes! You brood of vipers!" (Matthew 23:29, 33). As NOFX describes Jesus, "He's not the white child hippy / He looks and acts more like an indignant Ice-T" ("I'm Going to Hell for This One").

Focusing on the texts, I make no claims about the *historical* Jesus or religious leaders whom Jesus reportedly criticizes. By Jesus I mean Jesus of the Gospels. By "Pharisee," I mean a pharisaical person, not a member of a Jewish sect. Those "Christians" who egregiously make Jesus complicit in their anti-Semitism by quoting Jesus's reported criticisms of this sect are precisely the sort of *pharisaical* people that Jesus (who was Jewish and might have belonged to this sect) criticizes.

Jesus, who blasphemed the religious with the best of punks, lived way outside the box. He was "homeless, propertyless, peripatetic, socially marginalized, disdainful of kinfolk, without a trade or occupation, a friend of outcasts and pariahs, averse to material possessions, without fear for his own safety, a thorn in the side of the establishment" (*Terry Eagleton Presents Jesus*

Christ the Gospels, p. xxii). Call to mind the arrest of Pussy Riot, as reported by Jeffery Taylor, after the band members stormed a cathedral in Moscow with bags on their heads to scream, "Virgin [Mary] . . . become a feminist" ("A Punk Prayer")—or the backlash against Craig Duke when this pastor in a small town in Indiana strutted the stage in full drag to support the LGBTQIA+ community. You'll then have a modern inkling of Jesus's offensiveness to his audience. The religious establishment reportedly considered Jesus so sinful, so blasphemous, and so threatening to their way of life that they plotted to have him crucified for sedition (Matthew 26:59, 27:1–2). Accordingly, when Jesus announced that those who follow him must "take up their cross" (Matthew 16:24), he certainly did not mean to put on a gold chain with one's "Sunday best," take a seat on a cushioned pew, and enjoy sing-alongs to the worship spectacle in comfortably air-conditioned "warehouses of the Lord."

If only congregations today perceived the tortured screams of the crucified and stench of rotting corpses, then the message would be clear: following Jesus originally meant sealing your fate as a complete and utter outcast, much like being punk originally meant marginalizing oneself from society (*Seditious Theology*, pp. 149–181). The sad irony is that churches today, in cases like their persecution of Pussy Riot and Pastor Duke, more often resemble the religious elite that had Jesus crucified than the seditious life of Jesus. Taking up one's cross more often gets interpreted as a call to crucify misfits than to be crucified as a misfit. Such "Christians," if they can be called that, apparently need to be thumped on the head with their own Bibles and lots of punk albums. Fortunately, if "Jesus Christ is coming back / He wants to kick Mel Gibson's ass / . . . and thinks Christians are insane" (NOFX, "I'm Going to Hell for This One").

The same criticism applies to so-called "punks" who have also assimilated into mainstream culture, which punks originally railed against. You won't find much "out of the box" fashion at punk shows, for example, but you will find plenty of black band T-shirts, spikes, and other homogenized fashion trends that have been mass-marketed and mass-produced. Just try dressing outside the norm by wearing your "Sunday best" at a punk show, and see how may dirty looks you get (unless you're the lead singer of T.S.O.L.). You may even get more cold shoulders than you'll get at church if you join the pews as a crossdresser. You may even feel like a crossdresser at church if you show up queer to the punk show (perhaps not even The Queers do that). As Leftöver Crack addresses the punk crowd, "You may be anti-racist, but then yer anti-gay"

("Gay Rude-Boys Unite"). It's time for punks to take a good look at themselves in the mirror and "admit we're all the same / . . . we're all prejudiced / Yeah, we're all hypocrites" (Face to Face, "I Want"). Once outsiders, both Christians and punks are now insiders who need a strong dose of their own original-gangster medicine. In short, both punks and Christians need to be more punk.

Methodology

Let's look at the striking resemblance between "Atheism Anthem" by Leftöver Crack and Jesus's words of woe to religious leaders in Matthew 23. Obviously, these artifacts do not exhaust punk or Christianity. Still, they are good places to begin our examination. If punk rock disagrees with Christian-ity, we would expect to uncover this disagreement in the more anti-religious messages of punk, so what better place to start than with "Atheist Anthem"? In the words of one punk reviewer of the album *Mediocre Generica*, "This is the punkest fucking album I've heard in a while" (Paxton, "Leftöver Crack"). The album, the production of which itself enjoys a punk story of rebellion against record producers (Logan and Gentile, *Oral History*), promotes prototypically punk values like "freedom in my thoughts" ("Born to Die") and "raising your motherfuckin' pipes in the air" (intro to "Homeo-Apathy"). The album continually "spits on the holy bible" ("The Good, the Bad, and the Leftöver Crack"), and this criticism of Christianity climaxes in "Atheism Anthem."

As for how to understand "Christianity" as we examine its compatibility with punk, we do well to focus on the reported words and ministry of Jesus, given that "Christian" means *follower of Christ*. Whereas "Christians" themselves often harshly criticize members of the LGBTQIA+ community, for example, Jesus never once does but reserves *his* harshest criticisms for *religious people* who throw proverbial stones at vulnerable members of society. Accordingly, such "Christians" need a punk-rock-Sunday-school lesson on that passage that presents Jesus's denunciation of stone throwers like them: Matthew 23.

In these respective artifacts, Jesus and punks occupy the position of social outsiders looking in at those who enjoy a privileged place in society due to alignment with hegemonic norms and values: religious leaders who exercise power on "Moses's seat" as authorized interpreters of the law, and Christians who fit comfortably within cultural norms of acceptability due to Christianity's ideological influence.

How the tide has turned! Whereas the cross used to symbolize the socially dammed gasping for breath, now it symbolizes

"Atheist Anthem" and Matthew 23

FROM HIGH-UP ON YER CRUCIFIX
YOU PREACH ABOUT MY TRIPLE-SIX
YOU SPIT ABOUT MY THIS AND THAT
AND YANK AWAY YER WELCOME MAT
WITH A COUPON JESUS CHRIST WILL
   SAVE
SO DON'T YOU CHRISTIANS MISBEHAVE
'CUZ SANTA MAKES THE LIST HIMSELF
AND HE'S ROTTING ON THE WAREHOUSE
   SHELF

*AND ALL THE BOYS IN THE STRAIGHT-
   EDGE SCENE
ARE IN THE BASEMENT HUFFIN' GASOLINE
DEAD–DEAD–DEAD–DEAD
YER GOD IS DEAD TO ME
AND WHEN THE LAWS OF GOD JUST
   MAKE 'YA PISSED
YA' BETTER BECOME AN ATHEIST
DEAD–DEAD–DEAD–DEAD
YER GOD IS DEAD TO ME

WHEN THE GREED OF MAN IS NOT
   APPEASED
ALL WILL ROT, SICK & DISEASED
ONCE AGAIN THE FALLEN TOWERS
THE TORTURED DEATH OF EVERY HOUR
AND AT THE TOLL OF THE FINAL BELL
YOU LEAD THE RIGHTEOUS DOWN TO
   HELL
WHEN ALL THE WORLD IS DEAD BY DAWN
ALL I ASK'S "BRING ME ALONG!"

*
NUCLEAR APOX SPELLS YER DOOM
WITH THE T.V. IN YOUR "LIVING" ROOM
EACH BOMB KILLS A MILLION DEAD
IT MELTS YER SKIN, IMPLODES YER HEAD
AND NOW YOU GET YER JUDGEMENT DAY
YOU THINK YOU'LL FLOAT UP, THEN AWAY
BUT YER GUILTY JUST LIKE EVERYONE
YOU'LL TURN TO ASH WHEN THE BURN-
   INGS DONE

*THERE'S A HUNGER WITHIN YOU
A TAPEWORM DEEP INSIDE
OR MAYBE IT'S JUST CANCER
THE DOCTORS CAN'T DECIDE
BUT YER STOMACH KEEPS ON GROWING
AS YER BODY WASTES AWAY
AND YER JUST GETTING ILL AND WEAKER
EVERY SINGLE FUCKING DAY

WE ARE ALONE
WE ARE ALONE (Leftöver Crack, "Atheist
   Anthem")

Then Jesus said to the crowds and to his disciples: "The teachers of the law and the Pharisees sit in Moses' seat. . . . But do not do what they do, for they do not practice what they preach. They tie up heavy, cumbersome loads and put them on other people's shoulders, but they themselves are not willing to lift a finger to move them. Everything they do is done for people to see: They make their phylacteries [boxes containing scripture versus, worn on forehead and arm] wide and the tassels on their garments long; they love the place of honor at banquets and the most important seats in the synagogues; they love to be greeted with respect in the marketplaces and to be called 'Rabbi' by others. . . . Woe to you, teachers of the law and Pharisees, you hypocrites! You shut the door of the kingdom of heaven in people's faces. You yourselves do not enter, nor will you let those enter who are trying to. Woe to you, scribes and Pharisees, hypocrites, because you swallow up widows' houses, and to cover it up you make long prayers; therefore you will receive the greater condemnation [verse 14, from *Amplified Bible* translation, is not included in all manuscripts]. Woe to you, teachers of the law and Pharisees, you hypocrites! You travel over land and sea to win a single convert, and when you have succeeded, you make them twice as much a child of hell as you are. Woe to you, blind guides! . . . You blind fools! . . . Woe to you, teachers of the law and Pharisees, you hypocrites! You give a tenth of your spices. . . . But you have neglected the more important matters of the law—justice, mercy and faithfulness. . . . You strain out a gnat but swallow a camel. Woe to you, teachers of the law and Pharisees, you hypocrites! You clean the outside of the cup and dish, but inside they are full of greed and self-indulgence. Blind Pharisee! First clean the inside of the cup and dish, and then the outside also will be clean. Woe to you, teachers of the law and Pharisees, you hypocrites! You are like whitewashed tombs, which look beautiful on the outside but on the inside are full of the bones of the dead and everything unclean. In the same way, on the outside you appear to people as righteous but on the inside you are full of hypocrisy and wickedness. Woe to you, teachers of the law and Pharisees, you hypocrites! You build tombs for the prophets and decorate the graves of the righteous. And you say, 'If we had lived in the days of our ancestors, we would not have taken part with them in shedding the blood of the prophets'. So you testify against yourselves that you are the descendants of those who murdered the prophets. Go ahead, then, and complete what your ancestors started! You snakes! You brood of vipers! How will you escape being condemned to hell? Therefore I am sending you prophets and sages and teachers. Some of them you will kill and crucify; others you will flog in your synagogues and pursue from town to town. And so upon you will come all the righteous blood that has been shed on earth." (Matthew 23:1–35) the dominant Christian society that leaves its downtrodden crying, "I give you money, you give me death / You think it's funny, I gasp for breath" (Choking Victim, "Death Song"). How quickly Christians forget that "Foxes have dens, and birds have nests, but the Son of Man [Jesus] has no place to lay his head" (Matthew 8:20). How often they ignore Jesus's warning: "Depart from me . . . into the eternal fire . . . For I was hungry and you gave me nothing to eat, I was thirsty and you gave me nothing to drink, I was a stranger and you did not invite me in, I needed clothes and you did not clothe me, I was sick and in prison and you did not look after me . . . Truly I tell you, whatever you did not do for one of the least of these, you did not do for me" (Matthew 25:41–45). Jesus calls people to look out for outcasts, not to "pray to the Holy Ghost when you suck your host" (PiL, "Religion"), as Jesus apparently believed religious leaders were exploiting widows in his community (Matthew 23:14). Jesus commands, "Love your neighbor as yourself" (Matthew 22:39) and "Do not judge" (Matthew 7:1), not to kick your own children to the curb for being gay. In yanking away their welcome mat to so-called "sinners," so-called "Christians" follow the holier-than-thou religious people who slammed the door in Jesus's face as they labeled him a "glutton and a drunkard, a friend of . . . sinners" (Matthew 11:19).

If readers find themselves on the receiving end of this religious hatred, "Hang in there you're the true thugs and to all you selfish, apathetic, non-empathetic, prejudiced pieces of shit out there . . . BEWARE THE WRATH OF THE VICTIM!!!" (Leftöver Crack, *Mediocre Generica* album notes).

In other words, punks have your back. Like Jesus, they adopt the prophetic posture of moral critics who rail against society's injustices—especially when society preaches oppressive "man-made ideas as commands of God" (Matthew 15:9). One tool in the punk's arsenal is blasphemy, and punks have done everything from decorating album covers with upside-down crosses and pentagrams to storming altars to scream "A Punk's Prayer" (Jeffery Taylor). Not surprisingly, religious people often denounce such acts, much like they denounced Jesus as a low-life deviant "sinner" (John 9:24, Matthew 11:18–19), accused him of blasphemy (Matthew 9:3, 26:65), and threatened to stone him to death and throw him off a cliff (Luke 4:28–29, John 5:18, 8:59, 10:31–33). Nor did society always accept the prophets when they protested injustices and warned of impending judgment using bizarre shock tactics—as when Isaiah reportedly roamed the city naked for three years (Isaiah 20) and Ezekiel baked bread over human feces and lay on his side for over a year (Ezekiel 4). According to theologian Michael Iafrate, ". . . perhaps one reliable indicator of how Christian and how punk something is, is how blasphemous it is" ("Blasphemy, Conversion, and Liberation," p. 190). As he explains, both punk and Christianity "need to be made more punk by being more disruptive of the political and religious status quo of which blasphemy is an important part. Christians in fact already believe that blasphemy is a necessary ingredient to their religious tradition, for . . . Christians worship a person who was executed, in part, for the crime of religious and political blasphemy." Rather than firing pastors who show up in drag to demonstrate love and solidarity for their queer children (Jack Peiser) then, churches ought to follow Jesus by inviting all the outsiders to the feast (Luke 14:13). Rather than spending "the majority of its tax money to stockpile an unusable arsenal of weapons with a potential for destruction on an apocalyptic scale" (Leftöver Crack, *Mediocre Generica* album notes), all for God and country, America ought to live up to its motto by "riding in on a donkey instead of a war horse" (Craig Greenfield, "Yes, Jesus Was a Subversive"). Or, we can keep worshipping the "American Jesus" (Bad Religion) and suffer Leftöver Crack's atheistic curse "to turn to ash when the burning's done" ("Atheist Anthem") or Jesus's theistic curse to be "condemned to hell" (Matthew 23:33).

Punks and Jesus reserve a special curse for the moral hypocrisy of the religious. Both Leftöver Crack and Jesus challenge the perceived hypocrisy of their respective contemporaries—namely, straight edge punks and pharisaical religious leaders. Etymologically, "hypocrisy" means "actor," someone who pretends to be something they aren't (straightedge in public when they huff gasoline in the basement). Hypocrisy is most salient in the form of doing the very thing you blame others for doing, and cautioned against in the phrase "Practice what you preach." Sanctimonious religious people like the ones Matthew describes put on a big dog and pony show so everyone thinks they are God's great gift to humankind, but they are morally bankrupt. They preach a whole lot to everyone else and find only fault. In the end of the passage, they are condemned to hell for violating the very standards that they uncompromisingly hold others to and mercilessly blame others for violating.

Perhaps, purely actors, they don't even believe what they preach but lord over others just to serve themselves. In that case, they are dangerous psychopaths who forfeit their chance for genuine human relationships. Or perhaps they believe what they preach but do not recognize how miserably guilty they are by their own standards—that's how blameworthy they are for doing what they all too eagerly blame others for doing. In that case, punks must continue to relieve these "whitewashed tombs" of such ignorance: "Stained glass windows keep the cold outside / While the hypocrites hide inside" (PiL, "Religion"). Or, perhaps they're just weak-willed like the rest of us who knowingly fail to live up to our own standards, doing what we judge we ought not do, with the added hypocrisy that they judge others instead of just themselves (or, in Jesus's words, "look at the speck of sawdust in their brother's eye and pay no attention to the plank in their own eye," Matthew 7:3). In that case, they do well to heed Jesus's warning, "Do not judge, or you too will be judged" (Matthew 7:1)—or in the words of Metallica and The Chats, "Judge not, lest ye be judged yourself" ("Holier than Thou"). And hopefully their own guilt for knowingly failing to do what they themselves believe they ought will motivate them to follow the Golden Rule (Matthew 7:12), which boils down to the principle *do as you would have others do*—that is, *practice what you preach*. If all else fails, Jesus promises to exact poetic justice in the afterlife: "For in the same way you judge others, you will be judged, and with the measure you use, it will be measured to you" (Matthew 7:2). This warning should lead all Christians to heed Jesus's charge to ". . . let the one who has never sinned throw the first stone" (John 8:7).

Jesus's Punk Rock Ethic

Punks should find Jesus's ethic quite attractive, despite the way they detest many Christians' "holier than thou . . . one way morality" (Pennywise, "My God"). From a personal perspective, Jesus offers an attractively *authentic* and *free* starting place in ethics. In calling us to do as we would have others do, to live up to *our own* moral standards, the ethic essentially calls us to live as *we* see fit. The ethic calls us not only to live authentically according to our own standards but also to live *freely*, insofar as free will theorists are correct that paradigm cases of acting freely involve acting as we see fit. The ethic also appeals to those who are skeptical of the value of conforming to particular societal or religious norms.

Society may tell us that we ought to submit like good, modest Christians when actually we prefer to speak our minds and join SlutWalks. In this case, having to measure up to what society prescribes diminishes our sense of free agency. Accordingly, punks who value individuality and autonomy ought to appreciate Jesus's ethic. Far from calling us to do what the world demands and we denounce, the ethic calls us to do what *we* demand in calling us to avoid the hypocrisy of doing the very thing we blame. An ethic that urges us to freely do what *we* demand and blames us for doing what *we* regard as blameworthy gives meaning to Jesus's words to the weary and burdened that his ". . . yoke is easy and . . . burden is light" (Matthew 11:28–30). If anything, we may regard Jesus's ethic as potentially too light, for fear of people's poor standards. If, however, we have faith in people's capacity for moral knowledge when aided by the moral protest of punks, Jesus's minimalistic ethic looks like a good place to start.

While debates about what's objectively right (or whether objective morals even exist) go on forever, we can at least work on living up to the moral standards we've got. If Jesus is right that we'll all be judged by our own standards in the afterlife, so that no one has an excuse, we had better live up to our subjective standards, for they are the objective standards by which we'll be judged.

Nor do we have to wait for the afterlife to be judged by our own standards. We already judge ourselves whenever we feel guilty or shameful for acting contrary to our better judgment. Others will also take great delight in blaming us for doing what we blame them for doing. So even in the here and now we do well to practice what we preach and judge not, lest we be judged. Punks run a particularly high risk in judging others because, let's face it, punks are no saints like Jesus and, thus, have little standing to start flipping tables in blame (Matthew 21:12). That's why punks should be quite tempted to turn the other cheek (Matthew 5:39). Still, somebody has to do the dirty job of calling people out on their hypocrisy, even if the blame probably will fly back in the blamer's hypocritical face.

The Hardcore Heritage

Jesus is a theist, and our track is "Atheist Anthem," so don't we have a logical contradiction—namely, that followers of Jesus believe that God exists, while punks believe that God doesn't exist? Our anthem not only alludes to Friedrich Nietzsche's proclamation that "God is dead" but also concludes by groaning "We are alone" after giving an object lesson on the problem of evil (which questions how God can exist in light of all the suffering in the world). Anyone who has seriously grappled with this problem knows that rote Christian responses like "God had to give Adam and Eve free will to sin in the Garden of Eden" are problematic. So, sweeping generalizations aside, we can understand why the intro to "Atheist Anthem" complains that Christians often look "for easy answers, and they're too close-minded to look anywhere beyond their local church, or whatever the ignorant masses say is true."

Nevertheless, in light of the striking similarity between Jesus's and punks' social station as misfits and messages about morality and religious hypocrisy, the suggestion that only atheists can be punks should strike us as equally closed-minded. What about agnostics, for instance, who believe neither that God exists nor that God does not exist, are they allowed into the punk show? Or what about queers, are they invited to the punk show or heaven?

Even Jesus tells sanctimonious religious hypocrites to go to hell, but pretty much everyone else gets invited to the party, even if they don't wear the same spikes or see the world in quite the same way. (The best seats in the house go to punk prophets, prostitutes, and thieves on the cross; those who practice what they preach; and those who feed the hungry, house the stranger, and visit the prisoner.) Otherwise, punks are just as guilty of the very intolerance, apathy, and hypocrisy they detest.

In this way, whether you're a punk seems to be less about where your beliefs happen to land on whether God exists, and more about whether you take up your cross like Jesus and Pussy Riot by risking social crucifixion for speaking truth to power and injustice. Punk rockers and Christians must ask themselves, "When did punk rock [and Christianity] become so safe? / When did the scene become a joke?" (NOFX, "Separation of Church and Skate"). Both must find a way to start living up to their own hardcore heritage, lest they get fully absorbed into the "masses of asses" (L7, "The Masses Are Asses").

Until all-too-comfortable "punks" and "Christians" do, they both risk becoming oxymorons.[1]

---

[1] Thanks to Josh Heter, Richard Greene, Kita Johnson, and René Baston for helpful comments on earlier drafts.

22
Punk Rock Saves Lives

R.W. Main

Despite popular conception, punk rock is not the product of cis, white, misogynist youth culture. Punk has, since its beginnings, been queer.

The iconic mid-Seventies punk look has its origins in BDSM gear and other items taken from sex shops. Among those shops was the aptly named "Sex," owned by Malcolm McLaren, who briefly managed the NY Dolls before becoming Svengali to the Sex Pistols: "And the store, Sex, had a definite ideology, it wasn't about selling anything, it was about creating attitude" (Malcolm McLaren, quoted in *Please Kill Me*). Stylistically and historically, punk overlaps with and draws on drag, Glam Rock, and gender androgyny, and whatever it is that John Waters and Divine were doing.

Even the word itself is rooted in queerness. The term "punk" has been variously used as a derogatory epithet since the sixteenth century. It's earliest usage (one employed by Shakespeare himself) indicated a prostitute. However, prior to the mid-twentieth century, the term was most commonly used to refer to a young man or boy who was made to be the sexual partner of an older man, often by force. Other uses refer simply to someone contemptible or unworthy of any recognition. According to James Grauerholz, who was William S. Burroughs' editor and business manager, "punk" was an allusion to characters in Burroughs's counter-culture novel *Junkie*. Burroughs himself said, "I always thought a punk was someone who took it up the ass" (quoted in *Please Kill Me*, p. 230).

This derogatory sense was appropriated in the early 1970s and used to refer an artistic movement and burgeoning culture. Punk itself becomes a celebration of the weird, rejected, othered, and outcast, a dialectical reflection of the contradictions of its time. It includes a loose set of philosophies that tend to endorse the most rejected and reviled ideas and practices. One thing that's clear from its name and history, but frequently overlooked, is its close association with queerness in gender and sexuality.

In his 1975 book on popular music, Serge Denisoff says: "Punk rock challenged the norms of social etiquette. Performers appear to be championing those aspects of life which society considers perverse, deviant, and grotesque. Violence, homosexuality, transvestism [sic] and infanticide all may be props for the act" (p. 26). This appropriation of the rejected actually has a supportive effect on the outcast and reviled, as (philosopher) Jesse Prinz notes:

> . . . while misogyny, homophobia, and other forms of hate speech have been common in punk, the movement itself also initially had many more openly gay and female performers than mainstream rock, paving the way for greater tolerance in music. Political incorrectness is used to mock bigotry and indict what is perceived as the hypocrisy of the prevailing social order. ("The Aesthetics of Punk Rock," p. 585)

Punk is a celebration of the weird, rejected, othered and outcast, and often endorses the most despised and reviled ideas and practices. As indicated by its name, punk appropriates such offensive and immoral identities, crafting its own values in opposition. People who have historically been treated as contemptible and whose very existence is seen as offensive can find in such a space the means by which to re-appropriate that which identifies them as "other" and regain some measure of agency. Often this takes the form of a deliberate inversion of status quo values and leads punk to develop as a celebration of the depraved and vile.

Hatred Is Purity

Of all the mistaken ideals that comprise the history of human thinking, perhaps the most insidious is that of purity. One could make the case that no other abstract concept resulted in as much concrete suffering, both explicitly and under the guise of care and protection. The very concept of purity relies on— and creates—an opposite that is necessarily undesirable, and methods are developed for assessing and excising all such impurities. To be pure is to be homogenous, and anything different is a threat to that purity. In moral terms, to be good is to be like us. Purity implicates value. "Pure gold" and "pure trash" represent the extremes of goodness and badness that purity generates. That which is pure is to be protected—or secured so as to protect us. Purity is what is valuable is to be pursued.

This ideal has guided and been used to justify the great majority of human injustices, like one-drop rules, the pathological focus on female virginity, the need for a priestly caste, eugenics, genocide, and other forms of oppression and suppression. It is also intrinsic to every (non-relativistic) morality. This is why, according to Friedrich Nietzsche, "morality *denies* life" (*The Case of Wagner*, p. xxx).

However, nothing pure appears in the living world. *Inter faeces et urinam nascimur* (We are born between shit and piss). Life is impure from the start, perhaps itself the product of the adulteration of proto-organic compounds. The exceptionless laws describing a world free from the influence of human opinion and limitation have continued to remain just out of reach of the best of our science. It is a myth in the sense that it guides belief and action but is unobservable empirically. Pure purity can only be posited, hoped for, and taken on faith.

Filth and Fury

There is, of course, an alternative mode of valuation that seems to have rid itself of a reliance on the purity myth: art. Here is a practice of creating values in the promotion of life. This is why Nietzsche also says, "Art saves him, and through art life saves him" (*The Birth of Tragedy*, p. 61). It's what leads so many to say things like, "Punk rock saved my life." Just as purity finds its greatest expression in the religious, filth expresses itself in art.

Philosophies of filth are contraries to the myth of purity. "Filth" is, by definition, impure. Philosophies of filth actually have a long history, and one of the first punks in the Western philosophical tradition may have been a contemporary to Plato: Diogenes the Cynic. As with many of the figures of that time, all that we know of Diogenes is second-hand and anecdotal. However, there are significant commonalities in all of these stories. He was named the "Cynic" ("dog") in part because of his practice of living on the streets of Athens and engaging in all forms of indecent behavior from begging to public defecation and masturbation. (When rebuked on the latter he is said to have replied, "Were that I could dispel my hunger by simply rubbing my belly!") Utterly Crust. Philosophically, Diogenes was a counterpoint to Plato's fascistic take on governance and its underlying metaphysical and epistemological principles.

Plato understood the true nature of reality to be located in an unchanging and perfect realm beyond or behind the world we experience through the senses and which could only be accessed by a trained intellect. Everything we take to be in the "real world" is actually a sort of imperfect copy of a perfect Form which is its essence. For example, every circle ever drawn by hand or machine is imperfect in some way. The only "perfect" circle (and therefore the only one that meets the definition of a circle and so is the only real circle) would be a line on which every point is equally distant from a single point not on the line. We can never produce such a circle, but we can know it and that knowledge is truer than any we might acquire by measuring circles in our sensory realm.

Since true knowledge is of this sort, and since philosophy is the only way to achieve such knowledge, the only figure fit to rule, according to Plato, is the philosopher king. Ushering in the reign of such a king and his ideal republic would require raising an entire generation of children separate from everyone else and indoctrinated in the system Plato lays out. The result would be a "pure" society with a rigid class structure, a single ruler and a militant focus. Artists, of course, would be exiled.

Diogenes seems to have thought this was all bullshit. He is said to have heckled Plato at his lectures, making a scene of eating while criticizing Plato's account of Socrates. Plato, Diogenes seems to be saying, was a poser. More importantly, Diogenes committed to living out his critique. He took poverty, nearness to nature and the rejection of prevailing social norms and practices as virtues—entirely at odds with Plato's model of reason and civilization as tending ever away from the natural and the physical toward a higher good. The Dog rejected all forms of authority and political association and supposedly mocked the hot-tempered Alexander the Great directly.

There are no texts from him but the stories about him include a great number of philosophical stunts, such as carrying a lit lantern in the daylight in search of a good man. Plato's mentor and hero Socrates had, by his own account, attempted to direct Athens away from their false beliefs masquerading as knowledge and toward vital matters such as how one ought to live in order to be a "good man." Moreover, he did so not by writing but by doing. He, like Diogenes, is said to have lived quite modestly, never taking money for teaching because he never taught, and of being more at home in his animal skin. He was untroubled by the weather and wore the same old clothing year-round, drank all others under the table without any visible effects and enjoyed many of the finest young lovers the youth of Athens had to offer. The Cynic was a walking rebuke of everything Plato espoused and a challenge to his place as Socrates' pupil. To Diogenes, Plato was a sell-out.

This is how culture "works," and grows. We interpret those who came before us, and with each interpretation things change a bit. This divergence leads to conflict, resistance, and the solidification of principles and positions. That is, culturally speaking, everything gives birth to its opposite. Giordano Bruno, another potential philosophical punk, called this the "coincidence of contraries" and it had a significant influence on James Joyce, who was certainly a literary punk. Socrates said and did things that Plato understood in a certain way. Diogenes understood them differently and responded by becoming the anti-Plato in thought and action. Punk indeed.

Subhumanism

The concepts of filth and purity are inexorably bound up with issues of class and its moralization. There are people whose very existence is offensive to others. The subcultures surrounding punk (and similar "counter-cultures" like drag and cult cinema) begin with and develop through the appropriation of abject identities. Punk appropriates the filthy as resistance to the tyranny of purity.

This is not necessarily a replacement of one value set with another (although it can be) nor the denial of the possibility of all values (though it can be this as well), but the defiance of an imposed value structure that inhibits freedom and human dignity. Dr. Greg Graffin, PhD and lead vocalist of Bad Religion emphasizes this in his "Punk Manifesto":

> Punk is: the personal expression of uniqueness that comes from the experiences of growing up in touch with our human ability to reason and ask questions; a movement that serves to refute social attitudes that have been perpetuated through willful ignorance of human nature; a process of questioning and commitment to understanding that results in self-progress, and through repetition, flowers into social evolution; a belief that this world is what we make of it, truth comes from our understanding of the way things are, not from the blind adherence to prescriptions about the way things should be; the constant struggle against fear of social repercussions. ("A Punk Manifesto")

Punk art is not redemptive. Rather, it maintains that redemption is unnecessary. Its immoralism does not seek to replace one set of values with another—it is the rejection of moralism and objective morality itself.

Live My Life to Destroy Your World

Punk is both destructive and creative. According to McLaren, "the establishment's notion of bad needed to be redefined. And the notion of good meant to me things that I felt absolutely needed to be destroyed" (quoted in *Please Kill Me*, p. 265). The only rule is to break all the rules, and this creates a sort of self-corrective momentum to punk. One could make a strong case that so-called "nazi punk" or even "pop punk" simply aren't (punk, that is). They could only be considered punk by virtue of a model of musical genre that treats art as autonomous and with its own set of recognized elements of artistic composition. Punk, however, is not reducible to a musical genre, nor a (contested) set of performances and recordings. Punk is not unique in this respect—the same can and has been said of hip hop, for example.

Like hip hop, any attempt at a definition of punk must be able to cope with its multi-modality—neither is just music. Neither can be captured solely in terms of genre, medium, style (although stylistic elements are recognizable and significant to both), nor in terms of a specific period or location (although scenes are a central feature of both). Moreover, the cultural and societal importance of each cannot be explained or understood by the majority of the prevailing theories of art. Both are cultures of a sort, in the sense that they provide the materials, possibilities, and conditions for the development of human persons.

In this way, punk is a microcosm of larger cultures. That is, we can view punk as it reflects the culture at large as both deal with issues of race, gender, sexuality, community and control. Punk develops and evolves, as perhaps all of culture does, as a number of intersecting dialectic tensions. It can be seen to be in conversation with itself about itself, what can be counted among its ranks, what will force itself in and what must be left out.

In its infancy and early years, punk rock in both England and America was, relatively, gender inclusive. For example, Alice Bag fronted one of Hollywood's early punk bands, The Bags, and, arguably, helped invent the hardcore punk style associated with the LA scene. After a hiatus to earn a BA in philosophy and teach in Nicaragua and LA, she has been working as a solo artist whose performances are just as intense as they were in 1978.

However, as punk begins to spread and develop into hardcore, it takes on a much more male-dominated character. Internally, this plays out as a dialectic of punkness. In its earliest days, punk did not have enough of a sense of its own identity to begin gatekeeping. The art and the artists themselves were relatively diverse and varied across a wide range. It was anarchic and creative. As it became more popular, it developed signature features (thanks in large part to the marketing genius of MacLaren) that quickly became cliché. Thus the fear, quickly weaponized, of being a poser. In the LA scene, punk develops into Hardcore and moves to the suburbs drawing a much less diverse population than the Hollywood locals.

Yet even in this exclusionary form, punk continues as a haven for the misfits. Take Steven Blush's comments on the hardcore scene he experienced and documented:

> Lots of fucked-up kids "found themselves" through Hardcore. Many now say things like, "I grew up thinking I was a weirdo, but I met like-minded people and figured out I wasn't such a freak after all." If that's what "HC" did for them, then the scene succeeded. For some, it served as a valuable social network; for others, it opened a rich musicological mine; but for all involved, Hardcore was a way of life, something they had to do. (*American Hardcore*, p. 9)

This violent, white-male-centric strand of punk remains dominant (with exceptions, of course) until the riot grrrl scene in the Pacific Northwest in the late Eighties and early Nineties. Bands like Bikini Kill insisted that the "girls move to the front" and reclaimed sexuality in performance detached from the male gaze. This enabled bands like the Red Aunts and Sleater-Kinney to be (despite press and critics who invariably struggle to catch up with the music they're describing) simply "bands," sans qualifier. Neither erases their gender in performance or content, but neither needs to devote so much of its identity to resisting the being characterized primarily as a "girl group."

There is a similar dialectic surrounding race. Punk begins as a (relatively) racially inclusive, as seen in bands like the The Bags, Bad Brains, The Dead Kennedys and Death. But punk becomes "bleached out" to the extent that an entire sub-genre of racist hardcore emerges and becomes an important recruitment tool for white supremacist organizations.

This helps us to understand some of the more troubling aspects of punk, both definitionally and in terms of its own values. Punk has been closely associated with anarchism but also with fascism. There's too much here to dismiss and the development is certainly the result of multiple factors (such as the working-class white youth who felt disenfranchised and sought an identity like the ones formed by various racial and ethnic groups). Part of the answer is also that there have always been racists and America thrives on white supremacy. What's important is that punk values opposition to all authorities and rules. "Fascist" is an insult for punks, as bad (or worse) than "poser" and "sell out." It thereby creates the tools for its own transformation and, at its best, punk challenges the very systems that perpetuate systemic oppression.

The Shit You Have to Crawl Through Is the Shit You Choose to Take

Sisyphus was a mythical king who had such a lust for life that he is said to have cheated death at least once. As punishment, the gods condemned to him to the "Sisyphean" task of pushing a giant boulder to the top of a mountain only to watch it roll back down and be forced to do it all over again. And again. And again. As Camus puts it, Sisyphus's "scorn of the gods, his hatred of death, and his passion for life won him that unspeakable penalty in which the whole being is exerted toward accomplishing nothing" (*The Myth of Sisyphus*, p. 119). However, Sisyphus finds in his condition the three things Camus says make life meaningful: freedom, passion, and revolt. In refusing to see his situation as a punishment, in not letting the bastards get him down, Sisyphus frees himself from the gods exercising complete power over him. He makes his afterlife meaningful through his resistance, knowing that it is absurdly pointless. He gives the gods the punk rock salute of the middle finger. This is Camus's philosophy of revolt, and it is what makes life worth living, despite its ultimate meaninglessness: "That revolt is the certainty of a crushing fate, without the resignation that ought to accompany it . . . That revolt gives life its value" (pp. 53–54).

Life itself is an absurd and doomed endeavor, and each of us is beset by forces that we cannot hope to overcome. For many of us, the only freedom available is that of saying "No," and rejecting structures and meanings imposed on us by those outside forces. But, as Camus also says, "there is no fate that cannot be surmounted by scorn" (p. 120). In other words (specifically those of Patti Smith), "Punk rock is just another word for freedom" ("Remembrances of the Punk Prose Poetess").

The Duncan Effect

Sometimes punks save lives in a more tangible way as well. I call this the "Duncan Effect" after a popular representation of the punk as anti-bully. I'm not prepared to argue that *Some*

Kind of Wonderful should be inducted into whatever the punk rock canon is, but I do think that it offers a memorable depiction of the role many punks have played. In the movie, Duncan is a skinhead punk who befriends the lead character—a poor, artsy outsider—in detention. This pays off at a critical point in the story where Duncan saves the lead character from a beating at the hands of the rich kids.

In the cowboy culture that dominated my rural high school, all the misfits, outcasts and leftovers of the student body grouped together out of necessity. The punks were the closest thing we had to muscle in an area that had seen Native Americans actually crucified in our grandparents' generation and "long hairs" beaten, dragged behind pickups and hanged when our parents were young. SHARPS (Skinheads Against Racial Prejudice) existed entirely to fight the racist skinhead movement. And while this may have only escalated the violence and hurt the scene in the long run, you can't argue that they didn't help save at least one kid from getting beat to death. Thanks to all the Duncans.

23
Punk and Disgust

Sara M. Bergstresser

These days, Punk can seem like a fashion statement or style trend of the past. Now that brightly-colored hair and facial piercings are ubiquitous, it all feels trivial. But in its early years, Punk was seen as anything but harmless. Punk and related genres were often perceived as dangerous and evil, and this was not an accident. Punk was designed to frighten, upset, and disgust mainstream people and to show disdain for social norms.

In the 1970s US and UK, many pre-Punk and Punk bands were rejecting the sociopolitical and economic order of the day. Punk was protest. It aimed to shock by breaking society's most basic and deeply held social conventions, including those related to bodily integrity and boundaries. Punk did not just pretend to show violent contempt, there were real instances of bands producing and using excrement, sexual acts, and physical self-harm on stage. The performative aspect of Punk concerts was often as important as the music, and many of the most shocking and controversial performative acts involved bodily transgression.

Punk's explicit embrace of shocking behaviors and ideas loudly opposed to society's most basic sense of morality, cleanliness, propriety, health, the law, and rationality became a central strategy of performative protest in this era. The horrified reactions were exactly as intended, with performers condemned by political leaders, threatened with imprisonment and arrest, and bands and music becoming symbols of and scapegoats for the social ills of younger generations.

This same trend continues into the present, but it has transmuted into new and shifting delivery systems. By the late

1980s and 1990s, heavy metal music was tied to the "Satanic Panics" of that era, and other forms of transgressive music and performance continue to evolve with society and its propensity towards moral panics. Though stage performances have become more rehearsed and theatrical over time, with fake blood, scary masks, and simulated sex, few have quite reached the level of genuine bodily transgression of the early proto-Punk and Hardcore Punk genres.

Punk as Performance Art

Throbbing Gristle: Thee [sic] involuntary muscular spasms of death perhaps, sound throbbing, body, blood, air, cunt, throbbing air conveying sound, affecting thee [sic] metabolism.

— P-ORRIDGE (Group member P-Orridge's explanation of the band's name "Throbbing Gristle")

The aesthetics of Punk grew out of a rejection of society, including broadly accepted definitions of art and beauty. The performance and visual art group COUM Transmissions, which later became the band Throbbing Gristle, is a key example. Though the band eventually self-classified as industrial, it emerged within many of the same places and traditions in the 1970s UK that later became defined as Punk. The group was called "too real" and "too extreme" for the Punk scene by the Sex Pistols' manager (Ford, *Wreckers of Civilisation*). They were known for presenting shocking imagery, performing sexually explicit acts in full nudity, and for in 1976 being called by a member of parliament "wreckers of civilisation."

Throbbing Gristle had four core band members. The only female of the group went by the stage name "Cosey Fanni Tutti," which is a play on an Italian phrase and an Opera by Mozart. In her memoir *Art Sex Music*, when describing how the band composed music, Cosey described how it was not chosen because they liked the sound, but rather because it best reflected the horrors of the world they lived in:

As TG we wanted a sound that hit people between the eyes and swirled in grinding, growling mayhem between their ears. A sound that caused an involuntary physical response in the body that would make people feel and think . . . there was nothing comfortable about a TG gig, for us or anyone else. (*Art Sex Music*, p. 244)

She went on to explain that the goal was real human connection intended to engage the audience in genuine thought beyond the everyday; they were "breaking down preconceived ideas of what was 'music' by ripping away the foundations and leaving the listener to discover their own point of entry" (p. 240). The group intended to make art.

Can the disgusting be art? Art has historically been connected to the concept of beauty and the sublime, and Kant connects the experience of beauty to morality. (Guyer, "Feeling and Freedom"). Can ugliness and a rejection of the accepted systems of morality also be art? In *Art and Outrage*, art historian John A. Walker asks the question "Can dirty nappies be art"? This question refers to the 1976 UK exhibition of *Post-Partum Document,* by Conceptual and Feminist artist Mary Kelly. Her exhibit displayed the everyday and material experiences of motherhood, including said dirty "nappies" (British for 'diapers'), and it sparked ridicule in the popular press. Walker concludes that the exhibit was challenging and intellectual, proved to be highly influential within feminist art, and did not deserve to be trivialized by the press.

Walker then addresses the COUM Transmission and Throbbing Gristle exhibit/performance *Prostitution,* which was held at London's Institute of Contemporary Arts, also in 1976. The exhibition itself was described as: "explicit photographs of lesbian love and macabre assemblages of rusty knives, syringes, blooded hair and used sanitary towels one of which is growing mould" (Walker, *Art and Outrage*, p. 89).

The sight of bloody tampons also drew expressions of disgust from journalists, and the performance was called "Sick, sadistic, obscene, filthy rubbish, pornography." Conservative politicians used the uproar as an excuse to attack the Arts Council and its liberal supporters, and even the artists were surprised at the fury they had drawn. This persistence in transgressing unspoken rules is also why Walker considers this performance to be a significant event in the history of art.

In the underground Punk fanzine *Maximum Rock'n'Roll* we can find recent articles bemoaning the current state of Punk, complaining that it has become commercialized and homogenized. Punk used to be something else: Local, about personal suffering, local politics, inside jokes, diatribes against the neighbors (Vargyai, "Awkward Raging"). Now that disgust and ugliness as art is more socially accepted, the current dichotomy is that of art versus commerce.

Perhaps people have become more squeamish over time. Though CGI blood and gore is great for a movie or a video game, they are mediated by a screen. Perhaps, if some of COUM and TG's stage performances would be brought back, blood and guts could become shocking once again:

In Amsterdam we did a performance in the red-light district . . . There was an audience of around 2,000 people. And each day it got heavier, so that on Easter Sunday I [P-Orridge] was crucified on a wooden cross, whipped with two bullwhips, covered in human vomit and chicken wings and chicken legs, while I had to hold burning torches— people in the audience could hear the skin burning on my hands. And then I urinated down Cosey's legs while she stuck lighted candles up her vagina, so there was flames coming out of her vagina. Just ordinary everyday ways of avoiding the commercials on the television.

Feces, Danger, and the Law

GERALDO RIVERA: Why, GG, did you feel a need to, uh, to defecate in front of a live audience?

GG ALLIN: Well, my body is the rock'n'roll temple, and my flesh, blood, and body fluids are a communion to the people, whether they like it or not . . . my rock'n'roll is more, not to entertain, but to annihilate. I'm trying to bring danger back into rock'n'roll. And there are no limits, and no laws, and I'll break down every barrier put in front of me until the day I die. (*Geraldo Rivera Show*, 1992)

In *Purity and Danger*, anthropologist Mary Douglas explains how cultural systems across time and place are organized and maintained by distinguishing the pure from the unclean. Hygiene is not only a ritual of physical purity, but it is also symbolic of moral purity. Though cultural moral systems are complex, in times of uncertainty and confusion, pollution rules can determine outcomes. Physical dirt is also tied to social pollution and danger, which can arise from transgressions of internal systems or a symbolic breaking of external boundaries, both cosmic and social. With this in mind, its clear how the sense of disgust felt when encountering dirt and feces clearly parallels the sense of 'moral disgust' at individuals who have broken the core rules of society. Psychological horror at learning of a terrible crime or violation can be followed by physical vomiting, paralleling the human reaction to rot or poison.

In *Hiding from Humanity*, Martha Nussbaum further examines disgust as social transgression. She examines the connections between disgust, shame, and the law, pointing out that disgust can be the sole reason that some acts are made illegal. Obscenity laws can rely on the disgust of the "average man," which historically connects to the criminalization and abuse of minority groups. Some examples are laws forbidding homosexual acts between consenting adults, the denigration of people with disabilities, or violence against women and ethnic minority communities.

Disgust marks the boundaries of enforced social norms, beyond which the surveillance, policing, and punishment of people and actions become commonplace. Punishments for those who defy these social norms often involve public humiliation, shaming, and stigma. Nussbaum describes how disgust structures everyday social relationships, with avoidance taking up a great deal of time and energy:

> Ways of dealing with repulsive animal substances such as feces, corpses, and rotten meat are pervasive sources of social custom. And most societies teach the avoidance of certain groups of people as physically disgusting, bearers of a contamination that the healthy element of society must be kept at bay. (*Hiding from Humanity*, p. 72)

Human bodies are animal bodies that excrete, leak, ooze, and die, and these substances must be denied because they are reminders of mortality.

Punk bands blatantly show anger, lust, and other impolite emotions, and they put the "animal body" and its material products on full display, all while refusing to show shame. Punk performances can show violations of bodily integrity in often violent and frightening ways. Violation of the most basic and taken-for-granted norms can be the one of most transgressive things imaginable, and it does overlap with violent acts that are clearly criminal.

GG Allin was an American Punk artist known for defecating on stage and flinging it at the audience and for physically assaulting audience members. He performed rage and lust at the same time, with shocking images of social transgression, often coupled with evocations of "repulsive animal substances" including feces, ejaculate, blood, and urine. The lyrics of the 1987 song "Eat My Diarrhea" expand on the theme:

> I'm gonna shit in your mouth
> I'm gonna shit in your face, your mouth
> And I wanna shit on your mother
> I'm gonna shit on you and your mother.

He was banned from NYU after a concert there where he shoved a banana in his rectum and threw chairs at the student audience.

Perhaps the most controversial moment came in 1993 during an interview on *The Jane Whitney Show,* which occurred not long before his death from a drug overdose. The host introduced him as someone who "wants to lead America's young people in a bloody revolution to take over the country." During an aggressive interview, Allin said he would commit suicide on stage and take his audience ("your children") with him. He also said he was the "underground Messiah," and that his actions on stage were not a performance, but a ritual.

The 1993 documentary movie *Hated: GG Allin and the Murder Junkies* (directed by Todd Phillips) starts with a quote on the screen: "GG Allin is an entertainer with a message to a sick society. He makes us look at it for what we really are . . ." The quote is then revealed to be from serial killer John Wayne Gacy, written from death row. The film goes on to describe multiple instances when Allin arrived at concerts under the influence of so much heroin that he could not perform, prompting the audience to kick him and break bottles over his head. The imagery is of the singer covered in blood. Allin and his band are shown performing, first with Allin on stage naked, hitting himself repeatedly in the head with a microphone yelling "die!", then the viewer sees a news clip discussing how Allin once smashed in his own teeth with a microphone. Chaos and violence ensue, interspersed with interviews of Allin, band members, and fans.

Allin's violent transgression was not confined to song lyrics and interviews. He bragged about being arrested at least fifty-two times, and he served a prison sentence for assaulting a young woman. In a spoken word interview "Bleedin' Stinkin' and Drinkin'," Allin casually discusses arrests, interactions with the Secret Service (for corresponding with John Hinkley), and being in prison. Allin's transgressions were performative but also very real, though whether his work constituted 'real' Punk or empty shock theater is still debated. Are certain types of people prohibited from creating art? If so, who decides?

Punk and the Abject

I've readied it all for her, you know
Clean sheets, incense, a lots of fluffy pillows
Now soiled.

—IGGY AND THE STOOGES, "Wet My Bed," 1973

In *Powers of Horror*, Julia Kristeva describes abjection as related to loathing and perversion. The abject is a "jettisoned object," that is "radically excluded" and "draws me toward the place where meaning collapses" (p. 2). The abject is connected to waste, to pus and bodily fluids, the unclean, and to the corpse as a reminder of death. Abjection arises at the breakdown of boundaries between self and other or subject and object:

> These body fluids, this defilement, this shit are what life withstands, hardly and with difficulty, on the part of death. There, I am at the border of my condition as a living being. (*Powers of Horror*, p. 3)

Abjection is the "other facet of religious, moral, and ideological codes." These codes are what can purify and repress the abject. For Kristeva, the psychoanalyst, the author, and the prophet are the ones who dare approach the horror of the abject. I suggest that we add Punk musicians to that list, since Punk itself performs the abject.

Iggy Pop is often deemed the "Godfather of Punk." During performances with his band The Stooges, he would self-mutilate and bleed freely on stage. He frequently exposed his penis to the audience and continued to perform with it on display. Pop also liked to spit and vomit on the audience (*Rolling Stone*). His first solo concert, *The Murder of a Virgin* in 1974, was described by Rolling Stone:

> "Do you want to see blood?" Iggy asked the crowd, which howled affirmatively back at him. Then, at Iggy's urging, guitarist Ron Asheton, wearing a Nazi outfit, whipped Iggy repeatedly. Iggy began hurling racial epithets at a black spectator, hoping to goad the man into stabbing him with the steak knife he'd brought onstage. No luck, so he closed the set by carving an X into his chest himself.

In Paul Trynka's biography of Iggy Pop, *Open Up and Bleed*, spectators from that day recount their reactions: "We were not at all easily shocked back then, but that was really, really shocking" (p. 184). Pop transgressed all of the boundaries at once, cutting his own body with a rusty knife and violently lashing out at social norms, shocking even jaded observers. He had faced the horror of the abject while on a rampage of violent contempt.

Later in his life, Pop befriended and collaborated with controversial French writer Michel Houellebecq, who has expressed a similar view of the artist's role:

> Every society has its weak points, its wounds. Put your finger on the wound and push nice and hard. Go deep into the subjects that no one wants to hear about. The other side of the décor. Insist on illness, agony, ugliness. Speak of death, and of nothingness. Speak of death, of oblivion. Of jealousy, of indifference, of frustration, of the lack of love. Be abject, you will be true. (p. 28)

Unlike GG Allin, Iggy Pop lived beyond the era and into the present day, though he and his legacy changed and aged with the times. His 1977 song "Lust for Life," which included the line (clearly sexual in context), "Of course, I've had it in the ear before," was later repurposed to become the background music for a cruise ship television advertisement (but without mention of the ear). In a recent song, he sings for a new era of bodily contamination: "Dirty little virus; Sleeping inside us . . . Covid-19."

Feminism, Art, and Bodies as Protest

Why are my lips so
Why are my are my
Why are my lips so swollen shut shut shut.

—JACK OFF JILL, "Swollen," *Sexless Demons and Scars*, 1997

Ugliness has been used as a form of protest for female musicians. Girl bands "deploy 'ugliness' as a resistant practice that challenges cultural representations of 'pretty' femininity" (Karina Eileraas). Perhaps because their bodies have long been defined as inherently dirty and disgusting, female musicians have continued in the tradition of presenting female bodies and substances as performative protest. There are protests against discrimination, policing of female bodies, restrictive societal roles, and the exclusion of women within Punk movements. This has been the case within many musical genres that have evolved directly or indirectly from elements of the Punk era, including Riot grrrl Punk, Industrial, Grunge, and shock Metal.

Mary Douglas discussed taboos surrounding menstrual blood, describing how in many cultural traditions, it was thought of as one of the most dangerous substances (to men). Julia Kristeva also identifies menstrual blood as one of the two main categories of pollution, with the other being excrement, which also covers disease, decay, and corpses. For Kristeva, Menstrual pollution is tied specifically to social transgressions and threats to the social order. This is reflected in the controversy sparked when female artists have included menstrual blood and used tampons in their work. In 1971, artist Judy Chicago depicted a woman in the act of removing a bloody tampon in "Red Flag," and in 1972, she exhibited a trash can holding used tampons in "Menstruation Bathroom." In 1992, Donita Sparks of the all-female punk/grunge band L7 pulled a bloody tampon out from her shorts and threw it at the crowd, yelling "Eat my used tampon, fuckers!" In a later interview, she described the event as "I went performance art on their asses" (Farnell 2013).

Though Punk had a rhetoric of egalitarianism, many women found that it did not extend to a reconsideration of female menstrual blood or certain female social roles. In *Pretty in Punk*, Lauraine Leblanc described it as a paradox: "On the one hand, punk gave us both a place to protest all manner of constraints; on the other, the subculture put many of the same pressures on us girls as did the mainstream culture we strove to oppose." Cosey also described this tension in her memoir:

> I felt like 'Mother'. Sleazy even called me 'Mum' at times—the boys got to play while I was Ms Domestic Goddess, food shopping, cooking, laundering . . . Keeping our TG family happy and united also meant I got to do my thing. Shit, I hate saying that, but that's how it was. And of course, when I wasn't 'Mother' I was there for sex, Gen's Scarlet woman . . .

American Riot grrrl band Jack off Jill was founded in 1992 by singer Jessicka. Many of the band's lyrics and performances were steeped in rage at society, childhood sexual abuse, and for the image of the "happy family" that concealed it. For example, the song "Don't Wake the Baby" includes the lyrics: "Daddy feeds the scary clown; He likes me more with his pants down; Fuck you!" As Karina Eileraas notes, "sexual abuse leaves the body with 'strange information,' often trapping this body . . . Girl-band music exposes violation in visceral, unspeakable ways that recall Nietzsche's notion of writing with one's own blood, Frida Kahlo's self-portraiture, and Sylvia Plath's poetry" (p. 127).

Jessika often cut herself on stage, and in a since-erased personal website FAQ, she wrote: "The question might be, why did I cut myself so much? In Jack Off Jill I guess a lot of what did on stage earned me the title of 'Patron Saint of Self-Injury.' I initially started cutting myself at an early age out of frustration. Cutting tends to relieve anger" (Jessicka.com). Blood crossing the bodily boundary is a visual representation of embodied pain. In this case, blood was simultaneously performative, a symbol of personal protest, and an attempt to combat anger and frustration with self-injury. This sets it apart from the rage-filled but still somewhat joyful cutting performances by Iggy Pop, who was celebrated in the song "Lollirot" for a memorable stage performance of his own: "Evil boy, still the best; Peanut butter smeared on his chest." Perhaps this reflects a sense of envy for when the bodies of men cease to be objects of disgust when the performance is over.

Punk and Passion

Are there universal ways in which people react to beauty? No, because beauty is detachment, absence of passion. Ugliness, by contrast, is passion.

—UMBERTO ECO, *On the Shoulders of Giants*

In his description of the aesthetics of Punk Rock, philosopher Jesse Prinz identifies three ideals: irreverence, nihilism, and amateurism. Punk aims to challenge prevailing social norms via expressions of contempt, themes of decay, despair, suicide, societal collapse, and purposeful adoption of low production values. Punk not only challenges social rules, its existence is also a challenge to normative definitions of art, aesthetics, and morality. By bringing in the experiences of the marginalized, new aesthetics are revealed—those which have been marginalized from the social concept of beauty.

Umberto Eco wrote that in order to have a definition of beauty, you must have a foil of ugliness; but close examination of ugliness exposes that beauty is also contextual and historically contingent. Punk is disgusting, ugly, passionate, irreverent, noisy, and bursting with hidden meaning.

Maybe Punk is also art.

24
ReMENbering the Punk Movement

GEORGINA H. MILLS

Typical girls try to be typical girls very well.

—"Typical Girls," The Slits

In 2016, Viv Albertine went to the British Library to speak at an event as part of the exhibition *Punk 1976–78* along with punk journalist Jon Savage. A short blurb displayed at the exhibition summarized some key points of the British punk scene, citing the Sex Pistols, The Clash, and the Buzzcocks as influential bands in the movement.

Albertine was furious at the blurb's failure to mention a single female artist or band with a female member. She defaced the display, writing X-Ray Spex, the Slits, and Siouxsie and the Banshees over the top of the all-male band names. What was it about this display that made Albertine want to correct it?

Naturally, she might have been annoyed at the lack of acknowledgement for her own contribution, or that of her bandmates or the other women in punk that she admired. We can also see this as another instance of the Matilda effect, historicizing an art movement by ignoring the contributions of women and celebrating the contributions of men. This is a problem worth pointing out, but when we look closer at punk specifically, there is another layer of injustice at work here. By historicizing the punk movement in terms of the men only, we do an injustice to the punk movement as a whole.

The Matilda Effect

The erasure of women from history is well documented. In her 1870 paper, "Woman as an Inventor," Matilda Gage documented a list of inventions with female originators that are commonly attributed to men. Rossiter's 1993 article dubbed this phenomenon "the Matilda effect." The Matilda effect is not limited to invention; all across science and art the Matilda effect is observed.

Men are often honored with patents, Nobel prizes, and publications for joint work that included a woman who is not named. Or, art movements are remembered by the aesthetic contributions of the men involved when female artists served as pioneers and influences of the movement. I don't think that we can characterize the punk movement in London as straightforwardly suffering from the Matilda effect. No woman's work is repackaged as a man's work, the correct artists are credited, and the contributions of some women to the punk movement's aesthetic quality are even more celebrated than the men's—Vivienne Westwood is far more widely known as the punk stylist of London than her husband Malcom Maclaren with whom she designed and sold clothing to most of the young musicians of the Seventies punk bands.

However, as the defaced blurb at the British library demonstrates, there's still a male bias in our collective memory of the punk movement. The Sex Pistols and The Clash are often the first names to spring to mind when someone is asked to think of a quintessential punk band. This might be for the simple reason that they are more popular with fans, and this is not necessarily the result of bias (though it might be) but being more popular doesn't necessarily mean that you're more punk.

The Sex Pistols are remembered as shocking, anti-establishment, and DIY, all the things most characteristic of punk, but the Sex Pistols do not have a monopoly on these characteristics. So why is it that the Sex Pistols have become the quintessential punk band in our collective memory when X-Ray Spex and the Slits were every bit as punk? We can see this as an instance of the Matilda effect, but we can also build on that to identify a distinctive form of bias that is at play here. This is not quite the same as simply erasing women from the narrative of punk, but actually filtering the movement as a whole through our still prevalent patriarchal norms of behavior and acceptability.

Anarchy in the UK

There are several reasons for looking at London specifically instead of considering all women in punk. Firstly, the women pioneering the London punk scene seem to be such close parallels to their male counterparts that the contrast in how they are remembered is very clear and easy to juxtapose. The same point could possibly be made about other punk women from other times and places, but the punk women of 1970s London make for a good illustrative example. Secondly, some of the women of the American punk scene such as Debbie Harry and Patti Smith are as well remembered, if not better, than some of their male counterparts, so it's possible that my claims don't work on the other side of the Atlantic.

Typical Girls

We remember the rebellious and anti-establishment Sex Pistols from the perspective where they've now achieved mainstream success, their rebelliousness is approved of instead of condemned, and whatever the establishment is now, it seems to condone them. However, when they first began, their music and style of dress would put these individuals distinctly outside of the mainstream. As the blurb at the British Library claimed, Johnny Rotten was "public enemy number one." So where were the women in all of this?

A particular point of contrast between the men and the women of the punk scene is the 1977 White Riot tour where the Slits toured with The Clash, along with the Buzzcocks, the Prefects, and Subway Sect. The Clash are considered paradigmatically punk, but whatever it was that the Slits were doing was somehow too much for some of the people they met on this tour. In her book, *Boys, Boys, Boys, Clothes, Clothes, Clothes, Music, Music, Music*, Slits guitarist Viv Albertine describes being serially excluded from the hotels that The Clash and the other bands were staying at.

> The manager looks up from his desk, clocks us—in a mixture of leather jeans, rubber dresses, and knickers on top of our trousers, matted hair and smudged black eye makeup—pulls Don aside, and says, "They are not staying in this hotel."

Albertine describes how the manager got hold of their call sheet and warned every hotel on their tour not to let the Slits stay, so most nights they were relegated to a different hotel than the rest of the performers, or made to go straight to their rooms without being seen. By the time the Slits left the hotel, the manager had called every hotel in Manchester, warning them not to allow the Slits in their lobby. In Albertine's words, they were "treated like a threat to national security."

So why was it that, while The Clash and the Buzzcocks can stay in any hotel in the UK regardless of their unconventional dress sense and irreverent lyrical and musical style, the Slits were considered so controversial? While being a punk was meant to be a rebellious and controversial subculture in itself, to be rebellious and counter-cultural while female was doubly controversial. Their dress style rejected not only prevalent norms of fashion, but also norms of femininity. The Slits even parodied femininity at times by pairing their rubber stockings and leather with brownie outfits and tutus. They made no attempt to embody feminine norms of either modesty and elegance, nor did they attempt to be desirable or appealing to the male gaze.

While there is certainly rebellion in rejecting traditional norms of masculinity by adopting a punk aesthetic, women often carry a heavier burden of aesthetic obligation (Archer and Ware, "Beyond the Call of Beauty"). The standards for how women should dress and appear are higher and more consistently policed and criticized, to the point where it seems like there is an obligation for women to fit in with certain aesthetic norms. To reject these norms so thoroughly is a vehement rebellion against this obligation.

Given that the punk movement as a whole was counter-cultural, it's very telling that women participating in it was more shocking to hotel managers than their male counterparts. To make anti-establishment music laced with profanity is one thing, but to do so as a woman is quite another. Albertine continues "Most of the audience have never seen girls play before, let alone with the fuck-off attitude that we've got."

It's this rebellion and rejection of the expectations of womanhood that make the contribution of women to the punk scene so integral. To rebel while female always involves a twofold rebellion, as women are under such societal pressure to be compliant and agreeable. For this reason, if we are to see punk as a movement characterized by anti-establishment sentiment, we cannot only remember the men involved. To neglect the women involved we tacitly endorse at least one of the kinds of establishment that punks raged against—the patriarchy. This adds an extra sting to the claim that Johnny Rotten was "public enemy number one" in the 1970s. It's not that the characterization was inaccurate, John Lydon certainly attracted his fair share of negative press coverage. But while he may have been kicked out of the occasional hotel room for urinating in the residents' shoes, there are no stories of him activating a hotel management phone-tree simply by looking too shocking. If men being punks was shocking, women being punks was thoroughly outrageous.

Retro-active Gatekeeping

Part of the anti-establishment sentiment of the punk scene lay in its DIY nature. There was no particular standard musical route to becoming a punk musician, and this meant that the usual factors that might exclude you from becoming part of a musical movement do not apply in the way that they might to other musicians. Attitude and stage-presence were a more important feature than musical prowess. This made the movement much more accessible.

Both Viv Albertine and Poly Styrene were inspired to go into music upon seeing the Sex Pistols perform. Albertine describes how she felt seeing them for the first time:

> I've always thought that my particular set of circumstances, poor, North London, comprehensive school, council flat, girl, haven't equipped me for success. As I watch the Sex Pistols I realise that this is the first time I've seen a band and felt there are no barriers between me and them. (*Clothes, Clothes, Clothes . . .*)

This set punk apart from other music; anyone could do it. Albertine sees the Sex Pistols as communicating a message— be yourself. After the concert she begins to learn guitar, but not by following any particular musical tradition, just by playing around to try to find her unique sound. Meanwhile, Poly Styrene started trying to put a band together, no longer deterred by having never seen a mixed-race woman singing in a rock band before.

This was part of what was characteristic of punk at that time, it circumvented most of the pre-existing barriers to musicianship such as class, wealth, or gender. The involvement of women was a big part of this. Poly Styrene, Siouxsie Sioux, and Ari Up were singing in ways that women didn't normally sing, and Poly especially famously dressed unlike anyone else, even within the punk scene. The inclusion of women is an essential part of this characteristic. This movement wasn't about your gender or wealth, but what you had to say. When we exclude women from our memory of punk, we erase part of its inclusivity, which is an inherent part of punk itself.

I-dentity—Remenbering the Punk Movement

When considering the erasure of female contributors to various fields, we tend to think of this as a kind of injustice to the women themselves or to women in general. In the case of punk, the exclusion of women from our historical account does more

than just an injustice to the women involved, but to the movement as a whole. So far, we've seen that defining characteristics of the punk movement are anti-establishment sentiment
and a circumvention of the norms that act as barriers to musicianship. These two elements are particularly relevant for
women, as to rebel as a woman is also rebelling against the
feminine norm of compliance, and woman's musicianship has
often been attached to her marketability and physical appearance, a barrier that the women of punk broke entirely.

What does it mean for punk as a whole if we take the
women out of it? I don't mean to suggest that the British punk
scene wouldn't have been rebellious and counter-cultural if
Poly Styrene, Siouxsie Sioux, or Ari Up had never appeared or
bothered to form a band. Sid Vicious still would have been just
shocking to the British press without his female counterparts
ever having picked up a guitar. Instead, what I'm suggesting is
that when we historicize the punk movement without the
women, we're blunting its characteristic features by watering
them down according to patriarchal norms.

We think of punk as rebellious, and rebellion as masculine,
and project this association back into the past. This does an
injustice to the punk movement by overlooking how ahead of
its time it was in terms of equality. The Clash took the Slits on
tour because they believed in their music, and while this seems
faint praise by today's standards, it was part of punk's nature
that it would facilitate female rebellion and break down the
barriers to women's success in music. By ignoring this, we
unfairly paint punk with patriarchal norms that it didn't
endorse.

One way to understand this phenomenon might be as a kind
of retro-active marginalization. Iris Young defines marginalization as confining a group of people to a lower social status, or
to the edge of society. Arguably, all punks experienced a form of
marginalization at the time, as mainstream radio would often
refuse to play their music regardless of its popularity in an
attempt to keep them on the edge of the music industry. However, by the time the British Library created the aforementioned Punk exhibition in 2016, four decades after this scene
originated, punk is a globally successful and celebrated genre
of music.

The more punk is valued in the mainstream, the more
women are left out of it. Punk gains a higher social status along
with its mainstream appreciation. While female artists were
celebrated at the time, we now historicize punk as if it were a
male-dominated scene. Punk is no longer marginalized, and as

it lost its marginalized status, the involvement of women is less included in the picture. As punk gains social status, punk women play a smaller part of our collective memory of the era, and this has the effect of retro-actively marginalizing them from a movement that they helped to forge. The low social-status condition of womanhood excludes you from the now high social status group of founding punks. This has the effect of unfairly claiming punk for the mainstream and filtering it through the pre-existing patriarchal norms that, at the time, it refused to adhere to.

There is a secondary effect at work here. In sugarcoating punk according to patriarchal norms, we also run the risk of mischaracterizing the parts of it that we do remember. It is common to hear that the point of punk was to shock people, that's why the Sex Pistols were named as they were. They were actually named to promote "Sex" which was Vivienne Westwood and Malcom Maclaren's boutique on the Kings Road. The Pistols created an impression that shock value for its own sake was what punk was all about, with their name and the offensive symbols that they'd paint on their jackets.

In understating the contribution of women in punk, the Sex Pistols are sometimes taken as an accurate representation of the punk ethos. This leads people to imagine that other punks are doing similar things, and to therefore imagine that the X-Ray Spex song "Oh Bondage, Up Yours!" is about sex, and written for shock value. Poly Styrene is repeatedly quoted in interviews as explaining that the song is in fact about the bondage of people to material possessions, as well as being inspired by books she read about slavery. This mischaracterization of Poly's work is possibly the result of our male-biased memory of punk aesthetics. We have so filtered punk through our patriarchal lens that even when we do remember to include the women involved, our expectations are projected onto them as well as the movement as a whole. Women's work within the punk genre is interpreted to fit in with narratives that are based off the work of male bands.

My Mind Is Like a Plastic Bag

We started by wondering why Viv Albertine was so annoyed by the British Library's punk display, which included mentions of several of the men from the London punk scene in the 1970s, but not one mention of a band with a woman in it. Albertine has a good enough answer if we consider this another case of the Matilda effect, she and her bandmates were left out of an exhibition about a time in music that they helped make, it seems that punk is one of many areas of artistic expression where the female contribution has been overlooked.

There are even further reasons not to exclude women from our collective punk memory. Punk was characterized by rebellion and by representing its own audience, and having little or no reverence for status and hierarchy. By minimizing the role of women in this movement, we diminish these essential elements. In a sense, this can be seen as a sort of backwards-looking marginalization. This is harmful not only for the women involved but for punk itself, as it is becoming historicized according to norms that it rebelled against at the time. In some sense, by doing this we take some of the punk out of punk. This does a disservice to the movement as a whole as well as the women involved.

As Poly Styrene once said "Some people think that little girls should be seen and not heard, but I think . . ."

25

Close Your Eyes, Breathe, and Stick It to the Man

SETH M. WALKER

Imagine waking up one morning, feeling an itch for some fresh air and a stroll through the land surrounding your home, but instead of taking what you thought would be a nice, relaxing trip outside, you return home wide-eyed and fairly shaken. And then you do it again. A few more times. Further shaken after each trip. Your guide—let's call him your *charioteer*—growing increasingly alarmed and uncertain of your next move, can start to sense the makings of what we'd call *the* sort of crisis existentialists like to trouble us over.

So, what do you do? You take one last look at your cushy life, family, friends, and luxurious home, leave all of your things behind, gallop away as fast as you can, shave your head, change out of your fine clothes and into some meager robes, and start wandering around for an indeterminate amount of time because you're unwilling to simply accept what society dictates, and no longer capable of living an ignorant life characterized by selfish desires and corruption.

Obviously.

At first glance, talking about Buddhism in a volume revolving around punk ideology might seem a little out of place. But that story above about a wealthy Indian heir is one that resembles the sort of rebelliousness and revolutionary action shared among many punks around the world. To give up a life of pleasure and comfort at a rather high social tier because you recognize how illusory, shallow, and fleeting such a life is, and that the "happiness" it's brought has only been at the expense of others' . . . that's pretty damn *punk*.

Still, I'm sure you're wondering how the rejection of a sappy palace life aligns with the values and ambitions of punk subcultures, or how we might link the two together as complementary models for attaining a similar sort of well-being and life without suffering. But, in many ways, they both embody and advocate principles that equally demand the raising of your fists in an attempt to put an end to an unsatisfying, oppressive, and cyclic existence. Punk-rocking monks like Brad Warner have actually been writing about their unique approaches to Buddhism (specifically Zen, in his case) since the early 2000s, and Noah Levine fleshed out the Buddha's revolutionary inner punk and started an entire movement based on it for addiction recovery around the same time. But the main point we'll see here is that some of those aggressive, violent, and solely individualistic sensibilities often associated with punk ideology are often just poorly-channeled manifestations of the pointed call for social reform, a shakedown of hierarchical and unjust structures, and collective revolt in pursuit of change that characterizes punk's underpinnings.

Sid, the Rebel . . . Not the Vicious

Let's backpedal first a bit to this . . . Buddha. We're told that Siddhārtha Gautama ("Buddha" is simply a title, translating to something like, "one who has awakened") was born and lived sometime between 566 and 400 B.C.E. The precision here gets a little tricky, based on the source material and its accuracy. But he hailed from a privileged upbringing as a member of the kṣatriya (warrior-leader) caste, second only to the brahmins (scholar-priests) in Indian society, and next in line to his father's leadership among the people of the area: the ākyas.

After leaving that life of his behind and spending years searching for answers to the angst and dissatisfaction he felt, he plopped down underneath a tree one day in deep meditation and *woke up*. And thus, the four *truths* about reality he discovered were conveyed to those who would listen, spreading and growing into varying schools and lineages for the next couple millennia: 1. life is unsatisfactory; 2. it's that way because of our incessant cravings and attachments; 3. we can put an end to that relationship; and 4. that end is through a middle path between austerity and indulgence.

This was all quite revolutionary at the time, too. Sid ("the original rebel," Levine nicknames and refers to him as in his work—not to be confused with the famed Sex Pistols' bassist) didn't discriminate, and caste was of no major concern. If you wanted to wake up like he did, then sit down, shut up, and listen to what I discovered. It's not that complicated. It just takes a dedicated shift in perspective and mindful approach to the conditional world around us and learning how to understand what makes it tick and how that makes us suffer—learning how to raise our fists and make it clear that we won't be held hostage by the cravings and attachments that keep us trapped in cyclic, unsatisfactory existence. That was Sid's message. In short: destroy ignorance, subvert the predominant traditions prevalent throughout the area—traditions that blindly accept what has been handed down to them without direct experience or observation and aren't quite strumming the right chords within their practices and teachings. Listen to what I'm saying, Sid told his followers, and you too can see through society's shortcomings and lies, and you too can dismantle the oppressive sensibilities of contemporary consumer . . . er, *ancient Indian*, culture. In his *Against the Stream* (2007), Levine frames Sid as a revolutionary who sought to overcome greed, hatred, and delusion by cultivating their opposite forms: generosity, compassion, and understanding. And underneath all the stereotypical subcultural features, this is exactly what it means to be a *punk*, too.

One of the most important sets of moral principles to emerge out of Sid's teachings, especially in terms of Buddhist laity (non-monastics), has become known as the five precepts. For our purposes here, let's call them the five punk-cepts (okay, maybe that's a bit of a stretch, but it's a fun label, isn't it?): 1. slam into each other all you want, destroy what you need to, just don't kill anyone; 2. if it doesn't belong to you, don't take it (although it might be okay to sabotage it . . . use your discretion); 3. sex is fantastic in a lot of ways and for a lot of different reasons, but remember, it can also be very emotive and invite quite a bit of vulnerability among those involved, so just be cool and take everyone's feelings and satisfaction into consideration; 4. you can't be trusted if you lie, so don't be a coward, stand up tall and speak your mind; and 5. mind-altering drugs and booze cloud our judgments, decisions, and perceptions, and even though the experiences under their influence can often be incredibly enjoyable and relaxing, you should steer clear of using any of those substances so you can keep to that middle path without any hindrances or supposed "short cuts" to ending your pain and dissatisfaction.

X Marks the Spot

Sticking to those punk-cepts (yep, we're going with that label) might sound like a bit of a nuisance along the revolutionary

path, but people like Levine and Warner, and those they've
mentored and influenced, attest to how *not* following at least
something similar enough can often result in a betrayal of the
very ideals that the inner punk in them aimed to embrace and
actualize in the world to begin with. Punk ideology has always
been about responding to a corrupt and messed up world—a
revolt for a new generation of people who were simply unwilling to accept such a state of affairs. And while numbing themselves and escaping that world through hard, destructive drugs
and misdirected violence and aggression offers some solace, it
doesn't really help solve the dilemma to which they see themselves responding. The thing is, that outer rebellion, the one
that is exciting and immediate, sensual and exhilarating, it's
only *part* of what needs to take place in order to change both
ourselves and the unsatisfactory conditions surrounding us. An
inner rebellion needs to take place just as much as that outer
rebellion—if not more. Because honestly, there's nothing really
revolutionary about losing yourself in violence, sex, and drugs.
How can you even begin to change the world you're critical of
if you've completely lost yourself to it as well?

For this reason, some punks have embraced what's known
as the Straight Edge movement (directly linked to Minor
Threat's 1981 song of the same name), which lines up really
well with Sid's five punk-cepts. To be *straight edge* effectively
means abstaining from mind-altering substances—booze,
tobacco, recreational drugs—and casual sex. It means staying
completely sober, in other words. Straight-Edgers can often be
spotted by the black Xs drawn on their hands or tattooed on
their bodies, demonstrating their dedication to still being punk
but without the distractions getting in the way of their affront
to the system.

But you might be asking yourself: what about therapeutic
drugs, or the very intentional and responsible use of certain
drugs to achieve heightened states of consciousness or awaken-
ings? Wouldn't that just be akin to something that might happen during deep meditation or in the ecstatic revelry of
moshing in a good ol' fashion pit? Well, if you're following the
punk-cepts to the *p* on this (that label is growing on you now,
isn't it?), then there really isn't a question here: don't justify,
don't rationalize, just abstain. You don't *need* a hit of acid. You
don't *need* to micro-dose any psylocibin. You don't *need* to roll
with some MDMA. You don't *need* to go on some post-colonial
escapade into the Peruvian jungle and participate in an
"ancient" DMT ceremony with a bunch of other tourists. Just
sit down and shut up. Just close your eyes and breathe. The

Buddha didn't need that stuff. Punks don't either. Sure, they feel great, but is that the goal? To be doing something that feels great? Or shaking society loose from the shackles it's unknowingly wearing?

While not everyone might feel this way, Warner—and especially punks like Levine who have approached Buddhist practice from a *recovery* standpoint—has been very adamant about a zero-tolerance perspective regarding drugs, therapeutic or not. For him, their use to attain some sort of enlightened state—to *wake up* like Sid—is on a par with some of the extreme, and unsuccessful, ascetic practices Sid put himself through before finding a comfy position under that tree. For Warner, there's no real difference here between starving yourself to trip out your mind in an unhealthy, unbalanced way and dabbling with substances that effectively do the same thing. He doesn't deny the therapeutic use of certain substances, of course. They just don't have a place in the sort of practice and lifestyle Sid was advocating. They're often perceived as shortcuts for a path that isn't meant to be traversed with a final *destination* anticipated at the end of it. The path itself is the practice and lifestyle—and the goal. Drug-induced states aren't the same as learning how to arrive at those states on your own. Buddhist practice is no more about a quick fix to an existential problem than punk ideology is about escaping the societal ills they're critiquing. It's about lifelong reform and the marked journey that characterizes the challenges being leveled against that former ignorance and oppression.

So, there we have it then, right? Just say 'No' and all that? Well, again, that's not exactly the only perspective here. Many *do* advocate for the use of such drugs in Buddhist practice, just as many punks have a beer and a smoke on a regular basis. Keep in mind that one of Sid's main platforms was to always question. Even him. And deciding whether to interpret teachings and instructions as literal, metaphorical, or symbolic tends to be at the heart of most cultural traditions anyway. And *questioning* certainly goes together with *challenging* among punks too. In Buddhist thought, there's a concept referred to as "skillful means" (upāya-kauśalya) that signals the method of adapting teachings for a particular audience—to suit specific contextual needs in order to successfully instruct and convey wisdom, and to perhaps provide those being instructed with the means to attain that wisdom too. There are *some* instances in Buddhist literature involving enlightened beings taking some liberties with even the five punk-cepts in order to get the message across (Sid included). So, who's to say that Sid's punk-cepts weren't just time- and place-specific? Can't we just, y'know, get mindfully hammered if that works for *us*? Well, all we can really do is defer to the imperative to test and question everything. It should seem pretty clear to both punks and Buddhists alike to abstain from certain things that would likely impede more than facilitate a revolutionary path, but if your experience would seem to allow for a little more wiggle room and interpretation, then by all means, wash those X's off your hands and *cheers*!

Direct Meditative Action

This idea of always questioning and always challenging is one of the pillars of both Buddhist and punk ideology. For Sid, the entire world around him was utterly unsatisfactory and filled with suffering and a level of discontent that would have had him picking up a guitar and strumming through the most dissonant combination of power chords he could muster to express it, if that option were available. He inherently questioned it. His advocated path through it inherently challenged it. Why on earth would he require those listening to him to not embark on a similar journey of self-discovery and wisdom? During an interview I did with Warner at *Nomos Journal* in 2014, one of the things he mentioned was the notion of "permanent revolution" in terms of Buddhism and punk: you can't just have *one* revolution, or a singular revolutionary *moment*, in either context. You have to keep fighting. You have to keep challenging. You have to keep *revolutionizing the revolution*, he said. And we see this imperative not just in punk movements, but across the millennia that Buddhist traditions developed throughout as well.

One of the ways this has manifested in Buddhist practice is through the sort of direct action and creation of radical social situations that we see characterizing punk subcultures in general—from the aesthetic, attitude, and language, to various progressive platforms, anti-establishment values, musical actualizations of such sensibilies, and everywhere in between. A major influential thread in the development of punk ideology during the latter part of the twentieth century was the philosophy and artistic activism of the French Situationist International (1957–1972), a mixed group of French political and cultural revolutionaries disgruntled with an inauthentic existence that had been shaped by capitalistic ideals and industries. The Situationists united around a common vision for a better future with the collapse of what they called "the spectacle": the world as we know it, but one that is effectively synonymous with capitalistic representations of reality, driven by a passive consumption of commodities. The only way out of this *spectacular* mess, the Situationists realized, was to disrupt and dismantle this (mis)representative reality and foster a more authentic existence. Thus, and hence their name, they sought to construct *situations* through direct action that did exactly this.

Subverting some sort of oppressive social system and its structures probably isn't the first thing that comes to mind to most people when hearing the word "Buddhism," but as we've been discussing throughout this chapter, that's exactly what Sid was doing all along, and what he implored his followers to do as well. And while we can flesh out this theme amid Sid's more familiar message of the four truths and middle path, it's more apparent and obvious within movements centered around what has become known as Socially Engaged Buddhism. The types of actions associated with engaged Buddhist groups (such as the Buddhist Peace Fellowship, the Zen Peacekeepers, and the Order of Interbeing) combine Buddhist thought and practice with forms of social protest and involvement that range from boycotts, protests, prison reform, humanitarian programs, the lives and well-being of non-human animals, and environmental activism, among so much more. Some examples can be fairly disruptive too, inciting criticism from within and without—such as the ordination of trees among Thai Buddhist monks in order to help resist deforestation. While other examples might feel more akin to a guitar being smashed right over your head.

On June 11th 1963, Thich Quang Duc, a Vietnamese Buddhist monk, sat down in the lotus position at a busy intersection in Saigon, covered himself in gasoline, and lit himself on fire. His self-immolation is one of the more famed instances of this practice, but it's certainly not alone. His act was in protest of the prolonged persecution of Buddhists by the South Vietnamese government, and he has been hailed and revered ever since by those who understood his sacrifice as one filled with compassion, courage, and inspiration. It called attention to the suffering taking place among so many people, and it was a direct, radical action that played a significant role in later toppling the oppressive regime. Self-immolation has always been a bit difficult for Westerners to stomach—to not just consider it suicide—and much of that has to do with how the "self" is conceived in Buddhist thought: there is no permanent *self*, just a conglomerate of parts that are in constant flux and intimately connected to everything surrounding them. But I think we can agree that if Sid's dismissal of a life filled with pleasure and privilege for the sake of helping others was pretty damn *punk*, then what Thich Quang Duc and others have done to shake down the system and stir emotive and political responses for the sake of others . . . well, there's no question about how punk *that* is.

Sit Down, Shut Up, and Take a Look at It

The social dimensions of that example raise another point we should address before wrapping up as well: community. Community is an important part of any cultural or subcultural movement. It's an important part of society in general. Punks have their communities with other punks—Straight-Edgers tend to hang with other Straight-Edgers, anarcho-punks tend to wreak their havoc together, punks promoting non-human animal rights often work together, Riot grrrls share in the same platforms and protests, and so on. Community is important in Buddhist traditions as well. It's actually one of the most important things a Buddhist should embrace, whether it's in a monastic context, or among other practitioners. Sid referred to this sort of thing as fostering "right association": we can't possibly begin to start tearing down society's stifling walls and shed the blinders if we're surrounding ourselves with those who would make that much less possible—those who care very little for anything even remotely resembling the five punkcepts, for instance (you're loving this label by now, I just know it!). So, in a way, it starts there just as much as it does with taking control of your own life. And since the rejection of authority is at the center of both Buddhist and punk ideology, the egalitarian and communal aspects of both become incredibly important considerations, especially as both also regularly are at risk of being co-opted or abused in other, alternative hierarchical forms of authority and control that can also be both corporatizing and commodifying.

Warner concludes his first book, *Hardcore Zen* (2003), with this line: "So sit down, shut up, and take a look at it" (p. 198). He's referring to our own lives, and everything in them. No one is going to transform them for us. It's up to us to take control and start understanding and working to reform the world we're unsatisfied with and rebelling against. Maybe we don't need to go as far as to drag our charioteers out beyond our palace walls, turn and dramatically raise our fists, stick out our tongues, and yell, "Hey, ho!" But I think we would do well to discern our own *skillful means* in starting a permanent revolution in ourselves, for ourselves, and for others. A good place to start could similarly be finding a nice, shady tree, taking a comfortable seat under it, and observing and appreciating everything around us. And I don't think Sid would have a problem with tossing on our headphones to let impassioned, distorted melodies serenade us into place either.

VI

Punk Aesthetics

26

Be Like Johnny

GEORGE A. DUNN

John Cummings had an epiphany one day in 1969. He heard a voice—maybe it was God, he later speculated—admonishing him, "What are you doing with your life? Is this what you are here for?" He was a twenty-year-old hooligan, the scourge of his Forest Hills neighborhood in Queens, with a taste for fighting and vandalism. He even dabbled in burglary and strong-arm robbery from time to time. And one of his favorite forms of self-expression was dropping discarded television sets from roof-tops, barely missing pedestrians on the sidewalk. So, the voice kind of had a point.

In his autobiography, *Commando: The Autobiography of Johnny Ramone*, John attributed his bad behavior to "boredom and frustration," two emotions that would figure prominently in many of the songs of the band he would form, The Ramones. In fact, his attitude toward life was well summed up in the title of a song from the band's 1978 album *Road to Ruin*: "I Just Wanna Have Something to Do." And he didn't care much that most of what he found to do was destructive, one might even say nihilistic. Friedrich Nietzsche (1844–1900), a philosopher who reflected deeply on modern nihilism, famously said that human beings "would much rather will *nothingness* than *not* will" (*Genealogy of Morality*). John would rather drop television sets from rooftops.

But after hearing that voice a new John began to emerge. He quit drinking and drugs. He got a job delivering dry cleaning and in time graduated to working construction, never missing a day of work in five years. John liked to work and work changed him. He learned punctuality, regularity, discipline, and self-restraint. Then he took the next step. He began thinking about his future.

No longer the passive plaything of a roiling storm of anti-social emotions, John recreated himself, making self-discipline and dedication to work his new watchwords. He became his own Do It Yourself project of self-repair. And in due course he even found a trade, one at which he became highly skilled.

Knew I Was Ready for It, Some Kind of Employment

And Johnny Ramone did indeed approach his job playing in The Ramones as a skilled tradesman. It was Johnny who handled The Ramones' business affairs and acted as foreman, even something of a taskmaster. He dictated every detail of how they would dress, stand, and perform on stage. Their iconic uniform of bowl-haircuts, leather jackets, ripped blue jeans, and sneakers; their brisk synchronized walk onto the stage, each proceeding directly to his assigned spot where he would remain for the duration of their set; Joey's growling "Take it, Dee Dee!" followed by Dee Dee's staccato count-off: "one-two-three-four"; Johnny's perpetual scowl, his wide-legged stance with eyes locked forward, and his fanatical insistence on downstrokes only; the lack of any dawdling between songs, which left the audience barely time to catch its breath; and then the brusque synchronized exit—all of this magnificent stage-craft was the work of Johnny. The group knew what they were there to do, got right down to business, and never wasted a moment on stage.

The unvarying nature of The Ramones' stagecraft and their blue-collar work ethic might be thought to violate the spontaneity that many associate with the punk ethos of "anarchy." But independence of spirit doesn't preclude aspiring to excellence. The seeming rigidity of Johnny's approach stemmed from his yeoman-like commitment to giving the audience what they came for. No noodling around on your instrument between songs, waiting for inspiration to descend. He knew the job he was there to do. That's why it's fitting to call him a tradesman, someone who had learned how to craft a product of consistent high quality and refused to settle for anything less.

This ethos of learning what works and then doing it consistently means that Johnny carried into his musical career many of the virtues acquired in his former job in the construction trade. As philosopher Matthew Crawford writes, "Craftsmanship means dwelling on a task for a long time and going deeply into it, because you want to get it right" (*Shop Class as Soulcraft*, p. 20). Does the self-discipline that entails sound like the antithesis of the freedom supposedly achieved when we set aside convention and tap into our own inner storehouse of creativity? To the contrary, Crawford reminds us that "creativity is a by-product of the mastery cultivated through long practice. It seems to be built up through *submission* (think of a musician practicing scales, or Einstein learning tensor algebra)" (p. 51). Or Johnny practicing barre chords.

As for freedom, consider Crawford's depiction of the experience of the disciplined tradesman in the modern world:

> One feels like a man, not a cog in a machine. The trades are then a natural home for anyone who would live by his own powers, free not only of deadening abstraction but also of the insidious hopes and rising insecurities that seem to be endemic in our current economic life. Freedom from hope and fear is the Stoic ideal. (*Shop Class as Soulcraft*, p. 53)

Stoicism was an ancient philosophy that identified freedom with self-sufficiency and not relying on external circumstances for happiness. When we rely on things we can't control, we can only hope for the best while fearing the worst, which is a recipe for anxiety. And, contrary to The Ramones song, it's not the case that "anxiety keeps me happy" ("Anxiety"). But the self-sufficiency sought by the ancient Stoics was mostly psychological in nature, an inner state of contentment that could be maintained no matter what curveballs life sends your way. That's probably not how most people would describe the notoriously irritable Johnny Ramone. In his autobiography, Johnny described how in his youth, he was "ready to go off at any time." He wrote, "I liked being angry. It energized me and made me feel strong." Still, what makes the independent tradesman Stoic-like are the skills and the capacity for self-reliance he cultivates, which give him much more control over his destiny, much more freedom, and a much less stultifying work environment than the ordinary cubicle-dweller will ever experience.

Now the Time Has Come

The self-sufficient tradesman is distinguished in part by his ability to set his own hours, at least to some extent. Admittedly, few people are entirely free of the constraints of time. If your trade is playing rock'n'roll, you not only must get to the show but you need to "make it on time," whether "in a wheelchair" or "on a plane," because "sound check's at 5:02" ("Make It on Time," "I Wanna Be Sedated," and "Danny Says"). But whether you take that gig in Idaho is up to you—or perhaps to Danny, but he still works for *you*. That's a lot more freedom than most of us have. (Danny Fields was The Ramones' manager and the subject of the song "Danny Says," the opening lines of which are "Danny says we gotta go / Gotta go to Idaho.")

The skilled tradesman also owns his own tools, which further reduces his dependence on others, and he has mastered them to such an extent that when functioning properly they become almost an extension of his own limbs. Wait! The Ramones—master musicians? Maybe not *technically*, but try playing that style of music with their level of conviction, "generating steam heat" ("Blitzkrieg Bop") on stage night after night without ever easing off. Try keeping up with those relentless downstrokes and drumbeats, producing a sound that Tommy Ramone described in the band's first press release as "not unlike a fast drill on a rear molar" (*Rock and Roll Explorer Guide to New York City*, p. 206), playing impossibly fast while vibrating perfectly in sync with your bandmates. That's craftsmanship of the first order and The Ramones were masters of their craft. "D-U-M-B, everyone's accusing me," they sang ("Pinhead"). Hardly! Their musical minimalism stripped away everything superfluous to lay bare the throbbing heart of rock'n'roll. It was sheer genius. There's nothing dumb about rescuing a musical genre from premature mellowness and simpering senescence—and The Ramones did it with the deft touch of a skilled mechanic restoring a classic automobile.

The only problem was that rock'n'roll—or at least the corporate suits drawing their paychecks from the "music business"—didn't know it was in need of repair. That's why the Do It Yourself (DYI) ethic, which found ways to sneak past the corporate gatekeepers, was such an inseparable part of punk rock from the beginning. "We used to sit around and listen to the radio and not hear anything like the stuff we like," Tommy reported, "so we decided to play it ourselves" (quoted by Betrock in *The Guardian*). First they taught themselves how to play their instruments. Then they wrote songs tailored to their musical abilities, tapping their irreverent imaginations to write lyrics full of dark humor unlike anything ever before heard in a pop song. Then they toured ceaselessly, playing over two thousand concerts before they finally disbanded, winning fans across the globe despite virtually no radio play. The key to getting played on the radio was to have already had some hits or, if you were new to the game, to sound like other bands that had hits. The Ramones sounded nothing like Journey or the Eagles, indeed like nothing anyone had heard before, so they had to build their own lane rather than ride the corporate turnpike.

A philosopher with some keen insights into the importance of DYI was Ivan Illich (1926–2002). He argued that contemporary society schools us to believed that we can't do *anything* for ourselves, that we need to rely on large governmental and corporate institutions to deliver the goods and services we need to live. Like The Ramones, we "don't wanna be taught to be no fool" ("Rock'n'Roll High School") but, according to Illich, that's precisely the hidden curriculum of our schools and the message we regularly hear from most of the other powerful institutions of society—You *can't* do it yourself, *fool!*—a message that is ultimately destructive of our humanity. "People need not only to obtain things," Illich writes, "they need above all the freedom to make things among which they can live, to give shape to them according to their own tastes, and to put them to use in caring for and about others." Genuine human flourishing requires what he calls "*conviviality*," the power to shape our own lives, "in contrast with the conditioned response of persons to the demands made upon them by others" (*Tools for Conviviality*, p. 24). The Ramones certainly weren't "D-U-M-B," but modern society wants to persuade the rest of us that we are, so it can slot us into jobs that make us even dumber.

Punk rock is to corporate rock what Illich's conviviality is to a nine-to-five job in an impersonal institution—and The Ramones made no secret of their loathing for the nine-to-five routine. In "It's Not My Place (in the 9 to 5 World)," they announced loud and clear:

> Don't wanna be a working stiff, lose my identity
> 'Cause when it comes to working nine to five, there ain't no place
> or me
> Ain't my reality, to me.

You Gotta Learn to Listen, Listen to Learn

Like any good tradesman, Johnny learned by shadowing others. "I'd seen five hundred concerts before I started a band," he said. "I'd sit there and I'd watch every little detail of everything they did. Then when it came to starting a band, at least it was all in my head of what looks good, what doesn't" (Johnny Ramone's blue check twitter feed). The band took a similar approach to crafting its sound. According to Johnny, "What we did was take out everything that we didn't like about rock'n'roll and use the rest, so there would be no blues influence, no long

guitar solos, nothing that would get in the way of the songs"
(*Commando*, pp. 100–01).

The Ramones would later inspire legions of imitators, but
they started their career imitating others, albeit only after
having first distinguished what was and wasn't worthy of
imitation. Does that make them unoriginal? No one wants to
be called a copycat, but the social theorist René Girard
(1923–2015) has argued that one of the most salient features
of human beings is precisely our capacity to imitate. Using
the Greek word *mimesis*, from which we derive our word
"imitate," Girard notes how our capacity to take others as
our models is what makes human culture possible. "Everything we know under the titles of apprenticeship, education,
and initiation rests on this capacity for mimesis," reports
Guy Lefort, one of Girard's dialogue partners, summariz-
ing Girard's view of the inescapability of imitation (*Things
Hidden*, p. 290).

But in the modern world, most of us are loath to admit
that we're imitators. Wanting to be seen as wholly original,
we like to tout how exceptional we are, pretending to be
entirely our own self-invention. In the early years of punk,
there was a lot of this "Year Zero" conceit, an insistence that
it was time to start from scratch, rejecting everything handed
down from the past. In their song "1977," the Clash
demanded, "No Elvis, Beatles, or the Rolling Stones in 1977,"
even though a couple of years later, on their album *London
Calling*, they were mining the buried treasures of past musical styles with unabashed relish. (On the other hand, there's
Generation X's song "Ready, Steady, Go," written by Tony
James and Billy Idol and also recorded in 1977: "I was in love
with the Beatles / I was in love with the Stones . . . Because I
was in love with rock'n'roll.") As Girard points out, the effort
to distinguish yourself from others is often just a way of imitating them negatively. "Modern society is no longer anything
but a negative imitation," observed Girard, "and the effort to
leave the beaten path leads everyone into the same ditch"
(*Deceit, Desire, and the Novel*, p. 100). The Ramones actually
were original, but not because they set that as their goal.
Their goal was to be excellent and that meant apprenticing
themselves to the best models they could find.

The Ramones have a pair of apprentices living today near
Liverpool, England, who wonderfully exemplify the philosophy
we've been discussing. Rose and Matilda Farrell are two sisters, ages fifteen and thirteen, whose band Yee Loi (Cantonese
for "two girls") takes its inspiration from The Ramones and

other punk bands of that era. Rose's fascination with The Ramones began five or six years ago when she heard The Ramones anthology *Hey! Ho! Let's Go!* while riding in her auntie's car. "I heard that record and it just completely changed me," she says. (This quote and the others by Rose and Matilda are from a conversation I had with them in January 2022.) Soon after, Rose picked up a guitar and began to teach herself to play. She had some lessons from her dad, who led a band called Ellery Bop in the 1980s, but she reports "there was only so much he could teach me." Interestingly—and perhaps presciently—the cut from the anthology that made the greatest initial impression on her was "It's Not My Place (in the 9 to 5 World)," about escaping the stultifying and degrading grind of the corporate work world.

When Matilda came to share Rose's passion, the Farrell sisters began uploading videos of themselves performing Ramones songs to YouTube. Recorded on their mother's iPhone, most of their earliest videos featured Rose on guitar and Matilda on lead vocals, with a backing track of bass and drums downloaded from the Internet or provided by a family friend. In due course, Matilda taught herself to play drums and Rose to play bass so they could provide their own backing. No Milli Vanilli, this pair!

It soon became evident that they were not only lovers of The Ramones' music, but also careful students of their wardrobe and stage presentation. Matilda would place one foot forward, tightly grip her microphone stand, and lean in dramatically as she stared intently through her Joey-style rose-tinted glasses. Meanwhile Rose played with her guitar slung low and legs splayed wide, except when flawlessly executing the iconic one-legged 360° spin that she learned from watching videos of Johnny. Their torn jeans, leather jackets, and sneakers left no doubt whom they were imitating. And the crowning touch was the replica of Johnny's Mosrite guitar, the one he played on all of The Ramones albums and on stage at just shy of two thousand shows, which Rose built with her dad. She now plays a real Mosrite, purchased for her as a present from her dad. If Johnny had to go to five hundred shows to learn his craft, Yee Loi is in the fortunate position of being able to learn from him everything he learned from studying others. In due course, they added songs from other bands to their repertoire— The Clash, The Sex Pistols, Thin Lizzy, Generation X, The Stooges—and began to venture into hard rock as well as punk, as well as writing their own songs. But their chief inspiration and musical home base always remained The Ramones.

Fun, Fun, Oh Baby

Initially, Yee Loi made their videos just for fun, though their kind of fun required countless hours of work rehearsing, mixing, recording, and latter writing their own songs. Their young age, along with the coronavirus pandemic that imprisoned them at home, meant that they didn't have the option of winning fans in the way The Ramones did, through persistent touring. So, they built their fandom online through dozens of videos that over three years underwent an exponential increase in quality. It turns out that iPhones and the internet are very much what Ivan Illich called "convivial" tools, "those which give each person who uses them the greatest opportunity to enrich the environment with the fruits of his or her vision" (*Tools for Conviviality*, p. 134). Yee Loi developed an international following, including many fans in South America where The Ramones had built a dedicated fanbase decades earlier. "I couldn't believe it was actually happening," says Rose. "We were getting attention just for having fun. I was like: Huh! You can *do* that!"

According to Matilda, the fun they were having was the sort that "pushes you to do it well." The philosopher Alasdair MacIntyre would say that such "fun" came from partaking in a unique sort of good, one "internal to the practice" in which they were engaged, the practice of playing rock'n'roll (*After Virtue*, p. 188). Other reasons people have for playing rock'n'roll—the desire to make lots of money, see their name in lights, or "get some chicks" ("Rock'n'Roll High School")—are what MacIntyre calls "external goods," since you can get them in ways other than pouring your heart into music. But what are the goods *internal* to playing rock and roll? They are the joy of rocking out, the exhilarating experience of focusing all of your powers on creating something thrilling, and the pride and pleasure that comes with attaining the highest excellence at this activity within your reach. Like few others, The Ramones model what it is to excel at the practice of rocking out, which is what makes them so worthy of imitation by a novice.

But, surely, it's no mark of excellence to remain *merely* an imitator.

I Can't Be Someone Else

Rose speaks eloquently on the subject of imitating the Ramones:

> We're not afraid to show what we're inspired by because it *is* what we're inspired by. But with the release of our new stuff, we'd like to

embrace a bit more individuality and uniqueness. For example, in our last Ramones cover, I didn't dress as much like Johnny and I added my own moves. Thing is, though, I've been doing the Johnny thing and quite a lot of it has become just a part of what I do now, my mannerisms, even the way I play barre chords. The thing is, it just has become *my* thing. Moving away from that too much would be moving away from myself, 'cause it *is* me.

When we consistently imitate someone we truly admire over a long period of time, what began as just an outward reproduction of someone else's gestures can become so internalized that it's no longer imitation. It becomes who we are. That's the outcome at which the painstaking apprentice aims, imitating the excellent master until the master's excellence becomes his own. And that excellence is a source of genuine freedom, the sort that facilitates creativity. As Matthew Crawford writes,

> In the trades, a master offers his apprentice good reasons for acting in one way rather than another, the better to realize ends the goodness of which is readily apparent . . . For the apprentice there is a progressive revelation of the reasonableness of the master's actions. He may not know why things have to be done a certain way at first, and have to take it on faith, but the rationale becomes apparent as he gains experience. (*Shop Class as Soulcraft*, p. 159)

As you progress from imitation to mastery, you acquire an intuitive understanding of why some things work and others don't. Once that happens, you can make creative use of what you've learned, as Johnny Ramone and all the other great masters have done.

In one respect, The Ramones were imitators. They took what they had learned from a misspent youth listening to hour upon hour of "rock and roll radio" and tried recreate its magic "before rock's just part of the past" ("Do You Remember Rock'n'Roll Radio?"). But they combined and modified elements of what they inherited from the past to birth something new, thus exemplifying another point made by MacIntyre: "To enter into a practice, is to enter into a relationship not only with its contemporary practitioners, but also with those who have preceded us in the practice, particularly those whose achievements extended the reach of the practice to its present point" (*After Virtue*, p. 194). By extending the "reach" of a practice, MacIntyre means incorporating new aspirations, new techniques, and new standards of excellence, which can sometimes be so substantial as to lead to a wholesale reevaluation of what that practice is about and what it can ultimately become. The list of those who have extended the practice of rock'n'roll in MacIntyre's sense include such luminaries as Chuck Berry, Elvis Presly, Buddy Holly, Gene Vincent, Bob Dylan, the Beatles, Lou Reed, The Ramones, and Jason and the Scorchers. Each artist on this far-from-exhaustive list started as an apprentice, taking instruction at the knee of past masters, even if his relationship with those masters was mediated through vinyl grooves. That's where it begins, but not necessarily where it ends. Building on what came before, they spearheaded new musical movements, unearthing hitherto unimagined possibilities for rock'n'roll.

Yee Loi's place in rock'n'roll history is as yet undetermined, but others are already beginning to take notice of them. They were invited to play at a tribute concert for Phil Lynott, the late singer and bassist of Thin Lizzy, though for various reasons they were only able to contributed two videos ("Don't Believe a Word" and "Rosalie") that were broadcast during the concert They also collaborated in a video with Mikey Hawdon ("Mikey and His Uke"), CJ Ramone, Mickey Leigh (Joey Ramone's brother), and others to cover "Something to Believe In," with musicians each contributing their parts from remote locations

The video received tens of thousands of views, with many comments singling out Yee Loi for praise. (These and other videos by Yee Loi can be found on YouTube. Look for them.) And they were even mentioned in a BBC radio broadcast about Johnny Ramone, with their song "Be Like Johnny" played as the outro.

They're also poster children for the DIY ethic. After performing only covers for a while, they decided to record their own album. Titled *No One Eats for Free* and released on vinyl—of course!—it contains eight original songs, along with four covers. They recently followed up thatfirst LP with an EP titled *Get Going*. With the help of their dad, they're building a recording studio in an unused building on their property, which means learning some carpentry skills. In the meantime, they use rooms of their home for recording, padding wardrobes with duvets to create makeshift recording booths. For mixing, they bought their own equipment and taught themselves to use the software and the various platforms. "We teach ourselves everything," says Rose, "all the instruments, all the ways to do stuff, the mixing and engineering and other things," adding, "You do want to stand on your own two feet."

Be Like Johnny

The first song on Yee Loi's album is also their first single, "Be Like Johnny," a homage to Johnny Ramone. "We wrote 'Be Like Johnny' about how we don't want to be the perfect little girl," says Rose. "We want to be bold and out there, not afraid to express ourselves in a way that nobody is really doing these days." They hope to inspire more girls—or just people in general—to imitate the "drive for music" they picked up from their musical heroes. Both their debt to what came before and their fierce spirit of independence are captured in their lyrics:

> You're always pushing me around
> But this time I'm gonna put you in the ground
> I don't know what to do, I just don't wanna be like you.
> Don't wanna be just pretty, don't wanna be just neat
> I wanna be like Johnny!

If it's true that "all good cretins go to heaven" ("Cretin Hop") there's at least one hard-working cretin smiling down in pride on the Farrell sisters. Better than dropping a television set on them.[1]

---

[1] The section titles of this chapter, with the exception of the last one, are all lyrics from Ramones songs. In case you are unable to guess the song titles, here they are: "I Wanted Everything,"; "Time Has Come Today"; "Rock'n'Roll High School," and "Something to Believe In."

27
The Filth and the Fury

Greg Littmann

Fuck this and fuck that.

—The Sex Pistols, "Bodies" (1977)

Ever since punk emerged as a distinct genre in the 1970s, the public has often been shocked by the negative emotions expressed by many punk songs. This negativity has been one of the many reasons for punk's undeserved bad reputation. To some, it's seemed clear that there must be something sick or degenerate about people who want to wallow in such black themes.

Punk has often been the music of misery. The New York Dolls suffer a "Personality Crisis" (1973), "when frustration, heartache is all you've got," Eddy and the Hotrods have the "Teenage Depression" (1976), while The Damned lament "I Just Can't be Happy Today" (1979). The Ramones' songs "I Wanna Be Well" (1977) and "Bad Brain" (1978) describe losing battles with mental illness. Alienation is a common theme, as in The Saints' "Stranded" (1976), The Ramones' "We're a Happy Family" (1977), Television's "Prove It" (1977), and The Clash's "Lost in the Supermarket" (1979). The Ramones' "Now I Wanna Sniff Some Glue" (1976) and The Clash's "Career Opportunities" (1977) and "London's Burning" (1977) are anthems to boredom, as is The Buzzcock's "Boredom" (1977).

Some punk songs seem nihilistic. In "God Save the Queen" (1977), Johnny Rotten of The Sex Pistols promises, "There is no future and England's dreaming." In "Pretty Vacant" (1977), he boasts "We're pretty, pretty vacant and we don't care." Richard Hell of Richard Hell and the Voidoids sings that he belongs to the "Blank Generation" (1977), "God's consolation prize." Jean-Jacques Burnel of The Stranglers complains that there are "No

More Heroes" (1977). In "I'm Against It" (1978), Joey Ramone assures us "I don't like anything."

Even more striking, punk has often been the music of anger, unleashing a torrent of vitriolic fury, the likes of which had never been heard. Some of these songs expressed anger at injustice, and arguably carried socially constructive messages. For example, The Clash's "Tommy Gun" (1978), The Jam's "Down in the Tube Station at Midnight" (1978) and Stiff Little Fingers' "Johnny Was" (1979) express horror at violence. Likewise, X-Ray Spex's "Oh Bondage! Up Yours!" (1978) champions feminism, Gang of Four's "I Found That Essence Rare" (1979) protests the exploitation of the working class, The Dead Kennedys' "Holidays in Cambodia" (1979) condemns Western indifference to foreign hardships, and The Clash's "Know Your Rights" (1982) denounces police corruption.

But sometimes the anger is personal, and even abusive. The Sex Pistols accuse the listener of being a "Liar" (1977) and a "Problem" (1977). "Don't come to me if you need pity" warns Johnny Rotten in "Problem." In "Sonic Reducer" (1977) the Dead Boys gloat, "I'll be ten feet tall and you'll be nothing at all." In "I Am the Fly" (1978), Wire fantasize about giving us diseases.

Some songs encourage political animosity, like the Sex Pistols' "Anarchy in the UK" (1977), The Clash's "Hate and War" (1977), and Sham 69's "Hersham Boys" (1979). Some express the urge to destroy. In "Search and Destroy" (1973), Iggy Pop of The Stooges is "The one who searches and destroys." In "Anarchy in the UK", Johnny Rotten of The Sex Pistols sings "I wanna be Anarchist, get pissed, destroy." In "Smash It Up" (1980), Dave Vanian of The Damned is "gonna smash it up till there's nothing left."

Some songs even seem to encourage or glorify violence. Joey Ramone advises you to "Beat on the Brat" (1976) with a baseball bat (oh yeah!). Johnny Rotten is going to kick you in the head as you kneel down to pray to your God because he has "No Feelings" (1977) for anybody else. Joe Strummer of The Clash yearns for a "White Riot" (1977) where whites can throw bricks like black people do. Nick Cash of 999 tells you he believes in "Homicide" (1978) and asks for your address.

Some songs seem designed to disgust and offend. The Sex Pistols' "Bodies" (1977) is a revolting song about abortion. Richard Hell and the Voidoids' "Love Comes in Spurts" (1977) is a revolting song about sex, as is The Buzzcocks' "Orgasm Addict" (1977), right down to Pete Shelley's simulated climax. The Dead Kennedys' make their political points by ironically urging us to place "California Über Alles" (1979) and to "Kill the Poor" (1980), while Siouxsie and the Banshees satirize racism in "Hong Kong Garden" (1978) by ironically singing racist things.

Obviously, punk isn't purely focused on the negative. Some songs celebrate good times, like The Ramones' "Rockaway Beach" (1977), Sham 69's "Hurry Up Harry" (1978), The Cockney Rejects' "The Greatest Cockney Rip Off" (1980), and Stiff Little Fingers' "Two Guitars Clash" (1983). Some songs celebrate solidarity, like The Sex Pistols' "EMI" (1977), Generation X's "100 Punks" (1978) and Sham 69's "If the Kids are United" (1979). Punk can be whimsically playful, as in The Rezillos' "Flying Saucer Attack" (1978), The Ramones' "Rock and Roll High School" (1979), and The Toy Dolls' "Spiders in the Dressing Room" (1983) (and most other Toy Dolls songs). And, of course, punks sing about love, as in The Ramones' "I Wanna Be Your Boyfriend" (1976), The Damned's "New Rose" (1977), and The Buzzcocks' "Ever Fallen in Love?" (1978).

Still, the darkness of so much punk music is striking. My examples above have all been drawn from early punk, which makes a convenient reference point, but punk's focus on negative emotions persisted beyond this first wave. Examples of all the themes tagged above could have been drawn instead from the likes of NOFX, Fugazi, Nirvana, Green Day, Rancid, and Blink 182, along with whatever bands you are angry that I haven't mentioned.

Why would we want to listen to music that deals with negative feelings? Don't we want to have as few negative feelings as possible? If we want to be happy, why wouldn't we stick to happy music?

The Puzzle of Dark Art

The puzzle of why we want dark art is raised dramatically by the pessimism and bile of so much punk. But the puzzle extends far beyond punk. In 1977, arguably the peak of punk creativity, the top hit in England was Swedish pop-group ABBA's "Knowing Me, Knowing You," a sad song about romantic breakup, followed by David Soul's "Don't Give Up on Us," with the same theme. The US charts in 1977 featured number one hits like Thelma Huston's cover of "Don't Leave Me This Way," Mary MacGregor's rendition of "Torn Between Two Lovers," and The Eagles' surreal nightmare about drug addiction, "Hotel California."

Even if we exclude the ubiquitous songs about romantic disappointment, negative emotion has been a part of popular music as far back as we can trace popular music's history, from

The Beatles grim "A Day in the Life" (1967) and The Who's vitriolic "My Generation" (1965) in the 1960s, through the likes of Eddie Cochran's "Summertime Blues" (1958) and Merle Travis's "Sixteen Tons" (1955) in the Fifties, through downbeat blues songs of the Forties, Thirties, and Twenties. Music Hall performers in the late nineteenth and early twentieth century performed maudlin songs like "Danny Boy" (1913), mourning the death of a child, while opera was frequently tragic right from its seventeenth-century beginnings, telling stories of death and misfortune like Wolfgang Amadeus Mozart's "Don Giovanni" (1787), Richard Wagner's "Der Ring des Nibelungen" (1874), and Giacomo Puccini's "Tosca" (1900).

Popular music is only one piece of the puzzle, since people enjoy negative emotions in all sorts of art. Take, for example, narrative art like novels, movies, and plays. People enjoy tales of hatred and conflict, especially violent conflict, as in George R.R. Martin's *Game of Thrones* novels (1996–), action films of all descriptions, and the legends of King Arthur and Robin Hood. People enjoy stories about angry and unhappy individuals seeking revenge, as in the film *Joker* (2019), Shakespeare's play *Hamlet* (1603), and the earliest surviving works of western literature, Homer's epics *Illiad* and *Odyssey* (circa ninth century B.C.E.). People enjoy stories about suffering and privation, like the series *The Walking Dead* (2010–), Charles Dickens's novel *Oliver Twist* (1838), and the Biblical story of the crucifixion. People enjoy stories about fear, like the series *Stranger Things* (2016–), the horror novels of Stephen King, and tales of monsters from folklore or mythology.

Aristotle Goes Punk

Given the antiquity of the puzzle of dark art, it should be no surprise that philosophers have been working on it for a long time. Punk is a very modern art form, but the foundations of an explanation of punk's appeal is provided by one of the first known theorists about art, the Greek philosopher Aristotle (384–322 B.C.E.). Aristotle was one of the first to theorize about a *lot* of subjects. Arguably the most influential philosopher of Western civilization, he wrote seminal works on ethics, politics, biology, botany, logic, metaphysics, and rhetoric, among other subjects.

Aristotle might have been more accepting of punk than many people today. He states in his book *Politics* that music is legitimate even if it does nothing more than bring relief from stress. He writes, "For the end is not desirable for the sake of any future good, nor do the pleasures which we have described exist for the sake of any future good but of the past, that is to say, they are the alleviation of past toils and pains. And we may infer this to be the reason why men seek happiness from these pleasures" (*Politics*, Book VIII, p. 2125).

Like other Greeks of good breeding, he looked down on the music of the working class. Still, he recognized it as important for the workers to get to hear the sort of music they like. He writes that

> for the vulgar crowd composed of artisans, laborers, and the like— there ought to be contests and exhibitions instituted for . . . their relaxation . . . And the music will correspond to their minds; for as their minds are perverted from the natural state, so there are perverted modes and highly strung and unnaturally colored melodies. A man receives pleasure from what is natural to him, and therefore professional musicians may be allowed to practice this lower sort of music before an audience of the lower type. (*Politics*, Book VIII, p. 2129)

Aristotle might even be pleased by the emphasis on politics of bands like The Clash, Gang of Four, Black Flag, and Dead Kennedys, even if he didn't approve of their specific political views. He claimed in his book *Poetics* that the difference between history and poetry is that "the one describes the thing that has been, and the other a kind of thing that might be. Hence poetry is something more philosophical and of graver import than history" (p. 2323). In other words, lyrics allow us to explore ideas and consider different possibilities. Aristotle thought that political participation from citizens is vital for a healthy society. While he didn't think that democracy is the best form of government, he did note in *Politics* that "If liberty and equality, as is thought by some, are chiefly to be found in democracy, they will be best attained when all persons alike share in the government to the utmost" (Book IV, p. 2050).

Most importantly for our purposes, Aristotle was a huge fan of dark art. In Aristotle's Greece, there were two genres of theater: comedy and tragedy. Aristotle loved tragic theater, an extremely dark artform where the story is always one of how the protagonist's life collapses into misery. Aristotle holds up Sophocles's play *Oedipus the King* as an example of excellent tragic theater. In the play, King Oedipus of Thebes is a righteous monarch, who happens not to know who his parents are. Then he learns that his father is a man he once killed in a brawl, and that his mother is his wife, with whom he has had several children. In horror, he tears out his own eyes and goes off to live as a wandering hermit for the rest of his life. As tales of family disfunction go, *Oedipus the King* makes The Ramones' "We're a Happy Family" look light and fluffy by comparison.

Aristotle wondered why people like himself got pleasure from watching horrible things. Shouldn't people want to view things that are beautiful and avoid seeing things that are ugly? Why wouldn't people rather see something pleasant at the theater instead of poor Oedipus ripping his eyes out? In *Poetics*, he comes up with an answer.

Aristotle concludes that people are attracted to tragedies because by feeling pity and fear on behalf of the hero of a tragedy, we purge our souls of these emotions. He calls this process "*katharsis*," source of our English word "catharsis." In Greek, *katharsis* refers to any kind of purging, including vomiting. Watching a good tragic play is a good vomit for the soul, clearing out negative feelings. In *Politics*, Aristotle notes that *katharsis* can also be provided by music, purging "for example, pity and fear, and also religious excitement" (p. 2044).

Applying this to dark punk songs is straightforward. By feeling a twinge of sympathetic misery when hearing "I Wanna Be Well," or hopelessness when hearing "Blank Generation," or rage when hearing "God Save the Queen," we purge these feelings from our system. Perhaps it's no wonder that punk bands so often associate themselves with nausea, what with musician names like Johnny Rotten, band names like Rancid, and album names like The Dead Kennedys' *Fresh Fruit for Rotting Vegetables* (1980). What better names for experts in making your soul vomit?

Aristotle doesn't mention anger, but the catharsis model seems like a particularly good fit for the way punk has so often been used to blow off steam. Often when people are angry, they want to get it out of their system by performing an angry activity, say by swearing or shouting, playing a violent video game, punching a punching bag, or kicking a malfunctioning printer to bits. Why shouldn't they get the same relief from rocking out to an angry song?

Aristotle's cathartic model might even explain why so many of the furious punk songs have been directed at authority, as in "God Save the Queen," Sham 69's "Borstal Breakout" (1978), The Clash's "The Guns of Brixton" (1979), Black Flag's "Rise Above" (1981), and many of the songs I've already mentioned above. After all, of the things that annoy and frustrate us, authority tends to be the one that we can least openly complain about. It would be little wonder then if frustration at authority is something we particularly need to purge from our soul by catharsis.

David Hume Gets a Mohawk

Aristotle's account may explain why we would seek dark art out, but it doesn't explain the pleasure we get from dark art. A good vomit can make you feel better afterwards, but the act of throwing up is not, in itself, a pleasure. I can't speak for you, but I get no joy from parking the tiger. But listening to punk *is* a pleasure, and that's why we do it. Vomiting is an unpleasant necessity on the way to better things, but listening to punk is something we do for its own sake.

Philosophers have continued to this day to wrestle with the puzzle of dark art. To my mind, the one who made the greatest contribution after Aristotle was Scottish philosopher David Hume (1711–1776). Hume was a big fan of tragic themes in theater, oratory, and poetry. Like Aristotle, he wondered what the appeal of tragedy could be.

In his 1757 essay "Of Tragedy," Hume wrote, "It seems an unaccountable pleasure which the spectators of a well-written tragedy receive from sorrow, terror, anxiety, and other passions, that are in themselves disagreeable and uneasy" ("Of Tragedy," p. 441). The pleasure is a mystery because "It is certain that the same object of distress which pleases in a tragedy, were it really set before us, would give the most unfeigned uneasiness." In other words, you wouldn't want to see someone rip their eyes out in real life, so why would you want to see Oedipus do it in a play? Or in punk terms, it would cause you only unhappiness (I hope) to see Joey Ramone beat on a brat with a baseball bat, or Johnny Rotten kick a worshipper in the head as they knelt down to pray, or to see Dave Vanian be unable to be happy today. So why should it bring you pleasure to hear about these things in song?

Hume's solution to the puzzle of dark art is that negative emotions caused by a work of art can be converted into positive emotions by mixing them with the experience of beauty. When we enjoy a work of dark art, our predominant emotion is appreciation of the artwork's beauty. But the power of that emotion is increased by harnessing and transforming the power of our subordinate negative emotions—emotions we feel in response to the artwork's darkness. Consider The Clash song "Somebody Got Murdered" (1980). According to Hume's theory, if we're enjoying the song, our predominant emotion is appreciation of the beauty of the music and lyrics. Our subordinate emotion is horror that somebody got murdered. Mixing these two emotions results in the primary emotion becoming more powerful, which is to say, we enjoy the song even more.

Dark themes are a powerful tool for inspiring feelings in us that can then be harnessed by the artist. Hume notes that applying artistic skill to a boring subject fails to stir emotion, leaving the mind "in absolute calmness and indifference," so that it won't enjoy the beauty of the art. If "Somebody Got Murdered" were rewritten with the same music and equally eloquent lyrics to be a song about somebody getting muffins, the boring subject matter would fail to raise any emotions in us, and we'd likely not notice the beauty of the song.

Still, even this model leaves much unexplained. When we have two conflicting emotions, the lesser emotion doesn't necessarily increase the intensity of the stronger emotion. If my strongest emotion is happiness that I'm getting a new stereo, but I'm also disappointed that punk doesn't get enough love, my disappointment doesn't necessarily make me feel happier about getting the stereo. If my strongest emotion is sadness that my cat died, but I'm also angry that you play *Never Mind the Bollocks* loudly at 3:00 A.M., my anger need not make me feel sadder about the death of my cat.

Lesser emotions need not strengthen more powerful ones even when the more powerful emotion is the enjoyment of art. If your primary emotion is enjoyment of *Never Mind the Bollocks*, but you're also irritated that I keep complaining about the volume, your irritation doesn't necessarily make you enjoy the album even more.

Lesser emotions need not strengthen an appreciation of art even when the lesser emotions are a direct response to the content of the art. For example, the first time I heard the Rezillos' cover of "Somebody's Gonna Get Their Head Kicked in Tonite" (1978), I wasn't sure if the band were being ironic or not, and I was bothered by the thought that the song was a celebration of meaningless violence. I still *liked* the song. But I certainly didn't like it more for the fact that I was bothered by it. Similarly, I like the Buzzcocks' song "Orgasm Addict," but I also find some of the explicit sexual references unpleasantly gross, repressed individual that I am. My prudish discomfort doesn't ruin the song for me, but it doesn't make me enjoy the song any more either. Even if it's true that the function of the sexual references are to stir up emotions of discomfort that can then be transformed into pleasure by being mixed with the beauty of the art, that transformation doesn't happen for me when hearing the song.

Since weaker emotions don't necessarily add force to stronger emotions, Hume hasn't given us a full explanation of why they should add force to stronger emotions in cases when we enjoy dark art. Hume tells us only that the displeasure is transformed into pleasure by the skill of the artist. Speaking about oratory, he writes,

> This extraordinary effect proceeds from that very eloquence, with which the melancholy scene is represented. The genius required to paint objects in a lively manner, the art employed in collecting all the pathetic circumstances, the judgment displayed in disposing them: the exercise, I say, of these noble talents . . .

But what Hume doesn't tell us is exactly what the artist does with their skill to turn negative emotions into positive ones. We aren't told precisely how negative emotions are used to make the artwork more appealing.

Should We Stay or Should We Go?

Where does this leave us? Not with a complete explanation of why we listen to dark punk music. Perhaps it's inevitable that we fail to explain just how artists make art appealing. After all, to crack that secret would mean knowing exactly how to produce appealing art, and it seems unlikely that we're going to resolve such a deep mystery, not without some major new scientific breakthroughs in the study of the mind. If we knew just how to make songs that would move people, we could manufacture them to a formula, churning out as much as we liked rather than having to wait for a songwriter to be struck by inspiration.

But we do have the beginnings of an answer, and some clues as to why we love to listen to such negative punk songs. At the very least, a consideration of the history and philosophy of dark art should make clear how absurd it is to dismiss a love of dark punk music as something degenerate or unhealthy. As long as you don't actually beat on any brats with a baseball bat, or kick anyone in the head as they kneel down to pray, you should listen to whatever you like.

28

Riot Grrrl Punk as Feminist Creation

Patrick D. Anderson

The "Riot Grrrl Manifesto" appeared in the second issue of *Bikini Kill Zine*, published in 1991 by the Olympia, Washington-based band Bikini Kill. Announcing that a new era of punk had arrived, the manifesto told readers just what Riot Grrrl was all about: "Girls constitute a revolutionary soul force that can, and will change the world for real."

Bikini Kill consisted of Kathleen Hanna (vocals), Tobi Vail (drums), Kathi Wilcox (bass), and Billy Karren (guitar). Hanna, Vail, and Wilcox met while attending Evergreen State College. Hanna had been active in the local art scene for several years, and after she picked up a copy of Vail's zine *Jigsaw*, they formed a band in late 1990.

Bikini Kill was not the first punk band to feature women performers, but they were among the first to take an explicitly feminist stance. Alongside Bratmobile, Heavens to Betsy, Huggy Bear, Sleater-Kinney, and others, Bikini Kill led the Riot Grrrl revolution in punk, vowing to confront not only sexism and patriarchy but also, as the manifesto stated, "bullshit like racism, able-bodieism, ageism, speciesism, classism, thinism, sexism, antisemitism, and heterosexism."

Riot Grrrl punk flourished between two explicitly un-feminist eras of music. Before Riot Grrrl, women rockers like Janis Joplin, Joni Mitchell, and even Patti Smith and The Runaways openly disavowed feminism. After Riot Grrrl, corporate record labels co-opted the fiery spirit of Riot Grrrl to market commercialized acts like the Spice Girls, Alanis Morissette, and Fiona Apple. But Riot Grrrl bands believed that women could do more than participate in rock music—they could change the genre and the world. As Tobi Vail says, Riot Grrrls believed that "if girls started bands, it would transform culture—and not just empower them as individuals, but change society. It would not just put them in a position of power, but the world would actually change" (Meltzer, *Girl Power*, p. 11).

The Riot Grrrl movement has been widely recognized as feminist, which means it worked for gender equality by fighting sexism and patriarchy. But Riot Grrrl bands also stand as examples of *feminist aesthetic creation*. Aesthetics is a branch of philosophy that reflects upon standards of beauty and taste, especially with regard to artistic expression. Feminist aesthetics reflects upon the specifically male-centered values of traditional art, while simultaneously creating artworks that disrupt male dominated forms of expression. When you mix feminist politics, aesthetic theory, and punk rock, you get Riot Grrrl.

Sexist Society and the Punk Scene

Not all feminists agree that patriarchy is universal across all cultures, but there is wide agreement that western societies have been and still are patriarchal, meaning they are dominated by men, particularly white men. One of the basic arguments of feminist philosophy is that patriarchal social arrangements harm women, not only by denying them access to independent political and economic power but also by fostering sexist attitudes in both men and women. Because men control culture, cultural values often represent men's point of view. Insofar as women adopt the values of male-dominated cultures, they, too, can internalize sexist attitudes, using those attitudes to keep other women—and even themselves—subordinate to men.

Many feminists argue that the beauty standards of the dominant culture are created by men and for men, and whenever a woman adopts those beauty standards as her own, she is reinforcing patriarchy. Other feminists go farther, arguing that patriarchal social structures position women as objects, property to be owned and traded. To be sure, the term "feminist" is not synonymous with "woman": not all women are feminists, and not all feminists are women.

Feminists disagree about how to best to describe patriarchy and sexism; they also disagree about the best remedy for these problems. Some feminists argue that women must form their own societies separate from men, while others argue that patriarchy (rule by men) should be replaced with matriarchy (rule by women) because "feminine" values are more nurturing and less violent than "masculine" values. Most feminists, however, argue not for separation or matriarchy but for the reconfiguration of society along egalitarian lines. Such feminists advocate reorganizing societies so all humans, regardless of sex or gender, are equally empowered to participate in politics, economics, and culture. There is no consensus regarding the "progress" of the feminist cause. Many feminists believe that progress has been made *and* that there is still a long way to go before we achieve gender equality.

Punk subculture differentiates itself from mainstream culture by rejecting mainstream cultural norms, including the norms of sexism and patriarchy. Men and women in the punk scene are more open to feminist ideals of gender egalitarianism than those in the mainstream culture. Some mainstream feminists argue that women should have "access" to positions of establishment power. They want to see more women CEOs and even a woman president. Punks largely reject this view because it just means letting women use the tools of capitalism and imperialism to exploit and kill people like men. As Craig O'Hara explains, "Punks' conception of feminism does not involve applauding women who rise (or sink) to men's stereotype of toughness. Women fighting in Desert Storm, female politicians such as Margaret Thatcher, or women who gain authority and prominence in exploitative multinational corporations are not looked upon as inspirations" (O'Hara, p. 105). Many punks believe that patriarchal structures and sexist attitudes harm women *and* men because they are inauthentic conceptions of the self and because they contribute to harmful social practices: war, exploitation, domination, and ecological destruction.

Despite rejecting mainstream cultural norms, not all punks embrace feminism and gender equality. Some men in the punk scene have retained the sexist attitudes of mainstream culture, seeking to dismantle punk rock egalitarianism and transform the scene into a space for alternative macho expression. Some commentators blame the emergence of hardcore punk, while others blame the suburbanization of punk. Regardless of the explanation, there are pockets within the punk scene where men might reject preppy or jock versions of masculinity but nevertheless still believe they have a right to control and "own" social spaces. At punk shows, macho punks grope and sexually assault women. They use their superior size and strength to drive women from the pit. They jeer women bands, calling them "dykes" and pressuring them to "take it off." Women punks have testified that they avoid shows in such scenes because they fear for their safety. Even male-led bands have criticized sexism within the punk scene. Songs such as Dead Kennedys'

"Macho Insecurity," Fugazi's "Suggestion," Propagandhi's "Refusing to be a Man," and Good Riddance's "A Credit to His Gender" come to mind as examples. But the fact remains that the punk scene has not expunged all sexism from its midst.

Riot Grrrls certainly objected to the patriarchy and sexism of mainstream culture and establishment politics, yet the primary concern of the movement was to call out and challenge the sexism *within* punk. At their shows, Riot Grrrl bands used a variety of tactics to address women's issues, looking to transform the concert space—the stage, the pit—from a hostile, violent environment into a welcoming atmosphere. Using a "women to the front" tactic, Riot Grrrl bands encouraged girls to congregate near the stage and encouraged men to move out of the way. This practice was intended to remove the male-centered culture of the pit and equalize space at the barricades along gender lines.

This reversal of privileged spectator positions was accompanied by a reversal of privileged concerns. In male-dominated scenes, men treat shows as a space to expresses entitled masculinity, but at Riot Grrrl shows, bands would frequently stop playing to address immediate concerns of women audience members. Instances of sexism, harassment, and sexual assault were immediately and publicly addressed, shaming or otherwise punishing the offender and deterring future instances of male aggression. Some Riot Grrrl bands began holding women-only gigs, creating a space for women and women's culture. Riot Grrrl shows were meant to disrupt the sexist, male-dominated spaces of punk shows, "fostering and supporting girl scenes and girl artists of all kinds," as the Riot Grrrl Manifesto demanded.

Feminist Aesthetic Criticism and the Male Gaze

When the Riot Grrrl movement emerged, they represented not just feminist politics but also feminist aesthetics. There are two aspects to feminist aesthetics. The first aspect is *feminist aesthetic criticism*, which involves interpreting existing artworks and art forms to reveal the explicit or implicit sexist, patriarchal values expressed in those works. While the male-dominated tradition of aesthetic criticism in western philosophy has often treated artworks as ahistorical, transcendent objects uncontaminated by time, place, and culture, feminist critics argue that all art is situated in specific historical and cultural contexts and created by living, breathing humans. While traditional aesthetic critics view artists as geniuses who tap into the truths of a universal human experience, feminist critics view artists as embodied people who think about the world using the cultural values of their time, place, and identity. Since almost all art has been produced by men (and women) who live in patriarchal, sexist societies, most art will reflect patriarchal, sexist values.

The central concept of feminist aesthetic criticism is "the male gaze." As it is discussed by feminist critics, the male gaze is a phenomenon reflected in artworks. This gaze reflects the perspective a masculine and often heterosexual artist or "subject," as philosophers say, and depicts women and the world as objects of pleasure for male "subjects." In this framing, men are creative agents who make art, while women are passive objects depicted in art. As a result, artworks that express the male gaze determine how women are "seen."

There is a kind of taxonomy in how the male gaze "sees" women. On the one hand, women are sometimes *sexed*, becoming an object of erotic desire. Some sexed women are depicted as muses, the angelic, innocent good girls who men are to worship and love. Other sexed women are depicted as whores, the lascivious temptresses who threaten to seduce men into debauchery. On the other hand, women are sometimes *desexed*, being placed outside boundaries of acceptable erotic desires. Some desexed women are depicted as "one of the guys," the non-threatening platonic female friend. Other desexed women are depicted as "the girl with balls," the tough or even "masculine" women who exert enough power to threaten men who are insecure in their manhood.

These four depictions of women are common in heterosexual teenage dating culture. A guy wants to get laid with the whore, but he wants to bring home the muse to meet mother. Likewise, a guy isn't threatened by his best male friend's sister, who might hang around like one of the guys, but he is threatened by the "butch" or the "dyke" who humiliates him or tells him to fuck off.

To understand how the male gaze informs art, let's take movies as an example. Philosopher Mary Devereaux argues that the sexism of the male gaze is reproduced at three levels within filmmaking: production, narrative, and spectator. On the level of *production*, men are largely in control. They decide how money is spent, who it is spent on, and what should take priority. Even though women do make movies, they operate within a male-dominated space. After all, the male gaze is not biologically male but socially male. On the level of *narrative*, film storylines often take a male-centric perspective. Female characters are often secondary characters who are rewarded for being a good girl or dutiful wife, or they are punished for being a vamp or whore. This system of rewards and punishments is oriented by what is in the male interest along the lines of male desires. On the level of the *spectator*, the person watching the film, film audiences are led to identify with the objectives, concerns, values, and desires of male lead characters. By identifying with the male protagonist, film audiences—men and women—learn to adopt the male gaze as their own. Because the male gaze informs the productions and the narrative structure of most films, audiences are taught to "see" the world through the maze gaze. Men and women, then, end up "seeing" men as subjects and women as objects, not only when watching movies, but in their lives more generally.

By rejecting the practice of having all-male bands, Riot Grrrls engaged in feminist aesthetic criticism. As the Riot Grrrl Manifesto stated, "we don't wanna assimilate to someone else's (boy) standards of what is or isn't," and "we are unwilling to let our real and valid anger be diffused and/or turned against us via the internalization of sexism as witnessed in girl/girl jealousism and self defeating girltype behaviors." In other words, Riot Grrrl bands were unwilling to "see" themselves or other through the male gaze. They refused to be sexed or desexed based on what men believed was desirable, and they disrupted the dichotomies of muse/whore and "one of the guys"/"the girl with balls." By forming female-led bands and hitting the stage, Riot Grrrls countered the male gaze with an entirely different value system, one in which women and girls could be more than objects of male "seeing."

In Riot Grrrl art, women reclaimed a role denied to them by traditional western art: they became subjects who expressed their own values and created their own identities. As folk pop musician Liz Phair explains, women watching women rock performers is "like having someone in a movie that you can follow. It's like having a character you can live through…You go to a rock show because you want the guy to stare at you. You want to be noticed and singled out as an object. And this time, they are watching someone and pretending they are her" (*Girl Power*, p. 20). Because Riot Grrrls controlled the production and therefore the narratives of their performances, they challenged female (and male) audience members to identify with a different gaze.

Riot Grrrl and Feminist Aesthetic Creation

The second aspect of feminist aesthetics is *feminist aesthetic creation*, which involves producing artworks and art forms that

supply or enable a female voice or a female gaze. Unlike traditional western art, which pretends that the male gaze is a universal human perspective, feminist art or aesthetic creations
present audiences with an alternative female gaze without pretending that this perspective is universally human. Instead,
feminist aesthetic creation seeks to pluralize the available
human perspectives, contributing to the diversity of possible
ways of being in the world and understanding the world.
Importantly, feminist aesthetic creation is not simply "traditional art created by women artists." It is art, created by any
person, that adopts a non-male-centric perspective on values
and artistic expression.

Feminist philosophers have identified a few important characteristics of feminist aesthetic creation. Hilde Hein argues
that feminist artists innovate by violating and disrupting
existing standards of "good taste" in art, which means that feminist art is likely to offend or appear in "bad taste" to audiences
with traditional expectations. Hein also argues that feminist
artists intentionally reverse the standards of the male gaze,
revealing it to be but one possible gaze among many. Carolyn
Korsmeyer observes that feminist art incorporates two important practices: the use of non-standard materials and the use
of the body as part of the artwork. These practices are often
found in performance art, which takes art out of the museum
and puts it in our everyday spaces. Such art eliminates the traditional distinction between "crafts" (like quilting) and "fine
art" (like painting and sculpting). Following Hein and
Korsmeyer, we can say that feminist aesthetic creation revolu-
tionizes the gaze by incorporating non-traditional materials,
including the human body, into artistic expression.

In the context of Riot Grrrl punk, feminist aesthetic creation
is not about simply giving women guitars. It is about creatively
using any artistic means available to disrupt male-dominated
aesthetic values. Let's bring this all together and see how Riot
Grrrl bands challenge the male gaze by reshaping punk on
three levels: production, narrative, and spectator.

On the level of production, Riot Grrrls sought to "take over
the means of production in order to create [their] own meanings," as the manifesto declared. Song writing was important to
Riot Grrrl bands, but picking up instruments and microphones
was not the only way they put artistic production back into the
hands of women. They also published zines, reorganized concert spaces, and collaborated with feminist-friendly independent music labels (or started their own labels). Putting women
in charge of production, Riot Grrrls followed the feminist

aesthetic tradition of using non-traditional materials—Xerox machines, cheap guitars, markers, and more—to engender a reversal of production norms, which are usually male-centered and male-dominated. The movement used all of these means of expression to create a national and international network of Riot Grrrl clubs and scenes. Through these organizations, greater numbers of feminist women and men contributed to the movement.

On the level of narrative, Riot Grrrls wrote songs in which women were the protagonists and in which women-women relationships were prioritized over male-female relationships. Songs about women from the male perspective usually describe women as objects of desire within heterosexual gaze. In such songs, women are the worshiped muse, the heartbreaking whore, the cool chick from the show, or the aggressive lesbian. Lyrically, Riot Grrrl bands reversed the tropes in songs about girls, describing women in terms of friendship and bonding. In the Bikini Kill song "Rebel Girl," for instance, Kathleen Hanna sings as a girl, about a girl. The female protagonist of the song does not seek to out-compete a female antagonist by stealing her boyfriend or destroying her self-esteem. Instead, the protagonist seeks solidarity with her counterpart. "That girl thinks she's the queen of the neighborhood," Hanna sings, "I got news for you, she is!" The first half of this lyric suggests that the protagonist dislikes the other girl, but the second half eliminates that interpretation, affirming the value of the other girl. Once the chorus hits, "Rebel girl you are the queen of my world," there is no question that the song is about solidarity among women. Unlike songs informed by the male gaze, the rebel girl does not remove her clothes—she *shares* her clothes with her best friend.

On the level of the spectator, Riot Grrrls pushed audiences to dis-identify with the male gaze and instead adopt a female gaze. Many Riot Grrrls treated their stage performances as performance art, employing the body for subversive ends. In doing so, they disrupted the all the dichotomies of the male gaze. Hanna, for example, famously performed in a skirt and sports bra with "SLUT" scrawled across her midriff in black marker. This tummy message renders visible the implicit sexist assumptions of the male gaze. A male audience member might "see" Hanna as a muse to be loved or a whore to be fucked, but the message in black marker indicated that there's no difference between the muse and whore. Both are merely objectifications of women from the male gaze perspective. The muse is just a whore on a pedestal.

Hanna's performance also breaks down the dichotomy between being "one of the guys" and being "the girl with balls." Her scantily clad clothing undermines any attempted desexing, while her tough, aggressive performance style makes it difficult for male audience members to determine whether she is "one of them" or a threat to their fragile masculinity. Importantly, as Liz Phair's comments above suggest, the girls at the show are provided an opportunity to identify with women, as women, without those identifications being filtered through the male gaze.

Riot Grrrl aesthetic creation therefore not only puts materials into the hands of women. It questions and transforms the underlying ideological and material structures that produce women's oppression. By taking sexuality back through dressing in a certain way, screaming, holding phallic guitars, and asserting control over concert space, Riot Grrrls take up the feminist tactic of employing the body for subversive ends and reverse the values of sexist ideologies.

The Legacy of Riot Grrrl

Riot Grrrl bands thrived during the early 1990s, but the movement left a lasting legacy. On the positive side, some movement's founders are still active. Kathleen Hanna has performed with Le Tigre and The Julie Ruin, and Sleater-Kinney reunited in 2014 to tour and record new music. Riot Grrrl's international influence also inspired the creation of new bands, including War on Women (Baltimore), White Lung (Vancouver), and Pussy Riot (Moscow). On the negative side, the movement has been criticized from various perspectives. In the song "Kill Rock Stars," NOFX vocalist Fat Mike criticizes Hanna for being a militant feminist, telling her "You can't change the world by hating men." Others have criticized Riot Grrrl for representing only cisgender white middle-class women, arguing that the movement ignored—or even reinforced—racism, class exploitation, and transphobia.

Wishing to live up to the values of the Riot Grrrl Manifesto, most Riot Grrrls acknowledge the limitations of the movement and argue that it should be inclusive of all women. While the movement may have had its shortcomings, we should nevertheless recognize it not only for its feminist politics and punk rock ethos, but also for its practice of using feminist aesthetic creation to disrupt the heterosexual male gaze.

29
Anarchy in Aesthetics

S. EVAN KREIDER

Francis Hutcheson, one of the earliest philosophers to think about modern aesthetics, claimed that beauty is a kind of pleasure that we experience in response to the order and complexity of an object. The idea that an orderly and complex form makes something aesthetically pleasing is still quite popular, but are these characteristics really necessary for a work to have aesthetic value?

Punk rock certainly seems to challenge this notion. Evolving in part as a response to what they believed was an overly "artistic" progressive rock, punk purposefully aimed for less complexity and order and more simplicity and chaos—a kind of aesthetic anarchy, as it were. Indeed, it's precisely the simplicity and chaos that makes it such a worthwhile musical genre.

Order and Complexity

For Hutcheson, as for many early modern philosophers, a central concept in aesthetics is that of beauty. According to Hutcheson, beauty is a kind of aesthetic pleasure that humans experience, distinct from other kinds of pleasure, that specifically occurs as a response to an aesthetic idea that Hutcheson calls "uniformity amongst variety."

His account of uniformity amongst variety depends on the type of beauty under discussion, of which there are two: absolute and relative. Absolute beauty is the type relevant to the current discussion; the pleasure we experience is a response to uniformity amongst variety, where (in the case of absolute beauty) "uniformity" means "order" and "variety" means "complexity."

Hutcheson believes that the more of each of these, the greater its absolute beauty; that is, the more orderly and complex the experience of the object is, the more aesthetic pleasure we derive from it. Contrary to colloquial ways of putting it, Hutcheson does not think that objects themselves are beautiful, but rather that beauty is a response we have to certain properties that objects actually have. Following a typical early modern empiricism of philosophers such as John Locke, Hutcheson believes that objects themselves only have so-called "primary qualities" such as size and shape, qualities that are objective and quantifiable. However, those primary qualities give rise to "secondary qualities" such as visual color or audible pitch in the mind of the perceiver. This is also true in the case of beauty, though there's an additional step, as it were: an object has primarily qualities which give rise to secondary qualities in our minds, and then those in turn have the tertiary qualities of various formal relationships. Among those tertiary qualities is uniformity amongst variety, which strictly speaking is what gives rise to our experience of aesthetic pleasure: beauty.

Hutcheson would no doubt have approved of classical music, especially baroque compositions from such composers as Johan Sebastian Bach. As the name "baroque" itself suggests, such music is known for its complexity: ornamentation, including such devices as trills and grace notes, are very common ways to embellish the melody, and multiple simultaneous melodies, as found in fugues, were also widely used. Baroque compositions were also very orderly, tending to follow certain compositional forms: for example, a concerto typically has three movements (one fast, one slow, and another fast), with the orderly exposition and development of specific melodic themes, and a cadenza—a brief period in which the accompanying orchestra stops and the soloist improvises on her own—often punctuating each movement. J.S. Bach's Brandenburg Concertos are excellent examples of complexity and order in baroque music, as are Antonio Vivaldi's *The Four Seasons*.

Of course, complexity and order aren't limited to classical music. Jazz, particularly the subgenre known as "bebop," is known for its order. Most bebop tunes have a very orderly structure of specific chord changes that are played through over and over, first for the "head" (the main melody of the tune) which is itself usually played twice through, and then a number of additional choruses (repetitions of the chord changes) for each soloist, and then ending with the head again, which serves to bookend the entire tune. There is also the orderly correlation of various scales with which an instrumentalist plays his solo over each chord in the form; for a very simple example, a major scale would typically be used over a major chord.

Bebop is very much known for its complexity as well. Starting with a simple (pre-bebop) tune, the chord changes were often made much more complex by adding extra chords and chord substitutions; for example, a simple three chord blues tune usually has at least a couple of extra chords in bebop, and soloists might introduce additional chord substitutions and variations off-the-cuff as they solo. Particularly good examples of the order and complexity of bebop can be found in many of the works of masters such as Charlie Parker (such as "Confirmation") and John Coltrane (for instance "Giant Steps").

Many sub-genres of rock music tend to be simpler than baroque or bebop, but not all. The progressive rock (a.k.a. art rock) bands of the 1970s also strove for order and complexity, often through straightforward use of classical and jazz techniques. The band Emerson, Lake, and Palmer was particularly known for this, including rock interpretations of pieces by classical composers such as Alberto Ginastera and Modest Mussorgsky (admittedly not baroque composers, but broadly classical composers who still aimed for a degree of order and complexity), as well as Bach's "Two Part Invention in D Minor." However, many other sub-genres of rock music tended toward less complex and orderly forms and techniques, punk perhaps more than any. Indeed, much punk music arose specifically as a reaction to and rejection of the supposed excesses of progressive rock, and deliberately pursued a simpler and more chaotic style.

Much of the simplicity of punk can be seen in the song structure. Whereas a jazz tune is likely to have four or five chords as a minimum, many punk songs take that as a maximum. The Sex Pistols' "Problem" relies primarily on three chords, only introducing a fourth briefly during the bridge. The Ramones' "Blitzkrieg Bop" also has only four chords, while their "Judy Is Punk" has only three. Furthermore, punk music tends to use simpler chords, often sticking to three-note chords such as the major or minor, or even two-note "power chords" that lack a note that even identifies it as specifically major or minor. The chaotic nature of punk is more difficult to see on paper, as transcribed sheet music seems to indicate orderly chord progressions and song structure (verse, then bridge, then chorus—repeat as needed).

The chaos lies in the performance, whether as heard on an album or at a live show: drum parts often feature loud, random fills and cymbal crashes; guitars and bass often feature distorted sounds, with the guitars in particular adding screeching licks seemingly from nowhere; singers often "degenerate" from singing discernable melodies to speaking or even screaming atonally; and of course, live shows rarely featured calm, well-behaved performances from the members of the band, who typically opted to thrash around and gesticulate wildly, if not obscenely. The result is a style of music clearly inappropriate for Hutcheon's standards. However, there may be other ways of looking at the nature of music, from which punk may fare better.

Emotion and Expression

In contrast to focusing on formal properties such as order and complexity, we could instead consider art in terms of its emotional content and purpose. Leo Tolstoy, of *War and Peace* fame, believed that the defining feature of art was its emotional content, and that its primary purpose was to arouse emotions in the audience in a straightforward, literal manner. For example, a tragic story might contain emotion of sadness, and the purpose of the story is quite literally to make the audience feel sad.

For Tolstoy, this also serves not only as a means to understand the nature of art, but also to evaluate works of art. Specifically, a work of art is good if it arouses morally and spiritually appropriate emotions, and bad if it arouses inappropriate ones or none at all. Tolstoy himself spelled this out in terms of Christian values, so good works of art are ones that arouse Christian-approved emotions, and bad ones are those that do not. However, we can easily generalize this outside of Tolstoy's own very specific value system and say that good art serves the purpose of promoting various ethical, political, and perhaps even religious values, whatever those might be.

Some philosophers thought of Tolstoy's arousal approach to art and emotion as a bit too simplistic, while agreeing with his general point that art has something to do with emotion. Benedetto Croce and R.G. Collingwood argued instead that the purpose of art is not to arouse emotion, but to express it. As a result, the audiences' job is not to feel the emotions, but to be aware of the emotional content of the work, which then allows the audience to reflect on that content in a more removed manner.

According to this theory, a funeral scene in a novel should not cause the reader to burst into tears, but rather to contemplate the nature of sadness, death, and loss. For expression theories, there is no need for the work to contain moral, political, or religious values, though there is certainly no prohibition against such content either, so the emotions expressed may in some cases give the audience the opportunity to reflect on the emotional aspects of important issues in real life.

Emotion-centered theories of aesthetics certainly do capture a wide variety of artistic works, especially music. In the classical world, romanticism is known for its expressiveness, with composers such as Beethoven writing many pieces precisely to communicate emotional content. The second movement of Beethoven's seventh symphony is essentially a funeral march, and it clearly expresses grief and loss; indeed, it is often used in movie and television soundtracks precisely to accompany sad scenes. The final movement of his ninth symphony, the "Ode to Joy," is quite well-known for its use of vocals (and also used a great deal in soundtracks) and clearly communicates joyous feelings even if you don't understand the original German "O Freunde, nicht diese Töne! Sondern laßt uns angenehmere anstimmen, und freudenvollere!" ("Oh friends, not these sounds! Let us instead strike up more pleasing and more joyful ones!").

Despite its apparently academic and abstract nature, jazz too has its emotional variants. So-called "cool" jazz is a particularly accessible style of jazz, precisely due to its more expressive aspects, with more laid-back approaches to tempo and melody, much of which prioritizes emotional content over heady music theory. Vocal jazz pieces especially express emotion, wedding lyrics to music in order to communicate feelings, including straightforward love songs. When Nina Simone sings "I Put a Spell on You" and delivers the lyrics "I love you anyhow, and I don't care / If you don't want me, I'm yours right now," the listener knows just how she feels.

From the point of view of emotion-related theories of art, punk fares far better than it did under Hutcheson's formalist account. A great deal of punk seems designed specifically to arouse and express various emotions, especially anger and angst. The Sex Pistols' "Liar" lashes out: "You lie, lie, lie, tell me why, tell me why, why d'you have to lie . . . Now I wanna know why you never look me in the face, broke a confidence just to please your ego, should've realized you know what I know," we can hear the seething anger in Johnny Lydon's voice. So too, The Ramones' "I Wanna Be Sedated" hits the listener with the ironic but angst-filled lines: "Twenty-twenty-twenty-four hours to go, I wanna be sedated / Nothing to do, nowhere to go home, I wanna be sedated / Just, get me to the airport, put me on a plane, hurry, hurry, hurry, before I go insane / I can't control my fingers, I can't control my brain, oh no, oh-oh oh-oh."

Punk was also capable of much more than raw emotion, of course. Often the emotions expressed were meant to give the listener not just something to feel, but something to contemplate in a more distanced way (as Croce and Collingwood suggested), perhaps something that a particular listener may not have experienced for herself but of which she ought to be aware. For example, in "Know Your Rights" by the The Clash, we are told "You have the right not to be killed; murder is a crime / Unless it was done by a policeman or an aristocrat." Many listeners may not have suffered legal and political injustice themselves, but the song gives them the occasion to feel the injustice indirectly, for the purposes of political consciousness-raising. Similarly, "Tin Soldiers" by Stiff Little Fingers communicates the exploitation of the youth by the military: "Tin soldier, he signed away his name / Tin soldier, no chance for cash or fame / Tin soldier, now he knows the truth / Tin soldier, he signed away his youth." You don't have to be a member of the armed forces to appreciate the disillusionment so many young recruits must have felt.

Formalism Revisited

Hutcheson's formalist account of beauty required order and complexity, but not all formalist theories do. Many philosophers have incorporated formalist accounts into their aesthetics, but in a way that allow for simplicity and perhaps even a little chaos. One such philosopher is the great ancient Greek himself, Aristotle.

Though Aristotle's aesthetics is largely limited to an analysis of tragedy, and though his account incorporates other approaches such as *mimesis* ("representation") and didacticism (instruction), he does take the time to analyze the formal framework of tragedy, and in doing so, places great value on a kind of simplicity that he refers to as unity.

Unity of action is the requirement that the tragedy have a single set of events that are clearly causally related; that is, a single plotline, rather than multiple simultaneous plots or subplots. Unity of place is that the tragedy takes place in a single setting; no jumping around among multiple locations. Unity of time is that the tragedy takes place over a single day; no stories told over long periods of time, no flashbacks or flashforwards. In all of these, it's the simplicity of the story that makes it clear and coherent, according to Aristotle; additional complexity would simply get in the way of tragedy communicating its instructional (usually moral or political) message.

Admittedly, it's a bit harder to find the chaos in Aristotle: like Hutcheson, he probably would have approved of order for the most part. However, even in Aristotle, there's a dash of chaos in the dramatic element that we refer to these days as tragic irony. Irony of this kind involves an apparent inversion of cause and effect, especially with regard to human action. For example, Oedipus learns of the prophecy that he will kill his father and marry his mother, and so leaves home to avoid doing so. However, unbeknownst to him, he was adopted, so that the couple that raised him are not his biological parents. By leaving home, he actually brings about the prophecy he intended to avoid, when he runs into his (to him, unknown) father and kills him, and eventually (and again, unknowingly) marries his biological mother. This is still orderly in some sense—it's the causal result of Oedipus' actions—but it is unexpected (at least to the characters in the story), and it brings about the tragic events that shape the drama. In this way, the "chaos" of the unexpected turn of events is precisely what makes it dramatically interesting; there would not be much of a story if Oedipus had successfully avoided the prophecy.

Both classical and jazz music contain their share of simpler styles. In classical music, the period after the baroque period, featuring composers such as Mozart and Haydn, developed in reaction to what they saw as the overly complex baroque style; in fact, the word "baroque" literally means "misshapen" and was used as a criticism of the complex compositions of that period. So too, jazz had its reaction to the complexity of bebop, in the form of modal music, especially popularized by composers such as Miles Davis, and which featured very simple forms, sometimes only containing one or two chords, and very simple scale forms with which to solo over those chords. Chaos, admittedly, may be a bit rarer in classical and jazz, but there are certainly more experimental forms of classical music in the twentieth century (consider John Cage's *4 33*), and of course, there's free jazz (such as the album of the same name by Ornette Coleman), which featured wholly improvised tunes (rather than merely improvised solos over standard forms).

As previously described, punk definitely tends toward simplicity and chaos. However, whereas Hutcheson would have criticized this, Aristotle might have been more forgiving, precisely because it is not merely the formal properties that determine the aesthetic worth of the piece, but also its moral and political instructional value. Punk's simpler and more chaotic style was precisely the best way for it to communicate its sociopolitical content. The Sex Pistol's "Anarchy in the UK" (with its references to the conflicts in Ireland and their possible effects on Britain) and "God Save the Queen" (containing obvious criticisms of the British monarchy) are clear examples of this: the primary purpose of these tunes was to communicate dissatisfaction with politics, and the simple, chaotic style is precisely what is needed to do so. Similarly, The Clash's "Tommy Gun" (a reflection on terrorism) and "Rock the Casbah" (inspired by the censorship of Western music in certain Middle Eastern countries) make their points plain to hear; any more orderly or complex approach would simply dilute the message. The list of political punk tunes is a long one, and in each case, the simple and chaotic style is what allowed it to speak to Britain's "angry youth" much more effectively (they claimed) than the progressive rock to which they were responding.

Anarchy and Aesthetics

Francis Hutcheson's emphasis on order and complexity is found in aesthetics in general to one degree or another, not to mention many styles of music such as baroque, bebop, and progressive rock. However, Hutcheson was almost certainly wrong to think that order and complexity are better in all cases, and punk music serves as an excellent counter-example.

The aesthetics implicit in punk has almost certainly contributed to its appreciation and enjoyment by listeners. We hope that it could also influence philosophers to accept a bit more chaos and simplicity. We could all use a little more anarchy in our aesthetics.

VII

Punk Ethics

30
Good Guys Don't Wear White

LINDSEY J. SCHWARTZ

Philosophical revelations are often surprising. It might seem paradoxical to claim that punk rock—a notoriously defiant cultural phenomenon—is, essentially, the living, breathing embodiment of virtue ethics in action. Nevertheless, I will convince you that it is!

You see, in its own perfectly imperfect way, the punk scene exemplifies the essentially action-oriented process of becoming—ever *becoming*; never *being*—virtuous. At its core there is a DIY version of the Aristotelian process of virtue acquisition (Aristotle, *Nicomachean Ethics*) driven by a principled hostility toward the ugliness on display, daily, in millions of little ways the world over.

Punk rejects the world's ugliness, it disdains moral exhaustion, and it confronts us all with a litany of often contradictory moral demands. No matter who or what you are—an individual, an institution, a pacifist, an anarchist, a prince, a pauper—punk is going to stick it to you. In punk's view of the world (as in Aristotle's), *no one* is ever really good enough. No one is really *good* at all, because goodness is an ideal that remains out of reach for you so long as you are breathing. Still, it's an ideal worth striving to attain. So while none of us is quite the punk we take ourselves to be, it's the process of *becoming* that punk that leading a good life is really all about anyway.

What Is Virtue?

Good guys, bad guys—which is which?
The white collar worker or the digger in the ditch?
Man, who's to say who's the better man?
I'm always doing the best I can.

—Minor Threat, covering The Standells, "Good Guys (Don't Wear White)"

Moral philosophy covers a range of considerations about the good life: how to live well; how to judge people, actions, or events as right or wrong, good or bad; how we ought to treat each other; and so forth. Aristotle considered the ability to properly answer these questions a kind of "practical wisdom"— a kind of know-how.

Basically every time you ask yourself, *what should I do?*, in any context from choosing which color car to buy to deciding whether to give your money or your time to charity, you're engaged in the practice of normative reasoning. Moral reasoning is a special kind of normative reasoning. To Aristotle, virtue applies to the whole normative domain. You can virtuously choose a car color just as you can virtuously choose whether to give your time or money to charity. Importantly, because all normative questions are about what you ought to *do*, Aristotle took virtue to be essentially action-oriented. A virtuous person doesn't merely have the right thoughts and feelings or make the right value judgments. Rather, she's generally disposed—or *habituated*—to choose the right *course of action*, to *do the right thing*, in any situation. But how can you tell which is the *right* course of action?

You learn practical wisdom in two ways: by example and by understanding. But *practice* is what makes a person really practically wise. The action-orientation of punk is the first of many facets of the genre that support its characterization as virtue ethics in action. Punk began as a sort of action: a grand performative backlash to the alarmingly superficial political correctness of the mid-twentieth century. In 1950s America, politeness was largely taken to be part and parcel of goodness, but by the 1970s, a large chunk of the youth had the scales shaken from their eyes. They'd learned that being *polite* isn't the same thing as being *good*; that being easy to look at isn't the same thing as being respectable. In response to what they saw as a ridiculous cultural deference to mere appearances, detractors possessed of just the right amount of piss and vinegar declared themselves anarchists and antichrists, donned studded leather and shit-kicking boots, spiked their hair and pierced their faces, picked up loud instruments, and hurled sonic invective at not just the establishment, but all of those who perpetuated it by buying into it.

Soon, the somewhat bleary-eyed angst of the earliest punk rockers was joined by the likes of Crass, who used the same medium to challenge not just superficiality, but misogyny and male supremacy, religion as the arbiter of goodness and truth, homophobia, sexual repression, and myriad other social constructs that were taken to be paragons of righteousness.

They trashed these notions in spectacular fashion (perhaps none more spectacular than the scorched earth polemic that is "Reality Asylum"), and in so doing began to develop the moral spine of the punk rock movement.

By the 1980s, the ethos of punk had started to splinter into several loosely cohesive factions and the genre began to come into its own. Punk was all about action: raising money at shows to help feed the poor, supporting each other as an artistic community, taking underwing the homeless and disaffected youth, all the while sporting mohawks and liberty spikes because it isn't the haircut that makes a person respectable. The punk world had produced role models one could really look up to.

Punk Heroes Past

I don't need you to tell me what to do
And I don't need you to tell me what to be (Fuck you!)
I don't need you to tell me what to say
And I don't need you to tell me what to think.

—Anti-Flag, "Die for Your Government"

The story of punk rock is in large part the story of admiring, emulating, and rejecting punk heroes past. We learn practical wisdom in two ways: by example and by understanding. One crucial part of becoming a virtuous person is having an exemplar—a teacher who demonstrates the virtues in their day-to-day actions. It is impossible to understate the importance of this piece of virtue theory. Some introductory ethics books (such as Shafer-Landau's *Fundamentals*) focus on this aspect of the theory to the exclusion of nearly everything else about it. That's how important it is. But the second part is crucial, too, because the second part is learning how to figure out what to do once you're out there on your own. Many punk kids from the 1970s and 1980s know all about both of these avenues for growth first-hand.

You might say the first punk rock exemplars were *anti-*exemplars. They were shining beacons of what *not* to be like. But there were also proto-punks from the 1960s and 1970s. I quoted Minor Threat, but included in the attribution is the band they were covering, a 1960s LA garage band called The Standells. There were plenty of bands like this, quietly cultivating the punk rock mentality before it took off in the Seventies. These proto-punks gave rise to more than a few personalities the kids could be proud to model themselves after. Here are just a few of them.

I. Ian MacKaye (Minor Threat, Fugazi): DIY and Straight Edge

Ian MacKaye had plenty of musicians to look up to, but eventually became an exemplar in his own right. He exemplifies two virtues in particular: the virtue of self-reliance and that of self-respect. His bands' releases were one hundred percent independent and one hundred percent DIY, turned out on his co-owned label, Dischord Records, which supported several local D.C. bands with no corporate sponsor required. But that's just the tip of the iceberg.

On top of co-creating the label and releasing his own albums, he essentially birthed the "straight edge" movement in punk. Whatever else you want to say about it, it's made the scene an inclusive, welcoming place for both those who desperately need to get off of drugs and those wary of the perils of addiction to begin with. MacKaye wrote a song declaring that his choice to stay sober gave him a certain advantage, an edge—what he called a *straight edge*—that helped him keep on top of his game and his aspirations as a musician. Rock bands were cool in part because they got high, got drunk, wrecked hotel rooms, and got to play out the glamorous live-fast-and-die-young lifestyle. MacKaye didn't want that for himself. He made clear that his creative capacities are worthy of respect not despite, but because he rejected the crutch of substance use. A lot of people who might not be otherwise are alive today because of his influence and the influence of those who embraced the straight edge ethic alongside him.

II. Jeff Ott (Fifteen, Crimpshrine): Value Coherence and Ought Implies Ought

That band put out their own record
I think that's so fucking cool.
Even though their songs are sexist
They're DIY so I guess they changed the world.

    —Fifteen, "Punk Song"

Whatever your merits, improvement is always possible. Jeff Ott was one of many young punks in the Eighties and Nineties who resisted any dogmatic deference to the DIY ethic of the punk scene. It wasn't DIY *per se* that he found objectionable, but to the extent that keeping his art independent and thus "authentic" meant staying poor, destitute, and homeless, it seemed to leave something—*lots* of things—to be desired.

When Green Day hit it big and the scene renounced the band as pop-punk sellouts, Ott came to their defense. You see, his gigs were raising a couple bucks here and there for local causes, but Green Day's were netting *tens of thousands* (Jeff Ott, *My World*) When he really thought about it, it seemed pretty stupid to refuse to do something that would make your impact that much bigger. Why *not* go mainstream? Why *not* reach more people and do more good? What's so sacrosanct about poverty? Aristotle can relate! He taught for money, which made him, too, something of a sellout in his day. But there's a difference between selling out and enjoying commercial success. Ott didn't reject all things DIY. He just couldn't get behind the piety of being impoverished. He couldn't get behind a dogmatic worldview that refused to take a good, hard look in the mirror and conduct a genuine self-evaluation once in a while, especially in light of evidence that something you once thought was obviously good might be more complicated than you originally imagined.

That's Jeff Ott, though. His bands' catalogs are a wellspring of rage against every kind of injustice you can imagine, including the moral failings of his own one-time punk heroes. He learned from those who went before him and idolized them just like anyone else did. But he had the presence of mind to step back and look at things with an independent, hard-won sense of clarity. Proud as he was that his scene routinely ejected wayward neo-Nazi types who wandered in looking for a place to belong, he still noticed the dearth of non-white faces in the crowd. Proud as he was to have rejected the womanizing culture of the stereotypical high school jock, he couldn't help but notice the way women were treated like prizes or playthings in his own scene. The more he bothered to take notice, the more hypocrisy he saw. You think doing drugs is bad? Okay, sure. But get a load of these politicians who would rather you die on the street than let you get a hold of a clean needle! Why trash the addicts? Whose side are you on anyway?

Ott came for everybody: the landlords, the politicians, the cops, the media, his fans, his scene, even himself. What Ott brings to this story is commitment, a nearly obscene value coherence, and the rejection of the idea that *ought* implies *can*—that in order to be morally obligated to do something, it had better be possible to do it. Isn't it true that even if I don't have the money, it would be a better state of affairs if I were feeding the world's hungry? And doesn't that mean that there is a sense in which I am subject to a standing *ought*—that I *ought* to feed the hungry—whether or not I am capable of that at any given time? The same applies across the board. Jeff Ott is the only person I know who greets the death of each successive political figure with a resounding "good riddance to another war criminal." It would be great if becoming, say, President of the United States didn't mean also becoming a *de facto* war criminal, but it does. And the fact that it does is no excuse. It's crazy that someone has to say this aloud, but no matter what comes with the job, you still *should not do war crimes*. Ott tries every day to *live* his values. He's a real exemplar's exemplar. He's not always right, but he's doing his best, and his steadfast commitment to upholding his most deeply held beliefs is unassailable.

III. Billie Joe Armstrong (Green Day): Humility

Billie Joe Armstrong exemplifies the virtue of humility. The word has an unfortunately negative connotation, but for our purposes, consider what it means in contrast to *pride*. Green Day is a hugely successful, sometimes pop-y punk band, often maligned by the elders and the youth of its own scene. But the guys in the band are genuinely stand-up guys. They keep it humble, and for that, they are one hundred percent worthy of respect.

I saw Green Day play many years ago in Kansas City. Partway through the set they started inviting local musicians onto the stage and relinquishing their instruments to these people from the crowd who promised they *really could* play the drums, the bass, the guitar. "Anyone here play the drums? . . . Like really? . . . How long have you been playing? . . . Get up here." Each of them was given a quick rundown of what to play, and they proceeded to cover an Operation Ivy song—I don't remember which one—with Armstrong on vocals. Elated that they'd gotten to do this really cool thing, they started jumping off the stage to rejoin the crowd, but Armstrong stopped the guy he'd recruited to play guitar. "Hold on a sec. What do you think of that guitar? . . . It's yours." Only the kid who played Armstrong's guitar that night walked away with a tangible treasure, but each of them got something far more important than a famous guy's instrument. They got a *taste*. Armstrong had *supported* them the way the Gilman Street scene had supported him in his youth. He may have been on an enormous stage in front of thousands of people, but there was no reason he couldn't treat it the same way he'd treat a club gig: raising money for good causes, supporting the kids who are just coming up in the scene. And people call this guy, this band sellouts.

They're not the first or the only band to do something like that, but it has certainly earned them the title of Punk Rock Exemplar for tens of thousands more kids than they could have reached absent their commercial success.

In a recent interview with *Vulture Magazine* (Craig Jenkins), Armstrong said that his favorite band from his Gilman Street days was Crimpshrine, one of Ott's bands. He respected their DIY ethic, their friendship, and the way they cared for the scene, other people, and the things that really mattered to them. Say what you will about a massively successful band that tours in huge stadiums for beaucoup bucks a head. They have not forgotten where they came from. I doubt they ever will.

Protest the Hero and the Doctrine of the Mean

You don't just develop a virtuous disposition by emulating those who exemplify specific virtues; you must also learn to identify the virtuous action for yourself in any situation. There's an element of trial and error involved. Here's where you might think my inclusivity gets really questionable, but stay with me! The last band I want to talk about is Protest the Hero. You might question their punk rock credentials. I submit to you (and at this point it should be clear) that punk is not a sound, it's an ethos. It is perfectly possible to be quintessentially punk and compose songs that rock prog guitarmonies sick enough to bring a tear to your eye. Even if you think they've become something else, they started out squarely in the punk genre, and all justifications aside, just get out of here already with your elitism. I mean look at you, trying to be the arbiter of what's punk and what's not!

Protest the Hero exemplifies what it is to have internalized the virtues; to be the kind of person who habitually chooses the right course of action. They exemplify what it is to live according to the Aristotelian doctrine of the mean, and they do it in a way that makes clear that it is not a doctrine of moderation, as many think. Neither is it a doctrine of compromise. Rather, it's a doctrine of *relativity* intended to help its users hit a moving target.

You must learn in the course of becoming virtuous how to determine the right course of action relative to the circumstances and to the attributes of those involved. Your teachers won't always be there; you'll eventually have to fly on your own, so one thing it's important to cultivate in the process of becoming the punk you always wanted to be is the ability to discern for yourself what is right for you in the moment. You'll have to consider and appropriately weigh a host of factors to succeed. Ajax, famed strongman of Ancient Greece, should consume large quantities of proteins and carbohydrates in advance of a wrestling tournament, Aristotle says, but consuming the same quantity of food that's appropriate for Ajax in his circumstances is unlikely *ever* to be appropriate for, say, your typical radiologist. Being virtuous isn't a matter of simply following blanket prescriptions like *never be quick to anger*. Rather, it involves knowing *when it is and is not appropriate* for *you, in your circumstances* to be quick to anger. In Aristotle's terms, the virtuous action is the mean between two extremes. Courage, for instance, is a virtue beset on either side by the vices of rashness and cowardice. Courage is knowing when it is appropriate to stand firm in the face of danger. Rashness is running blindly toward danger without any good reason to do so; cowardice is to shrink from it even when something impor-tant depends on facing it. It isn't moderation; it's *calculation*.

Protest the Hero could never be accused of being moderate. Their lyrics cover nearly every contemporary moral question in the most quintessentially punk rock, confrontational way possible from rape culture ("No one is innocent if they go free / When we handraise the Beast and the Beast runs wild / We must speak of our own involvement in the rape of a child") to the food we produce and consume ("If I believed in meat, I'd eat a plateful of our dead") to breed specific legislation ("And if a pit bull is a weapon you'll have to pry them from my cold dead hands"). They are furious. And they are right to be.

Protest the Hero has played the whole game. As I said, they started out just like any other punk band, and when they made it (in a perhaps different but certainly adjacent genre!), they signed a standard (nevertheless predatory) three-record deal. By the end of that contract, they could not have been more vocal about wanting out:

> There's no such thing as unconditional
> No contracts bind you in the end
> Make no mistake, this is a killing ground
> Blood hungry and camouflaged as friends
> Select 'yes' at the end of this mess
> If you get there and it's your only fucking option left
> These days I don't know the people I'm supposed to trust
> And I don't trust these people that I'm supposed to know. (Protes
> the Hero, "Dunsel")

So, they got out. They crowd-sourced the funds to produce their fourth album at a quality recording studio, and they produced a masterpiece. As just one more middle finger to the industry that had nearly broken them, that album, *Volition*, contained eleven tracks, one more than the ten per album they'd produced each time before. What's right for this band, *in their circumstances*, is persisting without the backing of a record company through direct engagement with fans, and without compromising the sound quality their fans have come to expect. It's getting to keep musically conveying their sincere beliefs about what matters without compromising those beliefs for themselves. This is their mean: the virtuous space between being nobody and being compromised.

All virtue is beset on either side by vice. All virtue is relative. Punk's pendulum has swung back and forth over the decades between the vices of pious self-deprivation and soulless self-compromise. Protest the Hero has at times been mired in both. But they learned from it. They learned by *doing*. Virtue is essentially action-oriented.

Ever Becoming

You've learned from others and worked out how to decide for yourself. You have a good temperament, a good eye for things, a good sense of right and wrong like you have a good metabolism or a healthy resting heart rate. It's *physical*, in a sense. You build muscle by lifting; you build virtue by acting. Being good at anything requires practice.

Since virtue is essentially action-oriented, since it can only be acquired by practice, and since it depends on the circumstances, it is impossible ever to *be* a virtuous person. So long as you are alive, it is possible to devolve into viciousness. And yet, that means that no matter where you are at any moment, it is also possible to change for the better. It's never too late. It is never completely out of your hands. The point is: *being* virtuous was never the mortal goal. The goal is to keep your focus trained on *becoming* virtuous, to continue doing virtuous things.

The aging punks of the world are still out there trying, doing, behaving virtuously wherever they can, acknowledging their own shortcomings, trying to get anyone who will listen to come along for the ride. Jeff Ott is a registered nurse now. Having tired of watching people die of preventable overdoses, he got off his ass to do something about it. Henry Rollins is doing speaking gigs, inciting everyone he can to channel their righteous indignation for civic good. Pussy Riot keeps playing unapproved venues, getting thrown in prison, taking a stand against an authoritarian dictator who loses another battle against them—and validates them!—every time they call him to the mat and he answers with an iron fist. Plenty of the older bands are still touring, still making music, and new ones arrive on the scene every day. They're not quite the punks they want to be. Neither are you. Neither am I. But while none of us is quite there yet, it's the journey that ultimately matters.

For me, the clearest embodiment of the project of virtue ethics is punk rock, and since learning from our betters is crucial to that project, I'll let the exemplars play you out.

The only thing that matters, if you're in a band, can you successfully divert the next generation . . .

> . . . from accepting white racism?
> . . . from accepting misogyny and male domination?
> . . . from accepting homophobia and heterosexism?
> . . . from believing the lie that their first priority is their occupation?
> . . . from believing the lie of a middle class is falling for unintentional division?
> . . . from believing the lie that the Earth's rightful role is under human subjugation? (Fifteen, "Punk Song")

None of this is easy, but:

> What can we do, what can we do?
> Try.
> Try.
> Try.
> Try. (Minor Threat, "Look Back and Laugh")

Keep on becoming.

31
Out of Step with the World

GETTY L. LUSTILA AND JOHAN OLSTHOORN

Punk (and specifically hardcore punk) has from the start presented itself as a counterculture—and has prided itself on being so. From Minor Threat onwards, hardcore/punk artists have commended the value of living life "against the grain," in opposition to mainstream norms and practices.

This embrace of cultural independence is expressed in punk's *do-it-yourself* ethic, developed from the early 1980s onwards in conscious resistance to the music industry. Inspired by this ethic, youth across the world involved in hardcore/punk have created their own independent record labels, cut-and-pasted their own fanzines, organized their own shows, and formed and supported their own local music scenes. Countless hardcore/punk songs over the past forty years have developed and defended the value of being a *counter*culture—a culture that permits punks to live in defiance of "society and their rules" (Warzone, "It's Your Choice").

What are we to make of the cultural rebellion of hardcore/punks? Is there any ethical value in the pursuit of cultural nonconformity? Distinct moral justifications for cultural nonconformity can be teased from the lyrics of the hardcore/punk bands that we have grown up with and still love.

The best explanation of what makes cultural nonconformity morally valuable, we believe, comes from the English philosopher John Stuart Mill (1806–1873): it opens up new cultural space to oneself and to others, permitting "new and original experiments of living" (*On Liberty*, p. 281).

What Is Cultural Nonconformity?

How should we understand the idea of cultural nonconformity? Cultures are systems of values, embodied in social norms and practices. By "pursuing cultural nonconformity," we mean the adoption and development of ways of living in principled opposition to mainstream values, norms, and practices. These alternative ways of living—countercultures—are expressive of and shaped by interpretations of personal and moral values at odds with the rest of society. Cultural nonconformity, thus understood, has both critical and constructive dimensions. It criticizes prevailing norms and practices, and people's unquestioned commitment to them, while constructively fashioning cultural alternatives. The idea of cultural nonconformity becomes clearer by contrasting it to two related notions: autonomy, or "living by one's own rules," and authenticity, or "staying true to yourself" (Guiding Line, "Break the Chain"). While hardcore/punk artists have often praised autonomy and authenticity, our position is that cultural nonconformity is a distinct concept and value.

Consider first the idea of autonomy. Following the Enlightenment philosopher Immanuel Kant (1724–1804), Christine Korsgaard defines autonomy as the ability to "engage in conduct that is governed by laws that you give to yourself." Autonomy consists in self-governance, in living by rules of one's own making. The hardcore/punk ethic endorses living life on one's own terms and in pursuit of one's own aims, captured in the desire to be "master of my destiny" (Trail of Lies, "Master of My Destiny"). and "my own control" (Throwdown, "Program").

As the rules governing our lives are not our own creation, attempts to increase personal autonomy can prompt rebellion. Many hardcore/punk artists have objected to being compelled to live under rules set by others, on the ground that this disregards their capacity for self-determination. "Why should I listen to those fools / I'm going to live by my rules" (Void, "My Rules"). In "Can't Tell No One," Negative Approach even claim that rules as such, regardless of their content, make a mockery of our powers of self-governance: "Rules are made for idiots / People that can't think / I'm treated like I don't have a mind of my own". Others curse social structures stifling our agency. "Conditioned inside and out / to the point of no return / To what we may have been / without all this shit we were born into" (Tragedy, "The Point of No Return").

From the very start, hardcore/punk artists have portrayed themselves as critical and rational individuals—as "forward thinking youth" willing and able to "flex their head," and to decide for themselves what form of life is worth pursuing (Modern Life Is War, "Self-Preservation"). The phrase "flex your head" alludes to the seminal hardcore punk compilation *Flex Your Head*). Humans are "armed with a mind," as Have Heart put it: "It's the gift inside our heads not to take for granted / Because an unexamined life is a seed unplanted" (Have Heart, "Armed with a Mind"). There is moral value, these artists claim, in acting on the distinctly human capacity for self-direction. Even more, hardcore/punks were willing to act on their convictions, willing to turn their backs on society and to go it alone.

The idea of autonomy ("self-governance") is closely related to but distinct from that of authenticity ("acting in light of a proper view of oneself"). In *The Ethics of Authenticity*, Charles Taylor describes the last ideal as follows: "Being true to myself means being true to my own originality, and that is something only I can articulate and discover. In articulating it, I am also defining myself. I am realizing a potentiality that is properly my own" (p. 29). Authenticity requires self-realization, or the process of bringing about the unique potential found within ourselves.

Authenticity, thus understood, is a more demanding ideal than autonomy. It requires not only freely making our own choices but also choosing rightly—choosing that path which most accords with our own inner nature. The song "Godhead" by Burn captures the idea and value of authenticity: "Let me witness my true self, out in the bare / So I can realize my potential for greatness / or the possibility of failure." Inauthenticity is not the same as hypocrisy, although both involve inconsistencies revealed in behavior. According to Judith Shklar, actions or choices are inauthentic when they jar with our "true self"; hypocritical when they knowingly clash with our declared principles or attitudes. Crass duly called Steve Jones, guitarist for the Sex Pistols, a hypocrite: "preaching revolution, anarchy, and change / as he sucked from the system that had given him his name" ("Punk Is Dead").

Neither autonomy nor authenticity require cultural nonconformity. Indeed, Taylor dismissed the notion that "the enemy of authenticity . . . is social conformity." It is a mistake to think that we can only meet "the demands of self-truth" by rebelling against external norms (p. 63). People may find their true identity and life-satisfaction squarely within the confines of mainstream culture. Conversely, some punks are posers—their attachment to hardcore/punk culture is merely surface level, embracing the aesthetic trappings without being committed to the ideals that inform this aesthetic. As Ray Cappo pointed out, "Personality can't be purchased / in a skateboard store" ("Alternative Nation"). Some people adopt countercultural lifestyles for lousy reasons ("because it looks cool"). And yet, pursuing cultural nonconformity can be ethically valuable even if the punks in question are insincere or acting exclusively on peer pressure. The value in practicing cultural nonconformity cannot be reduced therefore to either authenticity or autonomy.

A Wrench in the System

Unlike autonomy and authenticity, cultural nonconformity presupposes rejection of some prevailing social norms and practices. Social criticism has been a staple of hardcore/punk lyrics from the start. We encourage readers to look up the lyrics of "Just Look Around" by Sick of It All—theirs is a particularly forceful condemnation of social injustice and of politicians' cynical encouragement of racial divisions. The punk band Poison Idea expressed their concerns slightly less eloquently: "The truth is as clear as a cesspool / I say piss on all your fucking rules / I'll bite the hand that feeds me shit / I am getting sick of the taste of it." Having declared those rules illegitimate, Poison Idea flatly denied to be bound by them: "What are they for? Why were rules made? To be broken!" ("Made to Be Broken"). The ethos in lyrics like these is one of alienation from a socio-political system perceived as broken and corrupt. A common identity is formed in that alienation, in opposition to mainstream norm-abiding behavior. Strike Anywhere put it in a nutshell: "To live in discontent / anti-establishment" ("Chorus of One"). Cultural nonconformity consists in more than just social critique, however. It also involves constructing new ways of living, in opposition to accepted social norms and practices.

Cultural nonconformity can be valuable in two ways: *contingent* and *general*. According to the contingent justification, the value in cultural nonconformity lies in replacing harmful societal norms and practices with morally better ones. Cultural nonconformity is morally valuable only in some conditions: *if* mainstream cultural practices are morally flawed and *if* the counterculture successfully embodies ways of living that are not similarly bankrupt. On the general justification, cultural nonconformity is valuable as such, regardless of the moral quality of the social norms it opposes and of the cultural alternatives it introduces.

The contingent line of justification is rife in both the vegan straight edge movement, inspired by the band Earth Crisis, and the revolutionary anarchism of groups like Crass. The vegan straight edge movement views cultural nonconformity as an act of moral purity in a world of evil. The nonconformist prefigures the just world to come and looks to save themselves from spiritual destruction through their nonconformity: "through my refusal to partake, I saved myself" (Earth Crisis, "The Discipline"). Self-righteous resignation proved a popular response to the perceived immorality of popular culture among hardcore/punks. Take the hardcore band The Path of Resistance: "Those brainless clones repulse me / So I'll walk alone / And all I need is one friend called Truth / and my heart is its home" (The Path of Resistance, "Counter"). Or the vegan warriors in Ecostrike: "I walk amongst the few / who swear their hearts to what they know is true" ("Amongst the Few"). So-called hardliners have taken a still more militant stance, advocating direct action to eradicate purported injustices. "Action must be taken to free the world from its sickness / Action for justice / leads to / freedom" (Arkangel, "Day of Apocalypse").

Many of the moral and political judgments voiced by vegan straightedge bands are questionable. Many will disagree with their hyperbolic cries about how morally degraded modern society. Is today's bioindustry truly "a common grave for our morals / an archaic way of thinking / so monstrous and absurd"? (Heaven Shall Burn, "The Voice of the Voiceless"). For the vegan straightedge counterculture to have moral value on the contingent justification, claims like these need not be true. Yet the contingent justification does require their counterculture to be morally superior to the mainstream cultural practices it opposes. Subcultures shaped by militancy, intolerance, and other illiberal values, like the hardline movement, clearly fail to meet this threshold (The band Vegan Reich popularized the term 'hardline'. Their eponymous EP (*Hardline*, 1990) contained a 'hardline manifesto' threatening violence to those harming innocent life—including the lives of fetuses and animals.) Hardline bands have proposed means of resistance bordering on terrorism—"a firestorm to purify" (Earth Crisis, "Firestorm"). Even vegans will agree that a counterculture built around such extremist views is morally worse than the mainstream cultural practices it seeks to replace.

Through its principled, constructive opposition to mainstream cultural practices, hardcore/punk helps provide the distance needed to critically evaluate obtaining norms and practices. Calling out complacency, Refused shouted: "It's not okay / to pretend everything's alright" (Refused, "It's Not Okay to Pretend Everything's Alright"). The anarcho-punk band,

Flux of Pink Indians, decry treating natural resources as exploitable commodities, irrespective of their meaning for others: "you don't want these trees / you only want towns and cities ... this is just a wood to you / but this is my home ... I don't want your progress / it tries to kill me / me / you / we." (Flux of Pink Indians, "Progress"). In questioning harmful norms and beliefs like these, cultural nonconformity places their content, and our commitment to them, under scrutiny. Moreover, by fashioning cultural alternatives, it shows that such norms are neither natural nor unavoidable. In this way, cultural nonconformity acts as a wrench in the machine of our common ways of living.

New Models of Living

Cultural nonconformity can have ethical value beyond it being a spark for moral progress. Developing countercultural alternatives might be valuable *in general*, regardless of the moral quality of the mainstream culture it opposes and regardless of whether one succeeds in developing morally superior cultural alternatives. It might seem silly to oppose benign cultural practices like disco music. And yet, we claim, cultural nonconformity enlarges the sphere of pluralism and freedom that underwrites the possibility of authenticity and self-governance. There is value in opposing "an oriented public whose magnetic force does pull / but away from the potential of the individual" (Bad Religion, "Against the Grain"). Resisting the magnetic pull of the masses opens up cultural space for everyone, and that is good in itself and thus morally valuable even in a reasonably just society.

The most eloquent philosophical defense of cultural rebellion is that of J.S. Mill in *On Liberty*.

> In this age, the mere example of nonconformity, the mere refusal to bend the knee to custom, is itself a service. Precisely because the tyranny of opinion is such as to make eccentricity a reproach, it is desirable, in order to break through that tyranny, that people should be eccentric. (p. 269)

Mill regarded opposing "the tyranny of the majority" especially useful in conformist Victorian England of his day and age, to help overcome debilitating popular mediocrity. Yet he stressed that cultural nonconformity has ethical value in general: it everywhere enables the "free development of individuality." Prevailing customs may suit some people, while crippling others. Given the diversity of human personalities, cultural freedom and pluralism is needed for all human beings to flourish. "Human beings are not like sheep; and even sheep are not undistinguishably alike" (p. 219). That thought resonates with the band Free: "Be yourself / not like the fucking masses" (Free, "MA Flex").

Mill's defense of cultural nonconformity was later taken up by the British-Latvian philosopher Isaiah Berlin (1909–1997). People should be free, Berlin argued, to seek and pursue their own conceptions of the good. Differences in ways of living should be celebrated rather than repressed. Berlin believed in value pluralism: no single way of living can capture all that is valuable. "If there are many and competing genuine values, then the greater the extent to which a society tends to be single-valued, the more genuine values it neglects or suppresses. More, to this extent, must mean better" (Bernard Williams, "Introduction," to *Isaiah Berlin*). Countercultures help prevent cultural homogenization and ensuing loss of value. "No rules, just be yourself / Don't rely on anyone else / No wrong or right / no certain way to be" (Insted, "No Rules").

Mill's defense of cultural nonconformity is elitist. He encouraged cultural dissent in part because he believed it allows for the free development of "persons of genius" who could overcome "collective mediocrity" (pp. 267–68). Our position, by contrast, is that cultural nonconformity is ethically valuable because it enlarges cultural space *for everyone*. Countercultures are sources of creativity, encouraging people to work together to develop truly alternative ways of living. Countercultures thus increase the number of cultural resources—models for living—available to people: resources on which they can draw to fashion their own social identity and way of life.

Hardcore/punk is and always has been "more than music" (Verbal Assault, "More than Music"). As a counterculture, it offers cultural resources for both personal identity-formation and purpose-creation. Having people pursue and develop genuinely alternative ways of living is good for everyone insofar as it increases the stock of culturally available lifestyles. Provided, of course, that the countercultural lifestyles are not themselves harmful (for instance by encouraging substance abuse or undue social conflict). The value of cultural enrichment is not conditional on mainstream cultural practices being harmful or unjust. Nor does it require widespread adoption of countercultural ideas and practices. Countercultures enhance cultural pluralism through their existence, not their popularity.

Pursuing cultural nonconformity is ethically valuable in general, we believe, since it increases the culturally available set of models of living. More such models make it easier for individuals to readily find ways of living that are authentic to them—without being hemmed in by societal expectations (as those generally diminish in force in conditions of cultural pluralism). Significantly, even those contributing to the hardcore/punk culture unthinkingly or insincerely help expand our cultural repertoire. Witness the common claim that the ideal of sober living will hold "true" regardless of how many "fakes" "break edge" (As an example, Carry On, "What Once Was").

A Positive Change?

For many hardcore/punk artists, the only meaningful form of cultural nonconformity left open to us today is total disengagement. If societal injustices are deemed irreparable, the only reasonable solution may be dropping out. The Youth of Today song "Disengage" captures this sentiment well: "In this age when everything's falling apart / disengage / don't think I'm crazy / for not wanting to take part" (Youth of Today, "Disengage"). Ceding in any way to prevailing norms and practices seemingly puts us right back where we started; a willing participant in a collapsing society.

Yet the "drop out" solution brings with it moral hazards of its own. If the prize of our own moral purity can only be attained at the expense of abandoning our social obligations and entanglements—say, the good of our dependents and compatriots—we might begin to question our commitment to moral purity. Other hardcore/punks have explored a rival solution: working together to prefigure or bring about positive change, however trivial. This strategy involves developing bonds of solidarity: "we gotta care together / and see this to the end." Kevin Seconds urges us to try even when risking falter: "you say we have no future / do we have a chance?" (7 Seconds, "The Crew"). Cultural nonconformity can therefore be compatible with societal *engagement*, with a positive commitment to partake in the larger political project of shaping our world.

Through its critical edge, cultural nonconformity creates the space required for new cultural norms and practices to develop. Constructively, it enlarges the set of cultural resources available to all for personal identity-formation and purpose-creation—thus bolstering the cultural preconditions for self-governance and authenticity. Many of us proceed through life feeling that "there's something wrong / I got a feeling that

I / I don't belong here" (Jerry's Kids, "I Don't Belong"). As Mindset writes: "I know I'll never know / what it means to live at ease in line with the status quo / I'll stand alone" (Mindset, "Counterpoint"). Cultural nonconformity helps counter such feelings of alienation and isolation by promoting and developing new experiments in living. Through its pursuit we can gain affirmation of our own manner of living. More emboweringly still, at its best it produces positive alternatives that are inspiring and that we can affirm, with clenched fists, open hearts, and open minds (an allusion to both The First Step, "Something Inside" and Mindset, "Leave No Doubt".

Bibliography

Abraham, Ibrahim, ed. 2020. *Christian Punk: Identity and Performance*. Bloomsbury Academic.

Addams, Jessicka. 2012. Jessicka.com <https://web.archive.org/web/20120226231639/http://www.jessicka.com/faq.html>.

Adorno, Theodor. 2002 [1931]. Why Is the New Art So Hard to Understand? In *Essays on Music*. University of California Press.

Albertine, Viv. 2014. *Clothes, Clothes, Clothes, Music, Music, Music, Boys, Boys, Boys: A Memoir*. Faber and Faber.

Alioto, Daisy. 2012. What the Killing of a Punk in Texas Says about America. *Vice News* (December 12th) <https://www.vice.com/en/article/434agp/what-the-killing-of-a-punk-in-texas-says-about-america>.

Ambrosch, Gerfried. 2018. *The Poetry of Punk: The Meaning Behind Punk Rock and Hardcore Lyrics*. Routledge.

Anonymous. *New Living Translation Bible, Bible Gateway* <https://www.biblegateway.com>.

Appiah, Kwame Anthony. 2005. *The Ethics of Identity*. Princeton University Press.

Archer, Alfred, and Lauren Ware. 2018. Beyond the Call of Beauty: Everyday Aesthetic Demands Under Patriarchy. *The Monist* 101: 1.

Arendt, Hannah. 1958. *The Human Condition*. Chicago University Press.

Aristotle. 1987. *Poetics*. Hackett.

———. 1998. *Politics*. Hackett.

———. 2019. *Nicomachean Ethics*. Third edition. Hackett.

Azerrad, Michael. 2002. *Our Band Could Be Your Life: Scenes from the American Indie Underground 1981–1991*. Back Bay.

Bad Religion, and Jim Ruland. 2020. *Do What You Want: The Story of Bad Religion*. Hachette.

Badiou, Alain. 2019 [2011]. *Wittgenstein's Antiphilosophy*. Verso.

Barile, Nancy. 2021. *I'm Not Holding Your Coat: My Bruises-and-All Memoir of Punk Rock Rebellion*. Bazillion Points.

Bartley, William Warren, III. 1999 [1973]. *Wittgenstein*. Open Court.

Beauvoir, Simone de. 2000. *The Ethics of Ambiguity*. Citadel.

———. 2011. *The Second Sex*. Vintage.

Becker, Howard S. 1963. *Outsiders: Studies in the Sociology of Deviance*. Free Press.

Bejgrowicz, Tom. 2019. *Scream with Me: The Enduring Legacy of the Misfits*. Abrams.

Bell, Celeste. 2019. *Dayglo! The Poly Styrene Story*. Omnibus.

Benardete, Seth. 1989. *Socrates' Second Sailing*. University of Chicago Press.

Bennett, Andy. 1999. *Subcultures or Neo-Tribes? Rethinking the Relationship between Youth, Style, and Musical Taste*. Cambridge University Press.

Bennett, Todd. 2002. The Celluloid War: State and Studio in Anglo-American Propaganda Film-Making, 1939–1941. *International History Review* 24:1.

Berlin, Isaiah. 1978. *Isaiah Berlin: Concepts and Categories*. Princeton University Press.

———. 2002. John Stuart Mill and the Ends of Life. In Berlin, *Liberty: Incorporating Four Essays on Liberty*. Oxford University Press.

Betrock, Alan. 2013. Ramones: "We Play Short Songs for People Who Don't Have a Lot of Spare Time"—Interview from the Vaults. *The Guardian* (April 17th).

Bickerdike, Jennifer Otter. 2014. *Fandom, Image, and Authenticity: Joy, Devotion, and the Second Lives of Kurt Cobain and Ian Curtis*. Palgrave Macmillan.

Blush, Steven. 2010. *American Hardcore: A Tribal History*. Feral House.

Bolton, Richard. 1992. In the American East: Richard Avedon Incorporated. In R. Bolton, ed., *The Contest of Meaning: Critical Histories of Photography*. MIT Press.

Boulware, Jack. And Silke Tudor. 2009. *Gimme Something Better: The Profound, Progressive, and Occasionally Pointless History of Bay Area Punk from Dead Kennedys to Green Day*. Penguin.

Bradley, John F.N. 1992. *Czechoslovakia's Velvet Revolution: A Political Analysis*. East European Monographs.

Breton, André. 1972 [1969]. *Manifestoes of Surrealism*. University of Michigan Press.

Callwood, Brett. 2011. *The Stooges—Head On: A Journey through the Michigan Underworld*. Wayne State University Press.

Camus, Albert. 2018. *The Myth of Sisyphus*. Vintage.

Chapkis, Wendy. 1986. *Beauty Secrets: Women and the Politics of Appearance*. South End Press.

Chicago, Judy. 1971. Red Flag (photo lithograph). *Museum of Menstruation* <www.mum.org/armenjc.htm>.

Coulter, Colin. 2019. *Working for the Clampdown: The Clash, the Dawn of Neoliberalism, and the Political Promise of Punk*. Manchester University Press.

Crawford, Matthew. 2010. *Shop Class as Soulcraft: An Inquiry into the Value of Work*. Penguin.

Crimethinc. 2019. Music as a Weapon: The Contentious Symbiosis of Punk Rock and Anarchism. *Rolling Thunder: Anarchist Journal of Dangerous Living* 7.

Crowther, Bosley. 1940. The War on the Screen. *New York Times*, Section 9 (27th October).

Cuffman, Timothy. 2015. Idle Musical Community: Dischord Records and Anarchic DIY Practice. *Contemporary Justice Review* 18.1.

Curtis, Deborah. 2014 [2005]. *Touching from a Distance: Ian Curtis and Joy Division*. Farrar, Straus, and Giroux.

D'Ambrosio, Antonio. 2004. *Let Fury Have the Hour: The Punk Rock Politics of Joe Strummer*. Nation Books.

Dao, James, and Serge Kovalski. 2012. Music Style Is Called Supremacist Recruiting Tool. *New York Times* <www.nytimes.com/2012/08/08/us/hatecore-music-is-called-white-supremacist-recruiting-tool.html>.

Davis, Ben. 2013. *9.5 Theses on Art and Class*. Haymarket.

Debies-Carl, Jeffrey S. 2014. *Punk Rock and the Politics of Place: Building a Better Tomorrow*. Routledge.

Debord, Guy. 1995 [1967]. *The Society of the Spectacle*. Zone.

Denisoff, R. Serge. 1975. *Solid Gold: The Popular Record Industry*. Transaction.

Diogenes Laertius. 2015. *Lives and Opinions of Eminent Philosophers*. Scholar's Choice.

Douglas, Mary. 2005. *Purity and Danger*. Routledge.

Eagleton, Terry. 2007. *Terry Eagleton Presents the Gospels*. Verso.

Eco, Umberto. 2019. On the Shoulders of Giants. Harvard University Press.

Edmonds, David, and John Eldinow. 2001. *Wittgenstein's Poker: The Story of a Ten-Minute Argument between Two Great Philosophers*. Ecco.

Edmondson, Jacqueline, ed. *Music in American Life: An Encyclopedia of the Songs, Stars, and Stories that Shaped Our Culture*. Four volumes. Greenwood.

Eileraas, Karina. 1997. Witches, Bitches, and Fluids: Girl Bands Performing Ugliness as Resistance. *The Drama Review* 41:3.

Ensminger, David. 2021. *Punk Women: 40 Years of Musicians Who Built Punk Rock, in Their Own Words (Punx)*. Microcosm.

Ferguson, Adam. 1996 [1767]. *An Essay on the History of Civil Society*. Cambridge University Press.

Fingerhut, Jeorg, Javier Gomez-Lavin, Claudia Winklmayr, and Jesse J. Prinz. 2021. The Aesthetic Self: The Importance of Aesthetic Taste in Music and Art for Our Perceived Identity. *Frontiers in Psychology* <https://doi.org/10.3389/fpsyg.2020.577703>.

Ford, Simon. 1999. *Wreckers of Civilisation: The Story of COUM Transmissions and Throbbing Gristle*. Black Dog.

Fresh Air. 2019. Punk Icon and Memoirist Viv Albertine on a Lifetime of Fighting the Patriarchy. *NPR Fresh Air* <www.npr.org/2019/11/01/775362224/punk-icon-and-memoirist-viv-albertine-on-a-lifetime-of-fighting-the-patriarchy>.

Freud, Sigmund. 1961. *Beyond the Pleasure Principle*. Norton.

Gage, Matilda Joslyn. 1870 *Woman as Inventor*. Darling.

Gall, Gregor. 2022. *The Punk Rock Politics of Joe Strummer: Radicalism, Resistance, and Rebellion*. Manchester University Press.

Geldof, Bob. 1986. *Is That It? The Autobiography*. Weidenfeld and Nicolson.

Gellner, Ernest. 1996. *Conditions of Liberty: Civil Society and Its Rivals*. Penguin.

Girard, René. 1976. *Deceit, Desire, and the Novel: Self and Other in Literary Structure*. Johns Hopkins University Press.

———. 1987. *Things Hidden Since the Foundation of the World*. Stanford University Press.

Glasper, Ian. 2014. *The Day the Country Died: A History of Anarcho-Punk 1980–1984*. PM Press.

Glynn, Paul. 2021. Sex Pistols at Lesser Free Trade Hall Films Sell for 15k <www.bbc.com/news/uk-england-manchester-58557782>.

Goldman, Vivien. 2019. *Revenge of the She-Punks: A Feminist Music History from Poly Styrene to Pussy Riot*. University of Chicago Press.

Gordon, Jane Anna, and Lewis R. Gordon. 2016 [2009]. *Of Divine Warning: Reading Disaster in the Modern Age*. Routledge.

Graeber, David, and David Wengrow. 2021. *The Dawn of Everything: A New History of Humanity*. Farrar, Straus, and Giroux.

Graffin, Greg. 2000. A Punk Manifesto. *Bad Times* 10.

Gramsci, Antonio. 1971. *Selections from the Prison Notebooks*. Lawrence and Wishart.

Gray, Obika. 2004. *Demeaned but Empowered: The Social Power of the Urban Poor in Jamaica*. University Press of the West Indies.

Grecco, Michael. 2020. *Punk, Post Punk, New Wave: Onstage, Backstage, in Your Face, 1978–1991*. Abrams.

Greenfield, Craig. 2016. Yes. Jesus Was a Subversive (18th April) <https://www.craiggreenfield.com/blog/2016/4/18/yes-jesus-was-subversive>.

Grigoriadis, Vanessa. 2010. Remembrances of the Punk Prose Poetess. Patti Smith interview. *New York Magazine* (7th January).

Guyer, Paul. 1990. Feeling and Freedom: Kant on Aesthetics and Morality. *The Journal of Aesthetics and Art Criticism* 48:2.

Haenfler, Ross. 2004. Rethinking Subcultural Resistance: Core Values of the Straight Edge Movement. *Journal of Contemporary Ethnography* 33.4.

———. 2006. *Straight Edge: Hardcore Punk, Clean Living Youth, and Social Change*. Rutgers University Press.

Hanscomb, Stuart. 2020. Shot by Both Sides: Punk Attitude and Existentialism. *Existential Analysis* 31:1.

Havel, Václav. 1986. *Václav Havel or Living in Truth*. Amsterdam: Meulenhoff.

———. 1991. *Open Letters: Selected Prose 1965–1990*. Faber and Faber.

———. 1994. *Toward a Civil Society: Selected Speeches and Writings 1990–1994*. Prague: Lidové Noviny.

Hebdige, Dick. 1979. *Subculture: The Meaning of Style*. Routledge.

Hegel, Georg Wilhelm Friedrich. 1821. *Grundlinien der Philosophie des Rechts: Naturrecht und Staatswissenschaft im Grundrisse*. Berlin: In der Nicolaischen Buchhandlung.

Heidegger, Martin. 2009. *Basic Concepts of Aristotelian Philosophy*. Indiana University Press.

Heylin, Clinton. 1993. *From the Velvets to the Voidoids: A Pre-Punk History for a Post-Punk World*. Penguin.

Holmstrom, John. 2012. *The Best of Punk Magazine*.

Hook, Peter. 2013. *Unknown Pleasures: Inside Joy Division*. It Books.

Horkheimer, Max, and Theodor W. Adorno. 1982. *Dialectic of Enlightenment*. Continuum.

Horne, Lydia. 2021. Bleeding Out: On the Use of Blood in Contemporary Art. *Art Papers* <www.artpapers.org/bleeding-out-on-the-use-of-blood-in-contemporary-art>.

Hume, David. 2001. *Four Dissertations and Essays on Suicide and the Immortality of the Soul*. St. Augustine's Press.

Hurchalla, George. 2016. *Going Underground: American Punk 1979–1989*. PM Press.

Iafrate, Michael J. 2020. Blasphemy, Conversion, and Liberation: 'Christian' 'Punk' in Theological Perspective. In Abraham 2020.

Illich, Ivan. 1973. *Tools for Conviviality*. Harper and Row.

Jacobson, Dan, and Ian Jeffrey. 2018. Tony Wilson's Bloody Contract: A Re-Enactment of the Faustian Bargain. In Power, Devereux, and Dillaine 2018.

Janovitz, Bill. 2022. Review of Iggy and the Stooges: *Search and Destroy*. AllMusic <www.allmusic.com/song/search-and-destroy-mt0001430752>.

Jarmusch, Jim, director. 2016. *Gimme Danger*. Magnolia Pictures.

Jenkins, Craig. 2021. The Best and Most Misunderstood of Green Day, According to Billie Joe Armstrong. *Vulture* (22nd April).

Johnson, Devon. 2021. *Black Nihilism and Antiblack Racism*. Rowman and Littlefield.

Johnson, Mark. 2014. *Seditious Theology: Punk and the Ministry of Jesus*. Routledge.

Joy Division Central. 1980. Ian Curtis Radio Blackburn Interview. <https://www.joydiv.org/rlinterview.htm>.

Kaufmann, Walter, ed. 1975 [1956]. *Existentialism from Dostoyevsky to Sartre*. New American Library.

Kimmerer, Robin Wall. 2013. *Braiding Sweetgrass: Indigenous Wisdom, Scientific Knowledge, and the Teachings of Plants*. Milkweed.

Kobayashi, Ron. 1986. Second Opinions Given on 'Back in Control'. *Fullerton Observer* (5th April).

Korsgaard, Christine. 2014. The Normative Constitution of Agency. In Vargas and Yaffe 2014.

Kristeva, Julia. 1982. *Powers of Horror: An Essay on Abjection*. Columbia University Press.

Kropotkin, Peter. 1995. *The Conquest of Bread and Other Writings*. Cambridge University Press.

Lahickey, Beth. 1997. *All Ages: Reflections on Straight Edge*. Revelation Records.

Lakes, Richard. 1999. Mosh Pit Politics: The Subcultural Style of Punk Rage. *Journal of Thought* 34:3 (Fall).

Leblanc, Lauraine. 1999. *Pretty in Punk: Girls' Gender Resistance in a Boys' Subculture*. Rutgers University Press.

Letts, Don. 2006. *Culture Clash: Dread Meets Punk Rockers*. SAF.

Levin, Harold G., and Steven H. Stumpf. 1983. Statements of Fear through Cultural Symbols: Punk Rock as a Reflective Subculture. *Youth and Society* 14.

Lipman, Natasha. 2020. Christian Picciolini: The Neo-Nazi Who Became an Anti-Nazi. *BBC World Service* (5th December) <www.bbc.com/news/stories-54526345>.

Logan, Brad, and John Gentile. 2021. *Architects of Self-Destruction: The Oral History of Leftöver Crack*. Rare Bird Books.

Loudwire. 2020. 10 Psycho Preachers Who Hate Rock + Metal. *YouTube* (27th January) <www.youtube.com/watch?v=YiqvBhQaAvU>.

Lukács, Georg. 1971 [1923]. *History and Class Consciousness*. Merlin.

Lure, Walter. 2020. *To Hell and Back: My Life in Johnny Thunder's Heartbreakers, in the Words of the Last Man Standing*. Backbeat.

Lydon, John [Johnny Rotten]. 2008 [1994]. *Rotten: No Irish, No Blacks, No Dogs*. Picador.

———. 2016 [2014]. *Anger Is an Energy: My Life Uncensored.* HarperCollins.

———. 2020. *I Could Be Wrong, I Could Be Right.* A Way with Media.

MacIntyre, Alasdair. 2007. *After Virtue: A Study in Moral Theory.* Third edition. University of Notre Dame Press.

Marcade, Phil. 2017. *Punk Avenue: Inside the New York City Underground, 1972–1982.* Three Rooms.

Marcus, Greil. 1990. *Lipstick Traces: A Secret History of the Twentieth Century.* Harvard University Press.

Marcus, Sara. 2010. *Girls to the Front: The True Story of the Riot Grrrl Revolution.* Harper Perennial.

Marmysz John. 2003. *Laughing at Nothing: Humor as a Response to Nihilism.* SUNY Press.

Marx, Karl H. 1844. Zur Judenfrage. *Deutsch-französische Jahrbücher.*

Matlock, Glenn. 1990. *I Was a Teenage Sex Pistol.* Faber and Faber.

McGuinness, Brian. 1988. *Wittgenstein: A Life. Young Ludwig, 1889–1921.* University of California Press.

McNeil, Legs, and Gillian McCain. 1997. *Please Kill Me: The Uncensored Oral History of Punk.* Penguin.

Meagher, Thomas. 2018. Creolization and Maturity: A Philosophical Sketch. *Contemporary Political Theory* 17:3.

———. 2020. The Spirit of Seriousness and Decolonisation. *Alternation* 33.

Mehr, Bob. 2016. *Trouble Boys: The True Story of the Replacements.* Da Capo.

Melly, George. 2013 [1970]. *Revolt into Style: The Pop Arts.* Faber and Faber.

Meltzer, Marisa. 2010. *Girl Power: The Nineties Revolution in Music.* Faber and Faber.

Mill, John Stuart. 1978. *On Liberty.* Hackett.

———. Mill, John Stuart. 2002. *Utilitarianism.* Hackett.

Miller, Jesse James, director. 2019. *Punk.* Four-part TV documentary. Epix.

Mohr, Tim. 2018 [2017]. *Burning Down the Haus: Punk Rock, Revolution, and the Fall of the Berlin Wall.* Algonquin.

Monk, Ray. 1990. *Ludwig Wittgenstein: The Duty of Genius.* Free Press.

Morris, Keith. 2017. *My Damage: The Story of a Punk Rock Survivor.* Da Capo.

Mullen, Brendan. 2002. *Lexicon Devil: The Fast Times and Short Life of Darby Crash and the Germs.* Feral House.

Nagel, Thomas. 1979. Subjective and Objective. In Nagel, *Moral Questions.* Cambridge University Press.

National School Safety Center. 1988. Gangs in Schools: Breaking Up Is Hard to Do. National School Safety Center/Pepperdine University.

New Musical Express. 2008. Sex Pistols on Bill Grundy's Today Show Most Requested Clip. *New Musical Express* (28th July).

Nicols, John. 2013. Lou Reed's Politics. *The Nation*, (27th October) <www.thenation.com/article/archive/lou-reeds-more-perfect-union-politics>.

Nikpour, Golnar. 2012. White Riot: Another Failure . . . *Maximum Rock'n'Roll* (17th January) <https://maximumrocknroll.com/white-riot-another-failure>.

Nietzsche, Friedrich. 1967. *Ecce Homo*. In *On the Genealogy of Morals and Ecce Homo*. Random House.

———. 1967. *The Birth of Tragedy*. In *Basic Writings of Nietzsche*. Random House.

———. 1988. *Also Sprach Zarathustra*. De Gruyter.

———. 1993. *Thus Spake Zarathustra*. Prometheus.

———. 1997. *Twilight of the Idols or How to Philosophize with the Hammer*. Hackett.

———. 1998. *On the Genealogy of Morality*. Hackett.

———. 2000. *The Antichrist*. Prometheus.

———. 2001. *The Gay Science*. Cambridge University Press.

———. 2016. *The Birth of Tragedy*. Project Gutenberg. <www.gutenberg.org/cache/epub/51356/pg51356-images.html>.

———. 2016. *The Case of Wagner*. Project Gutenberg. <www.gutenberg.org/cache/epub/52166/pg52166-images.html>.

Nussbaum, Martha C. 2004. *Hiding from Humanity: Disgust, Shame, and the Law*. Princeton University Press.

O'Hara, Craig. 1999. *The Philosophy of Punk: More than Noise!* Second edition. AK Press.

Ott, Jeff. 2000. *My World: Ramblings of an Aging Gutter Punk*. Subcity Records.

Ozzi, Dan. 2021. *Sellout: The Major-Label Feeding Frenzy that Swept Punk, Emo, and Hardcore 1994–2007*. Dey Street.

Partridge, Bernard Brook. Online interview <www.youtube.com/watch?v=bLBr98UOBX0>.

Paxton, Rob. 2001. Leftöver Crack: *Mediocre Generica*. *Punknews.org* (8th November) <www.punknews.org/review/694/leftover-crack-mediocre-generica>.

Peters, Michael A. 2019. Wittgenstein and the Ethics of Suicide: Homosexuality and Jewish Self-Hatred in Fin de Siècle Vienna. *Educational Philosophy and Theory* 51:10.

Peterson, Brian. 2009. *Burning Fight: The Nineties Hardcore Revolution in Ethics, Politics, Spirit, and Sound*. Revelation Records.

Picciolini, Christian. 2017. *White American Youth: My Descent into America's Most Violent Hate Movement—and How I Got Out*. Hachette.

Pop, Iggy. 1977. Interview with Peter Gzowski. *90 Minutes Live* (11th March) <www.dailymotion.com/video/x7smwcn>.

Power, M., E. Devereux, and A. Dillaine, eds. 2018. *Heart and Soul: Critical Essays on Joy Division*. Rowman and Littlefield.

Prinz, Jesse. 2014. The Aesthetics of Punk Rock. *Philosophy Compass* 9:9.

Putnam, Robert. 1993. *Making Democracy Work: Civic Traditions in Modern Italy*. Princeton University Press.

Ramone, Dee Dee. 2016. *Lobotomy: Surviving the Ramones*. Da Capo.

Ramone, Johnny. 2012. *Commando: The Autobiography of Johnny Ramone*. Abrams.

Ravok, Ashley, and Serenity Autumn. 2022. Before 1976 Revisited: How Punk became Punk. *Trash Theory* <www.youtube.com/watch?v=6lyoAczdMSM>.

Reddington, Helen. 2009 [2007]. *The Lost Women of Rock Music: Female Musicians of the Punk Era*. Routledge.

Reynolds, Simon. 2005. *Rip It Up and Start Again: Postpunk 1978–1984*. Penguin.

Rightwingwatch. 2013. Hagee: Rock Music Is 'Satanic Cyanide' that Should Be Taken Outside and Burned. *YouTube* (13th July) <www.youtube.com/watch?v=Lhpm5McxnhE>.

Robb, John. 2012. *Punk Rock: An Oral History*. PM Press.

Rolling Stone. 2021. 20 Wildest Iggy Pop Moments, *Rolling Stone* <www.rollingstone.com/music/music-lists/20-wildest-iggy-pop-moments-72545>.

Rollins, Henry. 2012. What Is Punk? Big Think (March 5th) <https://bigthink.com/videos/what-is-punk>.

Rorty, Richard. 1989. *Contingency, Irony, and Solidarity*. Cambridge University Press.

Rosenbaum, Jill Leslie, and Lorraine Prinsky. 1991. The Presumption of Influence: Recent Responses to Popular Music Subcultures. *Crime and Delinquency* 37:4 (October).

Rossiter, Margaret W. 1993 The Matthew Matilda Effect in Science. *Social Studies of Science* 23:2.

Rousseau, Jean-Jacques. 1992. *Reveries of a Solitary Walker*. Hackett.

Russell, Bertrand. 1998 [1967]. *The Autobiography of Bertrand Russell*. Routledge.

Salewicz, Chris. 2008. *Redemption Song: The Ballad of Joe Strummer*. Farrar, Straus, and Giroux.

Sartre, Jean-Paul. 1948. *Anti-Semite and Jew*. Schocken.

———. 1956 [1943]. *Being and Nothingness: A Phenomenological Essay on Ontology*. Washington Square.

———. 1976 [1960]. *Critique of Dialectical Reason*. New Left Books.

Savage, Jon. 2002 [1991]. *England's Dreaming: Anarchy, Sex Pistols, Punk Rock, and Beyond*. St. Martin's.

———. 2010. *The England's Dreaming Tapes*. University of Minnesota Press.

———. 2019. *This Searing Light, The Sun and Everything Else. Joy Division: The Oral History*. Faber and Faber.

Schechtman, Marya. 2007. *The Constitution of Selves*. Cornell University Press.

Schur, Edwin. 1980. *The Politics of Deviance: Stigma Contests and the Uses of Power*. Prentice Hall.

Sebetsyen, Victor. 2009. *Revolution 1989: The Fall of the Soviet Empire*. Pantheon.

Seligman, Adam B. 1992. *The Idea of Civil Society*. Princeton University Press.

Shafer-Landau, Russ. 2010. *The Fundamentals of Ethics*. Oxford University Press.

Shklar, Judith N. 1984. *Ordinary Vices*. Harvard University Press.

Silk, Michael S. 2002. *Aristophanes and the Definition of Comedy*. Oxford University Press.

Skilling, Gordon. 1981. *Charter 77 and Human Rights in Czechoslovakia*. Allen and Unwin.

Smith, Adam. 2010 [1759]. *The Theory of Moral Sentiments*. Penguin.

———. 2012 [1776]. *The Wealth of Nations*. Wordsworth.

Spitz, Marc. 2001. *We Got the Neutron Bomb: The Untold Story of L.A. Punk*. Crown.

Tadpolesandwich. 1999. Some Comments on Punk from December 1979 <https://www.youtube.com/watch?v=0GKiMvnpqW4>.

Taylor, Charles. 1991. *The Ethics of Authenticity*. Harvard University Press.

Taylor, Jeffery. 2012. What Pussy Riot's 'Punk Prayer' Really Said. *The Atlantic* (8th November) <www.theatlantic.com/international/archive/2012/11/what-pussy-riots-punk-prayer-really-said/264562>.

Temple, Julien, director. 1979. *Punk Can Take It*. UK Subs <www.youtube.com/watch?v=JDuAtJhqo2k>.

———. 2000. *The Filth and The Fury*. Film Four.

Thornton, Sarah. 1995. *Club Cultures: Music, Media, and the Subcultural Capital*. Polity.

Toothpaste, Lucy. 1977. *Jolt*, No. 3. Lucy Toothpaste.

True, Everett. 2005. *Hey Ho Let's Go: The Story of the Ramones*. Omnibus.

Trynka, Paul. 2007. *Iggy Pop: Open Up and Bleed*. Broadway Books.

Tutti, Cosey Fanni. 2017. *Art Sex Music*. Faber and Faber.

Vallee, Mickey. 2013. The Velvet Underground. In Edmondson 2013, Volume 4.

Varga, Somogy. 2011. *Authenticity as an Ethical Ideal*. Routledge.

Vargas, Manuel, and Gideon Yaffe, eds. 2014. *Rational and Social Action: The Philosophy of Michael Bratman*. Oxford University Press.

Vargyai, Viktor. 2022. Awkward Raging. <https://maximumrocknroll.com/column/awkward-raging>.

Walker, John A. 1999. *Art and Outrage: Provocation, Controversy, and the Visual Arts*. Pluto.

Walzer, Michael. 1991. The Idea of Civil Society. *Dissent* (Spring).

Wendell, Eric. 2014. *Patti Smith: America's Punk Rock Rhapsodist*. Rowman and Littlefield.

Wilcox, Zoë, Andy Linehan, and Stephen Cleary. 2016. From Shakespeare to Rock Music: The History of the Word 'Punk' (26th August) The British Library Blog: English and Drama. <https://blogs.bl.uk/english-and-drama/2016/08/from-shakespeare-to-rock-music-the-history-of-the-word-punk.html>.

Williams, Raymond. 1977. *Marxism and Literature*. Oxford University Press.

Winwood, Ian. 2018. *Smash! Green Day, The Offspring, NOFX, and the '90s Punk Explosion*. Da Capo.

Wittgenstein, Ludwig. 1973. *Philosophical Investigations*. Pearson.

———. 1984. *Culture and Value*. University of Chicago Press.

Wolff, Robert Paul. 1970. *In Defense of Anarchism*. Harper and Row.

Wong, Martin. 2009. Factory Man. Interview with Peter Saville. *Giant Robot* 60 (September–October).

Worley, Matthew. 2017. *No Future: Punk, Politics, and British Youth Culture, 1976–1984*. Cambridge University Press.

Young, Iris Marion. 1990. *Throwing Like a Girl: And Other Essays in Feminist Philosophy and Social Theory*. Indiana University Press.

Young, Julian. 2010. *Friedrich Nietzsche: A Philosophical Biography*. Cambridge University Press.

The Lineup

PATRICK D. ANDERSON is an Assistant Professor of Philosophy at Central State University in Wilberforce, Ohio, where he researches Black radical philosophy and the ethics of digital technology. He is the author of *Cypherpunk Ethics: Radical Ethics for the Digital Age*. Patrick is a self-taught guitarist and bassist who has played in over a dozen punk bands over the years; his favorite bands include Dead Kennedys, Bad Religion, War on Women, Municipal Waste, and Propagandhi. He was born in the same city as Iggy Pop.

RANDALL E. AUXIER is Professor of Philosophy and Communication Studies at Southern Illinois University Carbondale. His favorite punk bands are, without question and in this order, The Clash, The Sex Pistols, and The Ramones. In 1981 he dropped out of college in Memphis to play rock music for a living, if such a living was to be had. During this hiatus he played bass for a New Wave band called The Shakes, a hardcore Band called Nobody's Fool, and was the drummer for a band we would now call Alt Punk, called Four Neat Guys. The first was the most successful, the last was the most popular, and during one three-month stretch he was playing in all three bands. It didn't pay the bills. He went back to college in defeat, thinking that studying philosophy might be a better path to fame and fortune and chicks. Two out of three ain't bad. He now plays Americana and blues and sometimes jazz in respectable bars. He knows how to play country music but tries not to do it, unless it's Johnny Cash. His dream is to start a band called Johnny Clash, playing Clash tunes in boom-chicka country style and Johnny Cash tunes in Clash style.

PETER BRIAN BARRY is the Finkbeiner Professor in Ethics at Saginaw Valley State University. He is the author of *Evil and Moral Psychology* (2015) and *The Fiction of Evil* (2016). Never a punk, never in a punk band, but pretty sure that Bad Religion, the Buzzcocks, and the Stooges have it figured out.

SARA M. BERGSTRESSER is currently Lecturer in the Bioethics Program at Columbia University in New York. Her background is in anthropology, public health, and bioethics. People find it surprising that Sara's favorite music comes from the cusp of Punk, Industrial, and Metal, and she has enjoyed over-the-top concert performances featuring Genitorturers, GWAR, Sheep on Drugs, and Cradle of Filth.

JOSH CANGELOSI holds master's degrees in humanities and social thought (New York University) and philosophy (San Diego State University), and he is currently finishing his PhD in philosophy (University of Arizona). A longtime interdisciplinary humanities instructor, he currently lives in San Diego with his wife and dogs. Some of his favorite punk bands include Agent Orange and his friends' local bands, such as Tiltwheel, Madison Bloodbath, and Come Closer.

GEORGE A. DUNN has edited or co-edited several volumes dealing with philosophy and popular culture. He also recently edited a volume titled *A New Politics for Philosophy: Essays on Plato, Nietzsche, and Strauss* (2022). Currently affiliated with the Institute for Globalizing Civilizations in Hangzhou, China, he has taught philosophy in China and the United States. His favorite punk (and proto-punk) bands include the Modern Lovers, the New York Dolls, the Ramones, the Clash, Jason and the Scorchers, Yee Loi, and the band this book inspires you to form. With Steve Pick and Duwan Dunn, he interviewed the Ramones for the inaugural issue of the St. Louis fanzine *Jet Lag*.

RYAN FALCIONI is a Professor of Philosophy at Chaffey College, in Southern California. He specializes in philosophy of religion, philosophy of language, and philosophical anthropology. He is also a professor of Brazilian Jiu-Jitsu. A few of his favorite punk bands are Bad Brains, The Descendents, Propagandhi, Bad Religion, and NOFX. Fugazi and Hot Snakes are also in heavy rotation these days.

KAREN FOURNIER is the author of *The Words and Music of Alanis Morissette* and has published several essays that explore intersections between punk and gender, sexuality, and age. Karen is an Associate Professor of Music Theory and the Director of Research at the School of Music, Theatre, and Dance at the University of Michigan, Ann Arbor. Among her favorite punk bands are Patti Smith, Pussy Riot, Siouxsie and the Banshees, The Slits, and X-Ray Spex.

GWENDA-LIN GREWAL is currently the Onassis Lecturer in Ancient Greek Thought and Language at The New School for Social Research in New York City. Her recent publications include *Fashion I Sense: On Philosophy and Fashion* (2022) and *Thinking of Death in Plato's Euthydemus: A Close Reading and New Translation* (2022). Some of her favorite punk bands are The Cramps, The Damned, Patti Smith Group, Richard Hell and The Voidoids, and The Clash.

BRIAN HARDING is author of *Not Even a God Can Save Us Now: Reading Machiavelli after Heidegger* and editor of a few volumes on phenomenology. He is professor of philosophy at Texas Woman's University in Denton, Texas, and came into punk through an older brother and skateboarding; probably the first punk band he heard was DRI or Suicidal Tendencies; later came Rancid, the Clash, Minor Threat, NYHC and all those Nineties Epitaph bands.

JOSHUA HETER is co-editor of *Better Call Saul and Philosophy: I Think Therefore I Scam* (2022), *Westworld and Philosophy: Mind Equals Blown* (2019), and *The Man in the High Castle and Philosophy: Subversive Reports from Another Reality* (2017). He is an Assistant Professor of Philosophy at Jefferson College in Hillsboro, Missouri. Some of his favorite punk bands are The Clash, Bad Religion, The Police, and The Living End.

CHRISTOPHER M. INNES got his PhD from Goldsmiths College. This is the coolest and most musical college in the University of London with the 2014 Post Punk Then and Now podcasts being very popular. His favorite punk bands are the Sex Pistols, X-Ray Spex, Siouxsie and the Banshees, and Angelic Upstarts. Innes collects seven-inch vinyl punk singles indicating that he likes many more punk bands. He now teaches philosophy at Boise State University in Idaho. The fundamentals are still perplexing, but this does not stop him revising his textbook, *Philosophical Knowledge: The Limits of Critical Doubt* that he uses in his undergraduate philosophy classes. His specialism is in social and political philosophy where the questions about the mysteries of government and who should be in charge go unanswered.

MARKUS KOHL received his PhD in philosophy from the University of California, Berkeley, in 2012. He is currently Associate Professor of Philosophy at the University of North Carolina, Chapel Hill. Some of his favorite post-punk (and Goth) bands are Cocteau Twins, Cranes, Joy Division, Lycia, and The Sisters of Mercy.

S. EVAN KREIDER is a Professor of Philosophy at the Fox Cities campus of UW Oshkosh. In addition to studying ethics and aesthetics, he enjoys listening to punk and post-punk bands such as The Clash, Magazine, and Gang of Four. He also played bass in a punk band when he was sixteen; unfortunately, this did not stop him from playing prog rock as well.

TIMOTHY M. KWIATEK comes from the Boston punk scene. He spent his youth hitchhiking across the country to see some band play in some dirty basement. He is currently a PhD candidate in philosophy at Cornell University where he works on moral psychology and enjoys teaching Buddhist philosophy. Some of his favorite punk bands include Operation Ivy, Bane, The Blue Hearts, and Blondie.

GREG LITTMANN is Associate Professor of Philosophy at SIUE. He publishes on metaphysics, epistemology, philosophy of logic, philosophy of art, and the philosophy of professional philosophy, among other subjects. He's written numerous chapters for books like this that relate philosophy to popular culture, including volumes on Black Sabbath, David Bowie, and The Who. Greg's favorite punk bands are The Ramones, The Sex Pistols, Nirvana, and The Clash. Oh, sweet mercy, The Clash!

GETTY L. LUSTILA is Visiting Lecturer of Philosophy and Religion at Northeastern University in Boston, Massachusetts. His research focuses on topics in modern philosophy, indigenous philosophy, and the history of ethics. A few of his current favorite punk and hardcore bands are The Chisel, Sial, Amygdala, and Truth Cult.

R.W. MAIN is currently an Assistant Professor of Philosophy at West Chester University of Pennsylvania. Some of his favorite punks include Subhumans, Dead Kennedys, Nirvana, Alice Bag, and our lords and masters GWAR.

THOMAS MEAGHER is Assistant Professor of Philosophy at Sam Houston State University in Huntsville, Texas. He specializes in Africana philosophy, phenomenology, philosophy of race and gender, existentialism, and political theory. His favorite punk bands include the Patti Smith Group, the Germs, Subhumans (UK), and Propagandhi.

GEORGINA H. MILLS is a PhD candidate at Tilburg University working primarily on the philosophy of personality. Her other work includes philosophy of emotion, philosophy of disability, and philosophy of medicine, but she also writes frequently about philosophy and pop culture. She first got into punk music as a child, and aged fourteen she founded a punk band along with three friends from school. They were called Timewasters Anonymous but shortened it to T.W.A.ts and made four years of noise before disbanding to go to different universities. Her favorite punk bands are The Slits, X-Ray Spex, The Damned, and The Clash.

TIFFANY MONTOYA is currently a visiting assistant professor of philosophy at Muhlenberg College in Allentown, Pennsylvania. She specializes in political philosophy, ethics and theories of social change. While growing up in a musical household (a drummer and guitarist father, and a piano-playing mother) she was always exposed to a plethora of music genres and history. Since childhood she had been playing guitar by tabs and piano by ear, until a few years ago when she decided to "formally" learn an instrument and chose the drums. She discovered punk in her pre-teen years and has been hooked to its sound and devoted to its ethos ever since. Some of her favorite punk bands include the Dead Kennedys, AFI, Minor Threat, Rancid, and The Distillers.

JOHAN OLSTHOORN teaches political theory at the University of Amsterdam. He has been going to hardcore/punk and metal shows since the late 1990s. Preferring his hardcore/punk to be political, he enjoys most subgenres: Nineties metalcore, youth crew, melodic hardcore, d-beat crust, thrashcore, powerviolence, beatdown . . .

BAILIE PETERSON is an Assistant Professor at the University of Northern Colorado and a mom to five-year-old Johnny, who frequently demonstrates the punk attitude. Her philosophical interests include modal metaphysics and making philosophy accessible to First-Generation and K–12 students. Some of her favorite punk bands are Iggy and the Stooges, the Misfits, Sleater-Kinney, and Operation Ivy.

JESSE PRINZ is a Distinguished Professor at the City University of New York. He is the author of books and articles on a range of topics including categorization, emotions, ethics, consciousness, culture, identity, and aesthetics. His favorite bands include 999, Au Pairs, The Avengers, Bad Brains, Bikini Kill, The Brat, The Buzzcocks, The Dead Boys, Delta 5 ESG, The Eyes, The Heartbreakers, Maanam, Magazine, The Pagans, Patti Smith, Penetration, The Rentals, The Ruts, Stillettoe, The Stooges, Wire, The Weirdoes, Wreckless Eric, The X-Ray Spex, and a thousand one-hit, one-chord wonders

CASEY RENTMEESTER is the Director of General Education and Associate Professor of Philosophy at Bellin College in Green Bay, Wisconsin. He is the author of *Heidegger and the Environment*, co-editor of *Heidegger and Music*, and has written numerous peer-reviewed journal articles and book chapters. Some of his favorite proto-punk, punk, and punk(ish) bands include the Velvet Underground, the Stooges, Mogwai, and Godspeed You! Black Emperor.

JUNEKO J. ROBINSON, AKA GITTE SYNDROME is an AA-AA-BA-MA-JD-PhD independent scholar who was kicked out of high school for wearing a safety pin in her cheek and an attorney who defends refugees fleeing human rights abuses. Her research interests include existentialism, political philosophy, the politics of art and fashion, the philosophy of popular culture, and international human rights. Recent publications include, "The 45rpm Dress Revolution: Competing Temporalities in 1960s Fashion," in Fashion, Style, and Popular Culture and "The Fabric of Life: Technology, Ideology and the Environmental Impact of Clothing" in *Environmental Philosophy, Politics, and Policy*, edited by fellow punk John A. Duerk. Some of her favorite punk bands are Flipper, The Lewd, Black Flag, Agent Orange, The Didjits, Void Control, The Coathangers, and Sacripolitical.

LINDSEY J. SCHWARTZ is an Assistant Professor of Philosophy at Denison University in Granville, Ohio. She specializes in Philoso-phy of Law, Political Philosophy, Ethics, and Philosophy of Education.

Her favorite punk bands are Fifteen, The Offspring, Crass, and Dead Kennedys.

NICHOLAS H. SMITH played in a post-punk band while studying philosophy in England in the 1980s. He taught philosophy in Australia for over twenty years and is currently Visiting Professor in the Department of Philosophy at the University of Connecticut. Favorite punk bands include Buzzcocks, The Clash, The Ruts, The Saints, and Dead Kennedys.

MICHAEL STOCK is a Professor of Cinema and Media Studies at Southern California Institute of Architecture [SCI-Arc], where he teaches courses on American Film History, World Cinema, Film Aesthetics, and Film Genres—including many popular seminars on punk, cyberpunk, horror, science fiction, animation, and anime. His published work reflects these interests, with over a dozen published articles in scholarly anthologies and peer-review journals. Stock received his PhD in Cinema and Media Studies at UCLA, and his MA and BA in English at the University of Nebraska, Lincoln. His favorite punk records are usually filed in the DIY seven-inch section with band names like The Prats, The Seize, Zounds, Honey Bane, Il Ya Volkswagens, and The Desperate Bicycles (but he also loves The Slits, Wire, Buzzcocks, and of course the Original Punk, Iggy Pop).

MARTY SULAK is an independent scholar with interests in philosophy, political theory, and philanthropy. He has a BA in political science and philosophy from Mount Allison University, and an MA and PhD in philanthropy and philosophy from Indiana University. His favorite punk bands are The Boomtown Rats, The Sex Pistols, The Clash, The Jam, and The Stranglers, as well as the early, punk-inspired work of The Police, Blondie, and Devo. While an undergraduate, he lived with a punk band, The Strolling Clones, and partied with Teenage Head, and Nash the Slash.

ANNE-MARIE TIERNEY, who also writes as "Molly Tie," is a music journalist specializing in punk and has written for various publications including Punktuation, Loud Women, Vive Le Rock, and has her own blog series called Punk Rock Philosophy. She is a keen drummer and her favorite punk bands are The Clash, Minutemen, Green Day, and The Dead Kennedys.

SETH M. WALKER received his doctorate in religion at the University of Denver. His research revolves around popular culture, remix theory, pirate politics, and religion—especially Buddhism. He regularly writes and presents on topics in these areas. Seth's blog, publications, presentations, and current work can be found on his website: sethmwalker.com. Some of his favorite punk bands are The Misfits, The Ramones, The Clash, and The Pogues.

Index